SEX LIVES OF
AUSTRALIAN
TEENAGERS

SEX LIVES OF AUSTRALIAN TEENAGERS

JOAN SAUERS

RANDOM HOUSE AUSTRALIA

Random House Australia Pty Ltd
20 Alfred Street, Milsons Point, NSW 2061
http://www.randomhouse.com.au

Sydney New York Toronto
London Auckland Johannesburg

First published by Random House Australia 2007
Copyright © Joan Sauers 2007

National Library of Australia
Cataloguing-in-Publication Entry

Sauers, Joan, 1953–.
Sex lives of Australian teenagers.
Includes index.
ISBN 978 1 74166 512 3.
1. Teenagers – Sexual behavior – Australia. 2. Sexual behavior surveys – Australia. I. Title.
306.708350994

Cover and internal design by saso content & design pty ltd
Typeset by 1000monkeys.com.au
Printed and bound by Griffin Press, South Australia
10 9 8 7 6 5 4 3 2 1

This book is dedicated to all the teenagers who took part in the survey, and gave us a funny, surprising and moving account of their previously hidden worlds.

Contents

Introduction

How I got into this

Do 13-year-old girls really give blow jobs? What do 15-year-old boys think about when they masturbate? How often do teenagers regret having sex, and why? Do teenagers enjoy anal sex? What do teenagers think of sex education?

In 2005, I was working as a creative consultant on three film scripts that dealt with teenage sexuality, in some cases specifically with the questions posed above. To our dismay, the writers and I realised that most physical details as well as emotional truths of that hidden world were just that: hidden. At least from us. My job was to help the screenwriters find the dramatic essence of their characters and create realistic situations and behaviour. But if I didn't know what teenagers were really doing or how they felt about sex, what use was I?

I tried not to sound like a complete idiot, relying heavily on anecdotes, rumours and speculation provided by my teenage daughter, but I knew that she could only give me one version of what goes on, and no doubt a judiciously edited one at that. So I figured someone must have done a national study. Sure enough, in 2002 the Australian Research Centre in Sex, Health and Society (ARCSHS) surveyed 2388 Year 10 and 12 students about their sex lives, but the information they got wasn't that useful to me. For one thing, they weren't allowed to survey anyone younger than 15, and by then most kids are sexually active in some way. I needed to know what 13- and 14-year-olds were up to. For another thing, the survey had to be approved by school ethics committees, whose good intentions sometimes restricted the nature and scope of the questionnaire. In addition, all the kids who took part had to get written permission from their parents. So even though the respondents participated anonymously, the sample was skewed by parental preselection. The survey was weighed down by the heavy hand of adulthood before it had a chance to fly.

But the biggest limitation for me was that the study focused on the more clinical aspects of teenage sexuality. Primarily concerned with health issues, the survey featured a lot of questions about STIs (sexually transmitted infections), pregnancy, condom use, drinking and drugs. All the data gathered from this study was important and in many cases startling, and I applaud the efforts of the researchers and all who took part. But ultimately, I was looking for more intimate, emotional details. I wanted stories that put sexual experience in context. For example, I didn't just want to know how old a girl was when she first had sexual intercourse. I wanted to know if she liked it, whether she was pressured into it, if she had any regrets about it now, and whether she would have done things differently. I wanted to know about boys' sexual fantasies, whether they got off on porn, and whether they ever had chat room sex. I wanted to know things that probably fell outside the school ethics committees' boundaries of acceptability.

Around the same time, I saw the film *Kinsey*, a biopic of the pioneering sex researcher, Alfred Kinsey, and was floored by the way he and his associates researched the sex lives of American men and women in the late 1940s and 50s. Travelling around the country and conducting each interview in person, Kinsey and his team collected a mountain of information that, when published in Kinsey's two books, *Sexual Behavior in the Human Male* and *Sexual Behavior in the Human Female*, knocked the socks – or perhaps I should say the sheets – off a society that was largely in denial about the diversity of its sex life. Right away, as I was leaving the cinema, I thought, what I need is Kinsey-for-teenagers. And although unlike Kinsey I lacked the backing of a university, a team of researchers, and funding from the Rockefeller Foundation, I realised that I had access to something Kinsey didn't have. I had the internet.

The main problem with face-to-face interviews is that people are not always completely honest. Even when guaranteed anonymity, respondents to in-person surveys are likely to censor themselves or lie or both, tainting the integrity of the results. There is no question in my mind that teenagers are even *less* likely than adults to be completely candid in a face-to-face interview. Especially when the interviewer is a middle-aged woman. But protected by the complete anonymity of an internet survey, they might share their deepest, darkest secrets. They could talk about the most private, exciting, shocking, or embarrassing events and unload their emotions with total impunity. I bet Kinsey would have cut off his right arm, or at least his Rockefeller funding, for a chance to gather information like this.

These days, more and more university, government and private foundation studies are based on surveys conducted via the web. This is unsurprising, considering that people are generally more honest when their identities are protected so completely. And research shows that people (including teenagers) are as likely to be truthful in anonymous surveys about their sex lives as they are about their junk food consumption or TV-viewing habits.[1] So I decided to do a teenage sex survey online.

I am not a medical doctor or a psychologist or a social worker, and some may wonder what qualifies me to conduct such a survey. I believe that the main requirement for the job was curiosity and a concern for teenagers' emotional and physical welfare – along with a willingness to dive blindly into waters that medical and academic professionals had been either unwilling or unable to explore. Also, as the parent of a teenager, I have watched my daughter and her friends grow and change and try to navigate some of life's scarier hairpin turns, and I feel like I've been along for the ride. Deep down, I identify with people on the cusp of adulthood. Having written and edited scripts for and about teenagers, I felt somewhat empowered to help give them a voice. And finally, I did this survey because no-one else was doing it.

That said, I also knew my limitations, so I sought help and advice from a team of experts. In formulating the questionnaire and analysing the responses, I worked closely with psychologist Julie Catt, who brought years of clinical experience in sexual health and adolescent development to the project. Dr Gemma O'Brien, a physiologist at the University of New England, advised me on some of the neurological issues, particularly relating to female adolescent sexuality, and was generous enough to allow me to incorporate some of her revolutionary theories into my analysis. I was also advised by my lawyer, Shaun Miller, and my barrister, Dr Ian Freckelton, about what I could ask teenagers and under what circumstances, and in this regard they contributed to both the content and wording of the website. I was clueless about the IT side of the whole project, and relied heavily on the brilliance of Matt Fenton and Roy Cablewski of Monkii Media for the website design and data collection. This project was definitely a team effort, and I was lucky enough to work with the best.

Why we needed this survey

Although my initial reason for researching the sex lives of Australian teenagers was to inform the film scripts I was working on, I soon realised that the research itself was the story. If I could get a broad, random sample of respondents between the ages of 13 and 19, it could form the basis of a book – one that was desperately needed by parents, teachers, psychologists, and counsellors, but most of all by teenagers themselves.

According to a recent survey of Australian adults, 88% of men and 80% of women agreed that an active sex life is vital to their sense of wellbeing.[2] An American study showed that increasing the frequency of sex to at least once a week provides as much happiness as a $US50,000 a year pay rise.[3] To put it simply, sex makes us happy. At the risk of stating the bleeding obvious, marriages and other romantic unions thrive when sex between partners is good. When it's bad, unions dissolve and children suffer. Ignorance, incompetence, insensitivity and lack of communication about sex contribute to misery, infidelity and a high percentage of divorces. Yet we are all expected to bumble through our teen years, when most people have their first significant sexual experiences, with minimal or no guidance, and come through with flying colours as sexually well-adjusted adults. Unsurprisingly, this doesn't always happen.

As a result, adults often have an unhealthy attitude towards sex which they unwittingly pass along to their kids. In spite of having lived through or inherited the legacy of the so-called sexual revolution of the 1960s and 70s, adults today aren't necessarily sexually enlightened. As recently as 2005, *The Sydney Morning Herald* ran an article about sex counsellors wherein the author of the piece wrote that, 'The study of sex, whatever the rationalisation, has always struck me as faintly disreputable.' This sentiment reminded me that however progressive our society likes to think itself, when it comes to sex, many of us are still crippled by prudery, religious repression, political pig-headedness, physical squeamishness and just plain ignorance. Not to mention intolerance. There are still chemists around the country who refuse to sell condoms to minors, and many who won't stock them at all.

Another problem is that in a culture that is often driven by fear, many of us suspect that sexual predators lurk around every corner, and we've become overly protective. In our zeal to shield our kids from harm, we sometimes pretend that children and teenagers are not sexual beings. Aghast at the grotesquerie of raunch culture, Lingerie Barbie, and g-strings for 7-year-olds, we may recoil at the prospect of talking to our children candidly, worried that discussions about sex will further 'sexualise' them. Whatever that means.

The fact is that young people don't lose their innocence learning about sex. Innocence is freedom from moral wrong, not freedom from information. Research shows that children and teenagers who learn about sex in a healthy context don't get into trouble with STIs and pregnancy as often as kids who have had no sex education.[4] The US state of Texas has the highest percentage of teenagers who have sworn to preserve their virginity until marriage, but it also has the highest rate of teenage pregnancy. We shouldn't confuse innocence with ignorance, but many parents do. And when parents don't talk to their kids about sex, their kids don't talk to them. Which means that many parents have absolutely no idea what their teenagers get up to.

So parents needed this survey to open their eyes. They may not want to know, but they need to know. They don't necessarily need to hear the gory details of their own teenagers' sex lives, but they should at least have some understanding of the world their kids live in, and the sexual customs, expectations and behaviours that prevail.

Even more than their parents, teenagers needed this survey. Young people are under sometimes unbearable social pressures that can make it hard to be honest even with their best friends. Fear and anxiety about different forms of sex, embarrassment about their bodies, and confusion, regret or guilt about sexual encounters are all things that anyone – including adults – might not want to divulge. But it's even harder when you're 14. Sometimes it's easier to keep your mouth shut. The problem with this is that no-one knows what everyone else is going through. This survey was designed to explore some of the most private and difficult emotional terrain for the sake of teenagers, their self-esteem, their sexual health and their relationships. The book is an attempt to give teenagers a voice – to let teens speak freely about things that are often hard or impossible to talk about. Hopefully the girls and boys who took part in the survey as well as those reading the book will discover that they're not alone. They might even be able to make things easier and better for each other in the future.

The survey

The survey was open from 1 October 2005 to 31 January 2006, and appeared on a website at www.teenspeak.com.au. The biggest challenge was how to publicise the website and survey to the target group: 13- to 19-year-olds. Although a lot of media outlets expressed interest in publicising the book once it was published, there wasn't much enthusiasm for promoting the survey itself because there really wasn't a story yet. Fair enough. So I decided to take a more direct approach.

During the four months that the survey was open, I hired teenagers and young people in their twenties to hand out leaflets promoting 'teenspeak' in most capital cities and many regional centres around the country. I also travelled extensively myself, distributing leaflets and talking about the project to whoever would listen to me. Standing outside train stations, shopping malls, cinemas, schools, beaches, fast-food joints and parties (including schoolies' week on the Gold Coast), we only gave the leaflets to people who looked like teenagers. So those who answered the survey were either handed one of the leaflets or heard about the survey through friends. For this reason, we eventually got a small but carefully targeted and random (therefore significant) response.

After tossing out a number of the respondents who were either glaringly or suspiciously bogus, we ended up with exactly 300 solid participants. The suspect respondents were actually easier to spot than I would have thought. For example, in answer to the question about sexual fantasies, one boy described an audacious and painful activity involving him and our Prime

Minister, John Howard, which was clearly designed to get laughs. Another claimed that his first sexual experience had been with my mother. Both cases were easy to dismiss. When I wasn't sure, I would discuss the response with my consulting psychologist, Julie Catt, and if in doubt, we tossed it out. In general, the respondents who answered the questions honestly had the unmistakable ring of truth. But you can judge for yourself.

One of the most important features of the survey was its anonymity, so I only asked three identifying questions that could help us characterise the respondents: their sex, their age and their postcode. These questions weren't asked to compromise anyone's anonymity, but to give a better comparative picture of the responses from girls versus boys, younger teens versus older teens, and those from different parts of the country.

I expected more girls than boys to answer the survey, and although this was what happened, the boys made a pretty good showing: 190, or 63% of the respondents were girls, and 110, or 37% of the respondents were boys.

Happily, there was also a wide range of ages among the teenagers who took part:

Girls		Boys	
Ages	Numbers	Ages	Numbers
13	13	13	1
14	23	14	6
15	41	15	8
16	41	16	16
17	34	17	22
18	24	18	39
19	11	19	10
No age given	3	No age given	8

The biggest spike in responses among the girls was from age 15 to 17, with 61% of the respondents falling in those years. Among the boys, 70% were from 16 to 18 years old.

Thanks to the efforts of my leaflet distributors and good word-of-mouth, teenagers from all over Australia contributed to the survey. Just under a third, or 29%, came from New South Wales, 18% from South Australia, 16% from Queensland, 15% from Victoria, 13% from Western Australia, 1% from

Tasmania, 1% from the ACT, and 7% didn't identify themselves by postcode. Only the Northern Territory was unrepresented, and that's because unfortunately I failed to put a leaflet distributor on the ground there.

I allowed survey responses if the person stated their sex but left out their age or their postcode, as long as the response was credible. If they gave no personal information at all, their response was disallowed.

The survey itself had 50 questions. As I sought feedback from teenagers about the emotional rather than clinical aspects of sexuality, I avoided asking about infection rates and pregnancy, which have been extensively researched by groups like ARCSHS as well as a variety of government and health agencies. Instead, I wanted experiences, feelings, reactions, opinions. To get these, unlike most surveys, mine didn't ask only 'yes' or 'no' questions, or ones that could be answered by filling in a number, or an age, or ticking a box. In addition to those, I wanted stories and insights with emotional depth and detail that both teenagers and adults could really learn from. So after the appropriate questions, I left blank windows where participants could submit responses of unlimited length. I got everything I bargained for and more.

On the home page of the website it was stated clearly that it was a survey about sex for Australian 13- to 19-year-olds with the whole range of sexual experience from nothing to everything, and that a book based on the responses would be published. Teenagers were asked to take the time to respond fully either by ticking a box or writing longer responses. The importance of honesty was stressed and teenagers were reassured that there was no way their responses could be traced back to them.

For the parents

The survey website included a page for parents to assure them that we had their children's best interests at heart, with no interest in titillation or exploitation. It was emphasised that the information derived from the survey would be used in a book published by Random House, to expand knowledge of adolescent behaviour and promote discussion of issues that many people find difficult to face. It was our wish that the survey would build bridges, open doors and stimulate conversation where before there was silence.

About the responses

On the home page of the website, I encouraged teens to write in their own voices, using whatever slang words or terminology came naturally. I suggested they not respond too clinically, or tell me things they thought I wanted to hear. I made it clear their responses would not be censored.

Stylistically speaking, much of the 'teenspeak' used to respond to the survey has been significantly shaped by digital technology and mobile phones. It might take some adults a while to get used to the lack of capital letters and punctuation, as well as the new creative phonetics, contractions and abbreviations like lmao for 'laughed my arse off' or cbf for 'couldn't be fucked'. But teenagers who have grown up gabbing in chat rooms and sending text messages and emails at speed have developed a written language that those of us from an earlier generation will have to get used to if we don't want to be left behind. The use of this form of teenspeak is not a sign of ignorance or bad education, but technological sophistication and the inevitable evolution of language. It may be considered a form of dumbing down by some, but it is unstoppable.

I'm assured that most people under the age of 30 will understand everything. So I haven't changed the spelling, added capitals, or spelt out the abbreviations at the risk of stripping the responses of their fantastic character. Only occasionally have I added a full stop, a comma or a hyphen for clarity. The point is that to start understanding kids' linguistic vernacular is to start understanding who they are.

For those of us who can't work out what something means from its context, there is a glossary on page 15.

Some people will find some of what is contained in the survey responses shocking. No doubt adults will be more shocked than teenagers, but even teenagers might be startled or disturbed by some of the admissions, recollections and fantasies on the following pages. While there were some responses that I found seriously pathological, I've tried not to be judgemental in my presentation. How readers react will be up to them, and I'll leave it to the experts to more deeply analyse and comment on various responses that worried me. But I do encourage any teenagers who are troubled or confused, who have been hurt or manipulated, or those who are worried about their own sexual impulses, to talk to someone. These days there are all kinds of people who can help with sexual issues. No-one should have to cope with their problems alone. For more information, see the 'Resources for teens' section at the end of the book.

The layout

My original plan was to break each survey response into its component parts, so that all the answers to each question would be examined as a group. (For example, I would examine all the answers to question one together, then consider all the answers to question two, and so on.) I realised as soon as I started reading the material coming in that answers taken out of context are only interesting to a point. For me, the survey respondents really come alive when each individual is revealed as a whole, so I decided to take a different approach, and present the book in two parts. In Part I, I present my findings, drawing quotes from the histories, but focusing on statistics and trends. In Part II, I provide a selection of the complete individual histories, divided into age groups.

Respondents didn't always answer all the questions, especially when the questions didn't apply to them. So with the whole histories, I've included all the responses each individual gave, and left out the irrelevant or unanswered questions.

The questionnaire

1. How old were you when you first heard about sex?

2. What was the first thing you heard about sex?

3. How old were you when you started masturbating?

4. On average, how many times a week do you masturbate?

5. How do you masturbate?

6. How does masturbating make you feel? (The choices were 'very good', 'good', 'just okay', 'not very good'.)

7. Describe your sexual fantasies, even if they seem weird or boring or whatever.

8. How old were you when you had your first sexual experience with someone else? (I suggested that it might include anything from kissing to playing 'doctors and nurses' to intercourse.)

9. What happened in this first sexual experience with another person?

10. How old were you when you first had oral sex? (or 'never')

11. Describe what happened during this oral sex, and how you felt about it.

12a. On average, how many times a week do you have oral sex?

12b. If less frequent, how many times approximately has it occurred?

13. How old were you when you first had sexual intercourse? (or 'never')

14. Describe what happened during intercourse, and how you felt about it emotionally.

15a. How old were you when you first had anal sex? (or 'never')

15b. How often does this happen?

16. Describe what happens during anal sex and how you feel about having it.

17. On average, how many times a week do you have intercourse?

18. Would you like to have more sex? (The choices were 'yes', 'no', 'not sure'.)

19. How do you think sex could be better for you? (I suggested that they could describe physical and/or emotional issues.)

20. When you have intercourse, do you use protection? (The choices were 'always', 'sometimes', 'never'.)

21. What kind of protection do you use?

22. How often are your sexual experiences with someone of the same sex or gender as you? (The choices were 'always', 'sometimes', 'never'.)

23a. You think of yourself as ... (The choices were 'straight', 'gay', 'lesbian', 'bisexual', 'other'.)

23b. Other: (Fill in the blank.)

24. If you're gay or lesbian, are you 'out'? (Choices were 'yes' or 'no'.)

25. If you're gay or lesbian and you came out, was it hard? (Choices were 'very hard', 'a bit hard', 'not very hard', 'not hard at all'.)

26. Describe what happened when you came out and how you felt about it.

27. How old were you when you first saw pornography or erotica?

28. What kind of pornography have you seen? (I gave examples including films, photos, magazines, stories, books, websites and live shows.)

29. Does porn excite you sexually? (The choices were 'a lot', 'a bit', 'not much', 'not at all'.)

30. Does porn give you ideas about how to have sex? (Choices were 'always', 'sometimes', 'never'.)

31a. Do you think sexy films, music videos or advertising encourage you to have sex? (Choices were 'always', 'sometimes', 'never'.)

31b. Examples of media encouraging sex ...

32. Have you ever had phone sex, that is, sexually exciting yourself and someone else over the phone? (Choices were 'yes', 'no'.)

33. Have you ever sent or received sexual text messages? (Choices were 'yes', 'no'.)

34. Have you had a sexual experience in an internet chat room? (Choices were 'yes', 'no'.)

35. If so, did you also meet up with that person in real life? (Choices were 'yes', 'no'.)

36. Have you ever had a sexual experience with an adult? (Choices were 'yes', 'no'.)

37. If so, describe what happened and how you felt about it emotionally.

38. Have you ever had a sexual experience with more than one person at a time? (Choices were 'yes', 'no'.)

39. If so, describe what happened and how you felt about it.

40. Have you ever been pressured or forced into having sex? (Choices were 'yes', 'no'.)

41. If so, describe what happened and how you felt about it emotionally.

42. How often do you have sex while using drugs or alcohol? (Choices were 'always', 'most of the time', 'sometimes', 'never'.)

43. Do drugs or alcohol make sex better or worse? (Choices were 'better', 'worse', 'neither'.)

44. Does what you learn in sex education classes at school help you with your actual sexual experiences? (Choices were 'a lot', 'a bit', 'not much', 'not at all'.)

45. Do you think teenagers should be taught more or less about sex at school? (Choices were 'more', 'less', 'the same as now'.)

46. What do you think is the best age to start having sexual experiences? (I suggested that if they'd like, they should be specific and give their reasons.)

47. Do your parents have an influence on whether or not you have sex? (Choices were 'a lot', 'a bit', 'not much', 'not at all'.)

48. Does your religion have an influence on whether or not you have sex? (Choices were 'a lot', 'a bit', 'not much', 'not at all'.)

49. How important is it for you to have an emotional connection with your sexual partner? (Choices were 'very important', 'somewhat important', 'not very important', 'not important at all'.)

50. Is there anything else at all that you would like to say about sex or your own sexual experiences?

Glossary

The following 'teenspeak' translations will be required only by some adults, and my apologies to teenagers if some meanings have altered by the time of publication, as no doubt they will have.

atm	(abbreviation) at the moment
bd, b/d	(noun duo) bondage and discipline, often seen as BD/SM, meaning bondage and discipline and sadomasochism
bestie	(noun) best friend
bf	(noun) boyfriend or best friend, meaning construed from context
bj	(noun) blow job, head job, fellatio, oral sex on a boy
blow	(verb) to ejaculate or to give a blow job
cbf	(abbreviation) couldn't be fucked, i.e. couldn't be bothered to go on, or explain
cud	(verb form) could
dingers, dingaz	(noun) condoms
emo	(noun, adjective) first used to describe softcore punk music, now more commonly meaning an angsty, brooding teenager who is less dark than a goth (derived from 'emotional')
evry1, every1	(noun) everyone
furries	(noun) people who enjoy media that include fictional animal characters with human characteristics, sometimes in a sexual context
get	(noun) a person one 'gets with' (see below)
get with	(verb phrase) to kiss deeply and sexually, to French kiss, to 'hook up'
gf	(noun) girlfriend
handy	(noun) a hand job, also known as a 'wristy' or manual masturbation of another person

ho/hoes	(noun) whore or slutty girl
hook up	(verb phrase) to kiss deeply and sexually, to 'get with', to French kiss; can also mean to have sex with
leso, lezzo	(noun) lesbian
lick out	(verb phrase) give head or oral sex to a girl, cunnilingus
lmao	(abbreviation) laughed my arse off, laughing my arse off
lol, lols, lolz	(abbreviation) laugh out loud, laughing out loud, lots of laughs, lots of love; exact meaning must be construed from context
meh	(sound comment) used to express lack of enthusiasm; being underwhelmed
mwa	(sound message) a kiss
ppl	(noun) people
random	(noun) a stranger or unknown person met by chance, who exists outside one's social circle
s&m	(noun) sadomasochism, or sexual pleasure derived from giving and/or receiving pain
sik	(adjective) sick, meaning great
some1, sum1	(noun) someone
spoof	(verb) ejaculate
3some	(noun) threesome, or sex involving three people at once
ur	(pronoun and verb) your or you're, meaning construed from context
w/e	(noun) weekend
wristy	(noun) a hand job, or manual masturbation of another person
:)	(visual symbol) happy face
:(	(visual symbol) sad face

Part I

Survey results: Statistics and trends

Sex: rumour and innuendo

Whether the information was whispered in the playground, imparted by sensitive parents, or delivered in sex ed class at school, most of us have some memory of when we first heard about sex. When I was seven I heard that babies were born out of your bellybutton. Except when it's twins, and then they come out of your nipples. A year or so later I heard the rumour that sex was when the man put his penis into the woman's vagina. I knew that couldn't be true because my father wouldn't do that to my mother. None of this was adding up.

It's sad to say that we don't seem to have come all that far. At least when it comes to kids getting reliable information when they need it (before they start school) from reliable sources (their parents). Sex education in schools doesn't generally start until Year 6, and even then, the information is usually clinical and often deals with the microscopic (sperm enters egg) or mechanical (penis enters vagina) angles of sex rather than emotions, experience, attraction, pleasure. Some parents talk to their kids earlier on, but even then, it's usually about making babies, even though most sexual encounters don't result in babies and aren't intended to. Rarely does a child hear that sex is fun and people do it because it feels good. Or because they like each other. I guess some of us are afraid that if we tell kids how great sex is, they'll all rush out and try it.

Although responses were spread across the childhood years, most kids heard about sex somewhere between the ages of 5 and 12. For both girls and boys, the peak time that they remember first hearing anything is 10 years old, which is fairly late considering that these days a lot of 10-year-olds are already going through puberty and looking at demonstrations of deep-throating on the internet.

Age when girls first heard about sex		Age when boys first heard about sex	
3–4	4%	3–4	2%
5–7	26%	5–7	30%
8–10	45%	8–10	41%
11–13	23%	11–13	23%
14–17	2%	14–17	4%

By far the most common thing that children hear about sex is that it makes babies. Whether the more graphic scenario of intercourse is included in the explanation, or whether it's more about sperm and eggs, 36% of girls and 42% of boys were told that babies come from a man and woman having sex. So before anything like kissing, hugging or loving comes into it, kids learn that sex results in the birth of a child, which of course is only true in a tiny percentage of cases.

The next most frequent piece of information they get is that the penis goes in the vagina. Somehow it doesn't really paint the whole picture, does it? Nevertheless, 18% of girls and 23% of boys say this is the first thing they heard on the subject. Only one respondent said she remembered being told that the penis first becomes hard, which does help explain things somewhat, but still doesn't get beyond the mechanical.

A paltry 7% of girls and 5% of boys heard that sex has something to do with love. One 7-year-old girl was told that 'it was the ultimate way of showing love to someone'. At least a little feeling crept into some kids' understanding of one of nature's great enticements.

Contraception was the next most common thing that children heard about sex. Six per cent of girls and 5% of boys learned that when having sex you should use contraception like condoms for prevention of preg-nancy and infections. This is the useful but clinical side of sex that a lot of kids are introduced to in sex ed classes in Year 6. These messages are repeated throughout sex ed in high school, when there is a little more attention paid to the social and emotional aspects of sex, but by then most kids already have begun to 'experiment', as some grown-ups like to call it.

A small percentage of girls but no boys heard that sex hurts, and in several cases, this was the only thing they heard. Around the same percentage heard that kissing has something to do with sex and in some cases *is* sex. Of course this is only true if it's done right. Quite a few girls but no boys heard that sex is kissing while naked, and the combination at least begins to approach the truth.

Quite a number of both girls and boys heard that sex is something that only adults do. They were usually told that it's something that happens between a man and a woman, but never between two women or two men, even presumably when some of their parents were accepting of homosexuality. Or *were* homosexual. Perhaps the idea is that this information could be dangerous or confusing to unformed minds. And yet there's no evidence that informing young kids about homosexuality either confuses them or makes them gay.

A mere four kids said they heard about sex through books or pamphlets. Two mentioned the book *Where Did I Come From?*, which is a nice, direct, reliable source of information for young kids, especially when parents are unwilling or unable to explain sex the way they'd like to on their own.

When sex first came up, one or two kids said they heard about one or more of the following: puberty, masturbation, STIs, oral sex and positions including 69.

Two girls and two boys first heard about sex in sex education classes. As one girl said, 'our school was pretty big on sex education and gave us almost every detail … enough to scare us anyway!' Whatever the intention, it's another example of how information seems to make kids *more* rather than less cautious about sex.

And then there are the euphemisms that manage to obscure the real facts of life. One is that sex is 'a loving "embrace" between two people when they love each other'. It's sweet but kind of avoids the hard facts. Two girls described the one about how 'mums had a bush and daddys had a snake and the snake likes to hide in the bush'. Another master of linguistic precision told one girl that 'a man put his manly part in a woman's girly bit'. Another heard that 'the "doodle" goes into the "girl's part"'. One girl heard that 'guys and girls do it with theyre "things" down below' so she concluded that babies were made with pee. One boy heard that 'babies came from a ladies bottom … and I was amazed'. (I would be too.)

And then there are the myths. At the age of seven, one girl was told by her mother that she came from a cabbage patch. (I hope that didn't mean the girl thought she was related to one of those unattractive dolls.) Another girl said that there was a tree at her primary school with the words 'sex cradle' carved into it, and at the age of six she believed that if you fell into the sex cradle you'd had sex and would have a baby. My favourite is one girl's memory that at the age of five she was told that 'sperm flew from the man to the woman'. Someone was obviously comforted by the concept of reproduction without physical contact.

A few children were told that sex is actually fun, normal and cool. It doesn't appear to have turned them into raving sex fiends, but I guess we should give them time.

It's clear that there's huge variation in what children are told about sex, when they're told it, and by whom. By the time they start looking at websites, talking to other kids, and experiencing sexual contact themselves (even if it's just spin-the-bottle or doctors and nurses), they're at many different levels of knowledge. Socially and emotionally this makes for a very uneven playing field. Kids with information that they think is right or just pretend is right have power over kids who are uninformed. Ignorance has never protected anyone's innocence.

Either because they're uncomfortable about doing it themselves or because they don't think their children are ready for the information, parents too often leave the job of teaching their children about sex to others. Maybe they're hoping that their kids will get set straight at school, but that might be long after little Tommy has Googled the word 'boobs' and been treated to an eyeful of some of the most hardcore pornography you have ever seen. Parents should try it themselves and then decide how they want to play it. They can talk to their kids about sexuality in an honest, detailed way or let them find out on the internet what teenage girls and boys can do when they're short of cash.

For parents who think they're protecting their kids with a software program that filters porn, think again. Chances are they'll be spending time at friends' houses who don't have a filter, or they've figured out your password. Curiosity is the mother of all hackers.

Over half the pornography that kids see is from sources other than the internet anyway, such as DVDs and magazines. This is just one of the reasons that the government's obscenely expensive net-censoring plan is so lame-brained and nothing more than a cynical vote-grabbing exercise.

The point is not just to pre-empt or contextualise pornography. The point is to create a healthy and informed attitude to sexuality, which includes everything from puberty to attraction to kissing to penis-in-vagina, to homosexuality, to babies, to the media to paedophilia. An awareness and understanding of sexuality in families should be part of the wallpaper from the time children are born. It's not about coming up with the right moment or the right age to break the news to kids that sex happens. They should be able to look back on their childhood and not even remember when they first heard about sex because it was something they always knew about, like cooking or driving or politics, even though they weren't old enough to indulge in any of these activities at the time.

Masturbation

Although most teenagers (and adults) don't remember doing it, it's common for very young children to masturbate. Baby boys can get erections and baby girls can have clitoral erection and vaginal lubrication while breastfeeding. Many mothers will have had the experience of telling their toddlers that rubbing themselves that way is fine to do in private, but it's something that we shouldn't do in the supermarket, or waiting for a bus. (As much as we might like to.)

Whether by instinct or instruction, most of us have learned to masturbate in private, and this includes teenagers. Although they probably started earlier, most respondents remember starting to masturbate as they headed through puberty, when rising hormone levels stimulate stronger sexual feelings, thoughts, dreams and impulses.

Age when girls remember starting to masturbate		Age when boys remember starting to masturbate	
3–5	8%	3–4	1%
6–8	8%	6–8	7.35%
9–11	19%	9–11	18%
12–14	47%	12–14	67.34%
15–17	15%	15–17	6.31%
18–19	3%		

It's interesting that the ages girls remember starting to masturbate are spread out more evenly across their childhood, whereas boys have a much bigger concentration right in puberty, between the ages of 12 and 14. Perhaps boys are responding to their bodies' urgent physical changes, while girls may be stimulated by more emotional triggers. Although boys can have orgasms at any age, they only start to ejaculate at puberty, while at the same stage in life girls have less dramatic physical changes in their orgasms. As their responses to other questions will later confirm, boys tend to focus more on the physical and girls on the emotional aspects of sex, and with masturbation it's no different.

The gender differences in the age concentrations may also have something to do with the contrasting ways they think of masturbation. For boys, masturbation is a means to achieve orgasm, whereas for girls, it's a way of touching themselves to feel good.

The other huge difference between girls and boys when it comes to masturbation is how often they do it. The highest percentage of boys, 42%, say they masturbate more than five times a week. The highest percentage of girls, 38%, say they masturbate on average once a week, although once again, there is more of an even spread across the numbers with girls than with boys.

On average, how often teenage girls masturbate		On average, how often teenage boys masturbate	
Once a month	1%	Once a month	0%
Once a week	38%	Once a week	11.1%
Twice a week	19%	Twice a week	13.3%
Three times a week	21%	Three times a week	17.3%
Four times a week	6%	Four times a week	16.3%
Five times a week or more	15%	Five times a week or more	42.0%

Does this mean that the sexual impulse is stronger in boys, or just the *physical* sexual impulse, as opposed to the emotional sexual impulse?

Dr Gemma O'Brien of the University of New England is a leader in the field of the physiology of sex, and has a revolutionary theory about female adolescent masturbation and its possible outcomes. Because society is generally less accepting or encouraging of girls masturbating – with boys it's seen as an unavoidable part of adolescence – and because girls' relationship to their sexual impulses is different, they masturbate less. The problem with this is that, according to Dr O'Brien, if they don't use it, they'll lose it. In other words, if they don't stimulate their genitals as they go through puberty, nerve endings that aren't in use will be 'trimmed away', and the girls' ability to achieve orgasm later in life could be compromised.

Dr O'Brien says, 'various forms of masturbation should send helpful nerve signals to the brain to train the happy pathways'. If this approach is successful, we could see so-called female sexual dysfunction diminished and even largely eradicated in a generation. Wouldn't it be nice to think that while all the big pharmaceutical companies are scrambling to developing a female version of Viagra, all girls need to do is masturbate more often?

Much more similar are the ways that masturbation makes teenage girls and boys feel. The vast majority in both cases say that it makes them feel good or very good: 81% for girls and 87% for boys. Only 18% of girls and 13% of boys say that masturbation doesn't make them feel great.

Masturbation makes teenage girls feel		Masturbation makes teenage boys feel	
Very good	29%	Very good	31%
Good	52%	Good	56%
Just okay	14%	Just okay	9%
Not very good	5%	Not very good	4%

What's interesting but not particularly surprising is that the girls who feel better about masturbating are those with positive sexual experiences or no experience at all, whereas the ones who don't have sometimes been raped, abused or pressured into having sex.

Most teenage girls masturbate using their hands or fingers, some using lubricants, while some use objects such as vibrators or dildos. One girl sneaks into her mum's room and borrows her vibrator when she's out. It's illegal in Australia for teenagers under the age of 18 to enter adult shops that sell sex toys, so getting hold of something like a vibrator isn't that easy. This is part of the reason that many girls use found objects to stimulate themselves. Items mentioned include pillows, furniture, hairbrush handles, electric toothbrushes, a deodorant bottle, a cucumber wrapped in cling wrap, ice and a Barbie doll's foot. A couple of girls say that almost anything in the shape of a penis and vaguely rounded at one end will do in a pinch. But as one girl said, 'i always wanted a vibrator, i think they'd be awesome.' If people take Dr O'Brien's advice to heart, maybe girls will be given dildos and vibrators in their Christmas stockings.

While most girls masturbate through direct clitoral stimulation, many also go for vaginal penetration, while a few mention touching their breasts and nipples as well. One even described a whole body caress.

The vast majority of girls masturbate in their bedrooms, but a large number also use the bathroom. Some girls stimulate themselves directly with water running from the bath tap, and it seems that the detachable shower head isn't just great for shampooing. One girl explains, 'i twist the nozzle to almost full-force spray and stimulate my clitoris while sitting down in the shower. so now i usually do it everytime i have a shower, unless i'm in a real hurry.'

A number of girls masturbate while watching porn on TV or the internet, or reading sexy stories in magazines or books. One girl said that 'mild sex scenes in books that are absolutely not pornographic turn me on' and suggests that *The Time Traveller's Wife* has a good one. One girl mentioned stimulating herself while talking in an internet chat room, and a number arouse themselves in front of their partners, often as much for the partner's benefit as theirs.

One girl said she puts music on before she masturbates and several said they do it to relax. A handful said they don't masturbate at all because they have partners so they don't need to. Only one made a possible reference to the concept of guilt when she said that she only does it when there's 'no chance of getting caught', although this could be as much about privacy as guilt.

In spite of its far greater frequency, teenage male masturbation is pretty much the same as girls', although boys rely almost exclusively on manual stimulation rather than sex toys or found objects. A few mentioned using a sock. And unlike girls who have the options of clitoris and vagina, boys almost universally concentrate on the shaft of the penis. In response to the question, 'How do you masturbate?', one boy said, 'I just jack off i didnt know you could be fancy.' Most use no lube, except for a bit of spit.

Like girls, most boys masturbate in their bedrooms, but a high number also use the bathroom, particularly the shower, where some use shampoo or conditioner as lubricant and, as one boy said, it's easy to clean up afterwards. A handful of boys said they do it wherever, whenever. As one explained, 'generally anywhere that I have enough privacy and time to quickly squeeze one out'. Evidently, when you're masturbating more than five times a week you need to be fairly opportunistic.

Five times as many boys as girls say they look at porn while masturbating, most opting for the internet. Typical was the boy who, in answer to the 'How' question, said, 'in front of the computer watching porn. the normal way.' In one generation what was unheard of has become 'normal'. But many still just fantasise, hopefully demonstrating that imagination isn't dead, it's just waiting for broadband.

A few boys said they masturbate while in chat rooms, during phone sex, or while sending sexual text messages on their mobiles. (Nice to see they're being inspired by some of our sporting heroes.)

Some masturbate first thing in the morning, and others just before bed. As one boy said, 'Need a wank to get to sleep. otherwise i spend hours trying to get to sleep.'

And then there are the myths about masturbation, most of which seem to have died out. While teenage boys no longer believe that they will either go blind or grow hair on their palms, one said, 'I lie on my back and use my hands. I feel bad about doing it the same way everytime because I heard it decreases your ability to become aroused in a variety of ways later in life – so I try to do it differently some times e.g. standing up.' I don't think masturbation takes up much time in sex ed classes, but a little more information and myth-busting might help.

Sexual fantasies

Most teenagers have sexual fantasies, and as with adults, they imagine a huge range of diverse and colourful scenes. Unsurprisingly, what happens in their fantasy world is often wilder, riskier, raunchier than what they get up to in real life. Some of the most compelling insights that can be drawn from the responses to this question are about the differences between teenage girls and boys – or at least their fantasies.

Girls often describe elaborate stories, complete with lots of role-playing, costumes, narrative turning points and even musical scores. They're like scripts for short films, such as this one:

> … there was a knock on the door and there were three guys there who barged in and demanded that i get undress and then lye on the bed then they tied my arms and legs very tightly with rope to the bed stand and pulled out a video camera and one of them was filming while one of them was having sex with me and the other one stuck his dick in my mouth and then they all took it in turns and the last one to have sex with me was biting my nipples and pinching me very hardly then they got out a camera and masking tape and told me that if i skreamed that they would kill me and then ripped off my leg hair and pubic hairs with the masking tape while taking photos and then one of them stuck his dick in my mouth again and peed in there and then rubbed baby oil all over my body and robbed my house and before leaving cut three slits across my chest before going because they heard a car pull up [age 15]

In contrast, boys, especially straight boys, tend to set much simpler scenes when asked to describe their sexual fantasies, like these three:

> having sex with a chick [aged 18]

> fuckin chicks anywhere and everywhere [aged 18]

> lesbians [aged 18]

The difference reinforces the idea that for boys, sex is often more purely a simple, physical act, and for girls, it has a complex emotional context. Here are two more from the girls:

> Ummm ... I imagine the face of the guy I like on a really hot body, and meeting him outside the school, and standing on tip toes to kiss him, cos I'm shorter than him in this and I'm skinnier than I really am, and then getting into his car and going to his place, where there's a huge bed, and, well, things progressing from there. Pretty standard sex, you know ... [aged 15]

> i have a recurring sexual fantasy that i am staying at my friends house and i go to the toilet in the middle of the night. i find her mum watching porn on the sofa and she invites me to join in. we start to caress each other and erotically tickle each others nipples. basically, we have lesbian sex. [aged 15]

Role-playing in the appropriate wardrobe, even if it isn't in a story with a three-act structure, is frequently described by girls. One girl says she imagines 'i had a threesome in a car wearing a full fishnet suit'. Another one says 'id have to go with u know, lether and whip and boot type thing', while other girls picture themselves in lingerie or their school uniforms. The heterosexual male roles in their fantasies are often filled by schoolteachers, cops, doctors, footy players, lifeguards, celebrities (such as Daniel Radcliffe, Jared Leto, Usher, Ikon and Heath Ledger), older men, large men and the popular boys at school. In other words, traditional alpha males, especially ones with high physical status. In straight boys' fantasies, the status of the girls and what everyone is wearing are much less relevant. Quantity is more important. And hair colour. It seems that in this sense we have not evolved too far from gorillas and our other primate cousins.

A far greater percentage of girls than boys describe kidnapping, rape, bondage and discipline fantasies, usually with themselves in the passive role, like these two:

i like it rough and naughty or with older men although ive never had sex with an older man. i think that would be good to be under control with someone who is so mature and has great experience. rough sex and different positions is also good. i like variety and enthusiasm. [aged 17]

Role playing with a man kidnapping me and having intercourse with me, calling me dirty names & squeezing my nipples and choking me a little. Thats soo hot! [aged 19]

Most of these fantasies involve strangers, and often they are being filmed. A few of the girls who described violent fantasies where they're dominated by men had been violated in some way in real life, but not enough of them to be significant.

The critical things in so many of the girls' fantasies are detail and complexity. Like this one:

My fantasies are wide and varied, sometimes i will assume the role of a gay male, straight male, straight woman, but rarely a gay woman. [She describes herself as gay in real life.] they include bondage, latex, leather, whipping, gang-bangs, torture, fisting, role-play, use of food items, but as a rule are a variation of a situation seen on a tv show or in porn. generally the fantasies involve multiple participants with at least one under duress [aged 18]

Only two boys say they have submissive fantasies and describe them in much simpler ways: 'I wanna be tied up', and 'being dominated by a woman'. And two boys described overtly dominant fantasies. The first says:

BDSM, having little slave boys tied down to be victim to either myself with whips, matches or other pain-causing objects or have them victim to a large dog. [aged 19]

The other is also an exception to the rule that only girls describe detailed role-playing fantasies, and this boy imagines himself in a dominant situation with disturbing precision:

i think about being a parent and having a younger daughter and then i
think about the daughter doing something naughty and then i talk to
her and then i undo her pants and pull them down, and then i sit in a
chair and pull the girl over my knee and spank her bottom about 20
times with my hands on her panties, and then i slowly pull the panties
down and spank with my hand again for another 20. then i rub her
butt for a long time and sometimes i even turn her over and masturbate her pussy and slap it a little. then i turn her back over my lap and
continue spanking her ass for another 10, now this time it's paddle
time, so that's for another 20. and then lastly another 10 with the
hands. a lot of times i even fantasize about a girl dressing me up as a
girl (including and especially, in girls underwear) and then usually i get
spanked by that same girl too. [aged 15]

Another thing that's much more important to girls (and real estate agents)
than to boys is location. Again, context seems to be a key to the way girls
think about sex. Places they imagine doing it are the beach, the ocean, a
swimming pool filled with rose petals and lit by candles, a spa, a park, a
nightclub, a pool table, the bathroom on an aeroplane, a really nice hotel
with sexy music playing in the background, an elevator, a cupboard, on a
washing machine, in the shower, on a train, in the car, on a rocking chair,
an office chair, and at the following school locations: the toilets, the locker
bay, the gym and the hospitality fridge.

Boys occasionally mention locations but not often, and when they do
it's usually the beach. Although one managed to set his sexual fantasy in an
extreme sport scenario: 'To have sex while jumping out of an aeroplane.'

The other common fantasy described by girls that not a single boy
mentioned is the non-sexual sexual fantasy. In response to this question,
many girls imagine just being close with someone, in an emotional sense.
Like these:

just to feel good [aged 14]

My sexual fantasy would be just to be with someone i really like and
just be. [aged 14]

Not so much sex as just being affectionate with someone … [aged 18]

One i love just kissing and touching each other [aged 14]

all i want is a guy who doesnt care about the weight of a girl, to be completely genuine and not a complete sleazebag who only wants one thing. [aged 15]

The last big difference between the girls' and boys' fantasies is that a huge number of self-described 'straight' girls fantasise about sex with other girls or women. While the percentage of girls who describe themselves as lesbian or bisexual is higher than boys who call themselves gay or bi, as is the percentage of girls who describe themselves as straight but have had sexual encounters with other girls, there are even *more* straight girls who fantasise about it. Often these imagined encounters involve guys as well, but there is direct sexual contact and arousal between the girls, as in the following three examples, all from girls who define themselves as straight:

To have a woman "play with me" but I'm not a lesbian. [aged 15]

usually including a very sexual guy … sometimes even other girls

Sometimes I dream about having sex with another girl, though I don't know if I would ever actually do it coz I don't know if it would be weird. [aged 18]

In contrast, no boys who describe themselves as straight imagine having sex with other boys or men.

Girls and boys do have some things in common. The idea of multiple partners is obviously a huge turn-on for both genders and all sexual orientations. As two girls wrote when asked the question: 'To have raunchy sex with heaps of people … ', 'a three some – me and two other guys and they just grab me and do stuff to me'. Threesomes are high on teenagers' lists, and boys in particular like the idea of twins: 'two blonde twins', 'clearly to have a threesome with twins'. But basic threesomes will do for other boys as well: 'ive always wanted shower sex with 2 chicks, that would be sweetems', 'having a threesome with two hot chicks', 'hmm having a 3some with 2 chicks and me', 'in a sauna, two gorgeous girls, a blonde and a brunette … '

The other biggest common fantasy theme for both boys and girls was simply having sex with their girlfriends and boyfriends, or other friends for whom they have strong feelings. Like in these three from the boys:

mine usually involve a girl i like … they're usually romantic. sometimes i involve the story lines of final fantasy [a popular video game series] but incorporate my life into it [aged 19]

making sweet love to the girl of my dreams, who has a name but i will not mention it. i have been quietly in love with her since i met her. [aged 18]

im bisexual, and most of my fantasies involve my best friend who i have a major crush on. they usually just involve us foolin around or experimenting. [aged 17]

And these from three girls:

I always imagine myself having sex with people, never anything kinky but just having sex with people I like at the time. [aged 16]

i have dreams about guys that i think are hot that i know. [aged 16]

i want to have sex with the love of my life. i would want it to be very passionate. and for him to propose [aged 14]

Like girls, boys get off on imagining themselves with older members of the opposite sex, or the same sex if that's their preference. Teachers and their friends' mothers are very popular stars of boys' fantasies. The following are typical, and the first in particular fits a lot into his description:

I have fantasies about 2 different teachers at school. Both are young and attractive but the power thing is so hot. I want to have sex with a mother daughter combo and twins. [aged 18]

sex with hot older women [aged 18]

being with a hot teacher at school. being with a tutor in my school boarding house. Being with my friends mums [aged 18]

Although most boys don't describe any role-playing, one or two departed from the pack, like the one who wrote that 'I sometimes think about going to a strip club and the stripper finding me so attractive that we go into a back room and have sex.' And although there doesn't seem to be much of a role attached, some boys do imagine girls in costume, especially school uniforms. 'Naughty nurse suits' and 'a girl wearing a cowboy hat' were also mentioned, and as one boy wrote, 'Aliens, Secretaries, you name it, I've dreamed it.'

The only celebrities boys mention fantasising about are Paris Hilton and Britney Spears; the latter, as one boy said, 'before she became a mum back when she was depicted as a innocent school girl'. Actually, I think he's referring to her 'Hit Me Baby One More Time' years, when 'innocent' isn't really what she was aiming for. But it obviously worked.

Several boys' fantasies suggest they've grown up with even higher performance expectations than previous generations, perhaps due to all those endless Viagra-enhanced erections they see in lots of porn. Like these two:

my fantasy is being the best male lover of all time, i have three girls surrounding me and all of them leave in a wheel chair. [aged 19]

We fuck for hours and its complete ecstasy for hours. Starts slow and as we build up we peak and max amount of pleasure for hours. I have a super strong stamina! [aged 18]

Perhaps it's their tighter focus on the physical aspects of sex, but unlike the girls, boys seem to get into more fetishes. Two boys, one straight and one bisexual, fantasise about their foot fetishes:

Females in general as I am a heterosexual. But I especially love the lower part of their bodies namely the legs and feet. My main fantasy is having a woman rub me off with her feet so I can climax all over them. No one really knows about footsex here in this country, a huge shame. The above activity I described is called a footjob. Basically I like pretty females, and it's a huge plus if they have pretty feet. I like soft wrinkled soles and bright nailpolish is a huge turn on. [aged 18]

I would love to have sex with a skater boy. I love everything about them. I also have a kind of fetish for male feet, especially white-socked feet – weird i know … but hey, its cool. [aged 17]

Another boy has a fondness for fantasies about genitalia:

I really like the idea of women that ejaculate when they come for some reason. I've always thought that I'd like a woman to do that on my face while I was licking her out. Also, for ME to come all over a woman's face while she's kneeling and giving me head is high on the list. And I also find this weird enjoyment for watching girls pee. [no age given]

And then there are three boys who mention big breasts, although maybe with the rest of them it's a given:

having sex with chicks with big tits [aged 17]

Tits i can't get enough of them they need to be shaking in my face … hahaha and they have to at least be a C cup, i don't mind smaller but the bigger the better [aged 18]

The girl or girls have to have big tits. We fuck on a secluded tropical beach and go to wash the sand off in the water naked and we fuck out there in the water some more. [aged 18]

Finally there are three boys who fantasise about sex with animals, and you'll see from later chapters and the individual histories that they live out their fantasies as much as they can:

> Long lazy session of sex with a female Llama out in a field on a pleasantly sunny day. [aged 19]

> it's about animals [aged 18]

> Most tend to involve zoophilia or furry concepts, usually heterosexual acts, occasionally with genders swapped. Fantasised frequently about dolphins, lionesses and tigresses … occasionally dogs. [no age given]

So, perhaps as much as any other issue they responded to, teenagers' sexual fantasies illustrate their great diversity.

The first sexual experience

Respondents interpreted the questions about their first sexual experience in different ways. Many thought of early childhood instances of games like 'doctors and nurses' while most described their first post-puberty kiss. Others talked about the first time they had intercourse, or an orgasm. Whatever the case, when all the responses are taken together, the lines between early childhood sexual play and post-puberty 'real' sexual experiences blurs to nearly nothing, and sexual development emerges as an unbroken continuum rather than a succession of stages with distinct demarcations.

Another thing that has blurred the line between sexual play and the real thing is that for both girls and boys, the age of puberty has been getting lower. In 1900 the average age for the onset of menarche, or girls getting their periods, was 17. In 1992 when the latest large-scale study was done, it had dropped to $12^1/_2$. In the fifteen years since then, there is anecdotal evidence that girls are developing sexually even younger, and there are a number of possible reasons. Obesity is one trigger, as is the presence of stepfathers in many households. The absence of her biological father's pheromones tells a pre-pubescent girl's hormones to get going and attract a mate, as he's not around to provide and protect. We may think we're immune to the laws of the jungle but apparently we're not. Boys are displaying similar early pubescent symptoms, and both girls and boys are often now becoming physically and not just socially or culturally 'sexualised' at ages eight and nine.

For the record, responses to the question, 'How old were you when you had your first sexual experience with someone else?' were as follows:

	Girls		Boys
2–4	4%	2–4	0%
5–7	14%	5–7	18%
8–10	12.5%	8–10	13.5%
11–13	33%	11–13	23.5%
14–16	33.5%	14–16	38%
17–19	3%	17–19	7%

In general, whether talking about childhood games or the more serious business of oral sex and intercourse, girls often start a couple of years before boys. And while they both took part, a far higher percentage of girls remembered very early sex play. Adults tend to call this phase 'experimentation'; teenagers call it 'practice'.

Teenage girls remember playing sexual games between the ages of around three and seven, and calling them names like 'doctors and nurses', 'boyfriends and girlfriends', 'mums and dads' or as one called it, the game of 'teenagers'. They're often imitative games, either copying what they've seen in real life or more frequently in the movies, but sometimes they're just going on instinct. At other times, they're following instructions.

> when i first learnt about sex from my older sister and older cousin, [they] told me and my younger cousin (male) so we decided that we would try it out … we were three at the time!

> we were in the bath [at age 5] and i was pulling his penis and he was touching me and we kissed.

> My first sexual experience was when I was around 7 or 8, playing 'boyfriends and girlfriends' with a girlfriend (we would fight over who had to be the boy). It was pretty much just kissing and rubbing up on each other though.

> it was just me [at age 7] and my best friend (who was a guy) and we would play doctors and he would finger me and i would play with his doodle. At that stage we didn't think we were doing anything wrong.

Girls tend to remember a lot more happening, while boys generally focus on one thing, and describe it with less detail:

> a kiss … i dunno i think i got a boner afterwards [at age 5]

> um we kissed and i felt really good [at age 6]

> a kiss. i felt on top of the world. [at age 7]

Another difference is that the girls often wrote about their mixed emotions and guilt associated with childhood sex play, while the boys either didn't remember or didn't bother to mention it.

From a couple of the girls:

we [at age 7] played doctors and nurses it felt nice thats why we did it then mum walked in and caught us that made me sad coz i enjoyed it

Me and my best friend (a girl) used to close the door when we were at each other's house and kind of dry hump each other n kiss n stuff [at age 8]. I guess at the time I felt kinda naughty coz we knew that what we were doing was bad but I guess I loved it at the same time. Now I just feel disgusted by it, I guess coz I still think it's really wrong and also coz I'm not friends with her anymore. I always wonder if she remembers what we did and I get embarrassed bout it. I have never told anyone about it either.

Many other girls describe contradictory feeling after sex play, saying they liked it but felt guilty, or were filled with both 'repulsion and excitement'. One 6-year-old girl who played 'mums and dads' with her brother's 8-year-old friend, said she felt naughty, grown up, and excited all at once.

To lessen the weight of guilt and loosen their social inhibitions, a lot of children at this stage take part in sex play on a dare or during games of spin-the-bottle, where the onus of responsibility seems to be on others. 'I'll show you mine if you show me yours' is still a pretty tried-and-true method, although one boy wrote that he always showed his then the girls didn't hold up their end of the bargain, and ran away. For some guys, that still happens.

While all this appears distinctly to be sex play rather than real sexual engagement, the line starts blurring around the age of eight or nine, as these girls describe:

It was "french kissing" a family friend … and even some dry sex.
[at age 8]

a guy kissed me … it felt good, but it was scary and i wasn't really
sure what he was doing when he put his tongue in my mouth, but i
just went along with it … [at age 8]

This is also around the age when boys start giving their stories a bit more
detail:

kissed girl, did something similar to dry-sex in underwear. was fun
[at age 9]

played doctors and nurses with a girl who ended up just playing with
my penis which felt awesome [at age 8]

Another boy remembers touching and kissing a girl for hours behind a
locked door in her bedroom. He was nine.

By the age of 10 both boys and girls remember the occasional kiss, but
the deep, open mouth kiss, also described as 'getting with someone',
'pashing', 'hooking up' or 'French kissing', seems to start in earnest around
the age of 12 to 14 or so. For both boys and girls, these memories range
from wonderful to hideous, and it's around this time that the boys' descriptions start to be spiced with a few more emotional references.

kissed for ages, touching etc. FELT FANTASTIC!!! i had liked the guy
for ages so i loved it! [girl, age 13]

pashed at a party. it was cool. [boy, age 12]

Some guy I barely knew stuck his tongue down my throat. It felt kinda
gross, but I didn't really care because I knew I was eventually going to
have to have a first french kiss and it might as well be with a guy I
don't know too well so I don't embarrass myself with someone I do.
[girl, age 12]

hooked up with this chick at school dance … lol didn't feel shit i
musta been a shit get bak then [boy, age 12]

it was a pash … it was terrible, he was really bad and i never wanted to do it again. [girl, age 13]

just kissed. I thought it was lame [boy, age 12]

I kissed a boy i didn't even know … It felt weird at the time to have someone else's tongue in my mouth but after it felt good and I wanted to keep doing it. [girl, age 14]

i kissed a girl, she grabbed my dick. emotionally it was good, coz she was my girlfriend [boy, age 13]

kissing with boy on the last day of grade 7. just topped the year off!! [girl, age 12]

just kissing and pashing what ever you call it. it was great i felt very connectd with them [boy, age 13]

i started laughing half way into my first pash becuz the guy was dead ugly and i felt weird [girl, age 12]

just pashing on a school camp, i was happy at first but now i regret as the girl was not good looking. [boy, age 14]

My first kiss was also the first night i ever got drunk. i was so nervous and he was 6 years older than me! [girl, age 14]

It was my first kiss. It was great. All my friends had kissed people all the time and i felt like shit coz i hadn't yet and then when it happened i was over the moon and felt like i had finally got rid of the burden i had of not kissing someone. [boy, age 18]

It was with a guy, ummm it was a really really, really crap kiss.
[girl, age 13]

Even though it's just a kiss, this commencement of serious sexual engagement inevitably ushers in performance anxiety. One girl described how, at the age of 14, she was scared that she was kissing the wrong way, and only after a lot more experience realised that everyone had a different way they liked to kiss. In a totally deadpan understatement, one boy wrote that at the age of 12, 'A girl kissed me. I was somewhat apprehensive about the situation.'

As I said earlier, respondents interpreted the question slightly differently, and a lot of them described events that many adults would find pretty sophisticated for a 'first sexual experience'. But if I had to identify the biggest change in sexual behaviour since the last generation it would definitely be the new sequence of sexual events. In my generation, after the pashing and feeling-up stage, we generally went for intercourse, followed at some later time by oral sex and mutual masturbation. These days, it seems to be fairly customary that you go from pashing to 'handys' and 'oral' and *then* on to intercourse. And the interesting thing is that while pashing, hand jobs and blow jobs are obviously considered sexual, they're not called 'sex'. 'Sex' is vaginal or anal intercourse. (According to your average teenager, when Bill Clinton said that he did not have sex with that woman, he wasn't lying.) So there are a lot of kids out there who are technically, or by the old definition, virgins, but they've been having oral sex for years.

Some examples of girls' first sexual experiences that go beyond the kiss:

we kissed and i gave him a hand-job. i felt really close to him, it was nice being with someone who wanted you back as well. [at age 14]

I gave my boyfriend a handjob. i was scared, but also excited [at age 13]

a guy fingered me on the dance floor and it hurt but emotionally made me feel grown up and cool cause he was really hot. [at age 14]

i gave a head job to my boyfriend and he licked me out and dry sex [at age 14]

> it was with my best friend of the opposite sex. we were having a
> sleepover together and we decided, after talking about it, to experi-
> ment a bit. i gave him oral sex and he fingered me. we didn't kiss. i felt
> fine about it. [at age 15]

One girl wrote that at 13, she gave a guy a blow job and was proud because she was one of the first girls at school to do it.

These events are equally momentous for boys:

> I was fingering her and then she gave me a hand job [at age 14]

> I sat on the bus with my girlfriend and from underneath a newspaper
> masterbated her ... regularly. [at age 14]

> oral sex, how did it feel? Have a guess. [at age 14]

I can only speculate on the reasons for the change in order of sexual events, but there a few obvious possibilities. One is that since the advent of AIDS, and particularly the awareness on the part of young people that there is a sexually transmitted infection that can kill you, people are more careful about intercourse and rely on alternatives for satisfaction. And while you *can* contract HIV by giving head to an infected partner if you have open cuts in your mouth, it's a fairly low-risk activity.

Sex education programs went into high gear after the 1980s, when AIDS became more common in countries like Australia and the US, so every teenager in this country has grown up with the idea that oral sex and mutual masturbation are safe sex. And not just safe in terms of disease, but of course safe in terms of pregnancy. Nothing like a big-time bonus to make you get comfortable with what was previously considered an act more intimate than intercourse.

It has been said that in the US, one of the reasons that oral sex has become so popular among teenagers and now precedes intercourse is that there is a higher value placed on virginity than there was 20 years ago. Christian fundamentalism and a swing to more conservative values may have convinced some teenagers to keep their virginity intact while yielding to what they see as lesser temptations, but it's hard to say that the same shift has occurred in Australia.

There's another reason that teenagers may be more at ease with oral sex and mutual masturbation than they used to be, and that's pornography. Teenagers have always managed to get their hands on a little porn, but only since the proliferation of DVD burners and the internet has explicit, hard-core porn been so universally accessible. Whether they've seen it in films on DVD or on their computers straight from the web, most teenagers will have seen other people giving each other head before they've done it themselves. In this context, they've also seen all different kinds, sizes and shapes of genitalia, so not only the experience, but the equipment involved is more familiar to them than it was to previous generations. Oral sex has been demystified, and the apparent eagerness of men and women in porn to engage in the act certainly has had some influence.

There is no question that in a lot of cases, teenagers' first sexual experiences ain't what they used to be.

Oral sex

As already discussed in the chapter on teenagers' first sexual experience, oral sex appears to be more common among teenagers than ever before, and usually precedes intercourse. In fact, by the time they were 16 years old, 51% of girls and 65% of boys who participated in the survey had engaged in oral sex, either giving or receiving or both. But there were still a lot of teenagers who hadn't gone there yet.

In answer to the question, 'How old were you when you first had oral sex?' responses were as follows:

Girls, aged		Boys, aged	
11–12	3%	3–12	9%
13–14	24%	13–14	19%
15–16	24%	15–16	37%
17–19	7%	17–19	13%
Never	42%	Never	22%

Girls from New South Wales and Victoria often start a little younger (average age 14) than girls in other states and territories (average age 15).

When asked to describe what happened during their first oral sex and how they felt about it, as usual girls talked more about their emotions and anxieties than the boys did. But the biggest difference was how each of the sexes felt about the girls giving the boys head. For girls, those who had really bad experiences outnumbered the ones who'd had good experiences by over five-to-one. In contrast, and as will come as no surprise to anyone, the boys quite enjoyed themselves.

Here are some sample responses from girls who didn't have the time of their lives, followed by the ages they first performed oral sex on a boy:

dirty [age 13]

i gave a guy a blow job, HATED IT! [age 15]

well, i have arthritic sort of problems with my jaw and he expected too much of me … especially for my first time! I felt like I was going to vomit, having a fucking cock down your throat makes your stomach heave … [age 14]

yukkkie [age 15]

i didnt really want to do it. didnt feel too good about it … [age 14]

My boyfriend at the time kinda pressured me into doing it … I felt really bad about it, and I went home and cried afterwards. I didn't want to do it but I loved him and thought he'd break up with me if I didn't. I guess that was kinda dumb in hindsight. [age 13]

i didnt really want to do it. It was their "birthday present" [age 17]

I felt uncomfortable … I felt as if I didn't have much choice and this was the normal thing to do. [age 13]

… didn't like it but was willing to do it for the sake of experience. [age 12]

In the end he basically forced me. It wasn't too bad but its not some-thing i'd do just for fun. Afterwards i felt used. [age 13]

i gave the boy a blow job but not for long because i didnt like it [age 12]

In spite of all the advances in women's rights, it seems a lot of girls still do things they don't want to do because they're forced or pressured, or they're just afraid of rejection.

More from four girls who were drunk at the time and provide some of the saddest commentary that came out of the survey:

I was drunk and this guy took me out to the street and asked me to which i first said no to but then he just kinda pursuaded me so i did …

the whole time i was thinking it was gross [age 15]

i was drunk and … at a park with my boyfriend and his hot friends. my boyfriend kicked down a lampost and ran away from the police. all his friends followed except one. i proceeded to ask him how big his cock was, and then started sucking on it. it was quite good … i then decided dicks were disgusting and only go near them if the guy is special or if i am drunk (like last time when i gave my best mate head in a portaloo) [age 13]

i was very drunk. I just ended up giving him oral but i cant remember why because i had no idea how to do it. I wasnt pressured to do it, I just did it which is really weird and which im not really happy about. [age 16]

i was very drunk … and started kissing a guy that i had never met before … and i gave it to him, i was very drunk and felt a bit bad after doing it but i learnt from it for future, i would have liked my first to have meant more. [age 14]

But not all the girls had a terrible time. A few of them said it felt great. More typical were the girls who were a little ambivalent:

I felt very odd having someones genitals in my mouth [age 14]

fun but i'd rather receive than give any day. sperm does not taste the best [age 14]

when i first gave head to a guy i thought it so wasnt as big a deal as people had said. i had heard it was really disgusting but it wasn't as gross as people said it was [age 15]

pretty strange … i wasn't really sure what to do and i was really nervous … but i did it and it wasnt that bad [age 11]
i thought it was cool but also kinda gross [age 14]

And even though teenagers are more advanced in some ways, there is still some remarkable ignorance about how things work:

> A good guy friend … we started kissing and then he gently pushed my head down 'south' and then i just did it. I had to get it over and done with and the time may as well have been then. I swallowed and then later on that day he called me and asked if I should use the pill because he thought I could get pregnant. [age 15]

As already noted, boys were generally boundless in their enthusiasm for the blow job. A sample of their often endearingly straightforward reactions, and their ages when it first happened:

> it was on the pool table i got a blow job and it felt great [age 16]

> We were kissing and she slowly undid my pants and i was kindve hoping she would give me oral. She did and it was awesome. I ended up ejaculating into her mouth and she swallowed which was great. [age 15]

> She went down on me as she did not want to do intercourse. felt fantastic [age 15]

> it was sik felt amazing [age 14]

> i got a blowjob on a couch at a party. Of course it felt good, its a blowjob!! [age 15]

> it was at a party and was kissing before a girl asked me if i had been sucked, and i said ok and she did and swallowed which was really cool [age 12]

> awesome [age 12]

> I didnt have to do anything, it was great and she wasnt drunk either so there were no regrets. [age 14]

copped a headjob … headjobs gotta be the best thing in the world [age 15]

It was the best thing ever, it came as a complete surprise, she just went down on me and i remember thinking "holy shit is she really gonna do what i think she is gonna do". [age 15]

in the movies, absolutely awesome [age 15]

it was awesome i spoofed [age 15]

It was totally awesome how many 'awesomes' there were. But a few boys were a little underwhelmed by the experience of their first oral sex:

I thought it would feel better but it still feels good [age 17]

it did not feel that good – as in it wasn't that sexually exciting for me. It also hurt a little bit when teeth were involved. Overall it was a bit of a let down. [age 14]

I was boozed so didnt feel much [age 17]

was shit [age 15]

not very exciting … very meh ish [age 15]

Unsurprisingly, and in stark contrast to the way they feel about giving it, girls generally like to get head. Approximately five times as many girls enjoyed the experience of receiving oral sex as those who didn't. Many girls wrote that it felt 'great', 'nice', 'really good' and 'fantastic'. Some of the typically satisfied responses include:

well the guy licked me out and it felt really good! [age 14]

The first time i received it was at my cousins house with my cousins best mate … i absolutely loved it … i like it more than sex. [age 15]

It was gooood. Ha. Great. I climaxed. [age 17]

It felt really good and it made me go a little crazy e.g I wasn't really thinking straight. It wasn't awkward at all like I thought it would be … [age 15]

the first time he gave me oral sex i was just as awkward but i thoroughly enjoyed it. it feels just as good as sex. if not better [age 15]

its great. possibly my fav thing. i cum so quickly n so much. [age 16]

i felt weird because i had heard so much about oral sex but now i was actually experiencing it. it was really good and way better then i expected. [age 15]

But not all girls were as thrilled with the experience:

First time a guy went down on me … I was pretty out of it and eager as i heard it was pretty good, but, i was still nervous. What if it smells down there? What if im not normal? But i got over it. He just sorta licked around a bit … it was shit! [age 14]

when he first went down on me i really felt uncomfortable, didnt enjoy it at all. [age 14]

a boy … gave me head. I didn't enjoy it at all and never have since. It's very overrated and boring. Personally, I don't like the taste of kissing them after, and I'm uncomfortable about people seeing my private bits, especially people I've only known for about an hour. So basically it was a bad experience, and the fact that he expected something in return was pretty horrible, but expected. [age 15]

i just felt, oh my god is he really enjoying this? cause i think vaginas are
just weird and maybe he found mine gross and wasnt saying anything
but would go and tell his mates about this foul vagina [age 16]

From the boys' perspective, the experience of giving girls head mostly
seems to fill them with pride that they can have such a clearly positive
effect, even when it's not completely enjoyable for them. Like these:

i licked out my girl friend and she gave me a head job. i felt good
about it. felt grown up [age 15]

i ate out a chick ... felt real good [age 17]

I felt good because i pleasured my lady with my tongue. At the same
time i felt a little physically dirty because it smelt a bit and my face was
covered with giney juice. [age 16]

i gave this girl oral on the beach and it made me feel that i was good
enough to make her cum [age 17]

went down on a girl then she did the same to me ... it was real good
[age 15]

when first giving oral sex i thought it was a lot of fun, especially
because my partner got into it a lot, i felt empowered, i felt i was doing
it well. [age 16]

to be honest at first it tastes disgusting but you get used to it. [age 15]

While pornography may have demystified the act of oral sex and genitalia, it also may have increased expectations about what one's genitalia
should look like. Girls are at an extra disadvantage because, unlike boys,
they haven't been whipping their bits out in front of each other from an
early age, so they don't get a chance to see what other girls look and smell
like. But for both girls and boys, levels of performance anxiety have been

pumped up to new highs. I pity the poor girl who didn't quite come up to scratch according to one boy:

> The girl … was doing a good job. It got me relaxed as she was doing it. I felt great coz i didn't have to do anything. I just lay back and let her do it all. I was feeling really great and she was going for a while and then she pulled out before i cummed. I hadn't quite peaked yet which was a bit annoying but it felt great all the same [age 18]

Or this girl who was judged for not looking like the girls and women in porn, who almost always have their genitals waxed:

> I received it and was ashamed when he said i was too hairy, but it was his first time too [age 15]

But more common are the teenagers who have simply learned what to do from watching porn, like this girl:

> i was drunk, i wasnt fully aware of what i was doing but i was happy to do it … for experience, i just copied what i had seen from porn, he enjoyed it, but then it only lasted for about 2 minutes because i got bored haha [age 14]

It was refreshing to hear at least a few teenagers talk about how the closeness of their relationships and their ability to communicate was what made the first experience of oral sex positive:

> It felt awkward, and i had no clue. But neither did he. It was good to teach each other where the right places are and what not. [girl, age 15]

> It was with my girlfriend at the time, we were both nervous and self-conscious but we loved each other very much, and we tried it out. It was about 3am after having made out for several hours. [girl, age 14]

All this isn't intended to suggest that teenagers are having oral sex all the time. For many respondents, it had only happened once or a few times. To the question about how many times a week they had oral sex, the responses were as follows:

Girls		Boys	
Less than once a week	57%	Less than once a week	68.5%
Once a week	18%	Once a week	10%
Twice a week	10%	Twice a week	8%
Three times a week	5%	Three times a week	7%
Four times a week	4%	Four times a week	1.25%
Five times a week	2%	Five times a week	1.25%
More than five times a week	4%	More than five times a week	4%

And 42% of the girls and 22% of the boys said they had never tried it.

Sexual intercourse

These days, intercourse is seen by most teenagers as the final stage of sexual experience, after, as they would say, fingering, hand jobs and oral. And as mentioned earlier, intercourse is what they actually call 'sex'. In most states the legal age of consent for heterosexual sex is 16, except in Tasmania and South Australia, where it's 17. Male homosexuals in New South Wales are supposed to wait until they're 18, while in Western Australia they're meant to hold off until they're 21. Anal sex is forbidden in Queensland until the age of 18, and in the Northern Territory the age of consent for all gay and lesbian sex is 18. It's worth noting that the law has no apparent effect on the age when teenagers actually start having intercourse. For instance, I found that the average ages for first-timers are about the same in Victoria and South Australia, and the only state where a significant number of both boys and girls seem to wait a year or so longer than elsewhere is Western Australia.

Approximately one-third of all respondents had had sexual intercourse before the legal age of consent. Here are the ages at which they first had the experience:

Girls		Boys	
12 and under	2%	12 and under	2%
13	4%	13	1%
14	12%	14	11%
15	16%	15	20%
16	9%	16	18%
17	5%	17	11%
18	1%	18	4%
19	1%	19	2%
No age given	3%	No age given	2%
Never had sex	47%	Never had sex	29%

Even though many teenagers have had a variety of sexual experiences including oral sex and mutual masturbation, intercourse is still seen as a major step, and a lot of respondents talk about losing their virginity as the most important sexual rite of passage. (Although the 11-year-old virgin who gives blow jobs might be a challenging concept for many adults.)

The most interesting thing to emerge from the responses to the question about what happened during intercourse and how teenagers felt about it, is the fact that the age they first do it is almost irrelevant to how much they enjoy it. The single factor that most influences how much both boys and girls feel satisfied with their first experience of sexual intercourse is emotional closeness. The more emotionally intimate they are with their sexual partners, the better the experience will be, even if they have some physical difficulty or pain.

The next most significant factor is expectation. It seems that when they don't necessarily expect the earth to move or to have Angelina Jolie/Brad Pitt movie-style sex on their first outing, they'll feel good about it. As one girl explained who first had intercourse at the age of 14, she felt ready emotionally and didn't expect it to be amazing, so she liked it. But when teenagers' expectations for that first time are high, they're doomed to disappointment. Several boys aged between 12 and 19 when doing it for the first time felt let down and admitted that their expectations were way too high.

Among the girls, about half of the respondents had good first times, and half had either not very good or terrible encounters. Once again, the ones who were happy about losing their virginity, even if it hurt, were usually close to their partners. Here are some of their comments, followed by the ages when they first had intercourse:

It took a few times, and obviously it hurt a lot. But at the time I really felt for the person, so I don't regret it or anything. [age 16]

It hurt, it was passionate. I thought i was the most beautiful and luckiest girl ever. Not only because of the sex, but because I wanted the guy so much. I was head over heels for him. [age 15]

It was with someone i really cared about, it was very special to me [age 17]

we had a lot of trouble. My partner found it hard to keep hard ... when he went to put the condom on, when we finally did it, it hurt me a lot, but it made me and my partner feel very close and happy to experience that together. [age 16]

it hurt. but was beautiful. we were in love. [age 15]

In contrast, when there's no emotional relationship, girls usually have a bad first time. One girl described how she was ashamed to still be a virgin at the age of 19, so she had intercourse with a random guy she met at a club and got 'a pounding'. Afterwards, she bled a lot and became depressed to the point of feeling suicidal. A 14-year-old who did it with a boy who meant nothing to her in the back of his car was angry at him and felt like she wanted her innocence back. She said the experience made her feel old and guilty. Another girl had intercourse with a boy on their first date and he dumped her the next day. She said, 'i felt like shit, it still sticks with me, i regret it alot'. A couple of other girls felt the same:

I regret it. It was painful and not very enjoyable. Wasnt going out with the guy at the time [age 17]

i felt the first time disgusted. i couldnt believe i had wasted something so precious and important to such an ugly loser!!!!! [age 14]

It's distressing that several girls reported having a bad first time mainly because even though they were in pain, they let their partners keep going just to make them happy. A 15-year-old girl said that it was hard for her to get into a rhythm because she was in so much pain, but she put up with it because she was so eager to make it enjoyable for her boyfriend. As another girl put it:

it really hurt, i bled, but i let him keep going, he seemed happy, i really regreted it after doing it, but there wasnt much i could do, i just felt way too young and that it was too early [age 13]

At any age, girls need to be able to speak up. It would help if boys were more observant, too, like this one described by a 17-year-old girl:

> I was drunk at the time and he treated me nicely. He noticed I was finding it a bit painful so asked if I wanted to stop.

If I knew how to find this kid I would give him a medal.

Rape is always a terrible crime, but perhaps even more heartbreaking when it's someone's first experience of intercourse. A handful of girls endured this, including one 15-year-old who was raped by her boyfriend in 'a public toilet in the middle of nowhere'. Afterwards, she felt 'helpless, weakened and sick/damaged. i was emotionally crippled, never trusting anyone, crying myself to sleep.'

A far higher percentage of boys than girls had good first experiences of sexual intercourse. Probably twice as many boys were happy about it than not, and as with the girls, the ones who had the best times also had good emotional bonds with their partners.

> It was an amazing emotional moment as we had been together for about 4 months and were pretty serious. [age 16]

> Felt a deep connection with my girlfriend … Wasn't about pleasure it was about furthering a bond. [age 17]

> it was awsum i was with the girl for ages. she was a virgin 2 so it was pretty close [age 16]

> It took heaps of attempts for me to actually get it in the right area, we laughed about it as I made more and more mistakes, but we were both quite mature so I didnt let it hurt my pride … After a while I got it in, she gave a big gasp and winced … I got a rythum going, it lasted about 3 minutes then i quickly pulled out and about 2 seconds later I ejaculated. Later that day I felt really happy and couldnt get the smile off my face. I felt really proud. [age 17]

i was enjoying it alot and had been with a girl for a long time and i was just happy the whole time and wanted it to be good for her as well [age 14]

we had sex 3 times, i loved her. [age 14]

In contrast, boys who say the girl didn't mean anything to them often regret their first time. But probably one of the biggest dampeners for both boys and girls on the occasion of their first intercourse is being drunk.

i was very drunk and was told the next day. i cant remember it very clearly [boy, age 14]

it was the first time i got drunk and we had sex and i didnt like it because it hurt [girl, age 13]

i was drunk and my erection kept going down while i was getting the condom on. it worked after a few goes though. after that i didn't last as long as i would have liked but i wasnt that bad. [boy, age 17]

my boyfriend after 5 months, we didnt properly finish because he was so drunk ... he couldnt get very hard. very embarrassing story, kind of ruined our relationship, made us feel like we werent meant to be together because it didnt work. also i dont know if im a virgin or not, i mean he was inside me but we didnt finish?? [girl, age 16]

i was blind drunk. remember very little. I remember sitting on my bed naked, and i remember watching the roof spin. [boy, age 16]

I was drunk, it was really awkward and awful for me [boy, age 17]

And of course there are always exceptions to every rule. Sometimes, not knowing the person and being drunk don't necessarily make for a bad first time, as these two teenagers attest:

he was a random i was drunk it was good [girl, age 14]

umm well i was drunk … but dammmm it was awesome lol. umm wat didnt happen is tha question. i had only known the girl for a week and yeh we screwed like stoned monkeys for bout an hour [boy, age 15]

And of course there were teenagers who were nervous and self-conscious during their first time:

was very nervous … kinda awkward first time … [boy, age 15]

didn't last quite 5 minutes, was embarrased, but didn't show that embarrasment to the girl [boy, age 15]

I was frightened and nervous! It was fucking amazing though. [girl, age 13]

the girl of my dreams came over one day and we did it. during it was quiet and awkward being naked in front of the opposite sex. [boy, age 15]

Of those teenagers who have had intercourse, the assumption might be that once they try it they bonk like rabbits, but 56% of girls and 55% of boys say that it happens less than once a week and in many cases has only happened a few times. The rest of them describe the approximate frequency of their sexual intercourse as follows:

Girls		Boys	
Once a week	8%	Once a week	10%
Twice a week	15%	Twice a week	10%
Three times a week	8%	Three times a week	10%
Four times a week	6%	Four times a week	5%
Five times a week	2%	Five times a week	2%
More than five times a week	5%	More than five times a week	8%

Who knows when those in the last group have time for homework.

Anal sex

Many social commentators have recently speculated about how common anal sex has become, especially among heterosexuals, and particularly among young people. Ever since the emergence of AIDS, this once utterly taboo subject is now spoken of quite openly. An episode of *Sex and the City* had the four lead characters debating the pros and cons of 'up the butt' as they called it, and the practice has been made almost homey in films such as *Bridget Jones's Diary*, where it's just a bit of exotic fun that the characters played by Renée Zellweger and Hugh Grant get up to. Naomi Wolf recently announced that her next book will examine the sexual habits of American teenagers, particularly anal sex as an alternative to vaginal intercourse and a way of technically preserving virginity until marriage. It's the subject on everyone's lips.

But what's really happening with teenagers here in Australia? Responses to the question yielded these results:

Girls		Boys	
Have had anal sex	12%	Have had anal sex	25%
Never had anal sex	88%	Never had anal sex	75%

Of the boys who had engaged in anal sex, 25% were gay or bisexual, and 10% were zoosexual, or had anal sex with animals, usually dogs.

When the respondents who had had anal sex were asked to say how they felt about it, the biggest gulf in the survey between the genders was exposed. Seventy-one per cent of girls disliked the experience, usually ferociously, while 85% of boys had a much better time. Here are some of the girls' responses, followed by the age they were when they first had anal sex:

I hate anal sex! it happened once when this guy and i were doing it doggy style, but he jammed it up my arse in the middle of it all. I screamed in pain. Decked him, got dressed and walked off. [age 15]

I hate it! It disgusts me. this guy ... made me do it ... he actually raped me. [age 16]

i only recently tried to have anal sex with my boyfriend ... i really didn't enjoy it ... i feel uncomfortable, and really hate the feeling of it ... all i can think about is that my poo is getting pushed further and further back inside me ... gross! [age 17]

it felt like i was chucking a huge turd [age 16]

only once and lasted 1 sec, it was painful and sucked badly! i thought we were doggy styling and then he put it in my bum. i didnt like it one bit! [age 19]

Even with the few girls who say they enjoy anal sex, their pleasure is often qualified, and the experience can be emotionally jarring:

less than once a week, I dont like having it that much ... But when im feeling REALLY kinky and raunchy then i usually want it, or tell my bf to bring out the anal toys. [age 19]

at the time i liked it. it felt good. i never orgasmed though. [age 16]

my ex boyfriend would go down on me first, and while doing that put lube on his fingers and put them inside. he'd come up and turn me over, but keep kissing my neck and stroking my hair. He would slowly ease inside me, but i would hold his hand and squeeze if it hurt ... but the last time i started crying. It didn't hurt, and i still don't know why i cried, but i got sort of overwhelmed. [age 16]

it really hurt the first time but he really looks after me when we do it. After a while i get used to it and start to enjoy it. But i do like doing it because it makes him happy and yeah i like doing it because its different but i wouldn't do it all the time [age 18]

For both heterosexual and homosexual boys, it seems that it usually feels better to give than to receive:

> I enjoyed it – felt good, but the pain it caused my partner made me feel bad about it … it was pleasurable, but probably not worth the effort. It was a thrill and glad to have tried it. [age 17, straight]

> It still hurts because i have not had it enough but its starting to feel a lot better. I love to give it though [age 18, gay]

> I go in really gently, I let her guide me most of the way in, and then I start going in and out gently, eventually building up rythum and speed. We do it lying sideways, with her back facing me. I feel awkward having it with her, but sometime it's more fun for me, and she doesn't seem to mind, from what I can tell. [age 17, straight]

> I'm inside them and it feels great. When they're inside me I'm scared, I think I should stop in case I shit myself but want more. [age 19, gay]

All of the teenagers, including the gay male respondents, who said they have had anal sex say this happens less than once a week, and among all the straight couples, it's only happened once or twice. So what may have caught on in the movies has yet to really captivate most teenagers.

More sex, better sex

When asked whether they would like to have more sex, girls and boys typically displayed some differences:

	Girls		Boys
Yes	50%	Yes	76%
Not sure	33%	Not sure	18%
No	17%	No	6%

So a lot more boys than girls are sure they'd like more sex than they're getting at the moment, and there may be several reasons for this. For girls, sex is more associated with emotions than it is for boys, so the issues are more complicated. If girls do want more sex, it's often conditional on it being with a boy who can attend to their emotional needs, not just physical ones. This is why girls tend to be pickier than boys, and why there is a striking power imbalance between teenage boys and girls. Boys simply feel a more urgent need for sex, while girls can afford to shop around. This means that in the game of teenage sex, girls hold most of the cards.

But there are also issues of physical satisfaction, and there's no question that boys, like men, reach orgasm more frequently than girls and women for some obvious reasons and others that sexual health researchers are still trying to work out. Perhaps if girls came more often, they'd want sex as much as boys. Perhaps if they followed Dr O'Brien's advice and masturbated regularly, they'd experience the physical pleasures of sex in a more dominating way that is similar to boys. In any case, it is still a fairly small percentage of girls who are sure they don't want more sex than they're having currently.

When asked how sex could be better for them, the gender differences surprisingly seem to evaporate. The most common thing that both girls and boys are looking for to make their sex lives better is an emotional connection with their partner. Here is what some girls and boys have to say on the subject, followed by their current ages:

Emotional connection. A responsive and intuitive lover. good communication. sharing experiences – give and take [boy, age 19]

Sex could have more emotional attachment. I've had one night stands, they satisfy you physically but I feel used and dirty for a few days afterwards. [girl, age 18]

with someone i love as i dont know what love is yet as i am 15. i want to experience intercourse with someone i love [boy, age 15]

knowing the person better and having alot of trust in them [girl, age 16]

if i found the right girl it would be a better feeling as well, instead of just doing it for the hell of it. [boy, age 18]

Well getting a new boyfriend would be a start, as i don't want to sleep with some random. [girl, age 17]

If I was in a relationship with someone who i actually liked … Particularly if sex was not preceeded by the act of trying to procure it! [boy, age 18]

Being able to trust my lover implicitly, as well as being in a loving relationship. [girl, age 18]

i haven't been very close to my partners in the past, and i think i rushed into things too quickly. id like to know my partners better, that i might feel more comfortable with them … [boy, age 17]

if it were with someone i was in love with [girl, age 16]

So it's not just girls whose sexual experience is enhanced by emotions. Maybe in fundamental ways we're not that far apart. Perhaps if boys made more of an effort to communicate their emotional needs and desires while girls were doing all that masturbating, everybody would be better off.

The next biggest place where there's room for improvement is technique, and when asked how sex could be better, both girls and boys admit that the female orgasm is often proving too elusive:

> i want to have an orgasm ... ive never had 1. I still enjoy sex ... but ive never climaxed ... [girl, age 15]

> I wish i could give a girl real pleasure. I haven't given a girl an orgasm yet. [boy, age 18]

> if guys finished you off instead of just worrying about themselves blowing [girl, age 16]

> i wish the guy could be really intent on giving me an orgasm. if he accidentally comes or whatever, i dont want him to roll over and fall asleep, i want him to please me too, you know? give a little, get a little, that kind of thing. [girl, age 16]

> Wish the girl would come more often. She doesn't fake it or anything, it just doesn't happen. [boy, age 18]

> if i had an orgasm! i dunno i always just fake one cos i know its not gonna happen or probably take ages so i just fake it to keep my boyfriend happy. i would enjoy it more if we did it more slowly ... and i dunno its just never as good as it looks in movies and on tv and in books ... i dont know why! [girl, age 16]

Finally, one 19-year-old boy said he wished he had 'some kind of device' that told him every time 'she was "really" enjoying it'. I think it's called a vibrator. (Sorry, joking.)

The point is that in this day and age, in spite of how challenging it may be, girls need to try and take more responsibility for their own pleasure. If girls get into the habit of faking it when they're teenagers, they may never learn how to help their partners get them to climax. Boys aren't psychic. It's all about communication. Girls need to feel that they can tell their partners what stimulates them, and boys need to feel unthreatened when they're given a little direction. Especially when it comes to female orgasms, ignorance has never been bliss.

But it's not just about the orgasm. Once again, satisfaction is as much about the total experience as whether or not they come. For girls, sex (like their fantasies) often has a three-act structure: foreplay, climax and cuddling. As these girls say:

if there was a lot more kissing, and things like that and giving each other a massage instead of rushing right into it. [age 17]

if you take longer with the foreplay this being kissing as well, sex becomes so much better ... and its always so much better if you have your cuddling time after wards cos theres nothing worse then just having to leave after sex [age 18]

It could be more emotional ... the mood setting before it happens ... instead of stripping off climbing on top of one another and finishing really quickly ... a tease would be good [age 17]

I love sex but i wish i could lay in bed and hold someone i love after we'd just had mad passionate sex! [age 15]

Another aspect of their sexual experience that some girls and boys wanted to improve was their degree of confidence. I imagine that being insecure about themselves, their bodies and their level of expertise must be fairly universal, but these teenagers spelled it out:

Maybe if I was less self conscious. [girl, age 16]

maybe some more confidence. [boy, age 17]

confidence, mainly with a new partner u cant do it to ur full 'potential'. i guess u feel judged [girl, age 18] less tension … higher confidence [boy, age 18]

gaining more experience, and being more confident of my body.
[girl, age 17]

if i had a bigger penis … you watch the pornos and they do it with so
much ease because they have a huge one!! [boy, age 18]

if i was a bit more daring rather than shy [girl, age 17]

if i was good at it [boy, age 16]

if i felt better about my self. [girl, age 15]

There is no question that one of the factors that has contributed to teenagers feeling insecure about how they look and act in the sack is pornography. Often the women featured in X-rated films and magazines have had their genitals groomed to within an inch of their lives, complete with Brazilian waxes and anal bleaching, not to mention breast implants, fake tans, and other forms of artificial enhancement. And then there are the performance issues, like giving head to abnormally large males and happily receiving anal penetration. And the men featured in porn – often gym freaks – have also been waxed, implanted and Viagra'd to the point of being cybernetic. Boys are led to believe they have to go for hours and have cocks the size of wine bottles to put a smile on their girl's face.

Teenagers have a hard enough time dealing with body image issues in the face of mainstream media, but when you add pornography to the mix, boys and girls are growing up in particularly challenging times. The answer isn't to wipe out porn (impossible) or even to try to keep it away from children (also impossible), but to have well-rounded, early-starting sex education that comes from both schools and parents.

Both boys and girls also talked about wishing they had more privacy for sex. They wanted more times when they could actually sleep together so that sex wasn't such a rushed, furtive exercise. And of course if mum and dad were away a bit more, that would be sweet. Perhaps more parents should understand that if they don't provide a safe, private place for their sexually active teens, they'll do it in unsafe, semi-public places which can put girls, in particular, at risk.

Other things that teenagers mentioned that could improve their sex lives were more partners, more positions, more variety and greater frequency. And one 15-year-old boy, bless him, said sex would be better 'if girls couldn't get pregnant and there were no diseases'.

Protection

Perhaps the one thing we have to thank AIDS for is an increased aware-ness of all sexually transmitted infections (STIs) and a consequent rise in the use of condoms, even among teenagers. But there is still a long way to go.

Because other academic and government studies have been done on the rates of STIs and pregnancy among teenagers in Australia, and my focus is more on the social and psychological aspects of teen sex, I only asked two questions related to the subjects in this survey. The first was, 'When you have intercourse, do you use protection?' and the second was 'What kind of protection do you use?' In neither question did I distin-guish between protection against infection and protection against pregnancy.

An impressive percentage of teenagers appear to have got the message about condom use, although there is still some confusion about the func-tion of condoms versus the contraceptive pill.

In answer to the question, 'Do you use protection?' these were the responses:

Girls		Boys:	
Always	65%	Always	58%
Sometimes	20%	Sometimes	30%
Never	15%	Never	12%

In answer to 'What kind of protection do you use':

Girls		Boys	
Condoms (worn by partners)	81%	Condoms	83%
The pill	39%	The pill (girl uses)	28%

Twenty-eight per cent of girls and 15% of boys who said they use protec-tion use both condoms and the pill.

A few girls wrote that they use the contraceptive implant, Implanon, while one said her method of protection was to have her boyfriend pull out before ejaculation. Another said she relied on God.

One boy said that his partner used the morning-after pill, and one said he used a sock.

One of the most worrying myths apparently harboured by a lot of teenagers is that if the girl is on the pill, the boy doesn't need to use condoms. This is no doubt partly based on the theory that neither one of them has had other sexual partners, so pregnancy and not infection is the only thing to protect against. But unfortunately it is and will always be in our nature not to be entirely honest about something that might get us into trouble, see us rejected or at the very least, make someone jealous. So it's hard to be 100% sure. The simple fact is that the pill or implants can prevent pregnancy but not infection, and the condom can do both.

The problem with condoms will always be that they can make what is often an unwieldy experience even more awkward, but both boys and girls need to remember that it may get down to awkward versus pregnant, sick, infertile or even dead.

While the male homosexual teenage community has a very high rate of protection use and STI awareness, lesbians seem to have been somewhat neglected by educators. Although one lesbian girl mentioned using an oral dam for oral sex and condoms on sex toys, there is a misconception among some lesbian and bisexual girls that they don't need to use protection because they can't get STIs through girl-to-girl contact. The sad truth is that anything boys and girls can spread to each other, girls can spread to each other too. Especially if toys such as dildos or strap-ons are being shared, condoms should be used and changed every time the toy goes from one person to another.

In a perfect world there would be no such things as syphilis, gonor-rhoea, HIV, chlamydia, herpes, human papillomavirus, trichomoniasis, venereal warts and bacterial vaginosis. Unfortunately, we don't live in a perfect world, so let's be grateful they invented condoms. The tragedy is that there are a number of factions who are wittingly or unwittingly (dim-wittingly?) conspiring to limit condom use among teenagers. Some chemists refuse to sell condoms to 'underage' teens, and of course the

Catholic Church has declared it a sin to use condoms, even in marriage and even when one partner is infected with a terminal STI, although doctrine can always change. A few rebellious priests in Africa who have seen the devastation that HIV has wrought are standing against their own church and preaching the acceptability of limited condom use. In Columbia, one town plans to fine males over the age of 14 if they fail to carry a condom. The irony is that the local Catholic priest compared the plan to 'selling guns in the streets'. How this makes sense when it's diseases that can kill and condoms that can prevent disease, only the unique logic of the Catholic Church can explain.

In our own supposedly enlightened country we have a federal government that pays girls and women $4000 to have a baby. This insanely short-sighted incentive has resulted in girls as young as 13 and 14, usually from low-income backgrounds, risking sexually transmitted diseases while trying to fall pregnant. And after the successful ones burn through their baby-bonus and become long-term welfare dependents, they realise too late that they've been paid to throw away what was left of their childhood and their education.

One girl who responded to the survey said that she and her partner sometimes use condoms, but not all the time because they're too expensive. Hopefully soon we will come to our senses and distribute condoms for free to all teenagers whether they're sexually active or virgins, whether they're straight, gay, lesbian or bi. Hopefully some day the condom will be as common to every teenager as the toothbrush.

Sexual orientation

Sexual preference can evolve through one's life and be affected by many influences, and orientation is particularly fluid during the teenage years when curiosity and experimentation are more common than ever. Keeping this fluidity in mind, I asked teenagers whether they think of themselves as straight, gay, lesbian, bisexual or other. These were the results:

Girls		Boys	
Straight	72%	Straight	80%
Lesbian/gay	9%	Gay	4%
Bisexual	13%	Bisexual	9%
Other	6%	Other	7%

The girls who answered 'other' explained that they were 'bi-curious', 'not bisexual, just experimental', 'mainly straight, but sometimes I hook up with girls', 'straight but "adventurous"', and one said she was 'not sure'. The boys who described themselves as 'other' said they were 'curious', while one said he is 'zoosexual', one said he was 'pretty much gay with humans, straight otherwise' (meaning, with animals) and one said he was 'sort of bi, prefer a male dog to a male human'.

While these figures certainly convey some of the variety and mutability of sexual preference, as well as teenagers' eagerness to explore their sexuality and push boundaries, there were more surprises in store when I asked, 'How often are your sexual experiences with someone of the same sex or gender as you?':

Girls		Boys:	
Always	13%	Always	10%
Sometimes	29%	Sometimes	10%
Never	58%	Never	80%

What immediately leaps out from these dry statistics is the fact that while only 20% of boys have had sexual encounters with other boys, 42% of girls have had sexual encounters with other girls. Looking more closely at the numbers reveals that 41% of the girls who said they 'sometimes' had sexual experiences with other girls had actually described themselves as 'straight' in answer to the question about sexual preference.

The reasons girls seem more willing to experiment than boys are certainly partly social and cultural. We come from a society in which physical affection between females is more accepted and encouraged than between males, whether in sexual or non-sexual contexts. Female bisexuality is often presented as just one of the choices on all women's sexual menus, as suggested or depicted in films as diverse as *Basic Instinct*, *Bound* and *Kissing Jessica Stein*. When asked about their sexual fantasies, several straight boys in this survey answered simply 'lesbians', but only one girl imagined two boys kissing, and only if she were allowed to join in. In the film, *Y Tu Mamá También*, the two essentially straight teenage boys who have a sexual encounter with each other are only seen to do so when very drunk, and the next day when they realise what has happened they are physically sick and it isn't just the tequila.

Whether girls' natural mutual attraction has led to society's depiction of lesbianism and female bisexuality as more acceptable than sexual activity between boys, or whether society's depiction has encouraged girls to experiment more than boys is impossible to know for sure. Girls tend to be choosier than boys about their sexual partners, so perhaps with fewer alpha males to go around, girls opt more often for each other than what they perceive to be inferior boys.

The boys' responses also showed that some who describe themselves as 'straight' have also had same sex experiences, though their numbers are lower than the girls'. Twenty-nine per cent of boys who said they 'sometimes' have sexual encounters with someone of their own gender identified themselves as straight rather than gay or bisexual. This would appear to support the suggestion by many sex researchers including Kinsey that to some extent we're all bisexual, it's just a matter of degree.

An even more controversial revelation will probably be that three boys described themselves as zoosexual or as having sexual relationships with animals as well as humans, but this is actually nothing new. Other scientific surveys about sexual orientation estimate that anywhere from 2% to

10% of sexually active adults have had a sexual encounter with an animal.[5] Kinsey noted that among rural teenagers living on or near farms with live-stock, the figure could be over 40%.

Although having sex with animals is illegal here in Australia, as it is in the US and the UK, some countries such as Sweden and the Netherlands have decriminalised it as long as there has been no injury to the animal, and zoosexuality is no longer classified as a pathology, or disease, under the American Psychiatric Association Diagnostic and Statistical Manual. Philosopher and animal rights supporter Peter Singer has argued in his article, 'Heavy Petting', that zoosexuality is not necessarily abusive to the animal. Ingrid Newkirk, one-time president of the animal rights group, PETA, suggested that 'If a girl gets sexual pleasure from riding a horse, does the horse suffer? If not, who cares?'[6] The argument is that if the activity doesn't exploit or hurt the animal, it isn't inherently wrong.

In all cases of zoosexuality described by respondents to this survey, the consensuality of the acts was emphasised. In other words, the animal seemed to welcome the encounter, so presumably there is no inherent moral wrong. The most outspoken zoosexual pointed out that it is he who permits the dog to mount him, so there can be no question that the dog is being forced.

While most people won't be able to get past the 'yuck factor', also known by some as the wisdom of repugnance, the subject should certainly stir some lively debate.

Homosexuality and coming out

Our government is still fighting against gay marriages, but Australia is comparatively liberal when it comes to homosexuality. Every year, the Gay and Lesbian Mardi Gras celebration in Sydney becomes more of an affair for the whole family, and a recent study by the Australian Research Centre in Sex, Health and Society (ARCSHS) showed that teenagers in particular are more accepting of homosexuality than they were even seven years ago. But that doesn't mean that it's always easy to 'come out'.

I asked gay and lesbian teens whether or not they were they 'out', and they responded like this:

	Girls			Boys
Yes	52%		Yes	30%
No	48%		No	70%

These figures certainly back up the theory that society is more accepting of female than male homosexual activity, if proportionately so many fewer boys are open about their gay orientation. Some of the girls' comments do, however, suggest that we're less welcoming to butch-looking lesbians than traditionally feminine ones, and it begs the question: do straight boys only accept gay girls when they're the kind they like to fantasise about? Either way, coming out is still easier for both girls and boys than it used to be.

Boys appear to have had an easier time coming out than girls, but that might be because most boys who answered the survey are still in the closet. Those who were out responded like this:

	Girls			Boys
Very hard	28%		Not very hard	75%
A bit hard	39%		Not hard at all	25%
Not very hard	22%			
Not hard at all	11%			

Many indicated that they couldn't be clear-cut about whether it was hard or not because they had come out to some people and not others, and some are still unsure themselves. As one 16-year-old girl said, 'it hasent come out fully to my family and stuff but i don't really know myself if it's true and times i'm like yes u are and other times i don't want to admit it to myself so thats y i'd classify it as bi-sexuality.'

One boy said that he had come out to his friends, and it helped because a third of his friends are gay too, but his mother was shocked. She was in denial for a few months and is finally accepting the truth. But now he's worried about coming out to his straight friends. As he said, 'you don't hear others saying "hey ... I'm straight!"; so how do you tell them you're not so straight?'

The challenges are slightly different for one of the boys who said he's gay, but prefers a male dog to a male human: 'Well, when you have sex with dogs its very nervy coming out. Tho lately found out its quite commen in alot of farm boys and alot of older people.'

Often it's immediate families who are the harshest judges, as these teens wrote about their coming out experiences:

> my father tried killing me and i havent seen him since i came out about 2 years ago and my mother hates me and can barely speak to me. my sisters hate me. my mother physically and verbally abuses me. [girl, age 19]

> I told everyone and they were fine. They were like "Finally!" Except my dad. When [I] told him he said, after a long silence, "What makes you think that?" As if he didn't think I could make that decision. As if it's a decision. I didn't speak to him for three weeks. [boy, age 19]

> my dad was supportive but my mum ... kindov disowned me until she could get her head around it. [girl, age 17]

> I felt like the lowest piece of dirt on the planet. It was just swept under the carpet and then excuses like your too young to know were pulled out. I finally accepted me and my family couldnt. I felt like jumping back into the closet and bolt it shut. [girl, age 18]

Others aren't even going to try for a while. One 19-year-old girl says she has come out to close friends but not to her family because it would be too awkward. Her father and brother are homophobic so she's planning not to tell them until she moves out of home. At university, she often pretends to like guys so she doesn't scare off female friends: 'it kind of sucks ... i can sense when someone won't be very accepting of my sexuality, and i guess it stops me from making a lot of friends.'

Another girl said that coming out to her parents was hard at first but they trust her more now, although they constantly wonder if every girl she's friends with is gay, and she gets lectures about how 'unsavoury' the gay world can be. This attitude makes her feel guilty, as if she has made the wrong choice, even though she believes sexual preference isn't something you can choose.

Other girls, both lesbian and bisexual, had an easier time of it:

my mother figured it out before I did, and it wasn't an issue. I told my friends bit by bit, and there were no problems. [age 16]

I was nervous and scared. I came out to my friends first. Then about a year or two later, i came out to my mum and sisters. And well now its great, everyone is really good about it. Even at school. [age 17]

i was like ... i like boys and girls ... everyone was like thats nice. [age 18]

My parents must have guessed because they just came out with it and asked. Said yes. [age 18]

For the boys who said coming out wasn't very hard, it still wasn't a walk in the park:

I came out after school which was a good idea. Everyone was really supportive. i did not come out at school because didnt want to be known as the gay guy. when i first admitted to myself i was gay in high school i had suicidal thoughts. [age 19]

i told my best friend, he did not take it well at first, but was fine only days later. i think he feared that knowing it would ruin our friendship, which it didn't at all ... he also didn't understand why i felt i had to tell him ... i guess i just needed to talk to somebody about it. i was not ashamed of it ... [age 17]

In the ARCSHS study, teenagers said that television shows like *Will & Grace*, *Queer Eye for the Straight Guy* and *The L Word* had made it easier for them to come out and to be accepted. Let's hope the trend towards tolerance among young people continues to grow and extend to families, who are often our toughest critics about almost everything.

Pornography

Even though the average age that children are told about sex by their parents (if they *ever* are) hasn't changed much in a generation, the age that children first see graphic sexual images has. My earliest exposure to what could even remotely be called visual erotica wasn't until I saw an issue of *Playboy* magazine when I was around 10. I vaguely remember getting an eyeful of a young woman's bare breasts, including nipples(!), and she wore a string-knit bikini bottom. Nowadays, things are a little different.

By the time a lot of kids are 12 years old, they've seen a variety of hardcore, close-up images of group sex, oral sex, anal sex, bondage and discipline, use of sex toys, sex with animals, simulated vampirism, fetishism and even sex with children. Whether via the internet, magazines, or films on DVD or video, by the time they're 15 years old, almost *all* girls and boys have seen some kind of pornography.

Here are the ages respondents were when they *first* saw porn:

Girls		Boys	
6 and under	4%	6 and under	5%
7–8	11.5%	7–8	15%
9–10	11%	9–10	20%
11–12	27%	11–12	30%
13–14	32%	13–14	22%
15–16	11.5%	15	8%
17–18	3%		

Another way to look at it is that 15.5% of girls eight years old and under have seen porn, 53.5% of girls 12 years old and under have been there, and by the time they're 15, it's up to 97%. This is one area in which boys start a little earlier than girls. Twenty per cent of boys eight years old and under have looked at porn, and once they're 12, the number has risen to 70%. By the time they've reached the grand old age of 15, 100% of boys say they've seen pornography.

There are a number of questions to ask here. First, is this necessarily a bad thing? One conclusion that can be drawn from the survey responses is that the age at which teenagers first saw porn doesn't seem to have any correlation to how old they were when they first had sex. So it doesn't seem as though seeing it makes them necessarily want to rush out and do it. But there are other issues. It's not just the sex they see, it's what *kind* of sex.

Most pornography is still produced by and for men, so it depicts women giving pleasure to men, often in subservient positions – literally and figuratively. In both still photographs and films, freely available (without the use of credit cards!) on the internet, teenage girls and women are often shown delightedly performing oral sex on men with horse-sized penises, or receiving anal sex. But according to this survey, giving blow jobs and taking it up the bum aren't girls' favourite sexual activities.

And then there are the body-image and performance issues that affect both boys and girls. In a recent British survey, teenage boys were revealed to be as self-conscious about their bodies as teenage girls, with a majority being unhappy with their looks.[7] Fashion magazines and mainstream films already present beautiful bodies and love-making skills that are hard to live up to, especially when you're a pimply 14-year-old virgin. Add what can be seen in pornography to that mix, and teenagers are bound to feel even more insecure. Or just plain terrified.

Perhaps the worst thing about pornography is that most of it is devoid of any emotional content or context, which is the one thing above anything else that both boys and girls said would make their sex lives better.

No matter how teenagers, their parents, educators or politicians feel about it, the truth is that nobody can stop kids from seeing pornography. The federal government's plan to supply free porn filters to every home computer is doomed to fail because that's only *one* porn outlet that children can easily access. And no matter how you dress it up, it's still a form of censorship.

To get an idea of where teenagers find their pornography, I asked what kind of porn they had seen, giving as examples films, photos, magazines, stories, books, websites and live shows. I then worked out how much of the pornography they'd seen came from each of these forms of media. The answers surprised me. I expected the internet to dominate the list, even though I knew most would have seen porn from different sources. But the media were much more evenly spread out across the board. Here are the results, ranked from highest frequency to lowest:

Girls		Boys	
Films and videos	24%	Films and videos	19%
Magazines	22%	Internet	19%
Internet	22%	Magazines	18%
Photos	11%	Photos	15%
Stories and books	11%	Television (cable)	9%
Television (cable)	3%	Stories and books	9%
Live acts	3%	Live acts	7%
Drawings	3%	Drawings	4%
Comics	1%	Comics	0%

So spending all that money on net filters and slowing down everyone's computers isn't going to solve the problem. The only thing it will do is win a few votes, because it seems like a quick fix to a tough problem.

The point is that parents can no longer consider talking to their young children and their teenagers about sex as an optional extra. It's a must. For their own physical and emotional protection, from the moment they're born, children should be introduced to healthy attitudes about sexuality by their parents. Even if parents believe that sex is something young kids shouldn't know about, they'll have to start thinking otherwise or they're being irresponsible. The choices are: talk to kids openly about the importance of love and respect and emotional intimacy in sex, or let them get their information from Pink World's Teen Porn Archive on the internet.

To find out if pornography was actually anything more than a curiosity to teenagers, I asked whether or not it excited them sexually, and while there's a predictable difference between girls and boys, the answer in most cases is yes.

	Girls		Boys
A lot	17%	A lot	36%
A bit	41%	A bit	51%
Not much	19%	Not much	11%
Not at all	23%	Not at all	2%

It seems that around 58% of girls and 87% of boys are turned on by pornography, which is another reason that parents and educators should help them sort through what's acceptable and what's not. It's easy to dismiss all pornography as debasing but in fact one man's pornography is another man's erotica, and unless you believe that all erotic art or depictions of sex and sexuality in the media should be banned, it's important to discuss the subject openly.

When asked whether porn gives them ideas about how to have sex, the answer was an even more convincing 'yes' from the majority:

	Girls		Boys
Always	7%	Always	28%
Sometimes	63%	Sometimes	63%
Never	30%	Never	9%

So 70% of girls and 91% of boys always or sometimes get ideas about how to have sex from the pornography they see in a vast array of media.

I believe that future generations of adults will be much more sexually healthy if only *part* of what they learn but not *all* of what they learn about sex is rated X. I'm not on a crusade against pornography, I'm on a crusade against the lack of reliable information available to children and teenagers when they need it most. Parents have to pull their heads out of the sand and get over their own hang-ups in order to prepare their kids for a very different world to the one they grew up in. And if parents haven't seen any 'porn' since they flipped through *Playboy*, they'd better get on the internet and have a surf.

Aside from what would commonly be called pornography, all mainstream media seem to be brimming with sex. Sex is used to sell everything from cars to beer to cat food, and it features in films, television shows and certainly music videos in ways that wouldn't have been allowed a generation ago. Here in Australia we're more lenient about what can be shown in prime time on free-to-air (versus cable) TV than in countries like the US, where the idea of a show like *Sex and the City* running on a free-to-air channel is unthinkable.

But have teenagers got so used to all this in-your-face sex that they don't even notice it any more? Or do they no longer care? That's why I asked whether they thought sexy films, music videos or advertising encourage them to have sex. These were the results:

Girls		Boys	
Always	14%	Always	15%
Sometimes	61%	Sometimes	73%
Never	25%	Never	12%

A majority of teens – 75% of girls and 88% of boys – believe that the media encourages them to have sex, and that's just the direct influence they're conscious of. It's one more reason to open the lines of communication so that what they're directly and subliminally bombarded with every day can be placed in some kind of philosophical, emotional and economic context. Teenagers should be aware that sex is one of the tools used in a consumer society to reach their wallets. As one boy said, it's not that media encourage us to have sex as much as they exploit our natural urge for sex.

I also asked participants to give examples of media encouraging sex, and both boys and girls were happy to volunteer comments about particular ads and the advertising industry in general. As one girl said, 'i think its wrong, like they will have people naked driving cars or people moaning over shampoo. its kinda off putting.' One boy had a slightly different perspective about sex in ads: 'it makes it really hard to watch tv without thinkin bout it'. The cheapening effect is what bothered one girl who said, 'they make sex out not to be such a big thing'.

Specifically they mentioned ads for deodorant, cosmetics, condoms, perfume, clothing, fast food, alcohol and furniture. Brands that were singled out included Elle Macpherson, Calvin Klein, Skyy Blue, Ralph Lauren, Dior and Herbal Essences.

Teenagers also recognised the emphasis on sex in the cinema, and both boys and girls mentioned *American Pie* more than any other film. These boys put it quite simply:

Movies like American Pie push me to have as much sex as i can. [age 18]

Teen movies like 'American Pie' where all the guys are on a quest to 'get laid' makes me think I should be having more sex. [age 18]

Other films cited were *Road Trip, Cruel Intentions, Dirty Dancing, 40 Days and 40 Nights, Unfaithful,* the Austen Powers movies, and *Original Sin,* which one boy said, 'puts ideas in my head and even just makes me feel like having sex all the time'. While boys feel encouraged by films, girls tend to be more challenged, or find fault. As one said when referring to *Basic Instinct* and Sharon Stone's famous leg-crossing moment, 'girls feel that if they act like that (don't wear pants etc) boys will by default like them too'. Another girl pointed out that one of the problems with sex in films is that they make it look so perfect, and you never see them using condoms. Even in a film like *Something's Gotta Give* that features old people who should know better, the character played by Diane Keaton tells the Jack Nicholson character that he doesn't need to use a condom because she's gone through menopause – but Jack's character is famous for scoring with as many women as, well, Jack Nicholson, so what about STI protection?

A number of girls also talked about how movies idealise love and men, and lead you to expect too much. Romantic comedies generally have happy endings, even though life isn't always like that.

A lot of idealised sex and sexual relations were mentioned in television shows such as *Dawson's Creek, One Tree Hill, The Secret Life of Us* and even *Home and Away,* which in 2005 featured a wedding between a girl and a boy who were still teenagers and looked like they'd just come through puberty. The opposite problem exists with another show mentioned, *The OC*, where most of the lead actors playing Year 12 students are actually in their late twenties, and have both physical and emotional maturity clearly beyond the range of most 17- and 18-year-olds. In either case, it's hard for teenagers to feel like they can measure up.

By far the most criticism and occasional outrage was reserved for music videos, which a lot of girls see as too sexual, especially in the realm of R & B and hip-hop. The harshest dismissal came from the girls for featuring, 'women with perfect bodies', 'girls who are not respected by the guys', 'chicks dirty dancing and wearing hardly anything at all' and 'big booties, micro mini EVERYTHING, big jiggly breasts'. One girl said of rap videos, 'Like, they scream "sex is the best" and you kinda wonder why you aren't doing it'. Another said that rap videos 'with girls in bikinis (slapping their asses) encourages to be kinky or to do it at parties'. Another added that videos suggest that 'you will only ever get a boyfriend if you put out or if your gorgeous. an it is displaying guys who are treating girls like shit.'

At greater length, these girls didn't hold back their points of view about hip-hop videos:

They're absolutely pathetic, with a whole bunch of skanky girls practically having dry sex on the dance floor. Also a lot (if not all) of female artists sell themselves out and use their body to grab attention. It's not a good thing. There should be restrictions on TV about how sexually-orientated a video clip should be. [age 16]

... personally i think it is degrading and disgusting for girls to be portrayed like that. It's okay in private dressing up for your boyfriend but doing that stuff on TV for all to see is disgusting. [age 15]

I hate my bf watching it, I get annoyed. I think girls should have more respect about their bodies. [age 19]

Even a few of the boys agreed:

the commercial R&B bullshit that floods out tv screens and radios is the
worst offender. i dont understand why people arent sick of it. [age 18]

Another one pointed out that 'it's the cheap way out' while one said it
'tends to get bloody annoying'. But some boys responded exactly the way
they were meant to respond, at least from the point of view of the music
companies and the producers of the videos:

the females ... are behaving in ways that excite me, then i imagine
shagging them quite easily. Its exciting to see a girl in a video wear little
and wiggle or stretch herself and pose in sexually suggestive ways.
Britney Spears "hit me baby one more time" was sexy ... [age 19]

Britney was also mentioned by several of the girls, but not with the same
fondness: 'pop singers a.k.a. Britney Spears encourage girls to grow up too
fast – there are 9 year olds acting like hoes!'

The Pussycat Dolls, Sugababes and Christina Aguilera also push the
limits when it comes to music video sex, according to the girl respondents,
while 50 Cent, Snoop Dogg and Kanye West also got singled out for over-
selling sex. One of the boys recognised that a lot of male-dominated
hip-hop culture 'is about women being prizes and/or badges of pride'.

One girl boiled the powerful influence of ads and movies on teenagers
down to the simple fact that they want to be like celebrities. Sex helps sell
celebrities, of course. And everyone selling movies and music knows it.

Heavily sexualised imagery has provoked cries of outrage from many
social commentators who blame the media for creating raunch culture,
especially among young girls. But it's important to remember that raunch
culture exploits desires and needs that were already there, such as the need
to be attractive, to fit in, to feel sexy. Ad agencies didn't invent or fabricate
children's sexual instincts, but they're exploiting and encouraging them in
ways that both adults and teenagers need to be aware of.

It's been suggested that teenage girls, more so than teenage boys, are
having sex not because they want to but because it's cool. This is only true

some of the time, and blanket statements like that will throw us back to the bad old days when female sexuality was denied completely or associated only with sin, Eve and the poisoned apple. Hopefully, we've come too far to let anyone drag us back there.

Techno-sex

While the closest connection between teen sex and technology in previous generations was making out at a drive-in movie, today's teenagers have access to a wide selection of powerful technological tools that make it a lot easier to hook up. Whether with friend or stranger, child or adult, teenagers communicate about everything, including sex, using phones and computers in ways their parents never dreamed of.

Personal mobile phone use has revolutionised the way teenagers communicate. In the old days when they depended on home landlines, they would often have to go through a parent to talk to a friend, and both the length and privacy of the calls were often limited. Nowadays, when most teenagers have their own mobiles, they can be reached anywhere, anytime, and parents don't get to screen calls or callers. This means that kids can reach each other in their cars, walking home from school, or late at night under the covers after everyone else has gone to bed. Also, a lot of phones have cameras, so photographs and other images can be transmitted with impunity. A level of intimacy and privacy is possible that previous generations of teens would have died for.

When asked whether they had ever had phone sex, that is, sexually exciting themselves and someone else over the phone, teenagers had this to say:

	Girls		Boys
Yes	30%	Yes	40%
No	70%	No	60%

The percentage of teenagers who have had phone sex is actually lower than the percentage who have had either oral sex or sexual intercourse. This may at first seem surprising, until you remember how expensive it is to make calls on mobile phones, which, unlike local landline calls, are charged by the minute.

Compared to call charges, it's very cheap to send SMS (short message service) or text messages, via mobile phones, and it is the favoured method of communication between teenagers whether they're making plans for where to meet on a Saturday night, or turning each other on.

When asked whether they had ever sent or received sexual text messages, the response was almost a reverse of the answers about phone sex:

Girls		Boys	
Yes	68%	Yes	69%
No	32%	No	31%

Sometimes these sexual text messages are just a joke, and at other times are a form of harassment or even stalking, but there's no question that a lot of teenagers use their mobile phones as tools in courtship, flirting, sex play and mutual stimulation.

Then there's the internet. Forgetting for a moment about pornography, one of the web's biggest attractions for teenagers is its vast array of chat rooms, where anyone can talk to either friends or strangers in groups or individually about anything and everything. It offers not only privacy and anonymity, but of course once contact is made or if contact has been made by prior arrangement, individuals can identify themselves to each other if they choose. Teenagers can sit at their desks or in bed with their laptops, chatting happily to friends, lovers or strangers. It's instant communication between interested parties, and is frequently used for cybersexual encounters.

Such an encounter was notably featured in the film *Closer*, where the character played by Jude Law posed in a chat room as a desperately horny female who had raunchy cybersex with the character played by Clive Owen, a stranger. When the Clive Owen character wanted to meet up in 'real life' with the person he'd just had cybersex with (whom he presumed to be a woman), Jude Law's character sent him to meet Julia Roberts, whom Clive later married.

When asked whether they had ever had a sexual experience in an internet chat room, teenagers replied:

	Girls		Boys
Yes	43%	Yes	48%
No	57%	No	52%

Close to half of all teenage boy respondents and approaching half of the teenage girls said they'd had sexual dialogues in chat rooms, often with strangers. As several boys pointed out in answer to the question about masturbation, chat rooms are where they do it, comfortably sitting in their bedrooms in front of their computers, arousing or amusing themselves and others. There's no doubt that some kids do it as a joke, and even if not, it seems a fairly harmless pastime, although people tend to be much more adventurous in their cybersex, so it may create unrealistic expectations about the real thing.

The issue becomes a bit more complicated when looking at the responses to the next question. When asked whether, if they'd had a sexual experience with someone in an internet chat room, they had also met up with that person in real life, teenagers had this to say:

	Girls		Boys
Yes	14%	Yes	51%
No	86%	No	49%

That's a big disparity between boys and girls, the latter being more cautious about agreeing to meet with cyber-strangers. The problem with boys is that, while they may feel safer than girls, if they're meeting up with a stranger, they really have no idea how old that person is or even whether it's a man or a woman. While a lot of teenagers merely meet up in real life with people they know after chat room encounters, some will make dates with strangers and not many of them turn out to be a lot like Julia Roberts.

A recent internet poll in the US revealed that 25% of kids from 8 to 18 had talked online to a stranger about sex, and 12.5% had discovered that the person they were talking to turned out to be an adult pretending to be younger.[8]

Networking websites are another fast-growing form of cyberspace meeting place. Members can display photographs of themselves and friends online, as well as any personal details they choose. Seemingly in a nanosecond, sites like MySpace have become hugely popular, with an estimated 61% of British teens between the ages of 13 and 17 having their own profiles on a networking site. In Australia, the figures are probably comparable, and parents, sex educators and school counsellors should consider helping teenagers to design their sites so that they exclude surnames, addresses and even references to the school they attend, so that unwanted visitors to the site can't track them down.

Teenagers need to be careful, and it wouldn't hurt parents to explore the world of internet chat rooms and networking websites to get some idea of what's out there and how it works. It's hard to talk to teenagers about cyberspace if you've never been there. The idea isn't for parents to spy, but to familiarise themselves, to some small extent, with the world their teenagers are spending so much time in.

Sex with adults

Many if not most teenagers will be accosted, approached or hit on by an adult at one time or another. It may be someone only a few years older than they are, or the age gap may be significant. It may be a relative. Most teenagers know how to handle themselves in uncomfortable or potentially threatening situations like these, and few actually get into trouble. For this we owe a lot to child safety awareness campaigns about 'stranger danger' and the well-publicised realities of paedophilia, which have been part of primary school education for as long as most teenagers have been alive.

But some teenagers still make mistakes or fall prey to adults looking for sex. Others will simply have a sexual relationship with someone who is technically an adult while they are still in their late teens, or even someone older, but may not feel that the age gap is important.

When I asked whether teenagers had ever had a sexual experience with an adult, I didn't specify the circumstances because I wanted to get a full range of responses without negatively prejudging them. A full range was what I got. In answer to the question, they said:

	Girls		Boys
Yes:	26%	Yes:	25%
No:	74%	No:	75%

In spite of the fact that the girls' and boys' figures are almost identical, the descriptions of what happened and how they felt about it emotionally could not have been more different.

In approximately half of the cases where girls had sex with an adult, the age difference was minimal and they had a generally positive experience. There were a number of girls who were in their late teens when the guy they were seeing was in his early twenties, and one 14-year-old girl was with a 21-year-old guy whom she 'Practically had 2 beg for sex for hours before he got over his conscience and would sleep with me!' In these cases, the girls usually suggested that they and their partners were of equal maturity and there was nothing creepy about it.

In the other half, girls were taken advantage of, preyed upon, or raped. A few of them were assaulted as young children by their own relatives, as is all too often the case:

> … there was a couple of times when my uncle touched me while i was asleep. The first time it happened he'd fed me so much bourbon i was in fits of vomiting and he took advantage of me while i was out of it and in his care. I felt scared, betrayed and dirty. [age 15]

> When I was little my father sexually assaulted me for years until my mum found out and there was this whole courtcase and I was 10. He made me masturbate him, if that makes sense. I still hate him so much, and I was really scared of him back then … [age 15]

> They were supposedly a trusted relation and I wasn't willing to participate but was convinced to … [age 18]

Another girl and her cousin were repeatedly sexually assaulted by their grandfather when they stayed with him during the school holidays. She would pretend to be asleep and tried to avoid being alone with him, but couldn't always manage it. She said that she felt dirty and scared: 'deep down i knew it was wrong, or something wasnt right'.

There are dozens more stories of assault. And then there are the ones where the adult simply abused a young girl's trust:

> … he took me to his friends house and they got me drunk and his friend took me into the spare room and started fingering me and then he tried to have sex with me but I didn't want him to so he didn't. That time I really felt dirty and like I had been used. [age 16 at the time]

> The guy and me soon broke up and he said we were just having fun. I didn't know what I was doing … [age 14 now]

> i had a one night stand with a 40 year old, which i sorta regret, woke up in the morning feeling guilty and dirty, thinking i've got to get the

fuck out of here. she was buying me drinks all night and i sort of felt like i owed it to her, despite how stupid that sounds now, maybe i was just going through a bit of rebelion. hmmm she thought i was 18, still what sort of 40 year old picks up kids like me anyway ... [age 16 at the time]

Not good, he used me. I thought older men were supose to be more mature and respect people. [age 19 now]

In contrast, boys generally saw their sexual encounters with older partners as positive. As these boys said:

good experience cause ima guy. i can only gain not lose. [age 18]

I have no problems dating older women. [age 19]

nothing really emotional, just had sex with my girlfriends mum [age 19]

It made me feel very good about myself, in that I was able to secure the affection of a female that was older than me (who was not just some desperate mole). [age 18]

it felt fukn awsome i loved it [age 18]

Only two of the boys had regrets about their experiences:

it was my 1st and only gay sex i was 17 and i felt sick after but during it i was so horny i didnt care [age 18]

I freaked the fuck out! I was 19, she was 34. I was wasted, she was drunk ... everything was a bit too overwhelming for me. [no age given]

One zoosexual said simply 'All the animals I have sex with are adults.'

Cases of paedophilia, rape and exploitation are obviously wrong, and the laws we have are there to protect us. But is the age difference between sexual partners always relevant? And how does this relate to the age of consent? In other words, we may think it's acceptable for a 15-year-old and 17-year-old in love to have sex, but what about a 15-year-old and a 30-year-old? Or a 16-year-old, who is 'legal', with a 40-year-old? Roles, status and the power differential certainly make a difference. In other words, it may be okay for a 16-year-old to have a sexual relationship with a 22-year-old, but not if that 22-year-old is their teacher, their coach or their boss.

There is a Dutch political party trying to have the age of consent lowered from 16 to 12. Just one more reason that there should be open discussion about sexual responsibility not just between adults but between children and adults and between children themselves.

Multiple partners

While having sex with more than one partner at a time is a very common fantasy and features prominently in a lot of erotica and pornography, I wondered how many teenagers had actually been there and done that. Well, quite a few.

When asked whether they had ever had a sexual experience with more than one person at a time, the response was:

	Girls			Boys	
Yes	21%		Yes	29%
No	79%		No	71%

Often alcohol is involved as a disinhibitor, and the encounter is usually just seen as a bit of fun, as these girls explain:

It was with a few of my girl friends to impress this one guy. We were all a bit drunk and it was all in the name of fun. We had a good laugh about it [age 16]

It was with two of my girlfriends when we were about 14. We all felt fine about it at the time, then when we woke up in the morning we started laughing and vowed never to bring it up again but we do for a laugh sometimes now. [age 16]

with two girls ... very close friends ... it was just a bit of fun, and we all knew that ... [age 17]

ive had a few 3somes with my best friend and other guys but not full on ones where we have sex, pretty much just touching n making out. it was fun. ive also had a few 3somes with 3 girls where we fingered and licked each other out. i enjoyed it, we were all just friends having fun. [age 17]

It was too funny to explain. It was with my best girlfriend and a random guy we met. We were really drunk. We didn't have sex though. Everything but sex. [age 16]

But threesomes can be tricky, especially for girls, who attach more impor-tance to the emotional subtext of sexual experiences than boys do. Jealousy, loss of control and regret are common among the girls who reported these encounters:

was really drunk and ended up hookin up with a chick and a guy. At the time i wasn't really thinking but i regretted it heaps afterwards. [age 15]

At my home, my boyfriend, myself and a girl. Drinking alcohol and then "truth or dare" … Then we had a 3some … It was ok, but i felt jealous seeing my man do another girl … wasn't so great. Havent done it again. [age 19]

i didnt want it to happen, i only wanted one of the guys but the other guy wouldnt fuck off [age 17]

didn't really enjoy it, i felt uncomfortable. [age 17]

well me and my two best friends (one was a boy and the other was a girl) it was the guy's birthday and we went to his place to have a few drinks, we ended up drinking a lot. me and the girl started kissing and taking each others clothes off and masterbated each other. then we all performed oral sex on each other. it was quite an interesting experience and i regret it now because i have found someone i love and wish i didnt do anything sexual before i met him [age 16]

I felt that having multiple partners at once wasn't for me, I felt uncomfortable. [age 19]

ah I didnt like it too much, too much competition. I walked out. [age 18]

One girl insisted she was fine with it, but I'm not entirely convinced:

> I was having oral sex with a guy and then another guy saw us so, so that he wouldn't tell we invited him in. i didn't feel bad at all. [age 13]

Another girl used the internet for what she thought was a private encounter, with regrettable results:

> when i was doing a strip tease on my webcam to this guy he got his friends over and i didnt know, i felt really bad about it [age 15]

Once again, in unsurprising contrast, not a single boy described an experience with multiple partners that he regretted. Instead, boundless delight would better characterise their reactions. Their responses are followed by their current ages:

> my girlfriend and her friend came over and we had sex. i felt great fucking someone i didnt know very well and seeing my gf being leso [age 18]

> it was sweet [age 17]

> We'd been close friends for a fair while, and ecstatic would best sum up how I felt. [no age given]

> i was at the school dance and i was kissing 2 girls at the same time … they were both hot so i was pretty happy with it. it made me feel good about myself. [age 18]

> One of the best experiences of my life. Driving two girls home, I was able to convince them into taking their tops off. Then they started kissing each other, and I started fingering them, and then they started sucking my cock, and swapping turns while one fingered themself and kissed me and the other went down on me. We were all fairly good friends so it wasn't weird or anything like that. We've talked about it

since and we all seem to agree how much fun it was and how exciting and "on the edge" it seemed to be at the time. [no age given]

Simply kissing. I found it to be most enjoyable. [age 18]

i was with three girls which was kinda lucky and i hooked up with all of them and fingered all of them [age 18]

awesome, the more women the better [age 18]

The differences between the girls' comments and the boys' reflect the fact that for boys, sex is far more often a purely physical experience than it is for girls, who have more difficulty separating sexual acts from their emotional context.

Force and pressure

Although rape and sexual harassment are now reported more often than ever before, they are still the most under-reported crimes committed. Teens are particularly vulnerable – prone to peer pressure, high sexual expectations, confusing sexual politics, and their own general insecurities.

I asked both girls and boys whether they had ever been pressured or forced into having sex, and the responses are sad but not surprising, and consistent with other studies that have been done:

Girls		Boys	
Yes	28%	Yes	11%
No	72%	No	89%

Among the girls who answered yes, 63% had been raped, while 37% had been pressured. In the cases of rape, it was usually the girls' boyfriends or someone they'd met at a party, or even a relative. Here are stories from some of the girls who knew the person who forced them:

i was forced into having sex, i agreed to that but then it hurt and i told him to stop and he wouldnt but in the end i got him off me … [age 16]

i wasnt happy, i didnt want it to happen, just because he let me stay at his house gave him no right to do anything with me [age 17]

i was pressed against the wall and after i felt like i was dirty, contaminated and i thought he could do it because he was my boyfriend … i was really confused if he had raped me or if it was me. i did keep telling him to stop but i dont no if he heard cause his hand was over my mouth … [age 18]

I felt violated, used and worthless. I slept at my soon to be bf's house (in the process of dating). And he forced me face down into the pillow and clasped my hands behind my back and had sex with me … [age 19]

i was drugged, its wrong. i didnt know how to feel, he ws hot and the
guy that everyone was obsessed with so i was happy to start with but
when it sunk in, i was ashamed, and felt like something that i can
never have back was stolen, DIGNITY. my personal safety and respect
was violated. [age 17]

Other girls described being violated by family members when they were children, and one girl was raped on a train when she was drunk. Another girl fell
pregnant after she was raped and had an abortion, and said she will never be
the same. One 15-year-old girl said simply, 'There were 5 men, it was awful'.

One of the dreadful things about rape is the stain of guilt and pain it
leaves on its victims, and also the way it can interfere with a normal sex life
later. Sometimes girls who were raped were drinking or on drugs at the
time, and may feel partly responsible or even just stupid for making themselves targets, so they tend not to get counselling. And they never stop
blaming themselves.

Girls need to know that rape is never their fault. They should also be
aware that even once something starts, you can say no. Several girls
reported doing this, and one said, 'i felt disgusting thinking that a guy
would try to do that to me, i got up and stopped it'. There is no question
that the long-term psychic damage to this girl will be less than to those
who weren't able to stop the attacks.

Several girls reported the sneak attack, when they and their partners
were doing one thing and then it unexpectedly turned into another:

he was fingering me and i was giving him a handjob then he slipped
his dick in without me saying any thing. I told him i didnt want to and
he said ok and then i left. [age 19]

we were mucking around and he started to perform oral sex on
me then he put his penis in side me once then he pulled out and
ejaculated on the bed [age 16]

Whether these boys were doing something they knew the girls didn't want, or whether they thought they were both carried away in the moment, it shows that girls need to be really clear about what they're willing to do. Far too many girls are still prepared to do things they don't want to do just to please the boy, like these girls who said they felt pressured into having sex:

felt pressured to do it. also to make the guy like me ... DUMB IDEA [age 16]

I was with the guy at the time, I was a little bit pissed off because he knew I didn't want to have sex but I did it to please him. [age 19]

I was very drunk, and so was my boyfriend and he wanted to have sex and I didn't ... he just asked me and i sort of felt abliged ... In the end it was my fault, I could have said no quite easily. [age 16]

well guys put pressure on girls all the time ... enough for you to still be able to say no ... but you know they still want it and they get shitty if they dont get it so you may as well just give it to them and be over with it ... [age 16]

i would give it to him (ex boyfriend) because he would just be in a bad mood and it was worth giving him wat he wanted so he would leave me alone. that's why we arent together anymore [age 17]

It wasn't only the girls but some boys, too, who felt pressured into having sex. It's important to remember that just because they're males doesn't mean they're immune to sexual bullying, as these boys describe:

The lover at the time seriously wanted to have sex. i did not. i shagged her to shut her up. didn't particularly enjoy it but it was not so bad. [age 19]

just my ex girlfriend really horny and she just wanted to fuck so i did but i wasnt in the mood but she full made me [age 16] my ex-girlfriend it was a first cos usually i'm the horny one but this time she was and she wasn't takin no for an answer which was all good and i got the job done [age 18]

i know she would deny it, she would say, she allways asked if it was okay, but i didnt want to keep letting her down, so in a way i was pressured by my own guilt [age 17]

One 18-year-old boy was raped, and his agony is no less significant than the girls'. As he said, 'It destroyed me for months, even to this day im still sometimes reminded … i want to be sick.'

Unwanted sex can happen because of subtle and unspoken pressure or by violent force and everything in between. Teenagers are on the brink of adult independence, but haven't learned all the lessons yet, so they're especially vulnerable. Being drunk or excessively out of it on drugs will make them more so. When it comes to sexual issues, boys and girls need to be fully aware of what they want, what they don't want and how to communicate it. They also need to know that what might seem like the easy way out at the time – giving in, doing something to keep someone else happy – isn't really the easy way out at all. There's always a price – loss of dignity, shame, and regrets that can last a lifetime.

Drugs and alcohol

Some people might presume that teenagers usually drink or take drugs when engaging in sexual activities, but the responses to the survey suggest otherwise. When asked how often they have sex while using drugs or alcohol, they answered this way:

	Girls		Boys
Always	1%	Always	1%
Most of the time	11%	Most of the time	9%
Sometimes	34%	Sometimes	44%
Never	54%	Never	46%

Another way to look at it is that while approximately half of all teenagers are *never* stoned or pissed, 88% of girls and 90% of boys either never or only sometimes get drunk or high when they have sex. Only 12% of girls and 10% of boys say they are drunk or high either always or most of the time during sexual encounters.

To me, this suggests that teenagers aren't usually having sex because they're out of it, they're having sex because they want to have sex. The exceptions are with *excessive* drinking in particular, where both girls and boys can lose control and bad things can happen. A lot of respondents, especially girls, described situations where they got very drunk and later regretted what happened sexually, whether it was due to a loss of willpower on their part, or actual cases of rape. Studies show that binge drinking is on the rise among girls, and the consequences can sometimes be terrible.

The point is that teenagers of all ages are going to drink, even though the law says they can't until they're 18, and parents and schools should be teaching them how to control their drinking. Like sex, it's going to happen no matter what the legal age is, so teenagers need to learn to be responsible, moderate, and to exercise personal choice when faced with group pressure.

I also asked teenagers whether drugs or alcohol make sex better, worse, or neither, and as always, the responses were interesting:

Girls		Boys	
Better	30%	Better	14%
Neither	60%	Neither	58%
Worse	10%	Worse	28%

What's fascinating here is that over twice as many girls as boys say that drugs or alcohol make sex better, and nearly three times as many boys as girls say they make sex worse. Perhaps once again, it comes back to the different ways in which the genders experience sex.

If girls need more of an emotional context for the experience of sex, drugs and alcohol may help them get in the mood. The way that a Breezer or a joint can loosen them up and, according to studies, actually make members of the opposite sex look more attractive, is probably the reason why some girls find their sexual experiences enhanced by chemicals.[9] For some first-timers, drugs or alcohol may also simply alleviate the pain of intercourse.

Boys, on the other hand, usually have a more purely physical relation-ship to sex, and alcohol and other kinds of drugs they may be taking, such as marijuana or speed, all inhibit erections when used in excess. A lot of boys in the survey described losing their hard-ons because they were drunk. One girl said that her boyfriend sort of got his penis into her, but then went limp because he was so drunk and to this day she doesn't know whether she's still a virgin or not.

It's reassuring that the majority of both girls and boys felt that drugs and alcohol don't affect the quality of their sexual experiences, because it suggests that excess is not the norm. I wouldn't be surprised if teenagers are generally as moderate if not *more* moderate than many adults in this regard. Maybe because it's often a school night. Or maybe adults just need more parental supervision.

Sex education

Sex education in schools is a good thing, and we are blessed to live in a country where it is allowed to take place at all. There are, however, no national standards, so sexual curricula vary greatly from state to state and from school to school. In some schools, there's no sex education at all. All this means that teenagers begin their sex lives with a huge disparity of knowledge about sex and, as in everything else, ignorance is a handicap. The US and Australia have higher teenage pregnancy rates than Denmark and the Netherlands, where they've had universal sex education programs running in schools for nearly 50 years. You don't need to be a rocket scientist to figure out what this tells us.

One of the problems is that even when sex education exists, it starts too late. As one girl said:

> i go to a catholic school, and we were taught to wait until marriage to lose our virginity, when half the school weren't virgins, which is pretty pointless ... children should be taught about sex earlier and be more open about it. we werent taught about sex until year 10, when i had already had sex. [age 17]

The other problem is that sex education generally focuses on the biological and clinical aspects of sex, rather than the emotional, social and cultural angles. Most Year 6 students will be able to tell you that babies start growing when the sperm fertilises the egg, but they won't understand how attraction leads to penile erection in boys and clitoral erection and vaginal lubrication in girls. They know more about the microscopic details of reproduction than the emotional possibilities and physical consequences of kissing. By Year 10, most students will know how to put on a condom, but they might not know how to vocalise their resistance if they just don't want sex. They can recite the list of common STIs, but they might be confused or guilty about their sexual preferences.

Although some STIs are on the rise because Australia has no universal sex education, the sex ed we do have has been fairly good at telling teenagers about pregnancy and disease prevention. Unfortunately, it has done little to educate them about the emotional and experiential realities of sex. A lot of this is due to the mistaken idea, shared by too many parents and educators, that information and open discussion of this kind will lead to the premature sexualisation of adolescents and possibly even promiscuity. Every study that has investigated what knowledge and communication impart shows that teenagers tend to be more conservative about sex, not less, when given more information.

When asked whether what they learned in sex education classes at school helped them with their actual sexual experiences, teenagers responded like this:

	Girls			Boys
A lot	3%		A lot	9%
A bit	21%		A bit	31%
Not much	43%		Not much	32.5%
Not at all	33%		Not at all	27.5%

In other words, 76% of girls and 60% of boys say that sex ed at school doesn't help much or at all. A lot of resources go into these courses, but are they a waste of time? Do they need to go further? Should they start earlier? Do they need to shift their focus or at least broaden their scope so that the emotional side of sex comes into view? We need a national review of sex education in this country and we should start with a more holistic philosophy of what sex education is about.

Teenagers agree. When asked whether they should be taught more, less or the same as now about sex at school, their answer was resounding:

	Girls			Boys
More	75%		More	72%
Same	24%		Same	25%
Less	1%		Less	3%

A huge majority of teenagers want more sex education in schools. They also want more discussion of the non-clinical aspects of sex. As both girls

and boys pointed out, they just want to know how to do it. More attention paid to the emotional side of sex would surely help boys, who are
sometimes lacking in this knowledge, to understand girls better. And a
deeper understanding of boys' physical urgency, as well as their own
physical needs, would undoubtedly make girls more sensitive to what
boys go through. Perhaps the function of masturbation for girls as a way
to stimulate development of the neural pathways needed to achieve
orgasm later is something that will one day be covered in schools too.
Can anything that fosters greater pleasure and understanding between
the sexes as well as between those of different sexual orientations be a
bad thing?

Here are some ideas and opinions from both girls and boys:

Obviously with the TV and magazines our children are being introduced
to Sex a lot earlier in life, therefore we need to teach them a lot earlier
whether it be sex ed in primary school or parents or booklets. I know
i made a mistake because i didnt understand anything really about sex
and by having it at such a young age it re-directed my life towards a
very bad angle. A lot of females as well believe that they can use sex to
get a male to like them, only to realise that they are abusing their bodies
which makes them feel even lower ... So i guess it all comes back to
the "we need to teach the kids of tomorrow that sex is very important
and it is a sign of affection from one person to another" [girl, age 17]

in school sex ed i think they should actually say what to do, like it
says what happens during sex but they dont actually say how to do it.
[girl, age 15]

I think that schools give the spin that sex is necessary yet slightly
wrong ... If you don't know what you're doing down there then it feels
akward and you're uncomfortable. When school teaches about sex
they give biological facts and slightly "old school" opinions. As
opposed to the truth which is it's fun. It can be casual and that's
nothing bad or immoral as long as you are responsible ... I feel
patronised when I get taught about sex as well as the feeling that I'm

not getting the whole story. I feel comfortable having sex now. and school did next to nothing for that to happen ... [boy, age 19]

I think sex education should talk about homosexuality more. I was clueless and I don't think the word was even mentioned. I went to a normal public school ... There are 180 people in my grade (I've just finished year 12). We advertised and held a coming out of sexual preferences group purely so we could all have support and there were 19 gay/lesbian/bisexual kids there. That's 12%, at 12% of the grade population we have some right to education too. [girl, age 18]

I think we should have more anonymous ways of asking questions, like have a box and everyone should write 1 question down a day so not only one question gets put in and people are able to guess who it was. Also, I have been having trouble coming out to myself that I'm bisexual. I think it would be nice to have more information at school about homosexuality too for people who feel out of place. All in all, people should start being more open and not so afraid. Sex is part of life not a sin. [girl, age 17]

We really need to start learning about what genetalia looks like, and how people's can differ! I had no idea about labia majora's and minora's and all that bullshit with flaps, and clits, and openings and ALL THAT KINDA STUFF! Same goes with penises. Everyone needs to know that their sexual organs are normal no matter what they look like. [boy, no age given]

... one thing I hate about sex ed at school is that even though it covers everything we need to know ... we have a male teacher and he's really gruff and kind of intimidating. It would be so much easier if we had a female teacher and it wasn't a mixed class, at least not all of the time. [girl, age 15]

schools need to teach better sex education. they need young people in year 9 class rooms teaching kids about sex because there are plenty of 12 and 13 year olds having sexual intercourse and encounters at that age ... i think i would hav benefitted from sexual education that was relevant from a younger age. People who are in their early 20s would be listened to more then older teachers would as kids can relate to and would feel more comfortable talking to a person closer to their age. [girl, age 17]

They should warn you in school how bad you feel after a one night stand! [boy, age 18]

Sex ed classes should be held both in girls-only and boys-only sessions, and in sessions with everyone together. These classes should create open and accepting environments for the discussion of all kinds of issues ranging from anal sex to oral sex to rape to bisexuality to zoosexuality to pornography.

A recent trial in the UK had teenagers in schools talking to other teenagers and leading discussions about sex, with great results. Students taught by their peers were more satisfied with what they learned and more significantly, fewer girls reported having had sex by the age of 16.[10] Teenagers tend to listen more closely to people their own age, especially about emotions and sexual experience, than they will to middle-aged men and women. It's nothing personal. But it's a touchy subject and teenagers deserve to feel as comfortable as they can when dealing with the complexities of sex.

If Dr Gemma O'Brien's use-it-or-lose-it theory about female sexual programming is right, being taught about masturbation is important for girls *and* boys. What a civilised world it would be if what's currently called female sexual dysfunction became rare. Men and women of future generations would be so grateful.

For far too long, we have kept sex education in a very small box and it's time that we started thinking outside it.

When to start

If anyone thinks that teenagers are vague in their opinions about when to start having sex, think again. Not a single respondent lacked an opinion, and they were often passionate and specific. When I asked about what age they think is best to start having sexual experiences, I added that they could be specific about what kind of sex, and I asked for reasons. I knew that these days it wasn't just going to be about intercourse.

Approximately a quarter of both boys and girls said that people should start having sex whenever they're ready. Great emphasis was placed on the idea that every individual is different, and people mature at different times. Readiness was also often associated with having the right partner and an emotional connection. Girls especially talked about feeling comfortable, consenting and emotionally satisfied:

I'm 15 and i have sex with my boyfriend of one year. i hate adults that look down on me because of that. i think sex is all about emotion and i dont think age can define emotion … i love him and thats all that really matters to me. [age 15]

I started when I was 13 but there are some of my mates who weren't ready till just recently. [age 16]

… depends on the individual, I don't think there should be a focus on what age because that implies everyone is the same emotionally and developmentally at a certain age. I think whenever the person feels mature and comfortable enough … [age 16]

i dont think age should matter. if you think ure ready then its on your back. [age 16]

I've met 16 year olds who are very self aware and I'd say go for it but I also know 19 year olds who are still getting drunk at parties and doing it because they are dared to. [age 18]

... whenever is right. I started at 15 and think that was too young for me, but i have friends who are still too young now, and other friends who were fine with sex at 14 or younger. [age 17]

someone once told me that if you can say vagina and then penis without giggling then your mature enough to have sex. but i know 20 year olds who still laugh ... [age 17]

above like 14 so ur kinda mature and as long as ur in a caring loving relationship i think its ok at any age [age 15]

Responding to the question about when to start having sex, boys saw the concepts of readiness and maturity from a slightly different angle than the girls, but agreed that it depends on the individual:

When ever u can get it [age 18]

as soon as you want as long as it aint with someone more than 2 years younger [age 15]

I think it's subjective. Personally I started having "experience" when I was 15. It was right for me. Some need time. Some need less. [no age given]

when you are ready. And your dick is big enough [age 18]

[any age] as long as its not forced upon them and preferably with people the same age. Then again, when I was 15 I dreamed of making it with my best mates mum ... [age 17]

When both parties feel mature about the situation and aren't emotionally confused. [age 18]

if you have morals follow them and try to make it someone that is worthwhile. [age 18]

young girls going out with old guys is creepy and wrong. thats the only
sexual age issue i have a problem with. [age 17]

Other respondents were more specific about the ages they thought were
appropriate, and a code of often strict sexual sequencing emerged from
both the girls and boys. Note that when the word 'sex' is used on its own,
it means sexual intercourse.

First from the girls:

... you should probably start off with the basics. Kissing, then
touching, then licking, then sex ... it helps you realise what you're
getting into. I started kissing and touching when I was about 14, oral
sex at 15 and sexual intercourse at 16 ... Any younger and you can
wind up emotionally scarred, any older and by the time you reach
University you're sexually and emotionally under-developed. [age 16]

14 or 15 start giving oral sex ... 16 sex [age 15]

Kissing: about 13, Fingering/handys: 14 or 15, Oral: 15 or 16,
Sex: when ever you feel ready but not before 15 [age 16]

foreplay and oral sex – about 15 or 16, intercourse – 17 or 18 [age 16]

14 – kiss, the person is old enough to realise what this means ...
16 – oral sex, by this age the child is mature enough
mentally/emotionally and physically and can express their emotions
towards another, 17 – more mentally mature for sex ... [age 17]

kissing, touching – anywhere from 13 onwards, oral sex – about 15,
sex from 15, 16 onwards ... [age 17]

kissing from 12 onwards but oral sex shouldnt start until 15 onwards
and sex shouldnt start until 16 onwards because i think sex has a lot
of responsibilities and u can get hurt if you arent emotionally ready
for it [age 16]

13 is a good age for kissing and touching, 15 ultimate age for sex, if it is with sum1 you really like [age 14]

… about 16 for sex and 9 upwords if you wan to masterbate [no age given]

Things that come before sex, I'd say 15yrs old. Sex itself should be waited until the right person comes along & your over the legal age. [age 15]

kissing at 11 … oral at 15, intercourse after 16 [age 15]

highschool would be the best age for sexually kissing and using the hands, late highschool as in end of yr 10 and above would be best for oral but i think sex is something that should be with a special person when u feel 100% safe, loved and respected. not fooled. [age 17]

The boys were no less specific about the right ages for the sequence of sexual events:

umm i rekon 15 is definetly the time wen teenagers should be getting into it full on … 14 should be a time for experimenting with oral and handys but anything under those ages is kinda wrong [age 14]

kissing 12/13, mutual mastubation 14/15, oral and intercourse around 16/17 [age 18]

kissing is fine when people get into high school, so 12 or 13 … they should wait till they are 15 till they get fingered or get a wristy … wen they are 16 it is ok to give and recieve oral sex, and have sex. [age 18]
14 for oral, 15–16 for sexual intercourse & anal [age 18]

I think year 7 (13 years) is kissing time, Year 8 (14) same and maybe a little over the sweater action. Oral sex and intercourse should not occur until you are at least 16 – and even then is a bit young. [age 17]

I think masturbation should begin around end of primary school, start of
high school, because that's when you actually become REALLY interested in girls, but really don't know how to do anything with them. Hand
jobs and fingering are a definite year 9 and 10 thing. It's a way of being
sexually experimental without the risks of sex. People can tell each other
their stories, and you can find out how different everyone's genetalia is.
Depending on what kind of person you are, I see year 11 and 12 as the
"sucking and fucking" years (I just made that term up – feel free to use
that shit in your book!). This is because you're wanting to try these things
before you go out into the big bad world of college interaction with the
opposite sex, and also, by this stage, your mind is so goddamn curious
as to what is SO GOOD about this frigging SEX thing! [no age given]

Although sexual experiences including oral sex, fingering and mutual
masturbation are almost universally seen as things that should precede it,
the *average* age recommended by teenagers for sexual intercourse was 15
or 16. As one girl pointed out, before that, everyone 'is so confused it's
not funny'. But there were many exceptions. Quite a number of both
girls and boys felt that sex (including intercourse) is okay for 12- to 14-
year-olds. One girl who recommended intercourse for 13- and
14-year-olds said:

   … its a good way to keep fit. it brings you together deeply in a
   relationship and it is very appealing and enjoyable. [age 14]

Most, though, would seem to agree with the girl who said:

   but seriously having sex at like 12 is just wrong, its disturbing and its
   like kiddie porn GROSS … like kissin n stuff wen ur like 12-14 is aiight.
   but if u do more than that before ur 15 its just kinda wrong. [age 14]

Then there were those at the other end of the spectrum. A few girls and
boys suggested that no-one is really emotionally mature enough until
around 17 to 19. As the boy who described himself as zoosexual believes,
before 18 or 19 there just isn't the emotional maturity.

Two girls and two boys said that people should wait until marriage before having sex.

One 14-year-old virgin hadn't made up his mind about the right age to start, and admitted to the confusion that other teenagers warn about getting past before being ready:

> i dont know, i want to have sex but i dont want to regret it, i dont think
> strait when im turned on! [age 14]

In spite of what some might see as possible negative influences of things like permissiveness and pornography, there is evidence in almost all these responses of a carefully considered moral and behavioural code. Even though adults might have a hard time wrapping their heads around the new sexual sequencing, it suggests that teenagers don't take sexual activity lightly or casually. It's interesting that the new moral code – what's right and appropriate to do at what ages – isn't something they've learned in sex education classes or from their parents. Instead, it's a distillation of information and instinct. It's been drummed into them that intercourse holds the potential dangers of pregnancy and disease, so alternatives such as oral sex and mutual masturbation now come earlier. But there is also the sense that intercourse represents a bigger emotional step, and should rightly occupy the final stage of intimacy.

Parents, religion, emotional connections

We've acknowledged pornography, mainstream media and sex education when considering outside influences, but what else has an effect on teenage sexual behaviour? I wanted to hear if teenagers think their parents have an influence on whether or not they have sex, and this is the result:

Girls		Boys	
A lot	12%	A lot	7%
A bit	23%	A bit	10%
Not much	27%	Not much	23%
Not at all	38%	Not at all	60%

Another way to slice it up is that 65% of girls and 83% of boys feel that their parents have little or no influence on their sex lives. Of course parents do have *unconscious* influences on teenagers, but teens feel that they are pretty independent. Which is not a bad thing. Adolescence is the time when children are becoming adults and only through their own experiences will they learn. If they're still listening to their parents and swallowing their opinions whole, they'll never make it on their own in the real world.

This doesn't mean that parents are irrelevant. It just means that values are absorbed earlier rather than later, so if parents wait until their kids are going through puberty to fill them in about sex it will be too late. By that point, adults' opinions about things like sexual behaviour couldn't be more meaningless. Most teenagers will do what they want to do, even if they feel guilty for lying to their parents about it. As this survey has shown, 13-year-olds already have their own very definite ideas about sex. However, parents *do* have an influence when their children are much younger and still may actually believe a thing or two that grown-ups have to say. Also, at the age of five or six, kids may not have seen much pornography yet, and parents have an opportunity to talk about sex in a way that includes love, mutual attraction, respect, and all those things that teenagers say they want in order to improve their sex lives – which are usually lacking from most vampire sex websites.

The point is that if parents think they have much influence on whether their teenagers have sex, they'd better reconsider.

That once great arbiter of morality – religion – no longer has a lot of authority or credibility with most teenagers, who often see the Bible as fanciful as *The Da Vinci Code*, if not more. When asked if their religion has an influence on whether or not they have sex, teenagers responded:

Girls		Boys	
A lot	4%	A lot	4%
A bit	4%	A bit	8%
Not much	6%	Not much	4%
Not at all	86%	Not at all	84%

Even parents fared better than religion, which was dismissed by 92% of girls and 88% of boys as having little or no influence on their sexual behaviour. A lot of these kids may still have religious beliefs and adhere to religious principles in other aspects of their lives, but in their eyes, churches, mosques and synagogues have proven over and over again how out-of-date, intolerant and dangerous their sexual tenets are, and teenagers aren't buying them.

Only two generations ago, it was still unusual for a couple to live together before they got married. Now it's the norm. Homosexuality was illegal, and gays and lesbians had to hide their preferences to hold down jobs. Now families attend the Mardi Gras parade, and films and television regularly feature homosexual relationships. Birth control and abortion were strictly limited or illegal. Now teenage girls can go into a family planning clinic and get the pill without their parents' permission. Even though there is still some distance to go, we've come a long way. But a lot of religions still seem to be caught somewhere between the Middle Ages and the 1950s when it comes to sex. When teenagers have grown up in a society that has become relatively enlightened, why would they want to turn back the clock and listen to voices of religious conservatism that say that gay people can't marry or that using condoms is a sin? As responses to this survey suggest, they don't.

Much more relevant to their sex lives – even the boys! – is an emotional component. When asked how important it is to have an emotional connection with their sexual partners, teenagers answered like this:

Girls		Boys	
Very important	55%	Very important	30%
Somewhat important	36%	Somewhat important	42%
Not very important	6%	Not very important	20%
Not important at all	3%	Not important at all	8%

In other words, 91% of girls and 72% of boys believe that an emotional connection is important in sex. The lower percentage of boys unsurprisingly reflects their greater emphasis on the physical experience, but a large majority of them still value an emotional bond. This is enormously encouraging, especially in the face of accusations of promiscuity and rampant meaningless hedonism that some alarmists aim at teenage society. I believe that once again, it shows that in spite of our permissive and highly materialistic and sexualised culture, most teenagers are on the right track.

Parting shots

At the end of the online survey, I asked whether there was anything else that teenagers would like to add about sex or their own sexual experiences. The subjects they covered ranged from sex education to parents to advice for other teens.

A lot of them just enjoyed the chance to rave on about how much they liked sex, and what makes it good.

i find it alot better when you really like the person your doing it with and sharing it with them. i used to just go out and pick up sluts, at the time it was fun but now i have a good girlfriend ... and much prefer staying with her [boy, age 17]

... our experiences are always romantic with sexy foreplay to excite us ... sometimes its just good to cuddle and kiss. [girl, age 17]

I'd shag all day if I had the chance but it's always better to get it every now and then, you appreciate it more [boy, age 18]

its goood [girl, age 15]

I am glad that my partner and myself have sex because it brings us closer and makes us more open to each other. Also its good to 'get it out' [boy, age 17]

i enjoy sex alot. i cant get enough of it. even though i had it 2 times in four days the other week. I STILL WANT MORE! [boy, age 18]

I love it. [girl, age 18]

i luv it and it definetly makes a good night awesome. my sexual experiences hav prodominently been oral and i got to say all types of sex is awesome [boy, age 15] the happiest times in my life were having sex with my ex boyfriend. I loved him, and being so close to him and knowing he loved me too was amazing. Sex is so important because it can bring you so close to someone you love. [girl, age 17]

But not everyone had such high opinions of all their sexual experiences so far, particularly girls:

I think sex is kinda over rated! [age 15]

I really dont think sex is how AMAZING as it used to be. Everyone these days is going out getting drunk and getting knocked up. And they do it to fit in with the crowd … [age 13]

i've had friends who were raped, sexually abused, i've been mollested, it's just really sad to feel disconnected from your own self … we've come nowhere from the sexual revolution in the 60's and 70's, there's still an immaturity, almost a tabboo about talking about it. [age 15]

I'd also like to make the point that being "licked out" by anyone … is usually not a pleasurable experience. I've spoken to a lot of people about it and the general concensus is that it's no good, I wish guys knew that! [age 16]

I find i am increasingly confused about sex, and instead of it getting clearer as i grow up it is all becoming more hazy. I have a real madonna/whore complex. I want sex but somehow i feel guilty or violated by it … [age 17]

At least one boy was disappointed, too:

i feel i want sex all the time except when i am actually doing it. and ive asked around and a lot of guys feel the same. Girls enjoy sex a lot more than guys … [age 18]

Most of the teenagers' advice relating to sex education had already been covered, but in general they felt overwhelmingly that it doesn't go far enough into the emotional side of sex, and that the information is too clinical and often unusable. And *way* too late. Both educators and parents got a serve from a number of girls who want more guidance:

> The best thing parents, teachers etc. can do is to prepare kids for sex by making them aware of what it is, how to be safe, be understanding and to make clear that sex isnt as the media and pornography industry portray it. The more pressure put on kids not to do it the more scared they are of being open about it. the only way parents are going to have any chance of knowing whats going on in their childrens lives is if they dont pressure them or try to enforce rules. If parents do this too much the less they know about their children and their sex lives [age 16]

> i see girls who are like 13, 14, doing drugs, having sex, clubbing, having fake IDs, wanting to be older than they are ... honestly there is no where to turn ... not parents, if my parents knew what goes on in my teen years i would be shot hahaha ... you cant talk to the school councellors about drugs or sex ... if you are under a certain age. i needed councelling and i couldnt pay, didnt want to tell my parents, there need to be more places available to teenagers with councellors open and teenagers need to know this! please! [age 16]

One girl talked about how grateful she was to her mother who explained sex to her when she was young without metaphors or lies so she never found sex scary or weird.

Among the virgins there is great contrast between the girls, who are full of fear and caution, and the boys, who are full of desire:

> It sucks being a nineteen year-old virgin. I want to have sex but I don't want to throw away my virginity on some guy who isn't worth it. I also feel like I have missed out on some very important parts of adolescence by not having very many sexual experiences. [girl, age 19]

I want sex [boy, age 15]

You hear things like "if you have sex you stop growing taller but start getting a bit wider on the side and more chubbier." (I'd like to know if this is true or not) You also have to think about protection and if your going to catch std's or anything like genital warts and even crabs ... [girl, age 15]

i feel like an ugly frigid person because i have not [had sex] although i have friendships with plenty of girls at school [boy, age 15]

i at the moment am not ready to have sex but wen i find the right person i will and being a lesbian is harder. i do want to have sex even if its just a one night stand but wen i'm ready. [girl, age 19]

I REALLY WANT TO HAVE SEX – I AM SO HORNY [boy, age 17]

sex scares me!!!!!!! [girl, no age given]

Perhaps any sex education course should start with the kind of advice that these teenagers gave for each other:

do what you feel comfortable with and never more ... when you are ready you will do more. and don't get caught up in the moment and do things you may regret. [girl, age 15]

I think that you should never rush into things that your not sure of or that you don't feel comfortable about and that way your safer and avoid being hurt emotionally or physically. [girl, age 13]

make sure u mention that having a connection makes it easier on both partners and it's the only way to realy get the most of what sex is realy about. [boy, age 19]

i think sex with randoms (ie ppl you dont know at all) is feral, esp for ppl our age [girl, age 17] people should take more pride in themselves and not have sex til they are physically and emotionally ready for it. [girl, age 16]

I think sex is a perfectly chilled thing to do. I think that you need to be careful about how you do it as far as protection etc ... I will only have sex with either someone I really like and think I can persue a relationship with or a complete random, because i dont want to give the girl the wrong impression. Ive learned that sex can mean more for other people than it does for me ... i have learnt that sex can be a very powerful tool of destruction! [boy, age 18]

Be careful with what you do and make sure that you know what your doing before you do it. Have fun. [girl, age 17]

... as long as teenagers can understand the realities and consequences of their actions, and know what they have to do to be safe and respectful, they can have sex at a young age and turn out just FINE. I'm living proof of that. [boy, age 18]

Dont have sex whilst under the impression of alcohol. and dont tell every1. its special and between you and your partner not everyone else. parents need to focus more on this with their children! [girl, age 15]

Always be yourself! everybody hates it when you are stuck up and think you're the best thing on the planet! Don't be embarressed either [boy, age 16]

I always wanted my first of everything (eg. oral sex, mutual masturbation, intercourse etc.) to be with my first serious boyfriend, and it was. That's how I planned it, and that's how it happened ... I stuck to my beliefs, no matter what others around me thought. That's the best advice teens can get, stick to your own feelings and follow them. [girl, age 18]

i think enough has been said mate [boy, age 18]

Part II

Case histories

About the case histories

There were simply too many responses to the survey to include them all here, so I selected those that I felt represented the wide range of experience, emotions and opinions among the participants.

Sometimes, respondents only filled in part of the survey, so they weren't included. I believe the value for the reader in the case histories is in seeing the big picture. When it comes to an individual's life, the more answers there are, the bigger the picture. In other words, when it came to each survey response, the whole was greater than the sum of the parts.

I didn't choose cases just because they were sensational, but I did choose ones that included more elaborate responses than just monosyllables, although sometimes the short responses were just as expressive in their own way, and where this was so, they also made the cut. In addition, I have tried to represent the ages, genders, states and sexual orientations as equally as possible.

Finally, each one of these histories had something interesting and unique to say. While most have things in common, not one is exactly like another, and the sample attempts to celebrate this diversity.

Being 13 isn't what it used to be. Even if the respondents were still virgins, they had seen porn and used technology (mobile phones, the internet) for sexual encounters. And while the term 'virgin' applies to sexual intercourse, it doesn't include oral sex, and at least one of the girls sampled here (all virgins) had given and received head at the age of eight. But if that sounds alarming, as if today's 13-year-olds seem to be an entirely new breed, their basic needs and desires are the same as every generation that preceded them. They want to be loved and they want to be safe.

Sexual preference for these 13-year-olds is often fluid and not yet set in stone, if it ever will be. Even more than many older adolescents and adults, these kids are still in the process of understanding their sexual identities, but they have a lot of time to make up their minds. And whether it's with opposite- or same-sex partners, they all want romance.

Girl, 13, New South Wales, bisexual

How old were you when you first heard about sex? **9**

What was the first thing you heard about sex?

It feels nice and the penis goes inside the girls vagina.

How old were you when you started masturbating? **13**

On average, how many times a week do you masturbate? **Once a week**

How do you masturbate?

I watch TV where someone is making out i go on a couch and touch myself.

How does masturbating make you feel? **Good**

Describe your sexual fantasies, even if they seem weird or boring or whatever.

I'm with me crush and we go on this yellow bus and kiss everywhere. He pushes himself in me and he softley kisses my neck.

How old were you when you had your first sexual experience with someone else? **12**

What happened in this first sexual experience with another person?

This is when i got my first kiss. I'm at school, i went to sickbay and this other boy was there. He was my crush. He told me how much he liked me. I told him i liked him too. He kissed me. It was the best moment of my life. I wanted to have sex with him right there and then.

How old were you when you first had oral sex? **Never had oral sex**

How old were you when you first had sexual intercourse? **Never**

How old were you when you first had anal sex? **Never**

Would you like to have more sex? **Yes**

How do you think sex could be better for you?

I have so much feelings i want to release them.

How often are your sexual experiences with someone of the same sex or gender as you? **Never**

You think of yourself as … **Bisexual**

If you're gay or lesbian, are you 'out'? **No**

How old were you when you first saw pornography or erotica? **12**

What kind of pornography have you seen? **Magazine.**

Does porn excite you sexually? **Not at all**

Does porn give you ideas about how to have sex? **Never**

Do you think sexy films, music videos or advertising encourage you to have sex? **Sometimes**

Have you ever had phone sex, that is, sexually exciting yourself and someone else over the phone? **No**

Have you ever sent or received sexual text messages? **Yes**

Have you had a sexual experience in an internet chat room? **Yes**

If so, did you also meet up with that person in real life? **No**

Have you ever had a sexual experience with an adult? **No**

Have you ever had a sexual experience with more than one person at a time? **No**

Have you ever been pressured or forced into having sex? **No**

How often do you have sex while using drugs or alcohol? **Never**

Do drugs or alcohol make sex better or worse? **Worse**

Does what you learn in sex education classes at school help you with your actual sexual experiences? **A bit**

Do you think teenagers should be taught more or less about sex at school?
More
What do you think is the best age to start having sexual experiences?
13 or 14? Good age.
Do your parents have an influence on whether or not you have sex? **A lot**
Does your religion have an influence on whether or not you have sex? **A lot**
How important is it for you to have an emotional connection with your sexual
partner? **Very important**
Is there anything else at all that you would like to say about sex or your own
sexual experiences?
Sometimes i imagine having sex.

Girl, 13, Western Australia, straight

How old were you when you first heard about sex? **9**
What was the first thing you heard about sex?
**The first thing I learnt was when someone told me that sex is when a
guys dick goes into a womans fanny.**
How old were you when you started masturbating? **12**
On average, how many times a week do you masturbate?
Five times a week
How do you masturbate?
**I do it in the bathroom, and I get my finger and rub my clitiros, i lick my
finger before i start as a lubricant.**
How does masturbating make you feel? **Good**
Describe your sexual fantasies, even if they seem weird or boring or whatever.
**I dream of kissing like every celebrity that I like and just yeah kissing
and pashing mainly.**
How old were you when you had your first sexual experience with someone
else? **4**
What happened in this first sexual experience with another person?
**We played doctors quite regularly in day care but it never got too sexual
so I felt pretty normal about it happening.**
How old were you when you first had oral sex? **8**

Describe what happened during this oral sex, and how you felt about it.

I sucked his dick and he licked my vagina then another guy joined in. It didn't go any further at the time it felt fine emotionally it happened at day care after school under the assembly. I didn't know anthing about it though but I didn't tell my mum or anything but when I learnt what it was I felt a bit guilty and dirty like I felt like I was way too young and I felt that I was abnormal to do that at that age.

On average, how many times a week do you have oral sex?

Less than once a week

If less frequent, how many times approximately has it occurred? **Twice**

How old were you when you first had sexual intercourse? **Never**

How old were you when you first had anal sex? **Never**

How often are your sexual experiences with someone of the same sex or gender as you? **Never**

You think of yourself as … **Straight**

How old were you when you first saw pornography or erotica? **10**

What kind of pornography have you seen?

Magazines at the corner deli and my friends magazines along with movies.

Does porn excite you sexually? **Not much**

Does porn give you ideas about how to have sex? **Sometimes**

Do you think sexy films, music videos or advertising encourage you to have sex? **Sometimes**

Examples of media encouraging sex:

I know that some movies do but I can't remeber anyones that I have seen that encourage people to have sex.

Have you ever had phone sex, that is, sexually exciting yourself and someone else over the phone? **Yes**

Have you ever sent or received sexual text messages? **Yes**

Have you had a sexual experience in an internet chat room? **Yes**

If so, did you also meet up with that person in real life? **No**

Have you ever had a sexual experience with an adult? **No**

Have you ever had a sexual experience with more than one person at a time? **Yes**

If so, describe what happened and how you felt about it.

**I was having oral sex with a guy and then another guy saw us so, so
that he wouldn't tell we invited him in. i didn't feel bad at all.**

Have you ever been pressured or forced into having sex? **Yes**

If so, describe what happened and how you felt about it emotionally.

**Well a guy a few years older then me kept nagging and if i said no he
would get angry but would never abuse me or actually force himself on
me he'd just keep on asking but at not one point was i scared coz i
knew he would not hurt i was just annoyed about him asking me all the
time but we never did do it.**

How often do you have sex while using drugs or alcohol? **Never**

Do drugs or alcohol make sex better or worse? **Neither**

Does what you learn in sex education classes at school help you with your
actual sexual experiences? **A bit**

Do you think teenagers should be taught more or less about sex at school?
More

What do you think is the best age to start having sexual experiences?

**around year 7 or just the start of high school before kids rush into it with
out knowing because around 12 or 13 you get your period and if
teenagers didn't know about sex and they just did it then they could get
pregnant so we need to warn them about the consequenses of what
could happen so they'll feel safe and know what's right and wrong.**

Do your parents have an influence on whether or not you have sex? **A bit**

Does your religion have an influence on whether or not you have sex?
Not much

How important is it for you to have an emotional connection with your sexual
partner? **Very important**

Is there anything else at all that you would like to say about sex or your own
sexual experiences?

**I think that you should never rush into things that your not sure of or
that you don't feel comfortable about and that way your safer and avoid
being hurt emotionally or physically.**

Girl, 13, Queensland, other

How old were you when you first heard about sex? **9**

What was the first thing you heard about sex?

That the 'doodle' goes into the 'girls part' and thats how you make a baby.

How old were you when you started masturbating? **13**

On average, how many times a week do you masturbate? **Twice a week**

How do you masturbate?

I stick me fingers in my vagina and move it around or just rub the out side of my vagina

How does masturbating make you feel? **Good**

Describe your sexual fantasies, even if they seem weird or boring or whatever.

i fantasize about the guy i like at that moment, coming over to my house pashing me, fingering me, and feeling me and me giving him blow jobs and stuff.

How old were you when you had your first sexual experience with someone else? **7**

What happened in this first sexual experience with another person?

It wasnt realy good it was just me and my best friend (who was a guy) and we would play doctors and he would finger me and i would play with his doodle. At that stage we didnt think we were doing anything wrong.

How old were you when you first had oral sex? **Never had oral sex**

How old were you when you first had sexual intercourse? **Never**

How old were you when you first had anal sex? **Never**

Describe what happens during anal sex and how you feel about having it.

i think its a bit dirty and its when the male stick his penis into the womens anus.

Would you like to have more sex? **Not sure**

How do you think sex could be better for you?

I think i would be more confident around guys because i would be experienced and i would think i was growing up a bit.

How often are your sexual experiences with someone of the same sex or gender as you? **Never**

You think of yourself as …

Other: i feel like i want to do things with girls but i wont admit to that but i like guys so im basically straight. i wouldnt date a woman

How old were you when you first saw pornography or erotica? **13**

What kind of pornography have you seen? **film and mags**

Does porn excite you sexually? **A lot**

Does porn give you ideas about how to have sex? **Sometimes**

Do you think sexy films, music videos or advertising encourage you to have sex? **Sometimes**

Examples of media encouraging sex:

music videos how singers sing about having sex and how hot girls are.

Have you ever had phone sex, that is, sexually exciting yourself and someone else over the phone? **No**

Have you ever sent or received sexual text messages? **Yes**

Have you had a sexual experience in an internet chat room? **Yes**

If so, did you also meet up with that person in real life? **No**

Have you ever had a sexual experience with an adult? **No**

Have you ever had a sexual experience with more than one person at a time? **No**

Have you ever been pressured or forced into having sex? **No**

How often do you have sex while using drugs or alcohol? **Never**

Do drugs or alcohol make sex better or worse? **Neither**

Does what you learn in sex education classes at school help you with your actual sexual experiences? **Not much**

Do you think teenagers should be taught more or less about sex at school? **More**

What do you think is the best age to start having sexual experiences?

16. Having sex. because that is when you have sort of found out who you are and as a TEENAGER, what YOU realy want.

Do your parents have an influence on whether or not you have sex? **A bit**

Does your religion have an influence on whether or not you have sex? **Not at all**

How important is it for you to have an emotional connection with your sexual partner? **Somewhat important**

Is there anything else at all that you would like to say about sex or your own sexual experiences?

I really dont think sex is how AMAZING as it use to be. Everyone these days is going out getting drunk and getting knocked up. And they do it to fit in with the crowd. Thats their path they are choosing in life ...

At the age of 14, the huge diversity that characterises all age groups' experiences and attitudes to sex is evident. Many 14-year-olds have already had intercourse but many are still virgins. Many have had oral sex, while others still find kissing funny. I guess depending on who you're kissing, that can be true at any age.

There is an increased instance of phone and chat room sex, and some at this age are already living to regret things they've done. There is a greater use of drugs and alcohol during sex.

The girls tend to talk more about their feelings, while boys have a bit of trouble (or little desire?) to express their emotions. As with so many other things, girls often start having various sexual experiences younger than boys.

Girl, 14, New South Wales, bisexual

How old were you when you first heard about sex? **4**

What was the first thing you heard about sex? **positions.**

How old were you when you started masturbating? **9**

On average, how many times a week do you masturbate?

More than five times a week

How do you masturbate? **vibrator, and fingers**

How does masturbating make you feel? **Very good**

Describe your sexual fantasies, even if they seem weird or boring or whatever.

Somtimes its girls pushing their chests up against mine or men making moaning noises.

How old were you when you had your first sexual experience with someone else? **7**

What happened in this first sexual experience with another person?

we played doctors and nurses it felt nice thats why we did it then mum walked in and caught us that made me sad as coz i enjoyed it

How old were you when you first had sexual intercourse? **12**

Describe what happened during intercourse, and how you felt about it
emotionally.

**we were lying on top of eachother rubbing up and down, naked but he
kept speeking of other people wich made me sad i feel guilty about
what we did but you cant change the past**

On average, how many times a week do you have intercourse?

Less than once a week

Would you like to have more sex? **Yes**

How do you think sex could be better for you?

with girls, that really liked me.

When you have intercourse, do you use protection? **Yes**

What kind of protection do you use? **condom**

How often are your sexual experiences with someone of the same sex or
gender as you? **Always**

You think of yourself as … **Bisexual**

If you're gay or lesbian, are you 'out'? **No**

How old were you when you first saw pornography or erotica? **8**

What kind of pornography have you seen?

magazines, internet, books, stories and films

Does porn excite you sexually? **A lot**

Does porn give you ideas about how to have sex? **Sometimes**

Do you think sexy films, music videos or advertising encourage you to have
sex? **Never**

Have you ever had phone sex, that is, sexually exciting yourself and
someone else over the phone? **Yes**

Have you ever sent or received sexual text messages? **Yes**

Have you had a sexual experience in an internet chat room? **Yes**

If so, did you also meet up with that person in real life? **No**

Have you ever had a sexual experience with an adult? **No**

Have you ever had a sexual experience with more than one person at a
time? **No**

Have you ever been pressured or forced into having sex? **No**

How often do you have sex while using drugs or alcohol? **Never**

Do drugs or alcohol make sex better or worse? **Neither**

Does what you learn in sex education classes at school help you with your actual sexual experiences? **Not much**

Do you think teenagers should be taught more or less about sex at school? **More**

What do you think is the best age to start having sexual experiences? **14+ but not actual sex just touching or oral sex or dry sex.**

Do your parents have an influence on whether or not you have sex? **A bit**

Does your religion have an influence on whether or not you have sex? **Not at all**

How important is it for you to have an emotional connection with your sexual partner? **Somewhat important**

Boy, 14, Queensland, straight

How old were you when you first heard about sex? **6**

What was the first thing you heard about sex? **that it was a male's penis going into a females vagina, and a baby being born.**

How old were you when you started masturbating? **12**

On average, how many times a week do you masturbate? **Three times a week**

How do you masturbate? **i just picture sex and wank.**

How does masturbating make you feel? **Very good**

Describe your sexual fantasies, even if they seem weird or boring or whatever. **screwing adults**

How old were you when you had your first sexual experience with someone else? **14**

What happened in this first sexual experience with another person? **dry sex, weird but good.**

How old were you when you first had oral sex? **Never**

How old were you when you first had sexual intercourse? **Never**

How old were you when you first had anal sex? **never**

Would you like to have more sex? **Yes**

You think of yourself as … **Straight**

How old were you when you first saw pornography or erotica? **14**

What kind of pornography have you seen? **websites**

Does porn excite you sexually? **A lot**

Does porn give you ideas about how to have sex? **Sometimes**

Do you think sexy films, music videos or advertising encourage you to have sex? **Sometimes**

Examples of media encouraging sex: **can't**

Have you ever had phone sex, that is, sexually exciting yourself and someone else over the phone? **No**

Have you ever sent or received sexual text messages? **No**

Have you had a sexual experience in an internet chat room? **No**

Have you ever had a sexual experience with an adult? **No**

Have you ever had a sexual experience with more than one person at a time? **No**

Have you ever been pressured or forced into having sex? **No**

How often do you have sex while using drugs or alcohol? **Never**

Do drugs or alcohol make sex better or worse? **Neither**

Do you think teenagers should be taught more or less about sex at school? **More**

What do you think is the best age to start having sexual experiences? **i dont know, i want to have sex but i dont want to regret it, i dont think strait when im turned on!**

Do your parents have an influence on whether or not you have sex? **A bit**

Does your religion have an influence on whether or not you have sex? **Not at all**

How important is it for you to have an emotional connection with your sexual partner? **Very important**

Girl, 14, Victoria, straight

How old were you when you first heard about sex? **11**

What was the first thing you heard about sex? **it is how babies are made**

How old were you when you started masturbating? **3**

Describe your sexual fantasies, even if they seem weird or boring or whatever.

just to feel good

How old were you when you had your first sexual experience with someone else? **12**

What happened in this first sexual experience with another person?

it was just a kiss on the lips, it felt special at the time but means nothing now

How old were you when you first had oral sex? **Never had oral sex**

How old were you when you first had sexual intercourse? **Never**

How old were you when you first had anal sex? **Never**

Would you like to have more sex? **Not sure**

How do you think sex could be better for you?

i have personally never done it but it may be better if we had guaranteed pregancy protection because i defintely dont want to get pregnant

How often are your sexual experiences with someone of the same sex or gender as you? **Never**

You think of yourself as … **Straight**

How old were you when you first saw pornography or erotica? **Never**

Does porn excite you sexually? **Not at all**

Does porn give you ideas about how to have sex? **Never**

Do you think sexy films, music videos or advertising encourage you to have sex? **Sometimes**

Examples of media encouraging sex:

american rap videos with lots of black girls dancing all around one guy

Have you ever had phone sex, that is, sexually exciting yourself and someone else over the phone? **No**

Have you ever sent or received sexual text messages? **No**

Have you had a sexual experience in an internet chat room? **No** .

Have you ever had a sexual experience with an adult? **No**

Have you ever had a sexual experience with more than one person at a time? **No**

Have you ever been pressured or forced into having sex? **No**

Do drugs or alcohol make sex better or worse? **Neither**

Does what you learn in sex education classes at school help you with your actual sexual experiences? **A bit**

Do you think teenagers should be taught more or less about sex at school? **Same as now**

What do you think is the best age to start having sexual experiences?

i think that you probably should be 15 or 16 at least but it depends on the person and how mature they are. also how mature they think they are. People shouldn't be forced into sex and certainly shouldn't think that because the legal age is 16 you must have sex when you are 16! because that is stupid and once again peer pressure!

Do your parents have an influence on whether or not you have sex? **A bit**

Does your religion have an influence on whether or not you have sex? **Not at all**

How important is it for you to have an emotional connection with your sexual partner? **Somewhat important**

Is there anything else at all that you would like to say about sex or your own sexual experiences?

Some people can be unattached about sex and they don't care who they do it with as such, because they don't have that emotion involved. While other people 'save' their virginity for the right person. But it depends on the person. Personally i think sex is a personal thing in some ways but very casual in others. It dpends of what you make of it! Sex is like lerning to drive a car, you do it for the first time and it seems a really big deal but after a while it just happens. Some people make a big deal out of it, while others are casual, depnds on who you are.

Girl, 14, New South Wales, 'not sure'

How old were you when you first heard about sex? **9**

What was the first thing you heard about sex? **thats how babies are made**

How old were you when you started masturbating? **9**

On average, how many times a week do you masturbate? **Twice a week**

How do you masturbate?

umm in the shower with the shower head facing down on me

How does masturbating make you feel? **Good**

Describe your sexual fantasies, even if they seem weird or boring or whatever.

watching two emo guys pashing you and themselves at the same time

How old were you when you had your first sexual experience with someone else? **12**

What happened in this first sexual experience with another person?

i started laughing half way into my first pash becuz the guy was dead ugly and i felt weird

How old were you when you first had oral sex? **13**

Describe what happened during this oral sex, and how you felt about it.

i pissed myself laughing it was soo funny we had no idea what we were doing

On average, how many times a week do you have oral sex?

Less than once a week

How old were you when you first had sexual intercourse? **Never**

How old were you when you first had anal sex? **Never**

Would you like to have more sex? **Yes**

How do you think sex could be better for you?

itd be better than have to do all the work on ur own and have to fantasize stuff just to climax

When you have intercourse, do you use protection? **Yes**

What kind of protection do you use? **condoms**

How often are your sexual experiences with someone of the same sex or gender as you? **Sometimes**

You think of yourself as ... **Other: not sure**

If you're gay or lesbian, are you 'out'? **No**

What kind of pornography have you seen? **internet websites, movies.**

Does porn excite you sexually? **A bit**

Does porn give you ideas about how to have sex? **Sometimes**

Do you think sexy films, music videos or advertising encourage you to have sex? **Sometimes**

Examples of media encouraging sex:

that touch me one by that amerie chick i think thats her name shes full like 'touch me im not an innocent girl' or something like that

Have you ever had phone sex, that is, sexually exciting yourself and
someone else over the phone? **No**

Have you ever sent or received sexual text messages? **Yes**

Have you had a sexual experience in an internet chat room? **Yes**

If so, did you also meet up with that person in real life? **No**

Have you ever had a sexual experience with an adult? **No**

Have you ever had a sexual experience with more than one person at a
time? **No**

Have you ever been pressured or forced into having sex? **No**

How often do you have sex while using drugs or alcohol? **Never**

Do drugs or alcohol make sex better or worse? **Neither**

Does what you learn in sex education classes at school help you with your
actual sexual experiences? **Not at all**

Do you think teenagers should be taught more or less about sex at school?
More

What do you think is the best age to start having sexual experiences?
**i dunno whenever it feels right. but seriously having sex at like 12 is just
wrong, its disturbing and its like kiddie porn GROSS ... like kissin n stuff
wen ur like 12-14 is aiight. but if u do more than that before ur 15 its just
kinda wrong**

Do your parents have an influence on whether or not you have sex? **A bit**

Does your religion have an influence on whether or not you have sex?
Not at all

How important is it for you to have an emotional connection with your sexual
partner? **Somewhat important**

Girl, 14, Victoria, straight

How old were you when you first heard about sex? **4**

What was the first thing you heard about sex?
the penis touched the vagina and then a baby appears

How old were you when you started masturbating? **14**

On average, how many times a week do you masturbate?
More than five times a week

How do you masturbate?

I mastubate with my fingers

How does masturbating make you feel? **Good**

Describe your sexual fantasies, even if they seem weird or boring or whatever.

I wish that i had a threesome in a car wearing a full fishnet suit

How old were you when you had your first sexual experience with someone else? **2**

What happened in this first sexual experience with another person?

I was very happy because i didnt know what was happening really

How old were you when you first had oral sex? **14**

Describe what happened during this oral sex, and how you felt about it.

I felt very odd having someones genitals in my mouth

On average, how many times a week do you have oral sex?

Less than once a week

If less frequent, how many times approximately has it occurred? **Once**

How old were you when you first had sexual intercourse? **14**

Describe what happened during intercourse, and how you felt about it emotionally.

I felt ready but it hurt allot and i nearly cried

How old were you when you first had anal sex? **Never**

On average, how many times a week do you have intercourse?

Less than once a week

Would you like to have more sex? **Yes**

How do you think sex could be better for you?

If my boyfriend paid more attention to my body

When you have intercourse, do you use protection? **Yes**

What kind of protection do you use? **condoms**

How often are your sexual experiences with someone of the same sex or gender as you? **Never**

You think of yourself as … **Straight**

How old were you when you first saw pornography or erotica? **8**

What kind of pornography have you seen? **films, websites, books**

Does porn excite you sexually? **A bit**

Does porn give you ideas about how to have sex? **Always**

Do you think sexy films, music videos or advertising encourage you to have sex? **Sometimes**

Examples of media encouraging sex: **britney spears. madonna.**

Have you ever had phone sex, that is, sexually exciting yourself and someone else over the phone? **Yes**

Have you ever sent or received sexual text messages? **Yes**

Have you had a sexual experience in an internet chat room? **Yes**

If so, did you also meet up with that person in real life? **No**

Have you ever had a sexual experience with an adult? **No**

Have you ever had a sexual experience with more than one person at a time? **Yes**

If so, describe what happened and how you felt about it.

"person 1" was having sex with me and "person 2" was having oral sex with me

Have you ever been pressured or forced into having sex? **No**

How often do you have sex while using drugs or alcohol? **Sometimes**

Do drugs or alcohol make sex better or worse? **Better**

Does what you learn in sex education classes at school help you with your actual sexual experiences? **Not at all**

Do you think teenagers should be taught more or less about sex at school? **More**

What do you think is the best age to start having sexual experiences?

i say we should be able to have sexual intercourse at the age of 13 or 14 when we begin thinking about it and we should be able to have sex with any age.

Do your parents have an influence on whether or not you have sex? **Not at all**

Does your religion have an influence on whether or not you have sex? **Not at all**

How important is it for you to have an emotional connection with your sexual partner? **Not very important**

Girl, 14, Queensland, straight

How old were you when you first heard about sex? **8**

How old were you when you started masturbating? **Never**

Describe your sexual fantasies, even if they seem weird or boring or whatever.

I dont generally think about sex, mainly cos im ugly and have never gone out with anyone before either and stuff ... yeah life sucks

How old were you when you had your first sexual experience with someone else? **Never**

What happened in this first sexual experience with another person?

Dont think I've ever had one, I'm really misunderstood, different from most people ...

How old were you when you first had oral sex? **Never had oral sex**

How old were you when you first had sexual intercourse? **Never**

How old were you when you first had anal sex? **Never**

Would you like to have more sex? **Not sure**

How do you think sex could be better for you?

Not sure, never had sex, and at 14 most guys I would hate to have sex with, and most people wouldnt want to be with me anyway haha

How often are your sexual experiences with someone of the same sex or gender as you? **Never**

You think of yourself as ... **Straight**

How old were you when you first saw pornography or erotica? **13**

What kind of pornography have you seen?

Not proper porn just ... you know movies and that

Does porn excite you sexually? **Not much**

Does porn give you ideas about how to have sex? **Sometimes**

Do you think sexy films, music videos or advertising encourage you to have sex? **Sometimes**

Examples of media encouraging sex:

Not me as such but some people would probably ...

Have you ever had phone sex, that is, sexually exciting yourself and someone else over the phone? **No**

Have you ever sent or received sexual text messages? **No**

Have you had a sexual experience in an internet chat room? **No**

Have you ever had a sexual experience with an adult? **No**

Have you ever had a sexual experience with more than one person at a
time? **No**

Have you ever been pressured or forced into having sex? **No**

How often do you have sex while using drugs or alcohol? **Never**

Does what you learn in sex education classes at school help you with your
actual sexual experiences? **A lot**

Do you think teenagers should be taught more or less about sex at school?
Same as now

What do you think is the best age to start having sexual experiences?
Probably 16, when its legal

Do your parents have an influence on whether or not you have sex? **A lot**

Does your religion have an influence on whether or not you have sex?
Not at all

How important is it for you to have an emotional connection with your sexual
partner? **Very important**

Is there anything else at all that you would like to say about sex or your own
sexual experiences?
**WHAT SEX LIFE!?!?! I dont really mind, I would just like people to
understand me more**

Boy, 14, Queensland, bisexual

How old were you when you first heard about sex? **10**

What was the first thing you heard about sex?
kissing and you have to be in-love to have it!

How old were you when you started masturbating? **11**

On average, how many times a week do you masturbate?
More than five times a week

How do you masturbate?
i do it in bed as i thought any other guy does

How does masturbating make you feel? **Good**

Describe your sexual fantasies, even if they seem weird or boring or whatever.
i dunt know how to describe them

How old were you when you had your first sexual experience with someone else? **10**

What happened in this first sexual experience with another person?

   When i 1st kissed a girl i was happy

How old were you when you first had oral sex? **12**

Describe what happened during this oral sex, and how you felt about it.

   awesome and i cant tell u that

On average, how many times a week do you have oral sex?

   Less than once a week

If less frequent, how many times approximately has it occurred? **Three times**

How old were you when you first had sexual intercourse? **12**

Describe what happened during intercourse, and how you felt about it emotionally. **i felt weird**

How old were you when you first had anal sex? **12**

How often does this happen? **Less than once a week**

Describe what happens during anal sex and how you feel about having it.

   strange and that i shouldn't like it

On average, how many times a week do you have intercourse?

   Less than once a week

Would you like to have more sex? **Yes**

How do you think sex could be better for you? **more oral**

When you have intercourse, do you use protection? **Sometimes**

What kind of protection do you use? **condoms**

How often are your sexual experiences with someone of the same sex or gender as you? **Always**

You think of yourself as ... **Bisexual**

If you're gay or lesbian, are you 'out'? **No**

How old were you when you first saw pornography or erotica? **12**

What kind of pornography have you seen?

   mags, movies, photos, websites

Does porn excite you sexually? **A bit**

Does porn give you ideas about how to have sex? **Sometimes**

Do you think sexy films, music videos or advertising encourage you to have sex? **Sometimes**

Have you ever had phone sex, that is, sexually exciting yourself and
someone else over the phone? **No**

Have you ever sent or received sexual text messages? **No**

Have you had a sexual experience in an internet chat room? **Yes**

If so, did you also meet up with that person in real life? **No**

Have you ever had a sexual experience with an adult? **No**

Have you ever had a sexual experience with more than one person at a
time? **No**

Have you ever been pressured or forced into having sex? **No**

How often do you have sex while using drugs or alcohol? **Never**

Do drugs or alcohol make sex better or worse? **Worse**

Does what you learn in sex education classes at school help you with your
actual sexual experiences? **Not much**

Do you think teenagers should be taught more or less about sex at school?
More

What do you think is the best age to start having sexual experiences?
**14 coz i think they are old enough to make there own decisions about
what they can and can't do and i think sexuality shouldn't be a fault.**

Do your parents have an influence on whether or not you have sex?
Not at all

Does your religion have an influence on whether or not you have sex?
Not at all

How important is it for you to have an emotional connection with your sexual
partner? **Not very important**

Girl, 14, Tasmania, straight

How old were you when you first heard about sex? **8**

What was the first thing you heard about sex? **kissing is sex**

How old were you when you started masturbating? **12**

How do you masturbate? **i dont**

Describe your sexual fantasies, even if they seem weird or boring or whatever.
its disgusting

How old were you when you had your first sexual experience with someone else? **5**

What happened in this first sexual experience with another person?
    i was little n locked in a room n dared 2 kiss a boy so i did

How old were you when you first had oral sex? **Never had oral sex**

How old were you when you first had sexual intercourse? **Never**

How old were you when you first had anal sex? **Never**

Would you like to have more sex? **No**

How often are your sexual experiences with someone of the same sex or gender as you? **Sometimes**

You think of yourself as … **Straight**

How old were you when you first saw pornography or erotica? **9**

What kind of pornography have you seen? **web, movies, magazines**

Does porn excite you sexually? **Not much**

Does porn give you ideas about how to have sex? **Sometimes**

Do you think sexy films, music videos or advertising encourage you to have sex? **Never**

Have you ever had phone sex, that is, sexually exciting yourself and someone else over the phone? **Yes**

Have you ever sent or received sexual text messages? **Yes**

Have you had a sexual experience in an internet chat room? **Yes**

If so, did you also meet up with that person in real life? **No**

Have you ever had a sexual experience with an adult? **Yes**

If so, describe what happened and how you felt about it emotionally.
    uncomfortable coz i waz only little and he came on to me

Have you ever had a sexual experience with more than one person at a time? **No**

Have you ever been pressured or forced into having sex? **No**

How often do you have sex while using drugs or alcohol? **Never**

Does what you learn in sex education classes at school help you with your actual sexual experiences? **A lot**

Do you think teenagers should be taught more or less about sex at school?
    More

What do you think is the best age to start having sexual experiences?
little coz its usually litle kids dat get raped coz they dnt know wats goin on
Do your parents have an influence on whether or not you have sex? **A lot**
Does your religion have an influence on whether or not you have sex?
Not at all
How important is it for you to have an emotional connection with your sexual partner? **Not important at all**

Girl, 14, Queensland, straight

How old were you when you first heard about sex? **10**
What was the first thing you heard about sex? **how it is done**
How old were you when you started masturbating? **10**
On average, how many times a week do you masturbate? **Twice a week**
How do you masturbate?
in my room, i rub my clit
How does masturbating make you feel? **Good**
How old were you when you had your first sexual experience with someone else? **9**
What happened in this first sexual experience with another person?
i gave a hand job i was happy
How old were you when you first had oral sex? **13**
Describe what happened during this oral sex, and how you felt about it.
my boyfriend gave me head and i felt great
On average, how many times a week do you have oral sex?
Less than once a week
If less frequent, how many times approximately has it occurred? **Three times**
How old were you when you first had sexual intercourse? **13**
Describe what happened during intercourse, and how you felt about it emotionally.
we had sex and i felt kind of good and kind of bad at the same time. good because of the pleasure and bad because it was with someone who i didnt want to do it with that much

How old were you when you first had anal sex? **Never**

On average, how many times a week do you have intercourse?
Less than once a week

Would you like to have more sex? **Yes**

When you have intercourse, do you use protection? **Sometimes**

What kind of protection do you use? **condoms**

How often are your sexual experiences with someone of the same sex or
gender as you? **Never**

You think of yourself as … **Straight**

How old were you when you first saw pornography or erotica? **13**

What kind of pornography have you seen?
films, magazines, stories, internet websites

Does porn excite you sexually? **A bit**

Does porn give you ideas about how to have sex? **Sometimes**

Do you think sexy films, music videos or advertising encourage you to have
sex? **Always**

Have you ever had phone sex, that is, sexually exciting yourself and
someone else over the phone? **Yes**

Have you ever sent or received sexual text messages? **Yes**

Have you had a sexual experience in an internet chat room? **Yes**

If so, did you also meet up with that person in real life? **No**

Have you ever had a sexual experience with an adult? **No**

Have you ever had a sexual experience with more than one person at a
time? **No**

Have you ever been pressured or forced into having sex? **Yes**

If so, describe what happened and how you felt about it emotionally.
angrey because i wanted to wait

How often do you have sex while using drugs or alcohol? **Sometimes**

Do drugs or alcohol make sex better or worse? **Better**

Does what you learn in sex education classes at school help you with your
actual sexual experiences? **A bit**

Do you think teenagers should be taught more or less about sex at school?
More

What do you think is the best age to start having sexual experiences? **15**

Do your parents have an influence on whether or not you have sex?

Not much

Does your religion have an influence on whether or not you have sex?

Not much

How important is it for you to have an emotional connection with your sexual

partner? **Somewhat important**

Girl, 14, South Australia, straight

How old were you when you first heard about sex? **5**

What was the first thing you heard about sex?

i first learned that the boy put his penis into the girls bottom ... and it
was meant to be pleasurable.

How old were you when you started masturbating? **12**

On average, how many times a week do you masturbate? **Once a week**

How do you masturbate?

i dont actually masturbate on a regualar basis only when im feeling
horney. i sometimes sneak into my mums room and use her vibrator.
i have used a lubricant 3 times so it went in easier. i sometimes finger
myself but it doesnt affect me or do anything ... after masturbating i feel
dirty and disgusted

How old were you when you started masturbating? **Okay**

Describe your sexual fantasies, even if they seem weird or boring or whatever.

i want to have sex with the love of my life. i would want it to be very
passionate. and for him to propose

How old were you when you had your first sexual experience with someone

else? **14**

What happened in this first sexual experience with another person?

i had sex when i was 14. it was disgusting . i hated the person who i did
it with . it was my mums friends son and he kept pressuring me into it.
i went out 3 weeks later and had sex with my friends big brother who
was hot. it felt soo good. i enjoyed it lots. my third experience was even
better. i was on top and it was very sensual. i felt a lot of emotions and
feelings for my 2nd and 3rd sex. but nothing ever happened after that.

How old were you when you first had oral sex? **14**

Describe what happened during this oral sex, and how you felt about it.

i have gave oral sex 3 times. to a boy. i have never recieved oral sex.

On average, how many times a week do you have oral sex?

Less than once a week

If less frequent, how many times approximately has it occurred? **Four times**

How old were you when you first had sexual intercourse? **14**

Describe what happened during intercourse, and how you felt about it emotionally.

i felt the first time disgusted. i couldnt believe i had wasted something soo precious and important to such an ugly loser.!!!!!. my second i couldnt believe i scored so high. my third i scored okay but my friends werent too happy . i seemed to have lots of feelings for him after this. but he doesnt talk to me as alot of people found out due to his lack of respect.

How old were you when you first had anal sex? **Never**

On average, how many times a week do you have intercourse?

Less than once a week

Would you like to have more sex? **Yes**

How do you think sex could be better for you?

i love the feeling of sex. i think it brings you so much closer to the person you like. no matter if its just a quick sex. or if you have been boyfriend and girlfriend. i will defiantelty choose to have sex with the person i like at the moment

When you have intercourse, do you use protection? **Sometimes**

What kind of protection do you use?

i have used a condom 2 times. the third i didnt. and am not sure if i am pregnant as i was never getting a full period every month i was only getting some blood every 3 months but i feel as if i have because i bloated and got cramp for a couple of weekends but am too scared to take a test

How often are your sexual experiences with someone of the same sex or gender as you? **Never**

You think of yourself as … **Straight**

How old were you when you first saw pornography or erotica? **7**

What kind of pornography have you seen?

i have seen lots of films with sexual intercourse like close ups of the penis in the vagina and close ups on oral sex. and anal sex

Does porn excite you sexually? **A lot**

Does porn give you ideas about how to have sex? **Always**

Do you think sexy films, music videos or advertising encourage you to have sex? **Always**

Examples of media encouraging sex:

the sopranos ... american pie ... and 50 cent music videos

Have you ever had phone sex, that is, sexually exciting yourself and someone else over the phone? **No**

Have you ever sent or received sexual text messages? **Yes**

Have you had a sexual experience in an internet chat room? **Yes**

If so, did you also meet up with that person in real life? **No**

Have you ever had a sexual experience with an adult? **No**

Have you ever had a sexual experience with more than one person at a time? **No**

Have you ever been pressured or forced into having sex? **Yes**

How often do you have sex while using drugs or alcohol? **Always**

Do drugs or alcohol make sex better or worse? **Better**

Does what you learn in sex education classes at school help you with your actual sexual experiences? **Not at all**

Do you think teenagers should be taught more or less about sex at school? **More**

What do you think is the best age to start having sexual experiences?

13/14 i think intercourse is the best option.as its a good way to keep fit. it brings you together deeply in a relationship and it is very appealing and enjoyable.

Do your parents have an influence on whether or not you have sex? **A lot**

Does your religion have an influence on whether or not you have sex?

Not at all

How important is it for you to have an emotional connection with your sexual partner? **Somewhat important**

Is there anything else at all that you would like to say about sex or your own sexual experiences?

i met my second for 5 months before we had sex. my second he was my friends big brother. i had met him alot but didnt know him that well. my third i met 1 day and stayed at his house because i was hooking up with his lil bro and then we slept in the bed together with everyone in the room and everyone was asleep so we had sex.

By the age of 15, girls in particular have developed strong opinions about sex, especially the right age to do different things. In contrast to boys, they continue to emphasise the emotional, rather than the physical aspects of sex, but like boys, they often find themselves disappointed by their experiences. High expectations, fuelled by porn as well as mainstream media, combined with a lack of useful sex education, often lead to the conclusion that sex isn't what it's cracked up to be.

Fifteen-year-olds get drunk more often than younger teens, and some regret the bad sex that ensues, but a lot of them are enjoying their experiences, from pashing to hand jobs to blow jobs and intercourse. And while they're becoming more adventurous, for both boys and girls, the one thing that makes sex really good is having an emotional connection.

Girl, 15, New South Wales, straight

How old were you when you first heard about sex? **1**
What was the first thing you heard about sex?
> **I can't ever actually remember learning about sex ... I just remember knowing the basics already when we did a sex ed class in year five. I don't really remember much before that ...**

How old were you when you started masturbating?
> **Never**

Describe your sexual fantasies, even if they seem weird or boring or whatever.
> **Ummm ... I imagine the face of the guy I like on a really hot body, and meeting him outside the school, and standing on tip toes to kiss him, cos I'm shorter than him in this and I'm skinnier than I really am, and then getting into his car and going to his place, where there's a huge bed, and, well, things progressing from there. Pretty standard sex, you know ...**

How old were you when you had your first sexual experience with someone else? **Never**

How old were you when you first had sexual intercourse? **Never**

How old were you when you first had anal sex? **Never**

Would you like to have more sex? **Not sure**

How do you think sex could be better for you?

> **I'm really kind of withdrawn around guys, so I've never really had any real relationship at all.**

You think of yourself as … **Straight**

How old were you when you first saw pornography or erotica? **Never**

Does porn excite you sexually? **Not at all**

Does porn give you ideas about how to have sex? **Never**

Do you think sexy films, music videos or advertising encourage you to have sex? **Sometimes**

Examples of media encouraging sex:

> **Honestly, the romantic movies, the sort of things you feel really jealous of the leading actress to have a gorgeous guy like that who is entirely romantic.**

Have you ever had phone sex, that is, sexually exciting yourself and someone else over the phone? **No**

Have you ever sent or received sexual text messages? **No**

Have you had a sexual experience in an internet chat room? **No**

Have you ever had a sexual experience with an adult? **Yes**

If so, describe what happened and how you felt about it emotionally.

> **When I was little my father sexually assaulted me for years until my mum found out and there was this whole court case and I was 10. He made me masturbate him, if that makes sense. I still hate him so much, and I was really scared of him back then. I try not to let it effect anything I do now though.**

Have you ever had a sexual experience with more than one person at a time? **No**

Have you ever been pressured or forced into having sex? **No**

How often do you have sex while using drugs or alcohol? **Never**

Do you think teenagers should be taught more or less about sex at school?

> **Same as now**

What do you think is the best age to start having sexual experiences?

I think it really depends on the people having these 'experiences'. I definitely think though not before you are 15 because before that no one is really all that mature and just about everyone is so confused it's not funny ... lots of people are still like that after they are 15, but I think that would definitely be a lower limit.

Do your parents have an influence on whether or not you have sex?

Not at all

Does your religion have an influence on whether or not you have sex?

Not at all

How important is it for you to have an emotional connection with your sexual partner? **Somewhat important**

Is there anything else at all that you would like to say about sex or your own sexual experiences?

Well, I wanted to say that one thing I hate about sex ed at school is that even though it covers everything we need to know, I don't know about other schools but only ours, we have a male teacher and he's really gruff and kind of intimidating. It would be so much easier if we had a female teacher and it wasn't a mixed class, at least not all of the time. I'd also like to say that I think it is sooooo horrible for the government to suddenly decree that sure, go ahead, have all the heterosexual sex as you want as soon as you hit 16, but homosexual sex must wait until you are 18. How does that make sense? It's like saying that gay people are somehow inferior or dirty or not as intelligent as straight people, and even though I am not gay myself I know people who are and they are some of the nicest best people I know.

Boy, 15, Queensland, straight

How old were you when you first heard about sex? **10**

What was the first thing you heard about sex? **that everyone does it**

How old were you when you started masturbating? **11**

On average, how many times a week do you masturbate?

More than five times a week

How do you masturbate?

> i started off in bed and then went to the shower because the heat was more arousing i dont use lubricant nor objects but i hav tried lubricants before

How does masturbating make you feel? **Very good**

Describe your sexual fantasies, even if they seem weird or boring or whatever.

> **ive always wanted shower sex with 2 chicks, that would be sweetems**

How old were you when you had your first sexual experience with someone else? **14**

What happened in this first sexual experience with another person?

> **umm me and my gf hooked up it was very quick and basic but it felt great**

How old were you when you first had oral sex? **14**

Describe what happened during this oral sex, and how you felt about it.

> **i cant really remember but i did it with my gf who also was a first timer so it was not too great but still felt awesome**

On average, how many times a week do you have oral sex? **Twice a week**

How old were you when you first had sexual intercourse? **14**

Describe what happened during intercourse, and how you felt about it emotionally.

> **umm well i was drunk and it was under a stair case in mulch that grassy stuff ... but dammmm it was awesome lol. umm wat didnt happen is tha question. i had only known the girl for a week and yeh we screwed like stoned monkeys for bout an hour**

How old were you when you first had anal sex? **Never had anal sex**

On average, how many times a week do you have intercourse? **Once a week**

Would you like to have more sex? **Yes**

How do you think sex could be better for you?

> **umm probs just sex more frequently with a variety of different places and positions and maybe if i reached my climax a lil earlier but i guess its cause im usually incoherent**

When you have intercourse, do you use protection? **Yes**

What kind of protection do you use?

> **ansell condoms ... good stuff**

How often are your sexual experiences with someone of the same sex or gender as you? **Never**

You think of yourself as … **Straight**

How old were you when you first saw pornography or erotica? **7**

What kind of pornography have you seen?

ummm perty much all of it … wat havnt i seen lol

Does porn excite you sexually? **A lot**

Does porn give you ideas about how to have sex? **Always**

Do you think sexy films, music videos or advertising encourage you to have sex? **Sometimes**

Examples of media encouraging sex:

umm Unfaithful is pretty sexual as well as like teen movies encourage me such as American Pie

Have you ever had phone sex, that is, sexually exciting yourself and someone else over the phone? **Yes**

Have you ever sent or received sexual text messages? **Yes**

Have you had a sexual experience in an internet chat room? **No**

Have you ever had a sexual experience with an adult? **No**

Have you ever had a sexual experience with more than one person at a time? **No**

Have you ever been pressured or forced into having sex? **No**

How often do you have sex while using drugs or alcohol? **Most of the time**

Do drugs or alcohol make sex better or worse? **Worse**

Does what you learn in sex education classes at school help you with your actual sexual experiences? **Not much**

Do you think teenagers should be taught more or less about sex at school? **More**

What do you think is the best age to start having sexual experiences?

umm i rekon 15 is definetly the time wen teenagers should be getting into it full on … 14 should be a time for experimenting with oral and handys but anything under those ages is kinda wrong

Do your parents have an influence on whether or not you have sex? **Not much**

Does your religion have an influence on whether or not you have sex? **Not at all**

How important is it for you to have an emotional connection with your sexual partner? **Somewhat important**

Is there anything else at all that you would like to say about sex or your own sexual experiences?

ummm sex in general for me is definetly worth it … i luv it and it definetly makes a good night awesome my sexual experiences hav prodominently been oral and i got say all types of sex is awesome

Girl, 15, Queensland, bi/straight

How old were you when you first heard about sex? **5**

What was the first thing you heard about sex?

that sperm flew from the man to the woman

How old were you when you started masturbating? **Never**

Describe your sexual fantasies, even if they seem weird or boring or whatever.

hot boy. full stop.

How old were you when you had your first sexual experience with someone else? **10**

What happened in this first sexual experience with another person?

kissed a guy in my friends hot tub. kinda foul. but hot.

How old were you when you first had oral sex? **Never had oral sex**

How old were you when you first had sexual intercourse? **Never**

How often are your sexual experiences with someone of the same sex or gender as you? **Sometimes**

You think of yourself as …

Other: sometimes bi … mostly straight

How old were you when you first saw pornography or erotica? **8**

What kind of pornography have you seen?

stories, books movies, websites. haha

Does porn excite you sexually? **A bit**

Does porn give you ideas about how to have sex? **Sometimes**

Do you think sexy films, music videos or advertising encourage you to have sex? **Sometimes**

Examples of media encouraging sex:

some times makes me wanna

Have you ever had phone sex, that is, sexually exciting yourself and someone else over the phone? **Yes**

Have you ever sent or received sexual text messages? **Yes**

Have you had a sexual experience in an internet chat room? **No**

If so, did you also meet up with that person in real life? **No**

Have you ever had a sexual experience with an adult? **No**

Have you ever had a sexual experience with more than one person at a time? **Yes**

If so, describe what happened and how you felt about it.

me and my friend just kissed this guy cause he said he'd give us a bottle of malibu, he was also really hot.

Have you ever been pressured or forced into having sex? **Yes**

If so, describe what happened and how you felt about it emotionally.

been pressured, always said no.

How often do you have sex while using drugs or alcohol? **Never**

Do drugs or alcohol make sex better or worse? **Better**

Does what you learn in sex education classes at school help you with your actual sexual experiences? **Not at all**

Do you think teenagers should be taught more or less about sex at school?

Same as now

What do you think is the best age to start having sexual experiences?

umm i dont think theirs any problem with like kissing, kissings fun and not a big deal, the rest is up to the individual.

Do your parents have an influence on whether or not you have sex?

Not at all

Does your religion have an influence on whether or not you have sex?

Not at all

How important is it for you to have an emotional connection with your sexual partner? **Not very imporant**

Is there anything else at all that you would like to say about sex or your own sexual experiences?

i have never had sex, but i have been fingered and given guys hand jobs, neither of these was included in the questionaire, but

is kinda what most people i know are doing at the moment. just
thought id add that. Xxx

Boy, 15, Victoria, straight

How old were you when you first heard about sex? **11**
What was the first thing you heard about sex?
   that its how you make babies
How old were you when you started masturbating? **12**
On average, how many times a week do you masturbate? **Twice a week**
How do you masturbate?
   with finger and thumb making a ring around penis. the usuall
How does masturbating make you feel? **Good**
Describe your sexual fantasies, even if they seem weird or boring or whatever.
   sex with girls at school
How old were you when you had your first sexual experience with someone
   else? **14**
What happened in this first sexual experience with another person?
   **just pashing on a school camp, i was happy at first but now regret as
   the girl was not good looking.**
How old were you when you first had oral sex? **Never had oral sex**
How old were you when you first had sexual intercourse? **Never**
You think of yourself as … **Straight**
How old were you when you first saw pornography or erotica? **12**
What kind of pornography have you seen? **films mags etc**
Does porn excite you sexually? **A bit**
Does porn give you ideas about how to have sex? **Sometimes**
Do you think sexy films, music videos or advertising encourage you to have
   sex? **Sometimes**
Examples of media encouraging sex:
   slutty american girls on top of the pops shows
Have you ever had phone sex, that is, sexually exciting yourself and
   someone else over the phone? **Yes**
Have you ever sent or received sexual text messages? **Yes**

Have you had a sexual experience in an internet chat room? **No**

Have you ever had a sexual experience with an adult? **No**

Have you ever had a sexual experience with more than one person at a time? **No**

Have you ever been pressured or forced into having sex? **No**

How often do you have sex while using drugs or alcohol? **Never**

Does what you learn in sex education classes at school help you with your actual sexual experiences? **Not much**

Do you think teenagers should be taught more or less about sex at school? **More**

What do you think is the best age to start having sexual experiences?
14 - 15 you can start having sex because the laws are crap but if you arent really into it thats fine

Do your parents have an influence on whether or not you have sex?
Not much

Does your religion have an influence on whether or not you have sex?
Not at all

How important is it for you to have an emotional connection with your sexual partner? **Very important**

Is there anything else at all that you would like to say about sex or your own sexual experiences?
i feel like an ugly frigid person because i have not had sex although i have friendships with plenty of girls at school

Girl, 15, Victoria, straight

How old were you when you first heard about sex? **11**

What was the first thing you heard about sex?
that guys and girls do it with theyre 'things' down below, i thought babies were made with pee not with sperm ... lol

How old were you when you started masturbating? **14**

On average, how many times a week do you masturbate? **Once a week**

How do you masturbate?

i almost always just do it in my bedroom and i usually either use my fingers or an object in the shape of a penis eg. a handle of something

How does masturbating make you feel? **Good**

Describe your sexual fantasies, even if they seem weird or boring or whatever.

i wanna do it at school some time like in the locker bay

How old were you when you had your first sexual experience with someone else? **14**

What happened in this first sexual experience with another person?

making out with my boyfriend at the time or doing a strip tease

How old were you when you first had oral sex? **Never had oral sex**

How old were you when you first had sexual intercourse? **Never**

How old were you when you first had anal sex? **Never**

How do you think sex could be better for you? **actually having it!**

What kind of protection do you use? **i would use condoms**

You think of yourself as … **Straight**

How old were you when you first saw pornography or erotica? **14**

What kind of pornography have you seen? **photos on a website**

Does porn excite you sexually? **Not at all**

Does porn give you ideas about how to have sex? **Sometimes**

Do you think sexy films, music videos or advertising encourage you to have sex? **Sometimes**

Examples of media encouraging sex:

most hip hop film clips have sexually dancing girls in them and personally i think it is degrading and disgusting for girls to be portrayed like that. it may make you feel sexy dressing up like this with your boyfriend but doing those things on the television for everyone to see is disgusting

Have you ever had phone sex, that is, sexually exciting yourself and someone else over the phone? **No**

Have you ever sent or received sexual text messages? **Yes**

Have you had a sexual experience in an internet chat room? **Yes**

If so, did you also meet up with that person in real life? **Yes**

Have you ever had a sexual experience with an adult? **No**

Have you ever had a sexual experience with more than one person at a time? **Yes**

If so, describe what happened and how you felt about it.

when i was doing a strip tease on my webcam to this guy he got his friends over and i didnt know, i felt really bad about it

Have you ever been pressured or forced into having sex? **No**

How often do you have sex while using drugs or alcohol? **Never**

Do drugs or alcohol make sex better or worse? **Neither**

Does what you learn in sex education classes at school help you with your actual sexual experiences? **Not much**

Do you think teenagers should be taught more or less about sex at school? **More**

What do you think is the best age to start having sexual experiences?

17-18. by 16 most people have given or received head or hand and i think that that's ok but i think that that is too young to have sex

Do your parents have an influence on whether or not you have sex? **A bit**

Does your religion have an influence on whether or not you have sex? **Not at all**

How important is it for you to have an emotional connection with your sexual partner? **Very important**

Is there anything else at all that you would like to say about sex or your own sexual experiences?

do what you feel comfortable with and never more, don't test your boundaries. when you are ready you will do more. and don't get caught up in the moment and do things you may regret. i did this with my friends boyfriend, we organised and went to the movies togethor and made out the entire time, it was fun at the time but afterwoods i regreted it so much, i havent told ANYONE and now the guy is acting like a complete dick head and we barely talk any more :(:(we had liked each other for a REALLY long time as well and what we did ruined it because everything got really awkward but for some reason i still like him even though i hate him at the same time ...

Boy, 15, Queensland, straight

How old were you when you first heard about sex? **7**

What was the first thing you heard about sex?

it has to do with the word fuck

How old were you when you started masturbating? **8**

On average, how many times a week do you masturbate? **Twice a week**

How do you masturbate?

dick gets hard, then i take my pants off, and point the dick through my boxers (so it's sticking out), and then i move the nutsack around to loosen it up. then i slowly go up and down the dick with my right hand. the cock gets really hard (And during this time i am pretending i am a parent and that im spanking a girl), then when it hurts to go up and down on the penis, i rub it sideways back and forth with my right hand. after that i lift the dick up and down by itself (without using my hands) and then i feel all relaxed and warm ... then i let it cool off and still have my pants down and i dont put the pants back on till the cock softens.

How does masturbating make you feel? **Good**

Describe your sexual fantasies, even if they seem weird or boring or whatever.

i think about being a parent and having a younger daughter and then i think about the daughter doing something naughty and then i talk to her and then i undo her pants and pull them down, and then i sit in a chair and pull the girl over my knee & spank her bottom about 20 times with my hands on her panties, and then i slowly pull the panties down and spank with my hand again for another 20. then i rub her butt for a long time and sometimes i even turn her over and masturbate her pussy and slap it a little. then i turn her back over my lap and continue spanking her ass for another 10, now this time it's paddle time, so that's for another 20. and then lastly another 10 with the hands. a lot of times i even fantasize about a girl dressing me up as a girl (including and especially, in girls underwear) and then i usually get spanked by that same girl too.

How old were you when you had your first sexual experience with someone else? **9**

What happened in this first sexual experience with another person?

i dont remember

How old were you when you first had oral sex? **Never had oral sex**

How old were you when you first had sexual intercourse? **Never**

Describe what happened during intercourse, and how you felt about it

emotionally. **never have, but would LOVE to**

How old were you when you first had anal sex? **Never**

Describe what happens during anal sex and how you feel about having it.

i dont think I'd go for anal. itd hurt

On average, how many times a week do you have intercourse?

Less than once a week

Would you like to have more sex? **Yes**

How do you think sex could be better for you?

if it actually happened! that would improve it MAJORLY!!! haha.

How often are your sexual experiences with someone of the same sex or

gender as you? **Sometimes**

You think of yourself as … **Straight**

How old were you when you first saw pornography or erotica? **8**

What kind of pornography have you seen?

sex videos (many), spanking, dildo using, i even saw a video of a guy having sex with a horse and a dog. every once in a while i will start to feel sexually aroused extremely, so ill usually get on the computer and search for spanking photos and videos (teens and even younger), and i even usually download pictures of young kids too, mainly girls aged 9-13. there are some really awesome pictures out there you know. i just wish there were more spanking videos. i want to see videos of parents spanking their 9 year old daughters and sons and pulling their underwear down, etc. and even spanking teens, thatd be hot.

Does porn excite you sexually? **A bit**

Does porn give you ideas about how to have sex? **Sometimes**

Do you think sexy films, music videos or advertising encourage you to have

sex? **Sometimes**

Examples of media encouraging sex:

just seeing what underwear girls are wearing in person, ill look at their pants and particularly when theyre sitting down, their undies usually get

exposed when they start to lean over while theyre writing things. im sure there are many other things that trigger sexual things for me too

Have you ever had phone sex, that is, sexually exciting yourself and someone else over the phone? **No**

Have you ever sent or received sexual text messages? **No**

Have you had a sexual experience in an internet chat room? **Yes**

If so, did you also meet up with that person in real life? **No**

Have you ever had a sexual experience with an adult? **No**

Have you ever had a sexual experience with more than one person at a time? **No**

Have you ever been pressured or forced into having sex? **No**

How often do you have sex while using drugs or alcohol? **Never**

Does what you learn in sex education classes at school help you with your actual sexual experiences? **A bit**

Do you think teenagers should be taught more or less about sex at school? **Same as now**

What do you think is the best age to start having sexual experiences? **itd be different for everyone ... it might seriously confuse the hell out of younger people, like it did for me ... i didnt know why i was getting all these urges or what the hell was so special about some girls (now that i think of them) , till now im starting to understand it all a bit better ...**

Do your parents have an influence on whether or not you have sex? **A bit**

Does your religion have an influence on whether or not you have sex? **Not much**

How important is it for you to have an emotional connection with your sexual partner? **Very important**

Girl, 15, New South Wales, bisexual

How old were you when you first heard about sex? **13**

What was the first thing you heard about sex? **it hurt**

How old were you when you started masturbating? **13**

On average, how many times a week do you masturbate? **More than five times a week**

How do you masturbate? **hand**

How does masturbating make you feel? **Not very good**

Describe your sexual fantasies, even if they seem weird or boring or whatever.
  eating a carrot while having sex

How old were you when you had your first sexual experience with someone
  else? **13**

What happened in this first sexual experience with another person?
  didn't care, just wanted a baby.

How old were you when you first had oral sex? **13**

Describe what happened during this oral sex, and how you felt about it. **dirty**

On average, how many times a week do you have oral sex?
  More than five times a week

How old were you when you first had sexual intercourse? **14**

Describe what happened during intercourse, and how you felt about it
  emotionally. **happy**

How old were you when you first had anal sex? **13**

How often does this happen? **Less than once a week**

Describe what happens during anal sex and how you feel about having it.
  not happy

On average, how many times a week do you have intercourse?
  Five times a week

Would you like to have more sex? **Yes**

How do you think sex could be better for you? **more people**

When you have intercourse, do you use protection? **Never**

What kind of protection do you use? **don't**

How often are your sexual experiences with someone of the same sex or
  gender as you? **Sometimes**

You think of yourself as … **Bisexual**

If you're gay or lesbian, are you 'out'? **No**

Does porn excite you sexually? **A lot**

Does porn give you ideas about how to have sex? **Always**

Do you think sexy films, music videos or advertising encourage you to have
  sex? **Always**

Have you ever had phone sex, that is, sexually exciting yourself and
  someone else over the phone? **Yes**

Have you ever sent or received sexual text messages? **Yes**

Have you had a sexual experience in an internet chat room? **No**

Have you ever had a sexual experience with an adult? **Yes**

If so, describe what happened and how you felt about it emotionally.

horrible I wanted to cry for a week

Have you ever had a sexual experience with more than one person at a
time? **Yes**

If so, describe what happened and how you felt about it.

There were 5 men, it was awful

Have you ever been pressured or forced into having sex? **Yes**

If so, describe what happened and how you felt about it emotionally.

sad

How often do you have sex while using drugs or alcohol? **Sometimes**

Do drugs or alcohol make sex better or worse? **Better**

Does what you learn in sex education classes at school help you with your
actual sexual experiences? **Not much**

Do you think teenagers should be taught more or less about sex at school?

Same as now

What do you think is the best age to start having sexual experiences?

When ever you want to

Do your parents have an influence on whether or not you have sex?

Not much

Does your religion have an influence on whether or not you have sex?

Not at all

How important is it for you to have an emotional connection with your sexual
partner? **Not important at all**

Girl, 15, Victoria, straight

How old were you when you first heard about sex? **11**

What was the first thing you heard about sex? **i cant remember**

How old were you when you started masturbating? **Never**

Describe your sexual fantasies, even if they seem weird or boring or whatever.

ultimate sex fantasy- me and heath ledger.

How old were you when you had your first sexual experience with someone else? **14**

What happened in this first sexual experience with another person?
pashed a boy. i kinda regretted it on the first night because it felt weird but then the second night it was fun! we both met when we were holidaying.

How old were you when you first had oral sex? **Never had oral sex**

How old were you when you first had sexual intercourse? **Never**

How old were you when you first had anal sex? **Never**

How often are your sexual experiences with someone of the same sex or gender as you? **Never**

You think of yourself as … **Straight**

How old were you when you first saw pornography or erotica? **Never**

Do you think sexy films, music videos or advertising encourage you to have sex? **Sometimes**

Examples of media encouraging sex:
music videos nowadays are all about you will only ever get a boyfriend if you put out or if your gorgeous. an it is displaying guys that are treating girls like shit.

Have you ever had phone sex, that is, sexually exciting yourself and someone else over the phone? **No**

Have you ever sent or received sexual text messages? **No**

Have you had a sexual experience in an internet chat room? **Yes**

If so, did you also meet up with that person in real life? **No**

Have you ever had a sexual experience with an adult? **No**

Have you ever had a sexual experience with more than one person at a time? **No**

Have you ever been pressured or forced into having sex? **No**

How often do you have sex while using drugs or alcohol? **Never**

Does what you learn in sex education classes at school help you with your actual sexual experiences? **Not much**

Do you think teenagers should be taught more or less about sex at school?
More

What do you think is the best age to start having sexual experiences?

sexual intercourse - 17 to 18 years old. it just seems you are old enough to make your own decisions without being affected by pressure

Do your parents have an influence on whether or not you have sex?

Not much

Does your religion have an influence on whether or not you have sex?

Not at all

How important is it for you to have an emotional connection with your sexual partner? **Very important**

Is there anything else at all that you would like to say about sex or your own sexual experiences?

in school sex ed i think they should actually say what to do, like it says what happens during sex but they dont actually say how to do it.

Boy, 15, Western Australia, straight

How old were you when you first heard about sex? **10**

What was the first thing you heard about sex? **it was how i was born**

How old were you when you started masturbating? **12**

On average, how many times a week do you masturbate?

Four times a week

How do you masturbate? **wanking**

How does masturbating make you feel? **Good**

Describe your sexual fantasies, even if they seem weird or boring or whatever.

hmm having a 3some with 2 chicks and me

How old were you when you had your first sexual experience with someone else? **9**

What happened in this first sexual experience with another person?

pretty gud

How old were you when you first had oral sex? **14**

Describe what happened during this oral sex, and how you felt about it.

it was sik felt amazing

On average, how many times a week do you have oral sex?

Less than once a week

If less frequent, how many times approximately has it occurred? **Five times**

How old were you when you first had sexual intercourse? **15**

Describe what happened during intercourse, and how you felt about it
emotionally. **it wasnt as good as what it was made out to be**

How old were you when you first had anal sex? **Never**

Describe what happens during anal sex and how you feel about having it.
i dont see why any1 would want to its fuking rank

On average, how many times a week do you have intercourse?
Less than once a week

Would you like to have more sex? **Yes**

How do you think sex could be better for you?
**with someone i love as i dont know what love is yet as i am 15 i want to
experience intercourse with someone i love**

When you have intercourse, do you use protection? **Yes**

What kind of protection do you use? **condom**

How often are your sexual experiences with someone of the same sex or
gender as you? **Never**

You think of yourself as … **Straight**

How old were you when you first saw pornography or erotica? **12**

What kind of pornography have you seen?
pictures, internet websites, magizines

Does porn excite you sexually? **A bit**

Does porn give you ideas about how to have sex? **Sometimes**

Do you think sexy films, music videos or advertising encourage you to have
sex? **Sometimes**

Examples of media encouraging sex:
i dunno some music film clips are arousing to some people

Have you ever had phone sex, that is, sexually exciting yourself and
someone else over the phone? **No**

Have you ever sent or received sexual text messages? **Yes**

Have you had a sexual experience in an internet chat room? **Yes**

If so, did you also meet up with that person in real life? **No**

Have you ever had a sexual experience with an adult? **No**

Have you ever had a sexual experience with more than one person at a
time? **No**

Have you ever been pressured or forced into having sex? **No**
If so, describe what happened and how you felt about it emotionally.

but ive been drunk and not knowing wat i was doin

How often do you have sex while using drugs or alcohol? **Sometimes**
Do drugs or alcohol make sex better or worse? **Neither**
Does what you learn in sex education classes at school help you with your actual sexual experiences? **Not at all**
Do you think teenagers should be taught more or less about sex at school? **More**
Do your parents have an influence on whether or not you have sex? **Not at all**
Does your religion have an influence on whether or not you have sex? **Not at all**
How important is it for you to have an emotional connection with your sexual partner? **Not important at all**

Girl, 15, New South Wales, bisexual

How old were you when you first heard about sex? **9**
What was the first thing you heard about sex?

what sex was ... ??? u know, like penetration. I remember telling one of my friends at the time because she thought you just jumped on the bed with a guy ... lolz

How old were you when you started masturbating? **13**
On average, how many times a week do you masturbate? **Once a week**
How do you masturbate?

I like lubricant coz it feels so nice and cold when i insert my fingers ... i always wanted a vibrator, i think they'd be awesome.

How does masturbating make you feel? **Okay**
Describe your sexual fantasies, even if they seem weird or boring or whatever.

I would like to have sex with a guy and another chick. And we could handcuff the guy and let him watch while i lick melting chocolate off her naked body

How old were you when you had your first sexual experience with someone else? **14**

What happened in this first sexual experience with another person?

My first kiss was also the first night i ever got drunk. i was so nervous and he was 6 years older than me! I had sex for the first time in the back of my boyfriends car and i freaked out because we weren't that far out of town. I didnt bleed suprisingly enough ... but his dick was pretty small (seriously) ... lolz. I regretted that at the time because he meant nothing to me. The first time I had sex with a chick I was nervous because I was in love with her and I had a boyfriend, but we skipped school, got drunk and she ended up seducing me. I'll never say that i regret it because i didnt. I am still in love with her to this day but she moved towns and that shattered my heart. And this was all in the same year!

How old were you when you first had oral sex? **14**

Describe what happened during this oral sex, and how you felt about it.

the first time i gave a guy head ... well, i have arthritic sort of problems with my jaw and he expected too much of me ... especially for my first time! I felt like I was going to vomit, having a fucking cock down your throat makes your stomach heave ... He went round and told all his friends that I was crap ... First time a guy went down on me ... I was pretty out of it and eager as i heard it was pretty good, but, i was still nervous. What if it smells down there? What if im not normal? But i got over it. He just sorta licked around a bit ... it was shit! I met this guy who did know what he was doing! He'd softly massage my clit with his tongue like he was kissing it and he'd jam his tongue up my vagina ... god it was exciting!

On average, how many times a week do you have oral sex?

Less than once a week

If less frequent, how many times approximately has it occurred? **Ten times**

How old were you when you first had sexual intercourse? **14**

Describe what happened during intercourse, and how you felt about it emotionally.

i thought i was ready. One night when i got back from holidays i met up with my boyfriend and we did it in the back of his car. He'd had

problems getting it up (and he was 17 years old!) I was too scared about getting caught to think about it emotionally. I was impressed with myself … guess I wanted to know what all the fuss is about … Afterwards i felt like I'd lost my innocence and i was angry at him mostly because I wanted it back, i hated feeling so old and guilty …

How old were you when you first had anal sex? **15**

Describe what happens during anal sex and how you feel about having it.

I hate anal sex! it happened once when this guy and i were doing it doggy style, but he jammed it up my arse in the middle of it all.
I screamed in pain. Decked him, got dressed and walked off.

On average, how many times a week do you have intercourse?

Less than once a week

Would you like to have more sex? **Yes**

How do you think sex could be better for you?

I want a relationship! Im sick of having sex and getting ditched. I love sex but i wish i could lay in bed and hold someone i love after we'd just had mad passionate sex! I want someone to settle down with, whos devoted and faithful to me. And we could have sex every night! and i want to have an orgasm … ive never had 1. I still enjoy sex … but ive never climaxed …

When you have intercourse, do you use protection? **Yes**

What kind of protection do you use? **condoms/contraceptive pill**

How often are your sexual experiences with someone of the same sex or gender as you? **Sometimes**

You think of yourself as … **Bisexual**

If you're gay or lesbian, are you 'out'? **Yes**

If you're gay or lesbian and you came out, was it hard? **Not hard at all**

Describe what happened when you came out and how you felt about it.

I hooked up with a chick at a party and news spread fast. Ive never officially announced "i bat for both teams" but theres an unspoken knowledge.

How old were you when you first saw pornography or erotica? **6**

What kind of pornography have you seen?

porno flicks, i love the magazines … occassionally ill go 2 websites

Does porn excite you sexually? **A lot**

Does porn give you ideas about how to have sex? **Sometimes**

Do you think sexy films, music videos or advertising encourage you to have sex? **Sometimes**

Have you ever had phone sex, that is, sexually exciting yourself and someone else over the phone? **Yes**

Have you ever sent or received sexual text messages? **Yes**

Have you had a sexual experience in an internet chat room? **No**

Have you ever had a sexual experience with an adult? **Yes**

If so, describe what happened and how you felt about it emotionally.

uh i was 14, he was 21, i liked him, i seduced. Practically had 2 beg for sex for hours before he got over his conscience and would sleep with me! Then there was a couple of times when my uncle touched me while i was asleep. The first time it happened he'd fed me so much bourbon i was in fits of vomiting and he took advantage of me while i was out of it and in his care. I felt scared, betrayed and dirty.

Have you ever had a sexual experience with more than one person at a time? **Yes**

If so, describe what happened and how you felt about it.

I had sex with two girls and we just took turns touching and licking each other.

Have you ever been pressured or forced into having sex? **Yes**

If so, describe what happened and how you felt about it emotionally.

i was pressured, begged more like it, but i gave in of my own free will

How often do you have sex while using drugs or alcohol? **Sometimes**

Do drugs or alcohol make sex better or worse? **Better**

Does what you learn in sex education classes at school help you with your actual sexual experiences? **Not at all**

Do you think teenagers should be taught more or less about sex at school? **More**

What do you think is the best age to start having sexual experiences?

i think 15-16, for girls and about 16 for guys coz they dont mature as fast. it really depends on the person. whenever a person feels comfortable enough with themselves. They have 2 feel ready within there body and there mind.

Do your parents have an influence on whether or not you have sex?

Not much

Does your religion have an influence on whether or not you have sex?

Not at all

How important is it for you to have an emotional connection with your sexual partner? **Somewhat important**

Girl, 15, South Australia, straight

How old were you when you first heard about sex? **8**

What was the first thing you heard about sex?

wat is happening? the process eg where babies come from

Describe your sexual fantasies, even if they seem weird or boring or whatever.

have sex on a rocking chair, office chair, swimming pool.

How old were you when you had your first sexual experience with someone else? **3**

What happened in this first sexual experience with another person?

i kissed a boy on the cheeck that i liked.

How old were you when you first had oral sex? **14**

Describe what happened during this oral sex, and how you felt about it.

i was with my boyfriend in his house n i enjoyed it!

On average, how many times a week do you have oral sex?

Less than once a week

If less frequent, how many times approximately has it occurred? **Ten times**

How old were you when you first had sexual intercourse? **15**

Describe what happened during intercourse, and how you felt about it emotionally.

i was drunk but with my boyfriend who i love. didnt take note.

How old were you when you first had anal sex? **Never**

Would you like to have more sex? **Not sure**

When you have intercourse, do you use protection? **Yes**

What kind of protection do you use? **Condoms**

How often are your sexual experiences with someone of the same sex or gender as you? **Never**

You think of yourself as … **Straight**

How old were you when you first saw pornography or erotica? **14**

What kind of pornography have you seen? **films**

Does porn excite you sexually? **A bit**

Does porn give you ideas about how to have sex? **Sometimes**

Do you think sexy films, music videos or advertising encourage you to have sex? **Sometimes**

Have you ever had phone sex, that is, sexually exciting yourself and someone else over the phone? **No**

Have you ever sent or received sexual text messages? **No**

Have you had a sexual experience in an internet chat room? **No**

If so, did you also meet up with that person in real life? **No**

Have you ever had a sexual experience with an adult? **No**

Have you ever had a sexual experience with more than one person at a time? **No**

Have you ever been pressured or forced into having sex? **No**

How often do you have sex while using drugs or alcohol? **Sometimes**

Do drugs or alcohol make sex better or worse? **Neither**

Does what you learn in sex education classes at school help you with your actual sexual experiences? **Not much**

Do you think teenagers should be taught more or less about sex at school? **Same as now**

What do you think is the best age to start having sexual experiences? **when you feel comfortable with the person and you love one another after the age of 16! you have to both feel the same about the experience.**

Do your parents have an influence on whether or not you have sex? **Not at all**

Does your religion have an influence on whether or not you have sex? **Not much**

How important is it for you to have an emotional connection with your sexual partner? **Very important**

Is there anything else at all that you would like to say about sex or your own sexual experiences?

Dont have sex whilst under the impression of alcohol. and dont tell every1. its special and between you and your partner not everyone else. parents need to focus more on this with their children!

Girl, 15, Queensland, straight

How old were you when you first heard about sex? **7**
What was the first thing you heard about sex?

he puts his "thing" in your "thing"

How old were you when you started masturbating? **13**
On average, how many times a week do you masturbate? **Once a week**
How do you masturbate?

In bed. Don't really use anything. Just rub haha not really sure how to describe.

How does masturbating make you feel? **Good**
Describe your sexual fantasies, even if they seem weird or boring or whatever.

Strip clubs aaaannnd anything really. Anything kind of quirky.

How old were you when you had your first sexual experience with someone else? **10**
What happened in this first sexual experience with another person?

We would pretend we were at a club and then a guy would pick us up and we'd go home and "have sex". it wasn't actually sex just a hell of a lot of pretending.

How old were you when you first had oral sex? **13**
Describe what happened during this oral sex, and how you felt about it.

I didn't particularly want to do it. He had fingered me and said it was only fair i gave him something back. In the end he basically forced me. It wasn't too bad but its not something i'd do just for fun. Afterwards i felt used.

On average, how many times a week do you have oral sex?

Less than once a week

If less frequent, how many times approximately has it occurred? **Four times**

How old were you when you first had sexual intercourse? **14**

Describe what happened during intercourse, and how you felt about it
emotionally.

**We were at a party and we'd been going out for 7 months … we're still
going out. We had come to a mutual agreement about it so there was
no pressuring at all. It didn't turn out as planned … it wasn't in a
bedroom or anything and we got walked in on by someone who i dont
get on with very well. she made the whole party come in and turned
something that was happening everywhere into a big deal. The actual
sex … well it kind of hurt at first but it wasn't too bad. emotionally it
didnt feel particularly special but i know now it gets alot better.**

How old were you when you first had anal sex? **Never**

On average, how many times a week do you have intercourse? **Once a week**

Would you like to have more sex? **Yes**

How do you think sex could be better for you?

I don't think it could be better. i like it the way it is.

When you have intercourse, do you use protection? **Yes**

What kind of protection do you use? **Condoms, I'm going on the pill soon.**

How often are your sexual experiences with someone of the same sex or
gender as you? **Sometimes**

You think of yourself as … **Straight**

How old were you when you first saw pornography or erotica? **12**

What kind of pornography have you seen?

**internet web sites, covers of movies, some magazines and lots of
stories.**

Does porn excite you sexually? **A bit**

Does porn give you ideas about how to have sex? **Never**

Do you think sexy films, music videos or advertising encourage you to have
sex? **Sometimes**

Examples of media encouraging sex:

**Music videos with rap artists etc. are always all about sex. Ads and
movies influence people because they want to be like the celebrities.**

Have you ever had phone sex, that is, sexually exciting yourself and
someone else over the phone? **No**

Have you ever sent or received sexual text messages? **No**

Have you had a sexual experience in an internet chat room? **No**

Have you ever had a sexual experience with an adult? **No**

Have you ever had a sexual experience with more than one person at a time? **No**

Have you ever been pressured or forced into having sex? **No**

How often do you have sex while using drugs or alcohol? **Sometimes**

Do drugs or alcohol make sex better or worse? **Worse**

Does what you learn in sex education classes at school help you with your actual sexual experiences? **A bit**

Do you think teenagers should be taught more or less about sex at school? **More**

What do you think is the best age to start having sexual experiences?

i think it depends on the person. i dont think anyone should ever feel pressured for whatever reasons to feel like that have to have sex at the same time i dont think they should feel guilty for doing it. I'm 15 and i have sex with my boyfriend of one year. i hate adults that look down on me because of that. i think sex is all about emotion and i dont think age can define emotion. sounds stupid and cliched but i love him and thats all that really matters to me.

Do your parents have an influence on whether or not you have sex? **A bit**

Does your religion have an influence on whether or not you have sex? **Not at all**

How important is it for you to have an emotional connection with your sexual partner? **Very important**

Girl, 15, New South Wales, straight

How old were you when you first heard about sex? **5**

What was the first thing you heard about sex? **that its how we got here**

How old were you when you started masturbating? **13**

On average, how many times a week do you masturbate? **More than five times a week**

How do you masturbate? **using fingers**

How does masturbating make you feel? **Very good**

How old were you when you had your first sexual experience with someone else? **13**

What happened in this first sexual experience with another person?

i gave my boyfriend a handjob. i was scared, but also excited

How old were you when you first had oral sex? **14**

Describe what happened during this oral sex, and how you felt about it.

i thought it was cool but also kinda gross

On average, how many times a week do you have oral sex? **Once a week**

How old were you when you first had sexual intercourse? **14**

Describe what happened during intercourse, and how you felt about it emotionally.

penis entered vagina. i felt happy bcuz we had been trying for a while but it hurt too much to get it in, but when it happened i was elated

How old were you when you first had anal sex? **Never**

On average, how many times a week do you have intercourse?

Twice a week

Would you like to have more sex? **Not sure**

How do you think sex could be better for you?

it makes me feel closer to my bf

When you have intercourse, do you use protection? **Yes**

What kind of protection do you use? **condoms and the pill**

How often are your sexual experiences with someone of the same sex or gender as you? **Never**

You think of yourself as … **Straight**

How old were you when you first saw pornography or erotica? **13**

What kind of pornography have you seen?

mags, photos, lit erotica, films

Does porn excite you sexually? **A bit**

Does porn give you ideas about how to have sex? **Sometimes**

Do you think sexy films, music videos or advertising encourage you to have sex? **Never**

Have you ever had phone sex, that is, sexually exciting yourself and someone else over the phone? **No**

Have you ever sent or received sexual text messages? **Yes**

Have you had a sexual experience in an internet chat room? **No**

Have you ever had a sexual experience with an adult? **No**

Have you ever had a sexual experience with more than one person at a time? **No**

Have you ever been pressured or forced into having sex? **No**

How often do you have sex while using drugs or alcohol? **Never**

Do drugs or alcohol make sex better or worse? **Neither**

Does what you learn in sex education classes at school help you with your actual sexual experiences? **A bit**

Do you think teenagers should be taught more or less about sex at school? **More**

What do you think is the best age to start having sexual experiences? **any age above like 14 so ur kinda mature and as long as ur in a caring loving relationship i think its ok at any age**

Do your parents have an influence on whether or not you have sex? **Not much**

Does your religion have an influence on whether or not you have sex? **Not at all**

How important is it for you to have an emotional connection with your sexual partner? **Very important**

Girl, 15, New South Wales, straight

How old were you when you first heard about sex? **4**

What was the first thing you heard about sex? **snake enters her bush**

How old were you when you started masturbating? **11**

On average, how many times a week do you masturbate? **Four times a week**

How do you masturbate? **none of your bloody business**

How does masturbating make you feel? **Good**

Describe your sexual fantasies, even if they seem weird or boring or whatever. **guys ... der**

How old were you when you had your first sexual experience with someone else? **9**

What happened in this first sexual experience with another person?
kissing under the table at a christian primary skool

How old were you when you first had oral sex? **14**

Describe what happened during this oral sex, and how you felt about it.
oral sex happened

On average, how many times a week do you have oral sex?
Less than once a week

How old were you when you first had sexual intercourse? **14**

Describe what happened during intercourse, and how you felt about it
emotionally. **he was a random i was drunk it was good**

How old were you when you first had anal sex? **Never**

On average, how many times a week do you have intercourse? **Once a week**

Would you like to have more sex? **Not sure**

When you have intercourse, do you use protection? **Sometimes**

What kind of protection do you use? **condoms**

How often are your sexual experiences with someone of the same sex or
gender as you? **Never**

You think of yourself as … **Straight**

How old were you when you first saw pornography or erotica? **11**

What kind of pornography have you seen? **films mags internet**

Does porn excite you sexually? **Not much**

Does porn give you ideas about how to have sex? **Never**

Do you think sexy films, music videos or advertising encourage you to have
sex? **Sometimes**

Have you ever had phone sex, that is, sexually exciting yourself and
someone else over the phone? **No**

Have you ever sent or received sexual text messages? **Yes**

Have you had a sexual experience in an internet chat room? **No**

Have you ever had a sexual experience with an adult? **Yes**

If so, describe what happened and how you felt about it emotionally.
sex happened it was good

Have you ever had a sexual experience with more than one person at a
time? **No**

Have you ever been pressured or forced into having sex? **Yes**

How often do you have sex while using drugs or alcohol? **Most of the time**

Do drugs or alcohol make sex better or worse? **Better**

Does what you learn in sex education classes at school help you with your actual sexual experiences? **Not at all**

Do you think teenagers should be taught more or less about sex at school? **More**

What do you think is the best age to start having sexual experiences? **whenever u are ready**

Do your parents have an influence on whether or not you have sex? **Not at all**

Does your religion have an influence on whether or not you have sex? **Not at all**

How important is it for you to have an emotional connection with your sexual partner? **Not important at all**

Girl, 15, New South Wales, straight

What was the first thing you heard about sex?

I think it would have been that people have sex to make babies.

How old were you when you started masturbating? **13**

On average, how many times a week do you masturbate?

More than five times a week

How do you masturbate?

I do it in my room, before i sleep. How embarassing. I don't use anything. I would rather not go into anymore detail.

How does masturbating make you feel? **Very good**

Describe your sexual fantasies, even if they seem weird or boring or whatever.

I dont have many.

How old were you when you had your first sexual experience with someone else? **14**

What happened in this first sexual experience with another person?

I wouldnt say kissing is a sexual experience, my real one would be involving mine & a boys body parts. It was strange but seemed normal, it was something i was nervous about but when it happens it just seem right & you just forget whats happening.

How old were you when you first had oral sex? **Never had oral sex**

How old were you when you first had sexual intercourse? **Never**

How old were you when you first had anal sex? **Never**

How often are your sexual experiences with someone of the same sex or gender as you? **Never**

You think of yourself as … **Straight**

How old were you when you first saw pornography or erotica? **12**

What kind of pornography have you seen?

> **My bestie at the time, knew everything about sex etc. I was at her house & she said we were going to watch lord of the rings but instead she put on some porno.**

Does porn excite you sexually? **A bit**

Does porn give you ideas about how to have sex? **Sometimes**

Do you think sexy films, music videos or advertising encourage you to have sex? **Sometimes**

Have you ever had phone sex, that is, sexually exciting yourself and someone else over the phone? **No**

Have you ever sent or received sexual text messages? **Yes**

Have you had a sexual experience in an internet chat room? **No**

Have you ever had a sexual experience with an adult? **Yes**

If so, describe what happened and how you felt about it emotionally.

> **Well, it wasnt by choice. I was abused & i feel sick about it. i hate what happened & that nothing was done about it. It was wrong.**

Have you ever had a sexual experience with more than one person at a time? **No**

How often do you have sex while using drugs or alcohol? **Never**

Does what you learn in sex education classes at school help you with your actual sexual experiences? **Not much**

Do you think teenagers should be taught more or less about sex at school? **More**

What do you think is the best age to start having sexual experiences?

> **Things that come before sex, I'd say 15yrs old. Sex itself should be waited until the right person comes along & your over the legal age.**

Do your parents have an influence on whether or not you have sex? **A bit**

Does your religion have an influence on whether or not you have sex? **A bit**

How important is it for you to have an emotional connection with your sexual partner? **Very important**

Is there anything else at all that you would like to say about sex or your own sexual experiences?

I think sex is special. My body is a temple, my mum taught me. Im christian. But not full on, i dont go to church etc. just believe. I do think sex should be saved for marriage. But if you've been in loving relationship for a long time & it seems right. I would never waste mine, or have it before the legal age of 16. Something to look forward to, i think. I won't be pressured into sex or other things around sex. As i was abused im more careful of who things happen with, I Must trust them because trust was taken from me in a big way & its been hard for me to be close to boys for a loonnnggg time, until i found this one special guy, who is actually very horny but he never pressured me & for the first 6 months of our relationship it was all kissing until i knew i was ready. I dont regret any of it.

Girl, 15, New South Wales, straight

How old were you when you first heard about sex? **10**

What was the first thing you heard about sex?

That it is when people hug and kiss each other while they are naked

How old were you when you started masturbating? **13**

On average, how many times a week do you masturbate? **Once a week**

How do you masturbate?

i use one of my fingers most of the time and sometimes try to slip in another one. i once use a cucumber wrapped in cling wrap for hygenic reasons

How does masturbating make you feel? **Okay**

Describe your sexual fantasies, even if they seem weird or boring or whatever.

that i am with the guy i like and we play around and we have sex in a really nice hotel with sexy music playing in the background

How old were you when you had your first sexual experience with someone else? **14**

What happened in this first sexual experience with another person?
i have talked to guy of what i would like to do with him

How old were you when you first had oral sex? **Never had oral sex**

How old were you when you first had sexual intercourse? **Never**

How old were you when you first had anal sex? **Never**

Would you like to have more sex? **Yes**

How do you think sex could be better for you?
yes i think sex would take the stress out of me because it lets me release my self to someone i like and trust.

When you have intercourse, do you use protection? **Yes**

What kind of protection do you use? **condom**

How often are your sexual experiences with someone of the same sex or gender as you? **Never**

You think of yourself as … **Straight**

How old were you when you first saw pornography or erotica? **11**

What kind of pornography have you seen? **internet websites**

Does porn excite you sexually? **Not much**

Does porn give you ideas about how to have sex? **Sometimes**

Do you think sexy films, music videos or advertising encourage you to have sex? **Sometimes**

Examples of media encouraging sex:
romantic movies with really hot guys in it turn me on

Have you ever had phone sex, that is, sexually exciting yourself and someone else over the phone? **Yes**

Have you ever sent or received sexual text messages? **Yes**

Have you had a sexual experience in an internet chat room? **Yes**

If so, did you also meet up with that person in real life? **No**

Have you ever had a sexual experience with an adult? **No**

Have you ever had a sexual experience with more than one person at a time? **No**

Have you ever been pressured or forced into having sex? **No**

How often do you have sex while using drugs or alcohol? **Never**

Do drugs or alcohol make sex better or worse? **Neither**

Does what you learn in sex education classes at school help you with your actual sexual experiences? **Not much**

Do you think teenagers should be taught more or less about sex at school?

Same as now

What do you think is the best age to start having sexual experiences?

i think the right age will be for me 15 years and onwards. normal sex would be alright to start me off then i would experiment

Does your religion have an influence on whether or not you have sex?

Not at all

How important is it for you to have an emotional connection with your sexual partner? Somewhat important**

Is there anything else at all that you would like to say about sex or your own sexual experiences? **i am curious about it**

Boy, 15, Victoria, straight

How old were you when you first heard about sex? **8**

What was the first thing you heard about sex?

Thats where babies come from

How old were you when you started masturbating? **12**

On average, how many times a week do you masturbate?

More than five times a week

How do you masturbate? **In bed or in the shower**

How does masturbating make you feel? **Very good**

Describe your sexual fantasies, even if they seem weird or boring or whatever.

I wanna be tied up

How old were you when you had your first sexual experience with someone else? **6**

What happened in this first sexual experience with another person?

It was romantic

How old were you when you first had oral sex? **Never had oral sex**

How old were you when you first had sexual intercourse? **Never**

How old were you when you first had anal sex? **Never**

Would you like to have more sex? **Yes**

How do you think sex could be better for you? **I want it**

How often are your sexual experiences with someone of the same sex or
gender as you? **Never**

You think of yourself as … **Straight**

How old were you when you first saw pornography or erotica? **11**

What kind of pornography have you seen? **Movies and magazines**

Does porn excite you sexually? **Not much**

Does porn give you ideas about how to have sex? **Sometimes**

Do you think sexy films, music videos or advertising encourage you to have
sex? **Never**

Have you ever had phone sex, that is, sexually exciting yourself and
someone else over the phone? **No**

Have you ever sent or received sexual text messages? **Yes**

Have you had a sexual experience in an internet chat room? **Yes**

If so, did you also meet up with that person in real life? **Yes**

Have you ever had a sexual experience with an adult? **No**

Have you ever had a sexual experience with more than one person at a
time? **No**

Have you ever been pressured or forced into having sex? **No**

How often do you have sex while using drugs or alcohol? **Never**

Do drugs or alcohol make sex better or worse? **Neither**

Does what you learn in sex education classes at school help you with your
actual sexual experiences? **Not at all**

Do you think teenagers should be taught more or less about sex at school?
More

What do you think is the best age to start having sexual experiences?
**Well its legal so as soon as you want as long as it aint with someone
more than 2 years younger**

Do your parents have an influence on whether or not you have sex?
Not much

Does your religion have an influence on whether or not you have sex?
Not at all

How important is it for you to have an emotional connection with your sexual
partner? **Somewhat important**

Is there anything else at all that you would like to say about sex or your own
sexual experiences? **I want sex**

Girl, 15, Western Australia, straight

How old were you when you first heard about sex? **9**

What was the first thing you heard about sex?

That it's when the man's penis goes into the woman's vagina.

How old were you when you started masturbating? **14**

On average, how many times a week do you masturbate? **Once a week**

How do you masturbate?

Usually on the outside with my finger and reading a magazine with stories about sex, and sometimes with an electric toothbrush and on the outside.

How does masturbating make you feel? **Very good**

Describe your sexual fantasies, even if they seem weird or boring or whatever.

To have a woman "play with me" but I'm not a lesbian.

How old were you when you had your first sexual experience with someone else? **11**

What happened in this first sexual experience with another person?

Just kissing, like a peck on the lips and no tongue. It was weird.

How old were you when you first had oral sex? **Never had oral sex**

How old were you when you first had sexual intercourse? **Never**

How old were you when you first had anal sex? **Never**

How often are your sexual experiences with someone of the same sex or gender as you? **Never**

You think of yourself as … **Straight**

How old were you when you first saw pornography or erotica? **14**

What kind of pornography have you seen?

A photo of a woman with a bottle of alcohol sort of in her vagina. Real people's stories in Cosmopolitan magazine about sex

Does porn excite you sexually? **A lot**

Does porn give you ideas about how to have sex? **Sometimes**

Do you think sexy films, music videos or advertising encourage you to have sex? **Sometimes**

Have you ever had phone sex, that is, sexually exciting yourself and someone else over the phone? **No**

Have you ever sent or received sexual text messages? **Yes**

Have you had a sexual experience in an internet chat room? **Yes**

If so, did you also meet up with that person in real life? **No**

Have you ever had a sexual experience with an adult? **No**

Have you ever had a sexual experience with more than one person at a
time? **No**

Have you ever been pressured or forced into having sex? **No**

How often do you have sex while using drugs or alcohol? **Never**

Does what you learn in sex education classes at school help you with your
actual sexual experiences? **A bit**

Do you think teenagers should be taught more or less about sex at school?
More

What do you think is the best age to start having sexual experiences?
15 or 16 for oral sex or intercourse, maybe about 13 or 14 for kissing

Do your parents have an influence on whether or not you have sex?
Not much

Does your religion have an influence on whether or not you have sex?
Not at all

How important is it for you to have an emotional connection with your sexual
partner? **Very important**

Boy, 15, New South Wales, straight

How old were you when you first heard about sex? **10**

What was the first thing you heard about sex?
thats that how babies are made

How old were you when you started masturbating? **13**

On average, how many times a week do you masturbate?
Four times a week

How do you masturbate?
um in my bedroom on my bed masturbating the only way guys can

How does masturbating make you feel? **Good**

Describe your sexual fantasies, even if they seem weird or boring or whatever.
um i just think about my girlfriend n stuff

How old were you when you had your first sexual experience with someone else? **6**

What happened in this first sexual experience with another person?

um we kissed and i felt realy good

How old were you when you first had oral sex? **14**

Describe what happened during this oral sex, and how you felt about it.

um i got head and i felt natural about it

On average, how many times a week do you have oral sex?

Less than once a week

If less frequent, how many times approximately has it occurred? **Twice**

How old were you when you first had sexual intercourse? **15**

Describe what happened during intercourse, and how you felt about it emotionally.

um well we got caught the first time but the second time we did it we were all good and ye it felt realy good

How old were you when you first had anal sex? **Never**

On average, how many times a week do you have intercourse?

Less than once a week

Would you like to have more sex? **Not sure**

How do you think sex could be better for you?

um hav more privacy and have a better place to do it in. if girls couldn't get pregnant and there were no diseases then it would be heaps better because theres nothing to worry bout

When you have intercourse, do you use protection? **Yes**

What kind of protection do you use? **condom**

How often are your sexual experiences with someone of the same sex or gender as you? **Never**

You think of yourself as … **Straight**

How old were you when you first saw pornography or erotica? **10**

What kind of pornography have you seen?

websites,magazines,photos and films

Does porn excite you sexually? **A bit**

Does porn give you ideas about how to have sex? **Sometimes**

Do you think sexy films, music videos or advertising encourage you to have sex? **Sometimes**

Examples of media encouraging sex: **not sure**

Have you ever had phone sex, that is, sexually exciting yourself and someone else over the phone? **No**

Have you ever sent or received sexual text messages? **Yes**

Have you had a sexual experience in an internet chat room? **No**

Have you ever had a sexual experience with an adult? **No**

Have you ever had a sexual experience with more than one person at a time? **No**

Have you ever been pressured or forced into having sex? **No**

How often do you have sex while using drugs or alcohol? **Never**

Do drugs or alcohol make sex better or worse? **Neither**

Does what you learn in sex education classes at school help you with your actual sexual experiences? **A bit**

Do you think teenagers should be taught more or less about sex at school? **More**

What do you think is the best age to start having sexual experiences? **um well i personaly think i started too early but you can like make out and stuff when ur like 13 but don't actually have sex till ur older and more responsible and do it with sum1 u love like i did!**

Do your parents have an influence on whether or not you have sex? **Not much**

Does your religion have an influence on whether or not you have sex? **A bit**

How important is it for you to have an emotional connection with your sexual partner? **Very important**

Girl, 15, New South Wales, straight

How old were you when you first heard about sex? **8**

What was the first thing you heard about sex? **Can't really remember ... probably that it was how kids were made ...**

How old were you when you started masturbating? **10**

On average, how many times a week do you masturbate? **Three times a week**

How do you masturbate?

Just using my fingers, I usually rub my clit, sometimes I put my fingers into my vagina, occasionally I play around with my breasts and nipples too, it depends.

How does masturbating make you feel? **Very good**

How old were you when you had your first sexual experience with someone else? **12**

What happened in this first sexual experience with another person?

Basically just pashing and a bit of groping with both of us fully clothed. I wasn't opposed to it ... but I know now how different waiting can make everything.

How old were you when you first had oral sex? **Never had oral sex**

How old were you when you first had sexual intercourse? **Never**

How old were you when you first had anal sex? **Never**

Would you like to have more sex? **Not sure**

How often are your sexual experiences with someone of the same sex or gender as you? **Never**

You think of yourself as ... **Straight**

How old were you when you first saw pornography or erotica? **11**

What kind of pornography have you seen?

internet websites, books, magazines

Does porn excite you sexually? **A bit**

Does porn give you ideas about how to have sex? **Sometimes**

Do you think sexy films, music videos or advertising encourage you to have sex? **Sometimes**

Have you ever had phone sex, that is, sexually exciting yourself and someone else over the phone? **No**

Have you ever sent or received sexual text messages? **No**

Have you had a sexual experience in an internet chat room? **Yes**

If so, did you also meet up with that person in real life? **No**

Have you ever had a sexual experience with an adult? **No**

Have you ever had a sexual experience with more than one person at a time? **No**

Have you ever been pressured or forced into having sex? **Yes**

If so, describe what happened and how you felt about it emotionally.

(I don't consider this sexual intercourse … that is why I answered no before to previous questions …) I was raped 3 years ago. It was terrible, and not many people know what happened. I don't tell many people. There are only 2 or 3 of my friends outside my family who know.

How often do you have sex while using drugs or alcohol? **Never**

Do drugs or alcohol make sex better or worse? **Neither**

Does what you learn in sex education classes at school help you with your actual sexual experiences? **A bit**

Do you think teenagers should be taught more or less about sex at school? **More**

What do you think is the best age to start having sexual experiences?

I think you can't really specify an age – it's all about maturity and personal comfort. While one person may be ready for sex at 14, another may not be happy kissing someone until 18 …

Do your parents have an influence on whether or not you have sex? **Not much**

Does your religion have an influence on whether or not you have sex? **Not at all**

How important is it for you to have an emotional connection with your sexual partner? **Very important**

Girl, 15, New South Wales, straight

How old were you when you first heard about sex? **8**

What was the first thing you heard about sex?

I don't really remeber but I learned pretty early on that it was between a man and a woman and thats how babies were made.

How old were you when you started masturbating? **Never**

How old were you when you had your first sexual experience with someone else? **10**

What happened in this first sexual experience with another person?

I was lying in front of the fireplace at my farm next to a boy called [boy's name deleted], a family friend, with my twin sister on the otherside. He

hugged me from behind and kissed me on the top of my head. I immeadiately pushed him away and felt totally grossed out because I didn't like him at all. I considered him really wierd and a bit of a creep. In the moment it made me feel warm and fuzzy and maybe wanting more but not with him.

How old were you when you first had oral sex? **15**

Describe what happened during this oral sex, and how you felt about it.

It was with my first proper boyfriend in his room. I didn't really know what he was doing but eventually I was bottomless and being eaten out for the first time on his bed. It felt really good and it made me go a little crazy e.g I wasn't really thinking straight. It wasn't awkward at all like I thought it would be but then again I hadn't really been expecting it at all.

On average, how many times a week do you have oral sex?

Less than once a week

If less frequent, how many times approximately has it occurred? **Once**

How old were you when you first had sexual intercourse? **Never**

How old were you when you first had anal sex? **Never**

Would you like to have more sex? **Yes**

How do you think sex could be better for you?

I have never had sex but I would worry that I would have a few emotional issues if it was with a guy that I liked. I would probably feel insecure about wether he was just using me. To stop that I guess i would just have to think about sex with a different attitude. Think of it as something that gives pleasure rather than something that forms a special bond with the other person.

How often are your sexual experiences with someone of the same sex or gender as you? **Never**

You think of yourself as … **Straight**

How old were you when you first saw pornography or erotica? **12**

What kind of pornography have you seen?

I have seen a lot of older brother porn with magazines and video clips discovered on the computer or in secret places around their room.

Does porn excite you sexually? **A lot**

Does porn give you ideas about how to have sex? **Sometimes**

Do you think sexy films, music videos or advertising encourage you to have sex? **Never**

Have you ever had phone sex, that is, sexually exciting yourself and someone else over the phone? **No**

Have you ever sent or received sexual text messages? **Yes**

Have you had a sexual experience in an internet chat room? **No**

Have you ever had a sexual experience with an adult? **No**

Have you ever had a sexual experience with more than one person at a time? **No**

Have you ever been pressured or forced into having sex? **No**

How often do you have sex while using drugs or alcohol? **Sometimes**

Do drugs or alcohol make sex better or worse? **Neither**

Does what you learn in sex education classes at school help you with your actual sexual experiences? **A bit**

Do you think teenagers should be taught more or less about sex at school? **More**

What do you think is the best age to start having sexual experiences?
I would say start kissing around year 6 or the beginning of yr 7 and keep it at that until at least yr 8. By year 6 or 7 most people are mature enough to talk about it and accept it as ok. You wouldn't want to wait too long to start because the longer you wait it gets awkward because you have so much time to think about it. It is fun and pleasurable as well so it is your loss if you wait until later in high school to start having sexual experiences.

Do your parents have an influence on whether or not you have sex?
Not much

Does your religion have an influence on whether or not you have sex?
Not at all

How important is it for you to have an emotional connection with your sexual partner? **Somewhat important**

Is there anything else at all that you would like to say about sex or your own sexual experiences?
There is alot of stigma around it all. I wasn't really ready for my first proper kiss and so I was sort of scarred from it and it took me ages to get over the fear and let someone kiss me. Now I realized how stupid

my fear was but no one ever told me that it really isn't that big a deal. At the end of the day sex is a natural part of being human and so it comes naturally even if you aren't very good to begin with you have to start somewhere.

Girl, 15, (no postcode given), straight

How old were you when you first heard about sex? **8**
What was the first thing you heard about sex?
a friend told me that oral sex was called masturbation.
How old were you when you started masturbating? **Never**
Describe your sexual fantasies, even if they seem weird or boring or whatever.
all i want is a guy who doesnt care about the weight of a girl to be completely genuine and not a complete sleazebag who only wants one thing.
How old were you when you had your first sexual experience with someone else? **7**
What happened in this first sexual experience with another person?
my boyfriend at the time kissed me on the cheek. i was fine with it, it was weird though coz i hadnt had a boy my age kiss me anywhere before and three of my friends where watching.
How old were you when you first had oral sex? **Never had oral sex**
How old were you when you first had sexual intercourse? **Never**
How old were you when you first had anal sex? **Never**
Would you like to have more sex? **No**
You think of yourself as … **Straight**
How old were you when you first saw pornography or erotica? **10**
What kind of pornography have you seen?
i saw some girls boobs in a dolly magazine in the sealed section.
Does porn excite you sexually? **Not at all**
Does porn give you ideas about how to have sex? **Never**
Do you think sexy films, music videos or advertising encourage you to have sex? **Sometimes**

Examples of media encouraging sex:

well we see girls prancing around half naked shaking their butts and its like do any of the guys in the video clips actually have any respect for women. plus their are advertisments on the radio about condoms and strip clubs they just increase our intensity to know what sex is all about.

Have you ever had phone sex, that is, sexually exciting yourself and someone else over the phone? **No**

Have you ever sent or received sexual text messages? **Yes**

Have you had a sexual experience in an internet chat room? **No**

Have you ever had a sexual experience with an adult? **No**

Have you ever had a sexual experience with more than one person at a time? **No**

Have you ever been pressured or forced into having sex? **No**

How often do you have sex while using drugs or alcohol? **Never**

Do drugs or alcohol make sex better or worse? **Neither**

Does what you learn in sex education classes at school help you with your actual sexual experiences? **Not at all**

Do you think teenagers should be taught more or less about sex at school? **More**

What do you think is the best age to start having sexual experiences? **i think as long as people are comfortable, happy and are consenting to the experience then it is fine.**

Do your parents have an influence on whether or not you have sex? **Not at all**

Does your religion have an influence on whether or not you have sex? **Not at all**

How important is it for you to have an emotional connection with your sexual partner? **Very important**

Girl, 15, New South Wales, straight

How old were you when you first heard about sex? **10**

What was the first thing you heard about sex?

that a penis went into a vagina

Describe your sexual fantasies, even if they seem weird or boring or whatever.

an empty beach at night with the guy i like

How old were you when you had your first sexual experience with someone else? **11**

What happened in this first sexual experience with another person?

we were in a spa, and he started feeling my boobs under my costume, i felt weird about it because it was a first but at the same time comfortable because it was my best friend.

How old were you when you first had oral sex? **14**

Describe what happened during this oral sex, and how you felt about it.

i was very drunk at a party and started kissing a guy that i had never met before, and stupidly left the party with him we went down the road in some garage and i gave it to him, i was very drunk and felt a bit bad after doing it but i learnt from it for future, i would have liked my first to have meant more.

On average, how many times a week do you have oral sex?

Less than once a week

If less frequent, how many times approximately has it occurred? **Twice**

How old were you when you first had sexual intercourse? **Never**

How old were you when you first had anal sex? **Never**

Would you like to have more sex? **Yes**

How do you think sex could be better for you?

if i felt better about my self.

When you have intercourse, do you use protection? **Yes**

What kind of protection do you use? **condoms**

How often are your sexual experiences with someone of the same sex or gender as you? **Never**

You think of yourself as ... **Straight**

How old were you when you first saw pornography or erotica? **8**

What kind of pornography have you seen?

video, magazine, internet, films

Does porn excite you sexually? **Not much**

Does porn give you ideas about how to have sex? **Never**

Do you think sexy films, music videos or advertising encourage you to have sex? **Sometimes**

Examples of media encouraging sex: **music videos and some films**

Have you ever had phone sex, that is, sexually exciting yourself and someone else over the phone? **No**

Have you ever sent or received sexual text messages? **Yes**

Have you had a sexual experience in an internet chat room? **Yes**

If so, did you also meet up with that person in real life? **No**

Have you ever had a sexual experience with an adult? **Yes**

If so, describe what happened and how you felt about it emotionally.

i was drunk, it was new years eve and it was only a kiss, it was GREATTT!!!!!!

Have you ever had a sexual experience with more than one person at a time? **No**

Have you ever been pressured or forced into having sex? **Yes**

If so, describe what happened and how you felt about it emotionally.

i felt disgusting thinking that a guy would try do that to me, i got up and stopped it.

How often do you have sex while using drugs or alcohol? **Most of the time**

Do drugs or alcohol make sex better or worse? **Better**

Does what you learn in sex education classes at school help you with your actual sexual experiences? **Not much**

Do you think teenagers should be taught more or less about sex at school? **More**

What do you think is the best age to start having sexual experiences?

i think that kssing is fine at the age of 11, and that oral sex sould only start at around 15 and intercourse after 16

Do your parents have an influence on whether or not you have sex? **A bit**

Does your religion have an influence on whether or not you have sex? **Not at all**

How important is it for you to have an emotional connection with your sexual partner? **Very important**

By the age of 16, both boys and girls display more confidence and greater self-awareness about what works for them sexually. Boys in particular are starting to express themselves more, both verbally and physically. There's more experimentation as well as greater clarity about sexual persuasion, and they're very sophisticated and often cynical about how the media and advertisers use sex to sell their products.

Both boys and girls are more brazen about their sexual fantasies, and more inventive when it comes to masturbation. Girls are especially outspoken when it comes to what they want, and there is an increased expectation of and desire for orgasms. In spite of their greater awareness, many 16-year-olds are still not sure what to expect during sexual encounters and there is a universal hunger for more knowledge. School sex ed programs are mostly seen as pointless.

Girl, 16, Victoria, 'mainly straight'

How old were you when you first heard about sex? **7**

What was the first thing you heard about sex?

That it was between two people that "loved each other very much like mummy and daddy" only. But then again, I'd seen sex on TV since I was tiny, so I really did have a basic grasp of the concept.

How old were you when you started masturbating? **4**

On average, how many times a week do you masturbate?

Four times a week

How do you masturbate?

Using both of my hands I rub down in my nether regions, sort of an up and down motion.

How does masturbating make you feel? **Good**

Describe your sexual fantasies, even if they seem weird or boring or whatever.

I suppose I've always liked the thought of a hot international guy, or maybe the whole university sex scene. I don't really have any fantasies

as such. I have had a few lesbian fantasies, but haven't had any of them for a while. Once you live some of them out they lose their novel appeal. Basically I just fantasise about sex, pretty boring, hey? Not really a big whips and leather person myself.

How old were you when you had your first sexual experience with someone else? **8**

What happened in this first sexual experience with another person?

It was "french kissing" a family friend. I think we thought it was sex at the time. He climbed up on to my bunk one night when I was sleeping over and the next thing you know it was a lot of smooching and I think even some dry sex. I know, 8 years old! Bit extreme. Either way, his mum caught us and it was extremely embarresing.

How old were you when you first had oral sex? **15**

Describe what happened during this oral sex, and how you felt about it.

It was a couple of nights before New Years Eve in Lorne and a boy took me down to the "dunes" and gave me head. I didn't enjoy it at all, and never have since. It's very overrated and boring. Personally, I don't like the taste of kissing them after, and I'm uncomfortable about people seeing my private bits, especially people I've only known for about an hour. So basically it was a bad experience, and the fact that he expected something in return was pretty horrible, but expected.

On average, how many times a week do you have oral sex?

Less than once a week

If less frequent, how many times approximately has it occurred? **Ten times**

How old were you when you first had sexual intercourse? **16**

Describe what happened during intercourse, and how you felt about it emotionally.

We were both a bit confused and unsure as to what to do because you see, we were both virgins. I think we didn't really know where the penis went but after a few attempts we found out. It was quite painful the first couple of times. Emotionally, I was fine with it. I had wanted to have sex for a while and because I wasn't forced into it I knew that it was completely my own decision. And since my first encounters I have realised what works best. At the very beginning he went on top and I was really nervous. Now I'm on top and am very confident so it's a very enjoyable experience.

How old were you when you first had anal sex? **Never**

On average, how many times a week do you have intercourse?

Three times a week

Would you like to have more sex? **Yes**

How do you think sex could be better for you?

I like sex slow and only ever orgasm when I'm on top. I like to build it up to climax, slow to fast. Usually sex is unreal for me both physically and emotionally. As I've only had sex with the one person, and have been doing it for a while I really don't have any issues as yet. It's all about who you're doing it with, I suppose.

When you have intercourse, do you use protection? **Yes**

What kind of protection do you use?

I am on "The Pill" and we use condoms, always. Better to be safe than sorry!

How often are your sexual experiences with someone of the same sex or gender as you? **Sometimes**

You think of yourself as …

Other: Mainly straight, but sometimes I hook up with girls

How old were you when you first saw pornography or erotica? **7**

What kind of pornography have you seen?

Magazines and films, at my best friend's house. They were her older brothers.

Does porn excite you sexually? **A bit**

Does porn give you ideas about how to have sex? **Never**

Do you think sexy films, music videos or advertising encourage you to have sex? **Always**

Examples of media encouraging sex:

All those seedy hip-hop dance video clips and a lot of the rap ones. They're absolutely pathetic, with a whole bunchy of skanky girls practically having dry sex on the dance floor. Also, a lot (if not all) of female artists sell themselves out and use their body to grab attention. It's not a good thing. There should be restrictions on TV about how sexually-orientated a video clip should be.

Have you ever had phone sex, that is, sexually exciting yourself and someone else over the phone? **Yes**

Have you ever sent or received sexual text messages? **Yes**

Have you had a sexual experience in an internet chat room? **Yes**

If so, did you also meet up with that person in real life? **No**

Have you ever had a sexual experience with an adult? **No**

Have you ever had a sexual experience with more than one person at a
time? **Yes**

If so, describe what happened and how you felt about it.

> **I've never had a "threesome" but I have been to parties and hooked up
> with a whole lot of people the same night. I don't think that really
> counts.**

Have you ever been pressured or forced into having sex? **Yes**

If so, describe what happened and how you felt about it emotionally.

> **It wasn't really "forced", it was more like I was very drunk, and so was
> my boyfriend and he wanted to have sex and I didn't. He didn't force, he
> just asked me and I sort of felt abliged. Later on I told him that I really
> hadn't wanted to and he was really apologetic. In the end, it was my
> fault, I could have said no quite easily.**

How often do you have sex while using drugs or alcohol? **Sometimes**

Do drugs or alcohol make sex better or worse? **Worse**

Does what you learn in sex education classes at school help you with your
actual sexual experiences? **Not much**

Do you think teenagers should be taught more or less about sex at school?

> **Same as now**

What do you think is the best age to start having sexual experiences?

> **I think you should probably start off with the basics. Kissing, then
> touching, then licking, then sex. It's better that way and it helps you
> realize what you're getting into. I started kissing and touching when I
> was about 14, oral sex at 15 and sexual intercourse at 16. Personally,
> I think that is a good way to go. Any younger and you can wind up
> emotionally scarred, any older and by the time you reach University
> you're sexually and emotionally under-developed. There really isn't any
> age. I mean, you should begin having sexual experiences when you feel
> you're old enough, for me, it was through the ages of 14 and 16.**

Do your parents have an influence on whether or not you have sex?

> **Not at all**

Does your religion have an influence on whether or not you have sex?
Not at all

How important is it for you to have an emotional connection with your sexual partner? **Somewhat important**

Is there anything else at all that you would like to say about sex or your own sexual experiences?

Only that I wish girls would be more open about mastubation and sex. It's something that happens to all of us and there's no point in being ashamed. I mean, guys claim it and we hide it. It's pathetic. Also, I wish girls and guys weren't treated differently in terms of sex. I mean, I've got friends who's older brothers are allowed to have sex, but they can't because they're female. This puts a huge restriction on them that of course they're going to rebel against. It's not a good way to go because in the end they're worse off for having such restrictions. I'd also like to make the point that being "licked out" by anyone, in general, is usually not a pleasurable experience. I've spoken to a lot of people about it and the general concensus is that it's no good, I wish guys knew that!

Boy, 16, New South Wales, straight

How old were you when you first heard about sex? **10**

What was the first thing you heard about sex?

that sperm from the penis enters the vagina and a baby is formed didnt know how the sperm was produced though

How old were you when you started masturbating? **11**

On average, how many times a week do you masturbate?

Four times a week

How do you masturbate? **my bed room**

How does masturbating make you feel? **Good**

Describe your sexual fantasies, even if they seem weird or boring or whatever.

naughty nurse suits :) or hot mums

How old were you when you had your first sexual experience with someone else? **9**

What happened in this first sexual experience with another person?

we were kissing in primary school with a locked door for like hours in her bed room and i touched her and she touched me

How old were you when you first had oral sex? **12**

Describe what happened during this oral sex, and how you felt about it.

was fucking awsome had heaps of fun lol but i didnt finish off but it was really good plus the girl was older and had more experience than me

On average, how many times a week do you have oral sex? **Twice a week**

How old were you when you first had sexual intercourse? **14**

Describe what happened during intercourse, and how you felt about it emotionally.

i was enjoying it alot and had been with a girl for a long time and i was just happy the whole time and wanted it to be good for her as well

How old were you when you first had anal sex? **Never had anal sex**

On average, how many times a week do you have intercourse?

Twice a week

Would you like to have more sex? **Yes**

How do you think sex could be better for you?

im happy with the sex im having now more often would be better but dont have the time

When you have intercourse, do you use protection? **Sometimes**

What kind of protection do you use? **condoms**

How often are your sexual experiences with someone of the same sex or gender as you? **Never**

You think of yourself as … **Straight**

How old were you when you first saw pornography or erotica? **10**

What kind of pornography have you seen? **films, website, magazines**

Does porn excite you sexually? **A lot**

Does porn give you ideas about how to have sex? **Sometimes**

Do you think sexy films, music videos or advertising encourage you to have sex? **Sometimes**

Have you ever had phone sex, that is, sexually exciting yourself and someone else over the phone? **No**

Have you ever sent or received sexual text messages? **Yes**

Have you had a sexual experience in an internet chat room? **No**

Have you ever had a sexual experience with more than one person at a
    time? **No**

Have you ever been pressured or forced into having sex? **Yes**

If so, describe what happened and how you felt about it emotionally.

**just my ex girlfriend really horny and she just wanted to fuck so i did but
i wasnt in the mood but she full made me**

How often do you have sex while using drugs or alcohol? **Sometimes**

Do drugs or alcohol make sex better or worse? **Neither**

Does what you learn in sex education classes at school help you with your
    actual sexual experiences? **Not at all**

Do you think teenagers should be taught more or less about sex at school?
    More

What do you think is the best age to start having sexual experiences?

**anal not until 18 best age to start sex is 15 or so but like sexual
experiences like head or licking out a girl like but younger**

Do your parents have an influence on whether or not you have sex? **A bit**

Does your religion have an influence on whether or not you have sex?

Not at all

How important is it for you to have an emotional connection with your sexual
    partner? **Not important at all**

Girl, 16, New South Wales, lesbian

How old were you when you first heard about sex? **2**

What was the first thing you heard about sex?

**I was about 2 or 3. I never had the big sit down chats, it was just
casual information, it was no big deal. I learnt the basic biology of
sex; the penis puts sperm into the vagina which meets an egg and
makes a baby.**

How old were you when you started masturbating? **11**

On average, how many times a week do you masturbate?

Three times a week

How does masturbating make you feel? **Good**

How old were you when you had your first sexual experience with someone else? **14**

What happened in this first sexual experience with another person?

Again, there was playing "doctors and nurses" when I was much younger, say 5 or 6, but the first time I really kissed anyone (and went further) in a sexual context I would have been around 14.

How old were you when you first had oral sex? **14**

Describe what happened during this oral sex, and how you felt about it.

It was with my girlfriend at the time, we were both nervous and self-conscious but we loved each other very much, and we tried it out. It was about 3am after having made out for several hours.

On average, how many times a week do you have oral sex? **Twice a week**

How old were you when you first had sexual intercourse? **Never**

How old were you when you first had anal sex? **Never**

Would you like to have more sex? **Yes**

How do you think sex could be better for you?

Not sure really ... Maybe if I was less self conscious.

How often are your sexual experiences with someone of the same sex or gender as you? **Always**

You think of yourself as ... **Lesbian**

If you're gay or lesbian, are you 'out'? **Yes**

If you're gay or lesbian and you came out, was it hard? **Not very hard**

Describe what happened when you came out and how you felt about it.

My mother figured it out before I did, and it wasn't an issue. I told my friends bit by bit, and there were no problems.

How old were you when you first saw pornography or erotica? **15**

What kind of pornography have you seen? **Stories**

Does porn excite you sexually? **A bit**

Does porn give you ideas about how to have sex? **Sometimes**

Do you think sexy films, music videos or advertising encourage you to have sex? **Sometimes**

Have you ever had phone sex, that is, sexually exciting yourself and someone else over the phone? **No**

Have you ever sent or received sexual text messages? **No**

Have you had a sexual experience in an internet chat room? **No**

Have you ever had a sexual experience with an adult? **No**

Have you ever had a sexual experience with more than one person at a time? **No**

Have you ever been pressured or forced into having sex? **No**

How often do you have sex while using drugs or alcohol? **Sometimes**

Do drugs or alcohol make sex better or worse? **Worse**

Does what you learn in sex education classes at school help you with your actual sexual experiences? **Not much**

Do you think teenagers should be taught more or less about sex at school? **More**

What do you think is the best age to start having sexual experiences?
I really think it depends on the individual, I don't think there should be a focus on what age because that implies everyone is the same emotionally and developmentally at a certain age. I think whenever the person feels mature and comfortable enough to do so.

Do your parents have an influence on whether or not you have sex? **A bit**

Does your religion have an influence on whether or not you have sex?
Not at all

How important is it for you to have an emotional connection with your sexual partner? **Very important**

Girl, 16, Victoria, 'experimental'

How old were you when you first heard about sex? **10**

What was the first thing you heard about sex?
The first thing i learnt about sex was that only mummies and daddies were allowed to do it

How old were you when you started masturbating? **13**

On average, how many times a week do you masturbate?
Three times a week

How do you masturbate?
umm i do it in my bed after the rest of my family has gone to bed so i have no chance of getting caught, i usually use my deoderant bottle ...

How does masturbating make you feel? **Good**

Describe your sexual fantasies, even if they seem weird or boring or whatever.

i really like the whole lingerie thing and a bit of bondage never hurt anyone ... also a bit of role-playing

How old were you when you had your first sexual experience with someone else? **12**

What happened in this first sexual experience with another person?

i first kissed a guy when i was 12. he was my first boyfriend as well so i was very excited!!

How old were you when you first had oral sex? **12**

Describe what happened during this oral sex, and how you felt about it.

umm the first time i had oral sex was with my dads girlfriends son who is 4 years older than me and he fingered me an licked me out ... i was nervous but enjoying it all the same

On average, how many times a week do you have oral sex?

Less than once a week

If less frequent, how many times approximately has it occurred? **Ten times**

How old were you when you first had sexual intercourse? **15**

Describe what happened during intercourse, and how you felt about it emotionally.

well it really hurt the first time so we tried again later and that was better ... i was kind of drunk so i dont really remember how i felt ...

How old were you when you first had anal sex? **Never**

On average, how many times a week do you have intercourse?

Less than once a week

Would you like to have more sex? **Yes**

How do you think sex could be better for you?

if it were with someone i was in love with and if the guy knew what he was doing!!

When you have intercourse, do you use protection? **Yes**

What kind of protection do you use? **condoms ...**

How often are your sexual experiences with someone of the same sex or gender as you? **Sometimes**

You think of yourself as ... **Other: not bi sexual just experimental**

If you're gay or lesbian, are you 'out'? **No**

How old were you when you first saw pornography or erotica? **Never**

Do you think sexy films, music videos or advertising encourage you to have sex? **Sometimes**

Have you ever had phone sex, that is, sexually exciting yourself and someone else over the phone? **Yes**

Have you ever sent or received sexual text messages? **Yes**

Have you had a sexual experience in an internet chat room? **No**

Have you ever had a sexual experience with an adult? **Yes**

Have you ever had a sexual experience with more than one person at a time? **Yes**

Have you ever been pressured or forced into having sex? **Yes**

If so, describe what happened and how you felt about it emotionally.

i was forced into having sex, i agreed to that but then it hurt and i told him to stop and he wouldnt but in the end i got him off me.

How often do you have sex while using drugs or alcohol? **Sometimes**

Do drugs or alcohol make sex better or worse? **Neither**

Does what you learn in sex education classes at school help you with your actual sexual experiences? **Not at all**

Do you think teenagers should be taught more or less about sex at school? **More**

What do you think is the best age to start having sexual experiences?

kissing - 13years, oral sex - 15yrs, sex - 16 - 17 years

Do your parents have an influence on whether or not you have sex? **A bit**

Does your religion have an influence on whether or not you have sex? **Not at all**

How important is it for you to have an emotional connection with your sexual partner? **Somewhat important**

Is there anything else at all that you would like to say about sex or your own sexual experiences?

i once had a three-some with two guys and that was awesome ...
i always fantasise about other girls and i kiss them and stuff but im not a lesbian lol ...

Girl, 16, Queensland, straight

How old were you when you first heard about sex? **9**

What was the first thing you heard about sex?

that a boy's penis sent sperm into a woman creating a baby

How old were you when you started masturbating? **10**

On average, how many times a week do you masturbate? **Twice a week**

How do you masturbate? **rub clit in circular motion with finger**

How does masturbating make you feel? **Good**

Describe your sexual fantasies, even if they seem weird or boring or whatever.

being taken advantage of ... tied down ... not having control.

How old were you when you had your first sexual experience with someone else? **12**

What happened in this first sexual experience with another person?

kissing was my first sexual experience ... felt weird, afterwards i wanted to do it again straight away

How old were you when you first had oral sex? **14**

Describe what happened during this oral sex, and how you felt about it.

umm didnt really think about it i guess ... my boyfriend asked me to go down on him and i didnt think i could say no so i just did it, i didnt really care i guess. when he first went down on me i really felt uncomfortable, didnt enjoy it at all.

On average, how many times a week do you have oral sex?

Three times a week

How old were you when you first had sexual intercourse? **14**

Describe what happened during intercourse, and how you felt about it emotionally.

me and my boyfriend were fooling around (naked and everything) and he didnt ask or say anything he just slid his penis into me but he wasnt wearing a condom or anything so he got out of me really quickly ... it didnt hurt like some people said it would ... it was good, i liked it.

How old were you when you first had anal sex? **Never**

On average, how many times a week do you have intercourse?

Twice a week

Would you like to have more sex? **Not sure**

How do you think sex could be better for you?

> it could be better if i had an orgasm! i dunno i always just fake one cos i know its not gonna happen or probably take ages so i just fake it to keep my boyfriend happy. i would enjoy it more if we did it more slowly ... and i dunno its just never as good as it looks in movies and on tv and in books ... i dont know why!

When you have intercourse, do you use protection? **Yes**

What kind of protection do you use? **condoms**

How often are your sexual experiences with someone of the same sex or gender as you? **Never**

You think of yourself as ... **Straight**

How old were you when you first saw pornography or erotica? **14**

What kind of pornography have you seen? **internet webistes**

Does porn excite you sexually? **A bit**

Does porn give you ideas about how to have sex? **Never**

Do you think sexy films, music videos or advertising encourage you to have sex? **Sometimes**

Examples of media encouraging sex: **maybe shows like one tree hill**

Have you ever had phone sex, that is, sexually exciting yourself and someone else over the phone? **No**

Have you ever sent or received sexual text messages? **Yes**

Have you had a sexual experience in an internet chat room? **No**

Have you ever had a sexual experience with an adult? **No**

Have you ever had a sexual experience with more than one person at a time? **No**

Have you ever been pressured or forced into having sex? **Yes**

If so, describe what happened and how you felt about it emotionally.

> i dont know really ... but my boyfriend and i had broken up and it was his birthday on camp and so i snuck into his room to give him his present and i stayed the night and his friends left and everything and i rolled over in bed to look like i was going to sleep but he pulled me over and slid his finger into me and i felt forced into it but then i did help take off my clothes so i dunno

How often do you have sex while using drugs or alcohol? **Never**

Do drugs or alcohol make sex better or worse? **Neither**

Does what you learn in sex education classes at school help you with your actual sexual experiences? **Not at all**

Do you think teenagers should be taught more or less about sex at school? **More**

What do you think is the best age to start having sexual experiences?
i think sexual experiences such as kissing can start from 12 onwards but oral sex shouldnt start until 15 onwards and sex shouldnt start until 16 onwards because i think sex has a lot of responsibilites and u can get hurt if you arent emotionally ready for it

Do your parents have an influence on whether or not you have sex? **Not at all**

Does your religion have an influence on whether or not you have sex? **Not at all**

How important is it for you to have an emotional connection with your sexual partner? **Somewhat important**

Is there anything else at all that you would like to say about sex or your own sexual experiences? **sex should be taken more seriously i think**

Boy, 16, South Australia, straight

How old were you when you first heard about sex? **11**

What was the first thing you heard about sex? **fertilise**

How old were you when you started masturbating? **13**

On average, how many times a week do you masturbate?
Five times a week

How do you masturbate? **in my room, computer. stroke it**

How does masturbating make you feel? **Good**

Describe your sexual fantasies, even if they seem weird or boring or whatever.
legs baby

How old were you when you had your first sexual experience with someone else? **14**

What happened in this first sexual experience with another person?
kissing, confused

How old were you when you first had oral sex? **15**

Describe what happened during this oral sex, and how you felt about it.

was shit

On average, how many times a week do you have oral sex?

Three times a week

How old were you when you first had sexual intercourse? **Never**

How old were you when you first had anal sex? **Never**

Describe what happens during anal sex and how you feel about having it.

penis is inserted in the ass hole, its tighter and does not please the girl

On average, how many times a week do you have intercourse?

Less than once a week

Would you like to have more sex? **Yes**

How do you think sex could be better for you? **if i was good at it**

When you have intercourse, do you use protection? **Yes**

What kind of protection do you use? **condoms**

How often are your sexual experiences with someone of the same sex or

gender as you? **Never**

You think of yourself as … **Straight**

How old were you when you first saw pornography or erotica? **15**

What kind of pornography have you seen? **everything**

Does porn excite you sexually? **A lot**

Does porn give you ideas about how to have sex? **Sometimes**

Do you think sexy films, music videos or advertising encourage you to have

sex? **Sometimes**

Examples of media encouraging sex: **advertising**

Have you ever had phone sex, that is, sexually exciting yourself and

someone else over the phone? **No**

Have you ever sent or received sexual text messages? **Yes**

Have you had a sexual experience in an internet chat room? **No**

Have you ever had a sexual experience with an adult? **No**

Have you ever had a sexual experience with more than one person at a

time? **No**

Have you ever been pressured or forced into having sex? **No**

How often do you have sex while using drugs or alcohol? **Sometimes**

Do drugs or alcohol make sex better or worse? **Worse**

Does what you learn in sex education classes at school help you with your actual sexual experiences? **Not much**

Do you think teenagers should be taught more or less about sex at school? **More**

What do you think is the best age to start having sexual experiences? **16, all sex**

Do your parents have an influence on whether or not you have sex? **Not at all**

Does your religion have an influence on whether or not you have sex? **A bit**

How important is it for you to have an emotional connection with your sexual partner? **Somewhat important**

Is there anything else at all that you would like to say about sex or your own sexual experiences? **dont rush it, sex is very pleasing**

Girl, 16, New South Wales, trisexual

How old were you when you first heard about sex? **8**

What was the first thing you heard about sex? **It made babies and was what older people in love did.**

How old were you when you had your first sexual experience with someone else? **4**

What happened in this first sexual experience with another person? **Playing doctors and nurses-just mucking around and being silly. Not knowing what we were doing.**

How old were you when you first had oral sex? **13**

Describe what happened during this oral sex, and how you felt about it. **We (partner and I) did a 69er and it was fantastic.**

On average, how many times a week do you have oral sex? **Less than once a week**

If less frequent, how many times approximately has it occurred? **More than twenty**

How old were you when you first had sexual intercourse? **13**

Describe what happened during intercourse, and how you felt about it emotionally. **I was frigtened and nervous! It was fucking amazing though**

How old were you when you first had anal sex? **Never**

On average, how many times a week do you have intercourse?
Three times a week

Would you like to have more sex? **Yes**

How do you think sex could be better for you?
I love the sex I have with my partner-we have been together for 3 years and we are so in touch with each other.

When you have intercourse, do you use protection? **Sometimes**

What kind of protection do you use? **Condoms and The Pill.**

How often are your sexual experiences with someone of the same sex or gender as you? **Never**

You think of yourself as ... **Other: Tri Sexual**

How old were you when you first saw pornography or erotica? **Never**

Does porn excite you sexually? **Not at all**

Does porn give you ideas about how to have sex? **Never**

Do you think sexy films, music videos or advertising encourage you to have sex? **Sometimes**

Examples of media encouraging sex:
Hip Hop video clips are so sexual-also pop singers a.k.a Britney Spears encourage girls to grow up too fast-there are 9 year olds acting like hoes!

Have you ever had phone sex, that is, sexually exciting yourself and someone else over the phone? **Yes**

Have you ever sent or received sexual text messages? **Yes**

Have you had a sexual experience in an internet chat room? **No**

Have you ever had a sexual experience with an adult? **No**

Have you ever had a sexual experience with more than one person at a time? **No**

Have you ever been pressured or forced into having sex? **No**

How often do you have sex while using drugs or alcohol? **Most of the time**

Do drugs or alcohol make sex better or worse? **Better**

Does what you learn in sex education classes at school help you with your actual sexual experiences? **Not much**

Do you think teenagers should be taught more or less about sex at school?
More

What do you think is the best age to start having sexual experiences?

Whenever they are ready! I started when I was 13 but there are some of my mates who weren't ready till just recently. Start off by experimenting- feeling his cock, letting him poke you, sucking your tits ... then slowly putting his dick in your pussy! YEAH!!!!

Do your parents have an influence on whether or not you have sex? **A bit**

Does your religion have an influence on whether or not you have sex?

Not at all

How important is it for you to have an emotional connection with your sexual partner? **Very important**

Boy, 16, Western Australia, bisexual

How old were you when you first heard about sex? **12**

What was the first thing you heard about sex? **how to do it**

How old were you when you started masturbating? **12**

On average, how many times a week do you masturbate?

Three times a week

How do you masturbate?

i masturbate by rubbing my hand up and down my private part

How does masturbating make you feel? **Good**

Describe your sexual fantasies, even if they seem weird or boring or whatever.

i feel like i have been in space in a world of fantasie

How old were you when you had your first sexual experience with someone else? **12**

What happened in this first sexual experience with another person?

well we pashed under a tree afterschool and i felt great

How old were you when you first had oral sex? **Never had oral sex**

How old were you when you first had sexual intercourse? **15**

Describe what happened during intercourse, and how you felt about it emotionally. **well i felt happy excited and felt like i was having fun**

How old were you when you first had anal sex? **Never**

On average, how many times a week do you have intercourse?

Less than once a week

Would you like to have more sex? **Not sure**

How do you think sex could be better for you?

by it beeing a person that i actualy liked and we had somthing for each other if you know what i mean

When you have intercourse, do you use protection? **Yes**

What kind of protection do you use? **i used a condom**

How often are your sexual experiences with someone of the same sex or gender as you? **Sometimes**

You think of yourself as ... **Bisexual**

If you're gay or lesbian, are you 'out'? **No**

How old were you when you first saw pornography or erotica? **14**

What kind of pornography have you seen? **internet websites and movies**

Does porn excite you sexually? **Not much**

Does porn give you ideas about how to have sex? **Never**

Do you think sexy films, music videos or advertising encourage you to have sex? **Never**

Have you ever had phone sex, that is, sexually exciting yourself and someone else over the phone? **Yes**

Have you ever sent or received sexual text messages? **Yes**

Have you had a sexual experience in an internet chat room? **No**

Have you ever had a sexual experience with an adult? **No**

Have you ever had a sexual experience with more than one person at a time? **No**

Have you ever been pressured or forced into having sex? **No**

How often do you have sex while using drugs or alcohol? **Never**

Do drugs or alcohol make sex better or worse? **Neither**

Does what you learn in sex education classes at school help you with your actual sexual experiences? **Not much**

Do you think teenagers should be taught more or less about sex at school? **More**

What do you think is the best age to start having sexual experiences?

well i think 15 is a good age if protection is used anything under that age is just stupid

Do your parents have an influence on whether or not you have sex?

Not at all

Does your religion have an influence on whether or not you have sex?

Not at all

How important is it for you to have an emotional connection with your sexual partner? **Very important**

Is there anything else at all that you would like to say about sex or your own sexual experiences?

well i say you can have sex over the age of 15 and make sure you use protection unless your ready for the step of children

Girl, 16, Victoria, straight 'but adventurous'

What was the first thing you heard about sex?

my mum explained truthfully about "men's penises and women's vaginas" and how they "make a baby" when i was about 5.

Describe your sexual fantasies, even if they seem weird or boring or whatever.

feeling really close to someone emotionally, not neccessarily sexually.

How old were you when you had your first sexual experience with someone else? **14**

What happened in this first sexual experience with another person?

i had sex with my boyfriend twice, and haven't tried again since. i realise now that i was too young, and didn't feel comfortable about it. i knew what i was doing, and practised safe sex, but wasn't emotionally ready for it. Didn't feel 'sexy' like i thought i should.

How old were you when you first had oral sex? **14**

Describe what happened during this oral sex, and how you felt about it.

much better than my attempts at sex ... quite enjoyed it, but didn't really know what to say or do. Didn't feel 'sexy' at all.

On average, how many times a week do you have oral sex?

Less than once a week

If less frequent, how many times approximately has it occurred? **Three times**

How old were you when you first had sexual intercourse? **14**

Describe what happened during intercourse, and how you felt about it emotionally.

didn't find it particularly pleasurable, felt awkward and not 'sexy'.

How old were you when you first had anal sex? **Never had anal sex**

On average, how many times a week do you have intercourse?

Less than once a week

Would you like to have more sex? **Not sure**

How do you think sex could be better for you?

yes. i think i'm older now, and would feel more comfortable with my own body, and could say no if i needed to. i don't think I'll have sex again soon though. i would like to wait for a caring partner.

When you have intercourse, do you use protection? **Yes**

What kind of protection do you use? **condoms. i'm on the pill.**

How often are your sexual experiences with someone of the same sex or gender as you? **Sometimes**

You think of yourself as … **Other: straight, but 'adventurous'**

How old were you when you first saw pornography or erotica? **14**

What kind of pornography have you seen?

websites, with some photographs or films.

Does porn excite you sexually? **A bit**

Does porn give you ideas about how to have sex? **Sometimes**

Do you think sexy films, music videos or advertising encourage you to have sex? **Sometimes**

Examples of media encouraging sex:

tv shows such as 'the secret life of us', 'last man standing'

Have you ever had phone sex, that is, sexually exciting yourself and someone else over the phone? **No**

Have you ever sent or received sexual text messages? **Yes**

Have you had a sexual experience in an internet chat room? **No**

Have you ever had a sexual experience with an adult? **No**

Have you ever had a sexual experience with more than one person at a time? **Yes**

If so, describe what happened and how you felt about it.

kissing a girl whilst being 'fingered' by a guy. was ok.

Have you ever been pressured or forced into having sex? **Yes**

If so, describe what happened and how you felt about it emotionally.

there was no overt pressuring, just that feeling that my friend was fairly promiscuous, and i felt i needed to be 'like her'. at the time i didn't know, but now i regret some of my actions during that time.

How often do you have sex while using drugs or alcohol? **Sometimes**

Do drugs or alcohol make sex better or worse? **Neither**

Does what you learn in sex education classes at school help you with your actual sexual experiences? **Not much**

Do you think teenagers should be taught more or less about sex at school? **More**

What do you think is the best age to start having sexual experiences?

everyone's different. i would say, however, that around 15 I had developed emotionally to the point where i fully understood what i wanted, and didn't want.

Do your parents have an influence on whether or not you have sex? **A bit**

Does your religion have an influence on whether or not you have sex? **Not at all**

How important is it for you to have an emotional connection with your sexual partner? **Very important**

Is there anything else at all that you would like to say about sex or your own sexual experiences?

my mother explained sex to me truthfully, with no metaphors or ridiculous lies. I am very grateful to my mother for that, as it meant that i didn't find the idea of sex unusual or 'scary'. i also didn't have anything to rebel against, and as a result feel more in control of my sexual experiences.

i think it is unbelievably stupid the lengths some parents go to when 'explaining' sex to their children, e.g. stories about babies coming from tablets. They are not protecting their children, in fact i think the opposite! Sex education in schools may correct these ideas, but does not go far enough into the emotional side of things, it is very clinical and does not really teach kids much. I think kids need to be taught truthfully, looking at both the physical and emotional aspects of sex.

Girl, 16, Western Australia, lesbian

How old were you when you first heard about sex? **9**

What was the first thing you heard about sex?

that women had this womb inside them where babies grew. two years later i realised that the penis actually had to go INSIDE the vagina not just at the base!

How old were you when you started masturbating? **11**

On average, how many times a week do you masturbate?

Three times a week

How do you masturbate?

in my room duh, on my bed ... with my fingers

How does masturbating make you feel? **Good**

Describe your sexual fantasies, even if they seem weird or boring or whatever.

sometimes i like the idea of many big dirty men using me and treating me like a slut. other times i like to think of myself making other girls come.

How old were you when you had your first sexual experience with someone else? **6**

What happened in this first sexual experience with another person?

it was me and my step cousin, she was the same age as me, we used to play mums and dads, it's funny now i look at it, i was always the dominating male. we just made out and rubbed our crotches together. there was no emotional feelings as such apart from i suppose the idea of protecting this girl of mine.

How old were you when you first had oral sex? **15**

Describe what happened during this oral sex, and how you felt about it.

i met a bicurious girl that day and we ended up sharing the same bed that night, both of us were curious, i had no attraction towards her - but it was dark and yeh i wanted to make sure that girls were my thing. she went down on me first, then i went down on her.

On average, how many times a week do you have oral sex? **Once a week**

How old were you when you first had sexual intercourse? **15**

Describe what happened during intercourse, and how you felt about it emotionally.

i was drunk with a guy friend of mine, both of us were horny so we just did it, i was curious about what sex with guys was like so i thought id find out. emotionally there was no connection with him what so ever. personally i felt accomplishment, that i had gone through with it, and had the courage to give something a go. even if now i never want to have sex with guys again.

How old were you when you first had anal sex? **Never**

Would you like to have more sex? **Yes**

How do you think sex could be better for you?

if i had several hot lesbian sex buddies that i could call up at anytime when i'm horny. no i'm kidding, basically i've only had emotional sex with one person, all the rest have only been physical. so sex could be better for me if i could be with the one person i love, and if she didnt have the need to see heaps of other women.

When you have intercourse, do you use protection? **Yes**

What kind of protection do you use? **condom**

How often are your sexual experiences with someone of the same sex or gender as you? **Always**

You think of yourself as … **Lesbian**

If you're gay or lesbian, are you 'out'? **Yes**

If you're gay or lesbian and you came out, was it hard? **A bit hard**

Describe what happened when you came out and how you felt about it.

my friends guessed that i was when i was 13, and it took me two years until i admitted it myself and came out to them and my family.

How old were you when you first saw pornography or erotica? **7**

What kind of pornography have you seen? **movies, magazines, internet**

Does porn excite you sexually? **A lot**

Does porn give you ideas about how to have sex? **Sometimes**

Do you think sexy films, music videos or advertising encourage you to have sex? **Sometimes**

Examples of media encouraging sex:

any thing that has beautiful women, portraying women as sex objects!

Have you ever had phone sex, that is, sexually exciting yourself and
someone else over the phone? **No**

Have you ever sent or received sexual text messages? **Yes**

Have you had a sexual experience in an internet chat room? **No**

If so, did you also meet up with that person in real life? **No**

Have you ever had a sexual experience with an adult? **Yes**

If so, describe what happened and how you felt about it emotionally.

**all my sexual partners have been over 18 so does that make them all
adults ... i slept with this 28 year old a few times, at the time it was fine
and still doesnt bother me, i liked her for who she was, age didnt come
into the equation. but i had a one-night stand with a 40 year old, which
i sorta regret, woke up in the morning feeling guilty and dirty, thinking
i've got to get the fuck out of here. she was buying me drinks all night
and i sort of felt like i owed it to her, despite how stupid that sounds
now, maybe i was just going through a bit of rebelion. hmmm she
thought i was 18, still what sort of 40 year old picks up kids like me
anyway ...**

Have you ever had a sexual experience with more than one person at a
time? **No**

Have you ever been pressured or forced into having sex? **No**

How often do you have sex while using drugs or alcohol? **Most of the time**

Do drugs or alcohol make sex better or worse? **Better**

Does what you learn in sex education classes at school help you with your
actual sexual experiences? **Not at all**

Do you think teenagers should be taught more or less about sex at school?
Same as now

What do you think is the best age to start having sexual experiences?

**i was 15 and a half, with no regrets, still i think kids 13 and under can be
manipulated ... but yeh whenever they feel ready, some people mature
faster than others, it's up to the individual, as long as they're not being
pressured.**

Do your parents have an influence on whether or not you have sex?
Not at all

Does your religion have an influence on whether or not you have sex?
Not at all

How important is it for you to have an emotional connection with your sexual
partner? **Not very imporant**

Is there anything else at all that you would like to say about sex or your own
sexual experiences?

**there's definately two types of sex, emotional and physical. physical is
great if you're horny, just let the other person know thats all, i've broken
a few girls hearts because they've wanted more from me. hmmmm i
believe that you can be emotionally connected to someone and have
emotional (meaningful) sex with them while still maintaining physical sex
with others, as long as both people are honest about it ... so yeah i'm
all for open relationships is what i'm trying to say ...**

Girl, 16, Queensland, straight

How old were you when you first heard about sex? **6**

What was the first thing you heard about sex?

**My family was driving somewhere and my brother, he was eight at the
time, went into some service station toilets and came out asking about
the machine on the wall that sold condoms, so for the rest of the way
my mum explained the basics of sex to us.**

How old were you when you started masturbating? **13**

How do you masturbate?

I don't do it very often, only like once a month, and in the shower

How does masturbating make you feel? **Okay**

How old were you when you had your first sexual experience with someone
else? **14**

What happened in this first sexual experience with another person?

**i kissed another girl, i really regret it ... my first kiss ... with a girl that
i now hate**

How old were you when you first had oral sex? **15**

Describe what happened during this oral sex, and how you felt about it.

**I was drunk and this guy took me out into a street and asked me to
which i first said no to but then he just kinda pursuaded me so i did but
then we got interupted and i like ran back to the party, me and my**

friends had no where to stay that night so we went back to his place and i ended up doing it again ... the whole time i was thinking it was gross ... he promised he would never tell anyone, the next day he told one of my best friends boyfriends and then started spreading rumours that i had sex with him ... so all in all i'm not very happy about it.

On average, how many times a week do you have oral sex?

Less than once a week

If less frequent, how many times approximately has it occurred? **Once**

How old were you when you first had sexual intercourse? **Never had it**

How old were you when you first had anal sex? **Never had anal sex**

Would you like to have more sex? **Yes**

How often are your sexual experiences with someone of the same sex or gender as you? **Sometimes**

You think of yourself as ... **Straight**

How old were you when you first saw pornography or erotica? **10**

What kind of pornography have you seen? **magazines, films**

Does porn excite you sexually? **Not much**

Does porn give you ideas about how to have sex? **Sometimes**

Do you think sexy films, music videos or advertising encourage you to have sex? **Sometimes**

Have you ever had phone sex, that is, sexually exciting yourself and someone else over the phone? **No**

Have you ever sent or received sexual text messages? **Yes**

Have you had a sexual experience in an internet chat room? **Yes**

If so, did you also meet up with that person in real life? **No**

Have you ever had a sexual experience with an adult? **Yes**

If so, describe what happened and how you felt about it emotionally.

I got fingered by this guy who had just turned 18. I felt fine about it, we were actually going to go out after wards but then we decided the age gap was too big

Have you ever had a sexual experience with more than one person at a time? **Yes**

If so, describe what happened and how you felt about it.

I hooked up with two girls whilst we were all in the same bed. And once i kissed two guys whilst we were sitting on the same couch, but other than that nothing serious

Have you ever been pressured or forced into having sex? **No**

How often do you have sex while using drugs or alcohol? **Never**

Does what you learn in sex education classes at school help you with your actual sexual experiences? **Not at all**

Do you think teenagers should be taught more or less about sex at school? **More**

What do you think is the best age to start having sexual experiences? **Kissing: about 13, Fingering/ handys: 14 or 15, Oral: 15 or 16, Sex: when ever you feel ready but not before 15**

Do your parents have an influence on whether or not you have sex? **Not much**

Does your religion have an influence on whether or not you have sex? **Not at all**

How important is it for you to have an emotional connection with your sexual partner? **Somewhat important**

Boy, 16, Victoria, straight

How old were you when you first heard about sex? **8**

What was the first thing you heard about sex? **it makes babies**

How old were you when you started masturbating? **13**

On average, how many times a week do you masturbate? **Twice a week**

How do you masturbate?

in front of the computer watching porn. the normal way.

How does masturbating make you feel? **Very good**

Describe your sexual fantasies, even if they seem weird or boring or whatever.

having a threesome with two hot chicks.

How old were you when you had your first sexual experience with someone else? **7**

What happened in this first sexual experience with another person?

a kiss. i felt on top of the world.

How old were you when you first had oral sex? **14**

Describe what happened during this oral sex, and how you felt about it.

i got a head job off this girl at a party. it felt good but she was doing it for a while and i didn't cum.

On average, how many times a week do you have oral sex?

Less than once a week

If less frequent, how many times approximately has it occurred?

More than twenty

How old were you when you first had sexual intercourse? **15**

Describe what happened during intercourse, and how you felt about it emotionally.

the girl who i did it to wasnt sure about it so i didnt pressure her and i didnt even think it was gonna happen but she ended up really wanting it. it was a bit hard at first because i have a large penis and i felt kind of bad because she said it hurt but didnt want me to stop. it was a really good experience and felt really good.

How old were you when you first had anal sex? **Never**

Describe what happens during anal sex and how you feel about having it.

i really wouldnt have it because i think it is wrong. it just disgusts me

On average, how many times a week do you have intercourse?

Less than once a week

Would you like to have more sex? **Yes**

How do you think sex could be better for you?

i think the sex i hav had is great.

When you have intercourse, do you use protection? **Yes**

What kind of protection do you use? **a condom.**

How often are your sexual experiences with someone of the same sex or gender as you? **Never**

You think of yourself as … **Straight**

How old were you when you first saw pornography or erotica? **9**

What kind of pornography have you seen?

films, magazines, internet websights, tv

Does porn excite you sexually? **A lot**

Does porn give you ideas about how to have sex? **Sometimes**

Do you think sexy films, music videos or advertising encourage you to have sex? **Sometimes**

Have you ever had phone sex, that is, sexually exciting yourself and someone else over the phone? **No**

Have you ever sent or received sexual text messages? **Yes**

Have you had a sexual experience in an internet chat room? **No**

Have you ever had a sexual experience with an adult? **No**

Have you ever had a sexual experience with more than one person at a time? **No**

Have you ever been pressured or forced into having sex? **No**

How often do you have sex while using drugs or alcohol? **Sometimes**

Do drugs or alcohol make sex better or worse? **Neither**

Does what you learn in sex education classes at school help you with your actual sexual experiences? **Not much**

Do you think teenagers should be taught more or less about sex at school? **More**

What do you think is the best age to start having sexual experiences? **12 or 13. more about what to do when you are in positions when you can get sex.**

Do your parents have an influence on whether or not you have sex? **Not at all**

Does your religion have an influence on whether or not you have sex? **Not at all**

How important is it for you to have an emotional connection with your sexual partner? **Not very imporant**

Is there anything else at all that you would like to say about sex or your own sexual experiences? **all my sexual experiences have been great so i have not much to say.**

Girl, 16, Victoria, straight

How old were you when you first heard about sex? **7**

What was the first thing you heard about sex?

That it was something beautiful shared between two people in love, that was from my parents. but from the other kids at school it was just a big dirty joke that was worth a few giggles at the word 'penis'

How old were you when you started masturbating? **14**

On average, how many times a week do you masturbate?

Three times a week

How do you masturbate?

i usually do it late at night, in my bed. no objects or lube. i usually have music playing

How does masturbating make you feel? **Good**

Describe your sexual fantasies, even if they seem weird or boring or whatever.

schoolgirl/ teacher. groupie/musician, furries.

How old were you when you had your first sexual experience with someone else? **15**

What happened in this first sexual experience with another person?

it was with my best friend of the opposite sex. we were having a sleepover together and we decided, after talking about it, to experiment a bit. i gave him oral sex and he fingered me. we didn't kiss. i felt fine about it

How old were you when you first had oral sex? **15**

Describe what happened during this oral sex, and how you felt about it.

i was shy, and i guess i did a pretty bad job haha but it was a pretty big thing for me, so i wasnt embarrassed.

On average, how many times a week do you have oral sex?

Less than once a week

If less frequent, how many times approximately has it occurred? **Five times**

How old were you when you first had sexual intercourse? **16**

Describe what happened during intercourse, and how you felt about it emotionally.

we wore protection, it was late at night, in his bed. we weren't going out but we'd been fooling around for 2 weeks beforehand. he was 17, i was 16. years 10 and 12. we both wanted to, and i thought 'shouldnt i feel guilty about not going out with him, and not loving him?' but i didn't think those things at all.

How old were you when you first had anal sex? **Never**

Describe what happens during anal sex and how you feel about having it.

i feel slightly curious about it. i think it would feel good, but id need it to be as clean as possible etc hehe

On average, how many times a week do you have intercourse?

Less than once a week

Would you like to have more sex? **Yes**

How do you think sex could be better for you?

i wish the guy could be really intent on giving me an orgasm. if he acidentally comes or whatever, i dont want him to roll over and fall asleep, i want him to please me too, you know? give a little get a little, that kind of thing.

When you have intercourse, do you use protection? **Yes**

What kind of protection do you use? **condoms.**

How often are your sexual experiences with someone of the same sex or gender as you? **Never**

You think of yourself as … **Straight**

How old were you when you first saw pornography or erotica? **6**

What kind of pornography have you seen?

clips of film, photos, magazines, read stories, read books, websites, comics, ive seen a stripper at an 18th as well

Does porn excite you sexually? **A bit**

Does porn give you ideas about how to have sex? **Sometimes**

Do you think sexy films, music videos or advertising encourage you to have sex? **Never**

Have you ever had phone sex, that is, sexually exciting yourself and someone else over the phone? **Yes**

Have you ever sent or received sexual text messages? **Yes**

Have you had a sexual experience in an internet chat room? **Yes**

If so, did you also meet up with that person in real life? **Yes**

Have you ever had a sexual experience with an adult? **Yes**

If so, describe what happened and how you felt about it emotionally.

ive hooked up with a 20 year old friend before, one of my friends older brothers. i gave him head and we've made out in his room together at quite a few parties at his place. no-one knows about it

Have you ever had a sexual experience with more than one person at a
time? **Yes**

If so, describe what happened and how you felt about it.

**just internet Roleplaying with a few furries. i think there were 4 of us.
nothing in person though.**

Have you ever been pressured or forced into having sex? **No**

How often do you have sex while using drugs or alcohol? **Sometimes**

Do drugs or alcohol make sex better or worse? **Neither**

Does what you learn in sex education classes at school help you with your
actual sexual experiences? **Not at all**

Do you think teenagers should be taught more or less about sex at school?

More

What do you think is the best age to start having sexual experiences?

**i think the legal age is a good one, 16. but i think foreplay is okay after
14. kissing 8+ i guess, i dunno about kissing. it seems like nothing**

Do your parents have an influence on whether or not you have sex?

Not much

Does your religion have an influence on whether or not you have sex?

Not at all

How important is it for you to have an emotional connection with your sexual
partner? **Not very imporant**

Girl, 16, New South Wales, bisexual

What was the first thing you heard about sex?

**The first thing I really remember is just the basic details about what a
man does to a woman.**

How old were you when you started masturbating? **Never**

Describe your sexual fantasies, even if they seem weird or boring or whatever.

**I normally fantasise either about the boy I like at the time or someone
famous. The scenarios are very detailed and exact, but generally quite
normal. I allways like to be dressed in my school uniform though. I
normally put more effort into thinking about my own appearence, not
the guy's.**

What happened in this first sexual experience with another person?

My first sexual experience was when I was around 7 or 8, playing 'boyfriends and girlfriends' with a girlfriend (we would fight over who had to be the boy). It was pretty much just kissing and rubbing up on each other though.

How old were you when you first had oral sex? **14**

Describe what happened during this oral sex, and how you felt about it.

I gave it to a boy i was friends with. I don't remember the details but I remember regretting it because I didn't like him in a more than friends way. It wasn't forceful or unpleasant at the time though. I don't really like doing it and i've only given or recieved it a few times since then.

On average, how many times a week do you have oral sex?

Less than once a week

If less frequent, how many times approximately has it occurred? **Four times**

How old were you when you first had sexual intercourse? **14**

Describe what happened during intercourse, and how you felt about it emotionally.

I realy liked the boy and he really liked me but we weren't technically a couple. He was only 15 and it was at another friends house, in the little sister's room. It didn't go for very long, but it surprisingly didn't hurt much and I liked it. I felt I was emotionally ready, no regrets. I didn't expect it to be amazing.

How old were you when you first had anal sex? **Never**

On average, how many times a week do you have intercourse?

Less than once a week

Would you like to have more sex? **Yes**

How do you think sex could be better for you?

I've had sex with four boys (all around my age), but I was never really 'in love' with any of them. I liked it every time i did it but I havn't done it for almost a year because I decided then I would wait untill i'm really serious about someone.

When you have intercourse, do you use protection? **Yes**

What kind of protection do you use? **Condoms and the pill.**

How often are your sexual experiences with someone of the same sex or gender as you? **Sometimes**

You think of yourself as … **Bisexual**

How old were you when you first saw pornography or erotica? **13**

What kind of pornography have you seen?

I've seen videos, magazines and books mostly.

Does porn excite you sexually? **A bit**

Does porn give you ideas about how to have sex? **Sometimes**

Do you think sexy films, music videos or advertising encourage you to have sex? **Sometimes**

Examples of media encouraging sex:

Not music videos or advertising but films do. Films show the passionate and emotional joys of sex and make it look like so much fun.

Have you ever had phone sex, that is, sexually exciting yourself and someone else over the phone? **No**

Have you ever sent or received sexual text messages? **No**

Have you had a sexual experience in an internet chat room? **Yes**

If so, did you also meet up with that person in real life? **No**

Have you ever had a sexual experience with an adult? **No**

Have you ever had a sexual experience with more than one person at a time? **Yes**

If so, describe what happened and how you felt about it.

It was with two of my girlfriends when we were about 14. We all felt fine about it at the time, then when we woke up in the morning we started laughing and vowed never to bring it up again but we do for a laugh sometimes now.

Have you ever been pressured or forced into having sex? **No**

How often do you have sex while using drugs or alcohol? **Sometimes**

Do drugs or alcohol make sex better or worse? **Neither**

Does what you learn in sex education classes at school help you with your actual sexual experiences? **Not much**

Do you think teenagers should be taught more or less about sex at school? **Same as now**

What do you think is the best age to start having sexual experiences?

I think it depends on the individual. If your ready you know it. Theres really not that much pressure from peers these days where i'm from.

Do your parents have an influence on whether or not you have sex?

Not at all

Does your religion have an influence on whether or not you have sex?

Not at all

How important is it for you to have an emotional connection with your sexual partner? **Somewhat important**

Is there anything else at all that you would like to say about sex or your own sexual experiences?

I've probably had as much sex with girls as with boys but have never used any 'props' with girls. I think i prefer boys though. But girls are better kissers.

Girl, 16, Western Australia, straight

What was the first thing you heard about sex?

That it happened between a mummy and a daddy

How old were you when you started masturbating? **13**

How do you masturbate? **Lying down in a bath and turning on the tap.**

How does masturbating make you feel? **Good**

Describe your sexual fantasies, even if they seem weird or boring or whatever.

I always imagine myself having sex with people, never anything kinky but just having sex with people I like at the time.

How old were you when you had your first sexual experience with someone else? **14**

What happened in this first sexual experience with another person?

I kissed a boy i didn't even know ... It felt weird at the time to have someone else's tongue in my mouth but after it felt good and I wanted to keep doing it. The very same night he tried to put his hands up my skirt but I pushed him away because I was scared.

You think of yourself as ... **Straight**

How old were you when you first saw pornography or erotica? **13**

What kind of pornography have you seen? **photos in my brother's room etc.**

Does porn excite you sexually? **Not at all**

Do you think sexy films, music videos or advertising encourage you to have sex? **Sometimes**

Have you ever had phone sex, that is, sexually exciting yourself and someone else over the phone? **No**

Have you ever sent or received sexual text messages? **No**

Have you had a sexual experience in an internet chat room? **No**

If so, did you also meet up with that person in real life? **No**

Have you ever had a sexual experience with an adult? **Yes**

If so, describe what happened and how you felt about it emotionally.

We kissed and I had known him sometime before that anyway. We were both sexually attracted to each other and we were at the pub one night. We went outside and started kissing. His hands began to wander up my skirt and I pushed him off. I didn't want it to go any further and I felt scared (I don't know why)

Have you ever had a sexual experience with more than one person at a time? **Yes**

If so, describe what happened and how you felt about it.

It was with a few of my girl friends to impress this one guy. We were all a bit drunk and it was all in the name of fun. We had a good laugh about it

Have you ever been pressured or forced into having sex? **Yes**

If so, describe what happened and how you felt about it emotionally.

I never had sex with him though. He would always call and say "come over and spend the night with me". I got angry at one point because I kept saying no.

How often do you have sex while using drugs or alcohol? **Never**

Do drugs or alcohol make sex better or worse? **Neither**

Does what you learn in sex education classes at school help you with your actual sexual experiences? **Not at all**

Do you think teenagers should be taught more or less about sex at school? **More**

What do you think is the best age to start having sexual experiences?

I think by the start of high school people should start to kiss each other because it's a wonderful thing to share and is relatively harmless. I think they should be exposed to that kind of thing at that age because it makes them more mature in a way and able to handle to opposite sex better.

Do your parents have an influence on whether or not you have sex?

Not much

Does your religion have an influence on whether or not you have sex?

Not at all

How important is it for you to have an emotional connection with your sexual partner? **Somewhat important**

Is there anything else at all that you would like to say about sex or your own sexual experiences?

I haven't had sex yet but am thinking about it. I don't have a boyfriend but I have a few boy friends that i see. There's one who really wants to have sex with me and is slightly pushing me to have sex with him. I want to but I'm mostly scared about pregnancy and also what my other friends would think. I'm very relaxed about it, because the way i see it, if you really like the person and want to have that connection with them and it feels 100% right then why hold back? Some of my friends are a bit up tight about the whole sex issue and would probably judge me for it, also because this guy is a fair bit older than me. Those are the only reasons I hold back from having sex. 1) pregnancy 2) Friends and also 3) my parents (i would have to lie to spend the night with him and they don't even know him!)

Girl, 16, Western Australia, straight

How old were you when you first heard about sex? **6**

What was the first thing you heard about sex?

Babies come from sex, adults do it

How old were you when you started masturbating? **9**

On average, how many times a week do you masturbate? **Twice a week**

How do you masturbate?

i usually do it in my room on my bed. i usually play with my breasts for a while then i play with my clitoris

How does masturbating make you feel? **Good**

Describe your sexual fantasies, even if they seem weird or boring or whatever.

i have fantasies about role playing like nurses, cops etc. i always fantasise about doing sexual things in the water like a shower or bath or something like that.

How old were you when you had your first sexual experience with someone else? **10**

What happened in this first sexual experience with another person?

a boy kissed me, it wasnt that great

How old were you when you first had oral sex? **15**

Describe what happened during this oral sex, and how you felt about it.

i was staying at the boyfriends house of the time and it was late at night and we had been drinking, i was very nervous and it tickled a lot, it wasnt what i thought at the time it happend. Now im with my partner for life it is much more better

On average, how many times a week do you have oral sex? **Once a week**

How old were you when you first had sexual intercourse? **16**

Describe what happened during intercourse, and how you felt about it emotionally.

the first time i had sex, we had a lot of trouble. My partner found it hard to keep hard especially when he went to put the condom on, when we finally did it, it hurt me a lot, but it made me and my partner feel very close and happy to experience that together.

How old were you when you first had anal sex? **16**

How often does this happen? **Less than once a week**

Describe what happens during anal sex and how you feel about having it.

well its not the greatest thing in the world ... i dont always feel comfortable about doing it, i really have to relax for it to happen. But like my partner just inserted his penis into my bum and yeah it was weird and hurt way more then the first time i had sexual intercourse

On average, how many times a week do you have intercourse?

Three times a week

Would you like to have more sex? **Not sure**

How do you think sex could be better for you?

i think the sex me and my partner have it the best ever, its so good becuase we love each other very much, but it could be better sometimes if my partners penis was smaller

When you have intercourse, do you use protection? **Yes**

What kind of protection do you use?

well im on the pill and my partner sometimes uses condoms its just they cost too much money to buy.

How often are your sexual experiences with someone of the same sex or gender as you? **Never**

You think of yourself as … **Straight**

How old were you when you first saw pornography or erotica? **13**

What kind of pornography have you seen?

films, photos, magazines, websites

Does porn excite you sexually? **A bit**

Does porn give you ideas about how to have sex? **Sometimes**

Do you think sexy films, music videos or advertising encourage you to have sex? **Sometimes**

Examples of media encouraging sex:

a lot of ads these days use sex to sell there product i think its wrong, like they will have people naked driving in cars or people moaning over shampoo. its kinda off putting.

Have you ever had phone sex, that is, sexually exciting yourself and someone else over the phone? **Yes**

Have you ever sent or received sexual text messages? **Yes**

Have you had a sexual experience in an internet chat room? **No**

Have you ever had a sexual experience with an adult? **No**

Have you ever had a sexual experience with more than one person at a time? **Yes**

If so, describe what happened and how you felt about it.

well me and my two best friends (one was a boy and the other a girl) it was the guys birthday and we went to his place to have a few drinks, we ended up drinking a lot. me and the girl starting kissing and taking each others clothes off and masterbated each other. then we all performed oral sex on each other. it was quite an interesting experience

and i regret it now because i have found someone i love and wish i didnt do anything sexual before i met him

Have you ever been pressured or forced into having sex? **Yes**
If so, describe what happened and how you felt about it emotionally.

the guy liked me for over a year, and we were mucking around and he started to perform oral sex on me then he put his penis in side me once then he pulled out and ejaculated on the bed

How often do you have sex while using drugs or alcohol? **Sometimes**
Do drugs or alcohol make sex better or worse? **Neither**
Does what you learn in sex education classes at school help you with your actual sexual experiences? **Not at all**
Do you think teenagers should be taught more or less about sex at school?
More
What do you think is the best age to start having sexual experiences?

well i think people should wait until there in a settled relationship to start doing any sexual experiences except kissing because thats not that bad, other wise they will end up regreting everything they have done.

Do your parents have an influence on whether or not you have sex?
Not at all
Does your religion have an influence on whether or not you have sex?
Not at all
How important is it for you to have an emotional connection with your sexual partner? **Very important**
Is there anything else at all that you would like to say about sex or your own sexual experiences?

well i really wish i never did anything because now regret it all, and it really hurts me to think about it.

Girl, 16, New South Wales, straight

How old were you when you first heard about sex? **6**
What was the first thing you heard about sex?
what it was and it was how 'babies were made'
How old were you when you started masturbating? **12**

On average, how many times a week do you masturbate? **Once a week**

How does masturbating make you feel? **Good**

How old were you when you had your first sexual experience with someone else? **14**

What happened in this first sexual experience with another person?

i kissed the guy i was going out with, something i felt comfortable doing.

How old were you when you first had oral sex? **15**

Describe what happened during this oral sex, and how you felt about it.

rather self concious, i found it more intimidating than actual intercourse.

On average, how many times a week do you have oral sex? **Once a week**

How old were you when you first had sexual intercourse? **15**

Describe what happened during intercourse, and how you felt about it emotionally.

i had sex with my bf at the time, i kinda felt a bit pressured into it. it was actually a rather horrible experience. that i regret the whole thing was more about him then us. It never happened again. we broke up soon after for other reasons

How old were you when you first had anal sex? **Never**

On average, how many times a week do you have intercourse?

Less than once a week

Would you like to have more sex? **Yes**

How do you think sex could be better for you?

i think guys could be more aware of the girl they are with, for girls its alot more emotional. Alot of girls are afraid to speak up if they are uncomfortable or often feel bad for doing so. Guys need to be more aware of the fact that sex can be alot more than a bit of fun, if something goes wrong girls are the ones who end up pregnant

When you have intercourse, do you use protection? **Yes**

What kind of protection do you use?

condoms, i was considering going on the pill as i was in a long term relationship in which i was having sex quite frequently. The pill seemed like a good option. it would help remove alot of my anxieties about sex and the chance of pregnancy

How often are your sexual experiences with someone of the same sex or gender as you? **Never**

You think of yourself as … **Straight**

How old were you when you first saw pornography or erotica? **11**

What kind of pornography have you seen?

magazines, videos, photos its hard to say when i first saw it, as much as people try to shelter you, you do end up seeing it, its just whether you take it in or know what it is or not.

Does porn excite you sexually? **A bit**

Does porn give you ideas about how to have sex? **Sometimes**

Do you think sexy films, music videos or advertising encourage you to have sex? **Always**

Examples of media encouraging sex:

just generally the way sex is used in advertising and in the media. Sex appeal is excessivly used to target particular audiences

Have you ever had phone sex, that is, sexually exciting yourself and someone else over the phone? **No**

Have you ever sent or received sexual text messages? **Yes**

Have you had a sexual experience in an internet chat room? **No**

Have you ever had a sexual experience with an adult? **No**

Have you ever had a sexual experience with more than one person at a time? **No**

Have you ever been pressured or forced into having sex? **Yes**

If so, describe what happened and how you felt about it emotionally.

it was the first guy i slept with, i could've have said no, but i didnt. I didnt think it would really matter, i trusted him and thought it couldnt hurt to just do it anyway. He seemed rather eager i thought it meant something, the whole experience didnt feel right and i later realised i didnt actually love him like i thought i did. Having sex with my next boyfriend really confirmed these thoughts in my mind.

How often do you have sex while using drugs or alcohol? **Sometimes**

Do drugs or alcohol make sex better or worse? **Better**

Does what you learn in sex education classes at school help you with your actual sexual experiences? **Not much**

Do you think teenagers should be taught more or less about sex at school?
More

What do you think is the best age to start having sexual experiences?
I dont think there is a right or wrong age. People learn from thier experiences and will know what is right for them. It varies very dramatically between people and the relationships they are in.

Do your parents have an influence on whether or not you have sex?
Not much

Does your religion have an influence on whether or not you have sex?
Not at all

How important is it for you to have an emotional connection with your sexual partner? **Somewhat important**

Is there anything else at all that you would like to say about sex or your own sexual experiences?
I dont believe that anyone should have control or influence over another persons sex life. Its understandable that parents etc. want the best for thier children, but to do that you dont have to control them and who they see/have sex with. The best thing parents, teachers etc. can do is to prepare kids for sex by making them aware of what it is, how to be safe, be understanding and to make clear that sex isnt as the media and pornography industry portray it. The more pressure put on kids not to do it the more scared they are of being open about it, the only way parents are going to have any chance of knowing whats going on in thier childrens lives is if they dont pressure them or try to enforce rules. If parents do this too much the less they know about thier children and thier sex lives

Boy, 16, New South Wales, straight

How old were you when you first heard about sex? **11**
What was the first thing you heard about sex?
the penis goes into the vagina
How old were you when you started masturbating? **12**

On average, how many times a week do you masturbate?

More than five times a week

How do you masturbate?

i use my hands, i switch between left and right hand, letting other girls do it for me, in my room

How does masturbating make you feel? **Very good**

Describe your sexual fantasies, even if they seem weird or boring or whatever.

thinking of my girlfriend, different sexual positions

How old were you when you had your first sexual experience with someone else? **14**

What happened in this first sexual experience with another person?

it felt awesome, bit awkward at first but you get used to it

How old were you when you first had oral sex? **15**

Describe what happened during this oral sex, and how you felt about it.

the girl placed her mouth over my penis and licked it, it felt warm and it was a new experience for me. i returned the favour to her and to be honest at first it tastes disgusting but you get used to it.

On average, how many times a week do you have oral sex?

Less than once a week

If less frequent, how many times approximately has it occurred? **Five times**

How old were you when you first had sexual intercourse? **14**

Describe what happened during intercourse, and how you felt about it emotionally.

kissing, handjob - i felt estatic

How old were you when you first had anal sex? **Never**

Describe what happens during anal sex and how you feel about having it.

i would feel very comfortable having it with my girlfriend when she is ready

On average, how many times a week do you have intercourse?

Twice a week

Would you like to have more sex? **Yes**

How do you think sex could be better for you?

i could have sexual interecourse alot more often if parents went away

When you have intercourse, do you use protection? **Yes**

What kind of protection do you use? **condom, possible use of 'the pill'**

How often are your sexual experiences with someone of the same sex or gender as you? **Never**

You think of yourself as … **Straight**

Describe what happened when you came out and how you felt about it.
i'm not gay - they should b lined up agaisnt a wall and shot

How old were you when you first saw pornography or erotica? **11**

What kind of pornography have you seen?
movies, magazines, books, internet, tv

Does porn excite you sexually? **A lot**

Does porn give you ideas about how to have sex? **Always**

Do you think sexy films, music videos or advertising encourage you to have sex? **Sometimes**

Examples of media encouraging sex: **call on me**

Have you ever had phone sex, that is, sexually exciting yourself and someone else over the phone? **Yes**

Have you ever sent or received sexual text messages? **Yes**

Have you had a sexual experience in an internet chat room? **No**

Have you ever had a sexual experience with an adult? **No**

Have you ever had a sexual experience with more than one person at a time? **Yes**

If so, describe what happened and how you felt about it.
i got with both my girlfriend and her best friend at the same time

Have you ever been pressured or forced into having sex? **No**

How often do you have sex while using drugs or alcohol? **Never**

Do drugs or alcohol make sex better or worse? **Better**

Does what you learn in sex education classes at school help you with your actual sexual experiences? **Not at all**

Do you think teenagers should be taught more or less about sex at school?
More

What do you think is the best age to start having sexual experiences?
males - about 14-15, females - about 15-16 depending on maturity

Do your parents have an influence on whether or not you have sex? **A bit**

Does your religion have an influence on whether or not you have sex?
Not at all

How important is it for you to have an emotional connection with your sexual partner? **Very important**

Is there anything else at all that you would like to say about sex or your own sexual experiences?

Always be yourself! everybody hates it when you are stuck up and think you're the best thing on the planet! Don't be embarressed either

Girl, 16, New South Wales, straight

How old were you when you first heard about sex? **10**

What was the first thing you heard about sex? **that it hurts**

How old were you when you started masturbating? **10**

On average, how many times a week do you masturbate?

Three times a week

How do you masturbate? **in bed, fingers**

How does masturbating make you feel? **Good**

Describe your sexual fantasies, even if they seem weird or boring or whatever.

in the fucking ocean!!!!!!! hahaha

How old were you when you had your first sexual experience with someone else? **11**

What happened in this first sexual experience with another person?

kissed some guy, didnt know him and beacuse i was young i was like "oh i feel so used" hahaha, but ummm yeh, i always heard about all the different diseases u can get from hooking up, so i thought i was going to die!

How old were you when you first had oral sex? **14**

Describe what happened during this oral sex, and how you felt about it.

was going out with a guy in yr 8 and got a bit pissed n we had oral sex, i didnt really regret it strangly, i think oral sex muuuust be better for guys than girls

On average, how many times a week do you have oral sex?

Less than once a week

If less frequent, how many times approximately has it occurred? **Five times**

How old were you when you first had sexual intercourse? **14**

Describe what happened during intercourse, and how you felt about it
   emotionally.

**a guy i liked asked me out and the next night we had sex, he was my
first, and i really liked him even though i didnt know him very well, but
yeh, ummm he used me, dumped me the next day, i felt like shit, it still
sticks with me, i regret it alot**

How old were you when you first had anal sex? **Never**

On average, how many times a week do you have intercourse?

Less than once a week

Would you like to have more sex? **Not sure**

How do you think sex could be better for you?

**well i have had sex with 5 guys, and none of them i was in a proper
relationship, or knew very well, my first i like but he used me really
badly, my second was in bali and i was leaving to go back home the
next day, my third is a blur ... i was really stoned n ended up having sex
with this guy i pretty much didnt know, same with my 4th, and my 5th
was this guy, impulse it happened, havnt spoken to him since ... i never
intended it to be like this, cuz i sometimes feel used, but ive learnt now
i hope i dunno wateva**

When you have intercourse, do you use protection? **Yes**

What kind of protection do you use? **condom**

How often are your sexual experiences with someone of the same sex or
   gender as you? **Never**

You think of yourself as ... **Straight**

How old were you when you first saw pornography or erotica? **11**

What kind of pornography have you seen? **magazines n videos, they r funny**

Does porn excite you sexually? **A bit**

Does porn give you ideas about how to have sex? **Sometimes**

Do you think sexy films, music videos or advertising encourage you to have
   sex? **Sometimes**

Have you ever had phone sex, that is, sexually exciting yourself and
   someone else over the phone? **No**

Have you ever sent or received sexual text messages? **Yes**

Have you had a sexual experience in an internet chat room? **No**

Have you ever had a sexual experience with an adult? **Yes**

If so, describe what happened and how you felt about it emotionally.

adult as in what, like over 18? yes but he was 20, as i said it was a blur

Have you ever had a sexual experience with more than one person at a time? **No**

Have you ever been pressured or forced into having sex? **Yes**

If so, describe what happened and how you felt about it emotionally.

felt pressured to do it. also to make the guy like me ... DUMB IDEA

How often do you have sex while using drugs or alcohol? **Sometimes**

Do drugs or alcohol make sex better or worse? **Worse**

Does what you learn in sex education classes at school help you with your actual sexual experiences? **Not much**

What do you think is the best age to start having sexual experiences?

i think about 15 or 16, because before that its very hard to handle the emotional stress of it all

Do your parents have an influence on whether or not you have sex? **A lot**

Does your religion have an influence on whether or not you have sex?

Not at all

How important is it for you to have an emotional connection with your sexual partner? **Very important**

Is there anything else at all that you would like to say about sex or your own sexual experiences?

woohoo im anonymous hahaha, well i dont really have anything else to say, except as the years go on, the generations are getting younger and younger, if that makes any sense, as in ... i see girls who are like 13, 14, doing drugs having sex, clubbing, fake IDs, wanting to be older than they are ... i used to be like that, sometimes i still feel like that, but honestly there is no where to turn ... not parents, if my parents know what goes on in my teen years i would be shot hahaha, but yeah, because i dunno if this is true but you cant talk to the school councellors about drugs or sex or something like that if you are under a certain age, i needed councelling and i couldnt pay, didnt want to tell my parents, there need to be more places available to teenagers with councellors open and teenagers need to know this! please!

Girl, 16, Western Australia, straight

How old were you when you first heard about sex? **10**

What was the first thing you heard about sex?

that it was when you love someone and you wanna show them how much they mean to you

How old were you when you started masturbating? **14**

On average, how many times a week do you masturbate? **Once a week**

How do you masturbate? **well i use this shower head lol**

How does masturbating make you feel? **Very good**

Describe your sexual fantasies, even if they seem weird or boring or whatever.

i've always wanted to have hot dirty sex in the toilets at school

How old were you when you had your first sexual experience with someone else? **15**

What happened in this first sexual experience with another person?

well i was really really drunk and i had a boyfriend but i went to a party and was with three guys. it felt really good at the time but afterwards i felt cheated and used

How old were you when you first had oral sex? **15**

Describe what happened during this oral sex, and how you felt about it.

i felt weird because i had heard so much about oral sex but now i was actually experiencing it. it was really good and way better then i expected. he went down on me so many times that in the morning i was so sore but it felt great. i really enjoyed giving oral sex as well just the feeling of them blowing in my mouth was a full turn on

On average, how many times a week do you have oral sex?

Less than once a week

If less frequent, how many times approximately has it occurred?

Fifteen times

How old were you when you first had sexual intercourse? **16**

Describe what happened during intercourse, and how you felt about it emotionally. **it was good i felt sick afterwards though**

How old were you when you first had anal sex? **16**

How often does this happen? **Less than once a week**

Describe what happens during anal sex and how you feel about having it.

it felt like i was chucking a huge turd

On average, how many times a week do you have intercourse?

Less than once a week

Would you like to have more sex? **Yes**

How do you think sex could be better for you?

if guys finished you off instead of just worrying about themselves blowing

When you have intercourse, do you use protection? **Sometimes**

What kind of protection do you use? **i'm on the pill and a condom**

How often are your sexual experiences with someone of the same sex or gender as you? **Sometimes**

You think of yourself as … **Straight**

How old were you when you first saw pornography or erotica? **12**

What kind of pornography have you seen? **mags**

Does porn excite you sexually? **A bit**

Does porn give you ideas about how to have sex? **Always**

Do you think sexy films, music videos or advertising encourage you to have sex? **Always**

Have you ever had phone sex, that is, sexually exciting yourself and someone else over the phone? **No**

Have you ever sent or received sexual text messages? **Yes**

Have you had a sexual experience in an internet chat room? **Yes**

If so, did you also meet up with that person in real life? **No**

Have you ever had a sexual experience with an adult? **No**

Have you ever had a sexual experience with more than one person at a time? **No**

Have you ever been pressured or forced into having sex? **No**

How often do you have sex while using drugs or alcohol? **Never**

Do drugs or alcohol make sex better or worse? **Neither**

Does what you learn in sex education classes at school help you with your actual sexual experiences? **Not at all**

Do you think teenagers should be taught more or less about sex at school?

More

What do you think is the best age to start having sexual experiences?

you should be at least 16 i think personally but other things like oral 14 at least

Do your parents have an influence on whether or not you have sex?

Not much

Does your religion have an influence on whether or not you have sex?

Not at all

How important is it for you to have an emotional connection with your sexual partner? **Very important**

Girl, 16, New South Wales, straight

How old were you when you first heard about sex? **6**

What was the first thing you heard about sex?

The dick entering the vagina

How old were you when you started masturbating? **Never**

Describe your sexual fantasies, even if they seem weird or boring or whatever.

1. Sex on a pool table 2. Sex in the ocean 3. Sex in a bathroom on an aeroplane 4. Sex in a spa with the jets on

How old were you when you had your first sexual experience with someone else? **13**

What happened in this first sexual experience with another person?

It was a kiss. We were sitting on the couch together and I had no idea what to do. I just went with what he did. It felt really weird but it was a boost for my confidence having kissed a boy. I didnt like the boy afterwards but I was glad I had my first kiss.

How old were you when you first had oral sex? **15**

Describe what happened during this oral sex, and how you felt about it.

A good guy friend invited me over to his house on a Sunday and we started kissing and then he gently pushed my head down 'south' and then i just did it. I had to get it over and done with and the time may as well have been then. I swallowed and then later on that day he called me and asked if I should use the pill because he thought I could get pregnant.

On average, how many times a week do you have oral sex? **Once a week**

How old were you when you first had sexual intercourse? **15**

Describe what happened during intercourse, and how you felt about it emotionally.

I had met this 18 year old guy three times and he invited me onto his boat. I took some friends and he had some friends. I hadn't even kissed him before this. He took me to a room on the boat and we had sex. It was excrutiatingly painful. It hurt so much, I was grinding my teeth together. Emotionally I didnt really care, I was fine with it. I don't know why but I never seem to care about these sort of things. Alot of questions were asked by my friends and I dont think alot of them agreed with what I did.

How old were you when you first had anal sex? **Never**

On average, how many times a week do you have intercourse?

Less than once a week

Would you like to have more sex? **Yes**

How do you think sex could be better for you?

Find someone I absolutely trust and we can experiment and try and make it better for each other. Maybe even find a boyfriend (as easy as that sounds, its not) and have fun with him. Not getting a reputation for being a slut.

When you have intercourse, do you use protection? **Sometimes**

What kind of protection do you use? **Condoms.**

How often are your sexual experiences with someone of the same sex or gender as you? **Never**

You think of yourself as … **Straight**

How old were you when you first saw pornography or erotica? **9**

What kind of pornography have you seen?

Films, Magazines, internet Websites

Does porn excite you sexually? **Not at all**

Does porn give you ideas about how to have sex? **Sometimes**

Do you think sexy films, music videos or advertising encourage you to have sex? **Always**

Examples of media encouraging sex:

Skyy Blue advertising. Ralph Lauren Romance. Dior Addict.

Have you ever had phone sex, that is, sexually exciting yourself and someone else over the phone? **Yes**

Have you ever sent or received sexual text messages? **Yes**

Have you had a sexual experience in an internet chat room? **Yes**

If so, did you also meet up with that person in real life? **No**

Have you ever had a sexual experience with an adult? **No**

Have you ever had a sexual experience with more than one person at a time? **Yes**

If so, describe what happened and how you felt about it.

It was too funny to explain. It was with my best girlfriend and a random guy we met. We were really drunk. We didn't have sex though. Everything but sex.

Have you ever been pressured or forced into having sex? **No**

How often do you have sex while using drugs or alcohol? **Most of the time**

Do drugs or alcohol make sex better or worse? **Neither**

Does what you learn in sex education classes at school help you with your actual sexual experiences? **Not much**

Do you think teenagers should be taught more or less about sex at school? **More**

What do you think is the best age to start having sexual experiences?

I dont think it depends on age. It depends on maturity levels. If your mature at 14 and you think you can handle having sex and the post concequences then thats fine. It also depends on what you stand for. But to answer your question I would have to say 15 or 16. I dont think any sexual experiences excluding kissing should be done before 13-14.

Do your parents have an influence on whether or not you have sex?

Not at all

Does your religion have an influence on whether or not you have sex?

Not at all

How important is it for you to have an emotional connection with your sexual partner? **Not very important**

Girl, 16, New South Wales, straight

How old were you when you first heard about sex? **9**

What was the first thing you heard about sex? **the birds and the bees**

How old were you when you started masturbating? **Never**

Describe your sexual fantasies, even if they seem weird or boring or whatever.
fucking in a spa

How old were you when you had your first sexual experience with someone
else? **11**

What happened in this first sexual experience with another person?
nothing it was fun

How old were you when you first had oral sex? **15**

Describe what happened during this oral sex, and how you felt about it.
yukkkie

On average, how many times a week do you have oral sex?
Less than once a week

If less frequent, how many times approximately has it occurred? **Three times**

How old were you when you first had sexual intercourse? **16**

Describe what happened during intercourse, and how you felt about it
emotionally. **nothing i was drunk**

How old were you when you first had anal sex? **Never**

On average, how many times a week do you have intercourse?
Less than once a week

Would you like to have more sex? **Yes**

How do you think sex could be better for you? **i dont know**

When you have intercourse, do you use protection? **Sometimes**

What kind of protection do you use? **condom**

You think of yourself as … **Straight**

What kind of pornography have you seen? **films**

Does porn excite you sexually? **A lot**

Does porn give you ideas about how to have sex? **Always**

Do you think sexy films, music videos or advertising encourage you to have
sex? **Always**

Have you ever had phone sex, that is, sexually exciting yourself and
someone else over the phone? **Yes**

Have you ever sent or received sexual text messages? **Yes**

Have you had a sexual experience in an internet chat room? **No**

Have you ever had a sexual experience with an adult? **No**

Have you ever had a sexual experience with more than one person at a time? **No**

Have you ever been pressured or forced into having sex? **No**

How often do you have sex while using drugs or alcohol? **Always**

Do drugs or alcohol make sex better or worse? **Better**

Does what you learn in sex education classes at school help you with your actual sexual experiences? **Not much**

Do you think teenagers should be taught more or less about sex at school? **More**

What do you think is the best age to start having sexual experiences? **i think 15 or 16 as people are more mature and aware of what is right and what is wrong**

Do your parents have an influence on whether or not you have sex? **Not at all**

Does your religion have an influence on whether or not you have sex? **Not at all**

How important is it for you to have an emotional connection with your sexual partner? **Somewhat important**

Is there anything else at all that you would like to say about sex or your own sexual experiences? **i love sex i love sexi** love sexi love sexi love sexi love sexi love sexi love sexi love sexi love sexi love sexi love sexi love sexi love sexi love sex I AM A HORNY GOAT !!!!!!!!!!!

Girl, 16, New South Wales, straight

How old were you when you first heard about sex? **6**

What was the first thing you heard about sex? **that it made babies**

How old were you when you started masturbating? **13**

On average, how many times a week do you masturbate? **Twice a week**

How does masturbating make you feel? **Very good**

Describe your sexual fantasies, even if they seem weird or boring or whatever.
my sexual fantasies are always very interesting ... usually including a very sexual guy ... sometimes even other girls

How old were you when you had your first sexual experience with someone else? **7**

What happened in this first sexual experience with another person?
i was in primary school and it was a dare and i was the only one who was game enough to kiss and so we kissed ...

How old were you when you first had oral sex? **14**

Describe what happened during this oral sex, and how you felt about it.
my partner went down on me ... and i felt very strange at first and didnt know what to make of it and i then started to enjoy it and i began to loosen up a bit then got into it ... i found it quite enjoyable through to the end ...

On average, how many times a week do you have oral sex? **Once a week**

How old were you when you first had sexual intercourse? **14**

Describe what happened during intercourse, and how you felt about it emotionally.
the first time i was very wary of it and wasnt sure wat to expect, it was a painful experience but i began to feel comfortable about it, i wasnt comfortable about my age and so i was more scared about the reactions of my peers so i felt i shouldnt be doing it ...

How old were you when you first had anal sex? **Never**

On average, how many times a week do you have intercourse?

Four times a week

Would you like to have more sex? **Yes**

How do you think sex could be better for you?

i enjoy sex the way it is for me ... i dont feel that it needs to be better for me ...

When you have intercourse, do you use protection? **Yes**

What kind of protection do you use?

im on the pill but i also use condoms at times ...

How often are your sexual experiences with someone of the same sex or gender as you? **Sometimes**

You think of yourself as ... **Straight**

How old were you when you first saw pornography or erotica? **14**

What kind of pornography have you seen? **movies and magazines**

Does porn excite you sexually? **A bit**

Does porn give you ideas about how to have sex? **Sometimes**

Do you think sexy films, music videos or advertising encourage you to have sex? **Sometimes**

Have you ever had phone sex, that is, sexually exciting yourself and someone else over the phone? **No**

Have you ever sent or received sexual text messages? **Yes**

Have you had a sexual experience in an internet chat room? **No**

Have you ever had a sexual experience with an adult? **Yes**

Have you ever had a sexual experience with more than one person at a time? **No**

Have you ever been pressured or forced into having sex? **No**

How often do you have sex while using drugs or alcohol? **Sometimes**

Do drugs or alcohol make sex better or worse? **Neither**

Does what you learn in sex education classes at school help you with your actual sexual experiences? **A lot**

Do you think teenagers should be taught more or less about sex at school? **More**

What do you think is the best age to start having sexual experiences?

i think 16 is a good age but it depends on everyone as each person is at different stages and some people are alot more mature than others ...

i think this for sexual intercourse and for other sexual experiences

i beleive that around 14 or 15 is alright to start

Do your parents have an influence on whether or not you have sex?

Not much

Does your religion have an influence on whether or not you have sex?

Not at all

How important is it for you to have an emotional connection with your sexual partner? **Somewhat important**

Is there anything else at all that you would like to say about sex or your own sexual experiences?

i believe sex is very influenced by the media and alot of perceptions come from that ... i feel that many people are against it because of what is said but i also feel that even in your group of friends there can be a lot of stigma towards it ... i feel that our generation can be either very accepting or completely against it ... this also comes from what your parents have taught u and how u feel about it ...

Girl, 16, (no postcode given), straight

How old were you when you first heard about sex? **10**

What was the first thing you heard about sex?

that you can have babys from it.

How old were you when you started masturbating? **15**

On average, how many times a week do you masturbate? **Once a week**

How does masturbating make you feel? **Okay**

Describe your sexual fantasies, even if they seem weird or boring or whatever.

... i have dreams about guys that i think are hot that i know.

How old were you when you had your first sexual experience with someone else? **14**

What happened in this first sexual experience with another person?

i hooked up with a guy from my old skool, he was my first real kiss, he was really hot. i later found out that he was having a comp with his frend to c how many chicks they cud get with that night. wen i got told, i was like O'well it was good.

How old were you when you first had oral sex? **14**

Describe what happened during this oral sex, and how you felt about it.

i was at a party and i had had way too much to drink, i was throwing up every where. anyway i had passed out wen i woke up not long after, i was in a bed with my frend. her cuz decided to get in the bed next to me. i had never seen him b4 and he was feeling me up and then he fingered me, i didnt want him to, it hurt. but i didnt really know what to do i was so drunk. i hate him for it.

On average, how many times a week do you have oral sex?

Less than once a week

If less frequent, how many times approximately has it occurred?

More than twenty

How old were you when you first had sexual intercourse? **15**

How old were you when you first had anal sex? **Never**

On average, how many times a week do you have intercourse?

Less than once a week

Would you like to have more sex? **Yes**

How do you think sex could be better for you?

i wona know how to make it feel better and like get a book or sumthin to give tips. i wona have sex with a guy thats not judging.

When you have intercourse, do you use protection? **Sometimes**

What kind of protection do you use? **condoms**

How often are your sexual experiences with someone of the same sex or gender as you? **Never**

You think of yourself as … **Straight**

How old were you when you first saw pornography or erotica? **Never**

Do you think sexy films, music videos or advertising encourage you to have sex? **Sometimes**

Have you ever had phone sex, that is, sexually exciting yourself and someone else over the phone? **No**

Have you ever sent or received sexual text messages? **No**

Have you had a sexual experience in an internet chat room? **No**

Have you ever had a sexual experience with an adult? **No**

Have you ever had a sexual experience with more than one person at a time? **No**

Have you ever been pressured or forced into having sex? **Yes**

How often do you have sex while using drugs or alcohol? **Most of the time**

Do drugs or alcohol make sex better or worse? **Neither**

Does what you learn in sex education classes at school help you with your actual sexual experiences? **A bit**

Do you think teenagers should be taught more or less about sex at school? **More**

What do you think is the best age to start having sexual experiences? **i duno, if someone feels ready to have sex and stuff i suppose your age wouldnt matter, but probably 14,15,16.**

Do your parents have an influence on whether or not you have sex? **Not at all**

Does your religion have an influence on whether or not you have sex? **Not at all**

How important is it for you to have an emotional connection with your sexual partner? **Somewhat important**

Is there anything else at all that you would like to say about sex or your own sexual experiences? **the first time i had sex, i was at a party (really drunk) the party got broke up and every1 all split up, i went with my frend to the skate park (most ppl went there), i seen a guy from skool i was sorta frends with, he sed he wud drive me home. we sorta went for a drive around, he stopped the car and we started hooking up, i didnt mind coz he was a nice guy. but 1 thing led to a nother, i didnt really want to have sex, i was scared to say no, he was pushy, during the sex he was really rough and coz it was my first time, i bled. i was embarressed, it got on his jumper. i told him not to tell any body. i didnt talk to him at skool for a few weeks, when ever i walked past him or sumthing like that i looked away like i didnt see him. he must have told his frends what happend with the jumper and stuff and they sorta gave me shit about it for a day, i didnt care, i had already put it all behind me, but i was still sorta mad. the next time i saw him after that i ignored him, that night he sent me a msg saying 'are you annoyed at me' Of corse i was, but in my msg back i just wrote 'No y wud i be?' ... we talkd for a bit, that w/e i seen him at a party and we were talking heaps, it was good, we are frends agen.**

i regret having sex with him tho, theres nothing i can do about it now. but iv just learnt to say no to things i dont wona do now, and not to be scared to say it. hope u liked my story ... :)

Girl, 16, Western Australia, straight

How old were you when you first heard about sex? **8**

What was the first thing you heard about sex?

I was in the backseat of my car and found a pamphlet, explaining how the penis entered the vagina, me and my friend found it hilarious at that age.

How old were you when you started masturbating? **Never**

Describe your sexual fantasies, even if they seem weird or boring or whatever.

To be with someone hot, in control and popular.

How old were you when you had your first sexual experience with someone else? **13**

What happened in this first sexual experience with another person?

A friend and I had just met these guys at a holiday resort and we were sitting in a spa, suddenly the guy who my friend had a crush on started to touch me underneath the water. I remember thinking ew who does this guy think he his and kept pushing him away, but despite my efforts he kept trying until the night ended.

How old were you when you first had oral sex? **Never had oral sex**

How old were you when you first had sexual intercourse? **Never**

How old were you when you first had anal sex? **Never**

You think of yourself as ... **Straight**

How old were you when you first saw pornography or erotica? **6**

What kind of pornography have you seen?

A tricky question because all the films etc seam to be erotic these days, but most probably an anonymous email i was sent

Does porn excite you sexually? **A bit**

Does porn give you ideas about how to have sex? **Sometimes**

Do you think sexy films, music videos or advertising encourage you to have sex? **Always**

Examples of media encouraging sex:

Definately music video/film clips that involve woman prancing around men with perfect bodies. Teenage films also encourage it because it reanacts sex as a normal thing to do when your a teenager. American Pie and Road Trip are good axamples.

Have you ever had phone sex, that is, sexually exciting yourself and someone else over the phone? **No**

Have you ever sent or received sexual text messages? **Yes**

Have you had a sexual experience in an internet chat room? **No**

Have you ever had a sexual experience with an adult? **No**

Have you ever had a sexual experience with more than one person at a time? **No**

Have you ever been pressured or forced into having sex? **Yes**

If so, describe what happened and how you felt about it emotionally.

i was pressured but didnt end up doing it. I was however pretty close to giving in.

Do drugs or alcohol make sex better or worse? **Better**

Does what you learn in sex education classes at school help you with your actual sexual experiences? **Not at all**

Do you think teenagers should be taught more or less about sex at school? **Less**

Do your parents have an influence on whether or not you have sex? **A lot**

Does your religion have an influence on whether or not you have sex? **Not much**

How important is it for you to have an emotional connection with your sexual partner? **Very important**

Is there anything else at all that you would like to say about sex or your own sexual experiences?

Girls are the victims of sex almost all the time. If we dont have a sexual experience with a guy we are considored "tight" otherwise if we do have sex we are abused as sluts, skanks, whores or loose bitches. Guys on the other hand are either experienced hunks, or understanding gentle virgins.

The responses from 17-year-olds exhibit even greater certainty that sex is better when they're in a relationship. Whether they've been doing it for years or they're first-timers, both girls and boys appreciate emotional connections in enhancing the quality of sex. There are just as many regrets about sexual encounters among this older group as the younger teens when there is no emotional intimacy.

A lot more boys answered the survey in this age group, and they've become even better at expressing how they feel. They also display a new depth of self-awareness and sensitivity.

More kids are 'coming out' if they're gay, lesbian or bisexual, and both gay and straight seem more sure of their preferences.

Girl, 17, ACT, straight

How old were you when you first heard about sex? **9**

What was the first thing you heard about sex? **cant remember sorry**

How old were you when you started masturbating? **12**

On average, how many times a week do you masturbate? **Once a week**

How do you masturbate?

   its really none unless its part of foreplay with my boyfriend

How does masturbating make you feel? **Good**

Describe your sexual fantasies, even if they seem weird or boring or whatever.

   just that my bf's mum went away more often so we could do it more

How old were you when you had your first sexual experience with someone else? **12**

What happened in this first sexual experience with another person?

   hmm my first thing was masterbating, i didnt really know what it was,

   just that if felt good. i accidentaly discovered it. wen first time did

   something sexual with bf felt excited and wanted to tell everyone!

How old were you when you first had oral sex? **15**

Describe what happened during this oral sex, and how you felt about it.

I recieved it and was ashamed when he said i was too hairy, but it was his first time too

On average, how many times a week do you have oral sex?

Less than once a week

If less frequent, how many times approximately has it occurred?

Twenty times

How old were you when you first had sexual intercourse? **15**

Describe what happened during intercourse, and how you felt about it emotionally.

it didnt work properly for ages, but we didnt mind. it was just a natural progression from oral and fingering and handjobs

Describe what happens during anal sex and how you feel about having it.

tried once felt gross like backwards shitting

On average, how many times a week do you have intercourse?

Less than once a week

Would you like to have more sex? **Yes**

How do you think sex could be better for you?

more times when we could sleep over together, so more of it. less inhibitions

When you have intercourse, do you use protection? **Yes**

What kind of protection do you use? **the pill, sometimes condoms but rarely**

How often are your sexual experiences with someone of the same sex or gender as you? **Never**

You think of yourself as ... **Straight**

How old were you when you first saw pornography or erotica? **12**

What kind of pornography have you seen? **everything except live shows**

Does porn excite you sexually? **A lot**

Does porn give you ideas about how to have sex? **Sometimes**

Do you think sexy films, music videos or advertising encourage you to have sex? **Sometimes**

Have you ever had phone sex, that is, sexually exciting yourself and someone else over the phone? **Yes**

Have you ever sent or received sexual text messages? **Yes**

Have you had a sexual experience in an internet chat room? **No**

Have you ever had a sexual experience with an adult? **No**

Have you ever had a sexual experience with more than one person at a time? **No**

Have you ever been pressured or forced into having sex? **No**

How often do you have sex while using drugs or alcohol? **Sometimes**

Do drugs or alcohol make sex better or worse? **Better**

Does what you learn in sex education classes at school help you with your actual sexual experiences? **Not much**

Do you think teenagers should be taught more or less about sex at school? **More**

What do you think is the best age to start having sexual experiences? **shoudnt have sex till 16/17 (i did 15 but i sort of regret it, only becuse when i tell ppl they are shocked!!)**

Do your parents have an influence on whether or not you have sex? **Not at all**

Does your religion have an influence on whether or not you have sex? **Not at all**

How important is it for you to have an emotional connection with your sexual partner? **Very important**

Is there anything else at all that you would like to say about sex or your own sexual experiences? **i think sex with randoms (ie ppl you dont know at all) is feral, esp for ppl our age (17) i have only had sex with my bf of 2.5 years and very happy with that**

Boy, 17, New South Wales, bisexual

How old were you when you first heard about sex? **7**

What was the first thing you heard about sex? **That babies came from a ladies bottom ... lol ... I clearly remember my friend telling me ... and I was amazed**

How old were you when you started masturbating? **11**

On average, how many times a week do you masturbate? **More than five times a week**

How do you masturbate?

I usually wank the same way each time. I try all different material though. Porn from the net, self-fantasies, phone sex, text/cyber sex.

How does masturbating make you feel? **Good**

Describe your sexual fantasies, even if they seem weird or boring or whatever.

I would love to have sex with a skater boy. I love everything about them. I also have a kind of fetish for male feet, especially white-socked feet - weird i know … but hey, its cool.

How old were you when you had your first sexual experience with someone else? **16**

What happened in this first sexual experience with another person?

Well at 16 - i kinda of sucked on another guys toes and feet. At 17 i made out with a GIRL for the first time. That's about it … im quite reserved about sex with other people.

How old were you when you first had oral sex? **Never had oral sex**

How old were you when you first had sexual intercourse? **Never**

How old were you when you first had anal sex? **Never**

Would you like to have more sex? **Yes**

You think of yourself as … **Bisexual**

If you're gay or lesbian, are you 'out'? **No**

How old were you when you first saw pornography or erotica? **14**

What kind of pornography have you seen?

Magazines, photos, movies, internet websites, stories.

Does porn excite you sexually? **A lot**

Does porn give you ideas about how to have sex? **Always**

Do you think sexy films, music videos or advertising encourage you to have sex? **Sometimes**

Examples of media encouraging sex: **Queer As Folk - - lol**

Have you ever had phone sex, that is, sexually exciting yourself and someone else over the phone? **Yes**

Have you ever sent or received sexual text messages? **Yes**

Have you had a sexual experience in an internet chat room? **Yes**

If so, did you also meet up with that person in real life? **No**

Have you ever had a sexual experience with an adult? **No**

Have you ever had a sexual experience with more than one person at a time? **No**

Have you ever been pressured or forced into having sex? **No**

How often do you have sex while using drugs or alcohol? **Never**

Do drugs or alcohol make sex better or worse? **Neither**

Does what you learn in sex education classes at school help you with your actual sexual experiences? **Not at all**

Do you think teenagers should be taught more or less about sex at school? **More**

What do you think is the best age to start having sexual experiences?
I think year 7 (13 years) is kissing time, Year 8 (14) same and maybe a little over the sweater action. Oral sex and intercourse should not occur until you are at least 16 - and even then is a bit young.

Do your parents have an influence on whether or not you have sex?
Not much

Does your religion have an influence on whether or not you have sex?
Not at all

How important is it for you to have an emotional connection with your sexual partner? **Not important at all**

Is there anything else at all that you would like to say about sex or your own sexual experiences? **I REALLY WANT TO HAVE SEX - I AM SO HORNY**

Girl, 17, South Australia, bisexual

How old were you when you first heard about sex? **7**

What was the first thing you heard about sex?
thats how babies where made

How old were you when you started masturbating? **12**

On average, how many times a week do you masturbate? **Twice a week**

How do you masturbate?
usually with a viabrator or rubbing in circles on my clitoris, i do it usually in my room or at my boyfriends house in front of him.

How does masturbating make you feel? **Good**

Describe your sexual fantasies, even if they seem weird or boring or whatever.

i like it rough and naughty or with older men, although ive never had sex with an older man i think that would be good to be under control with someone who is so mature and has great experiance. rough sex and different positions and different places is also good. i like variety and enthusiasim.

How old were you when you had your first sexual experience with someone else? **6**

What happened in this first sexual experience with another person?

i was too young, it was my brothers friend who is 2 years older, during a sleep over. we slept next to each other on the floor while my brother slept on his bed. we played with two teddies and mum's and dads. i felt naughty, grown up, i can still remember the adrenalin rush and the excitment.

How old were you when you first had oral sex? **14**

Describe what happened during this oral sex, and how you felt about it.

well i was drunk, i wasnt fully aware of what i was doing but i was happy to do it with this particular person for experiance, i just copied what i had seen from porn, he enjoyed it, but then it only lasted about 2 minutes because i got bored haha

On average, how many times a week do you have oral sex?

Four times a week

How old were you when you first had sexual intercourse? **15**

Describe what happened during intercourse, and how you felt about it emotionally.

it was on my 15th birthday, it wasnt exactly intercourse at an extreme level, he put the condom on, and tried to put it in, but it wouldnt fit, it went a little in then i felt uncomfortable and not ready, i didnt know what to class that as. the first proper sex, i was drugged at a party.

How old were you when you first had anal sex? **Never had anal sex**

On average, how many times a week do you have intercourse?

Three times a week

Would you like to have more sex? **Not sure**

How do you think sex could be better for you?

i just like the feeling after i have climaxed, i love the person whom i am having sex with. it makes me feel loved and respected back. it releases so much feelings, i am unsure because i think sex is more special when its rare.

When you have intercourse, do you use protection? **Yes**

What kind of protection do you use?

i have the implanon, sometimes we use a condom.

How often are your sexual experiences with someone of the same sex or gender as you? **Sometimes**

You think of yourself as … **Bisexual**

If you're gay or lesbian, are you 'out'? **No**

How old were you when you first saw pornography or erotica? **7**

What kind of pornography have you seen?

all types except live shows. i shared a computer with my dad and older brother so it was kind of hard when ur at curious age

Does porn excite you sexually? **A lot**

Does porn give you ideas about how to have sex? **Always**

Do you think sexy films, music videos or advertising encourage you to have sex? **Sometimes**

Examples of media encouraging sex:

mostly female artists who 'sell sex' like christina agulira and britney spears. two song clips i can think of are dirty by Christina A and push the button by the sugar babes

Have you ever had phone sex, that is, sexually exciting yourself and someone else over the phone? **Yes**

Have you ever sent or received sexual text messages? **Yes**

Have you had a sexual experience in an internet chat room? **Yes**

If so, did you also meet up with that person in real life? **No**

Have you ever had a sexual experience with an adult? **Yes**

If so, describe what happened and how you felt about it emotionally.

i was too young that i didnt know what was happening to me, my cousin also was young and would have it happen to her by our grandad who we used to stay there with over school holidays. deep down i knew it was wrong, or something wasnt right. i didnt like it, i felt dirty and

scared, i used to pretend i was asleep and so did my cousin when he would come in our room, me and my cousin wouldnt leave each other, it was hard though when she didnt come to stay i wouldnt leave my brother and i was always trying to avoid being alone with him

Have you ever had a sexual experience with more than one person at a time? **No**

Have you ever been pressured or forced into having sex? **Yes**

If so, describe what happened and how you felt about it emotionally.

well i was drugged, its wrong. i didnt know how to feel, he ws hot and the guy that everyone was obsessed with so i was happy to start with but when it sunk in, i was ashamed, and felt like something that i can never have back was stolen, DIGNITY. my personal safety and respect was violated

How often do you have sex while using drugs or alcohol? **Sometimes**

Do drugs or alcohol make sex better or worse? **Better**

Does what you learn in sex education classes at school help you with your actual sexual experiences? **A bit**

Do you think teenagers should be taught more or less about sex at school? **More**

What do you think is the best age to start having sexual experiences?

i think it depends on the individual. highschool would be the best age for sexually kissing and using the hands, late highschool as in end of yr 10 and above would be best for oral but i think sex is something that should be with a special person when u feel 100 % safe, loved and respected. not fooled.

Do your parents have an influence on whether or not you have sex? **A bit**

Does your religion have an influence on whether or not you have sex? **Not much**

How important is it for you to have an emotional connection with your sexual partner? **Somewhat important**

Is there anything else at all that you would like to say about sex or your own sexual experiences?

i think that sex is all about the individual, i personally was exposed to some pretty extreme cases, they have had an effect on my emotional and pschycological thinking because i am afraid to tell anyone, i feel like

its all my fault, and how could someone be so cruel to another about their freedom and naivity. i believe your virginity is so important, you shouldnt rush into having sex, its not what its cracked up to be, its 10 times better when u love that person and they love u back. its not about how early or late u have it, ur time will come so make it be special, there are plenty of other ways to experience and enjoy your sexuality.

Girl, 17, New South Wales, straight

What was the first thing you heard about sex?

that it was a loving "embrace" between two people when they love each other (mum)

How old were you when you started masturbating? **16**

Describe your sexual fantasies, even if they seem weird or boring or whatever.

i'm not telling u that

How old were you when you had your first sexual experience with someone else? **15**

What happened in this first sexual experience with another person?

it was with a childhood friend "as mature adults" i didnt really like them, i just wanted to kiss someone.

How old were you when you first had oral sex? **17**

Describe what happened during this oral sex, and how you felt about it.

i didnt really want to do it. It was their "birthday present"

On average, how many times a week do you have oral sex?

Less than once a week

If less frequent, how many times approximately has it occurred? **Once**

How old were you when you first had sexual intercourse? **15**

Describe what happened during intercourse, and how you felt about it emotionally.

at the time i thought that i liked the person. It was his idea, and at the time it seemed like a good idea.

How old were you when you first had anal sex? **16**

How often does this happen? **Once a week**

Describe what happens during anal sex and how you feel about having it.

at the time i liked it. it felt good. i never orgasmed though.

Would you like to have more sex? **No**

How do you think sex could be better for you?

well i only have sex if i'm going out with someone, and i'm not with anyone so i'm not having sex. it would be better for me if i would orgasm.

When you have intercourse, do you use protection? **Yes**

What kind of protection do you use? **condom**

How often are your sexual experiences with someone of the same sex or gender as you? **Never**

You think of yourself as … **Straight**

How old were you when you first saw pornography or erotica? **14**

What kind of pornography have you seen? **magazines**

Does porn excite you sexually? **A bit**

Does porn give you ideas about how to have sex? **Sometimes**

Do you think sexy films, music videos or advertising encourage you to have sex? **Always**

Examples of media encouraging sex:

Lots of ads on tv. sex sells they make sex out not to be such a big thing. Which it is more so for girls then boys.

Have you ever had phone sex, that is, sexually exciting yourself and someone else over the phone? **Yes**

Have you ever sent or received sexual text messages? **Yes**

Have you had a sexual experience in an internet chat room? **Yes**

If so, did you also meet up with that person in real life? **No**

Have you ever had a sexual experience with an adult? **No**

Have you ever had a sexual experience with more than one person at a time? **No**

Have you ever been pressured or forced into having sex? **Yes**

If so, describe what happened and how you felt about it emotionally.

i dont care and i didnt go through with it.

How often do you have sex while using drugs or alcohol? **Never**

Does what you learn in sex education classes at school help you with your actual sexual experiences? **Not at all**

Do you think teenagers should be taught more or less about sex at school?

More

What do you think is the best age to start having sexual experiences?

when they meet the right person. i lost my virginity at 16 and half and i think that is young. i know people that lost it at 13 which is way too young. Everyone is going to lose it one day or another so they might as well be taught about safe sex and the right way to do it. i go to a catholic school, and we were taught to wait until marriage to lose our virginity, when half the school weren't virgins, which is pretty pointless. i think that children should be taugh about sex earlier and be more open about it. we werent taught about sex until year 10, when i had already had sex.

Do your parents have an influence on whether or not you have sex? **A lot**

Does your religion have an influence on whether or not you have sex?

Not at all

How important is it for you to have an emotional connection with your sexual partner? **Very important**

Is there anything else at all that you would like to say about sex or your own sexual experiences?

Well i have only slept with two people and i am very close to my mum and she knew when it happened and was cool about it, if more parents were like that then it would be a much easier for people when they have sex.

Boy, 17, Queensland, straight

How old were you when you first heard about sex? **11**

What was the first thing you heard about sex?

That two people are involved

How old were you when you started masturbating? **11**

On average, how many times a week do you masturbate? **Once a week**

How do you masturbate?

In the shower thinking of my girlfriend and sometimes porn images that i have seen before. I masturbate by tossing my self. I masturbate in the shower because it is easy to clean up.

How does masturbating make you feel? **Good**

Describe your sexual fantasies, even if they seem weird or boring or whatever.

Britney Spears before she became a mum back when she was depicted as a innocent school girl.

How old were you when you had your first sexual experience with someone else? **12**

What happened in this first sexual experience with another person?

I kissed a girl and i felt that i shouldn't have because i felt that i was too young. Despite that it was very enjoyable at the time.

How old were you when you first had oral sex? **16**

Describe what happened during this oral sex, and how you felt about it.

I felt good because i pleasured my lady with my tongue. At the same time i felt a little physically dirty because it smelt a bit and my face was covered in giney juice.

On average, how many times a week do you have oral sex?

Less than once a week

If less frequent, how many times approximately has it occurred? **Four times**

How old were you when you first had sexual intercourse? **15**

Describe what happened during intercourse, and how you felt about it emotionally.

At the time i felt that it was the best time of my life. It was with someone who i had been with for .... long enough and im glad because im still with her today. We both climaxed at the same time.

On average, how many times a week do you have intercourse?

Twice a week

Would you like to have more sex? **Not sure**

How do you think sex could be better for you?

If i could go quicker because my lady nearly always goes before me.

When you have intercourse, do you use protection? **Sometimes**

What kind of protection do you use? **Condom**

How often are your sexual experiences with someone of the same sex or
gender as you? **Never**

You think of yourself as … **Straight**

How old were you when you first saw pornography or erotica? **8**

What kind of pornography have you seen?
Magazines, movies, stories, websites

Does porn excite you sexually? **A lot**

Does porn give you ideas about how to have sex? **Sometimes**

Do you think sexy films, music videos or advertising encourage you to have
sex? **Sometimes**

Examples of media encouraging sex: **Lingerie magazines etc**

Have you ever had phone sex, that is, sexually exciting yourself and
someone else over the phone? **Yes**

Have you ever sent or received sexual text messages? **Yes**

Have you had a sexual experience in an internet chat room? **No**

Have you ever had a sexual experience with an adult? **No**

Have you ever had a sexual experience with more than one person at a
time? **No**

Have you ever been pressured or forced into having sex? **No**

How often do you have sex while using drugs or alcohol? **Sometimes**

Do drugs or alcohol make sex better or worse? **Better**

Does what you learn in sex education classes at school help you with your
actual sexual experiences? **A lot**

Do you think teenagers should be taught more or less about sex at school?
More

What do you think is the best age to start having sexual experiences?
**I think that due to the current laws which we should abide by the
earliest age should be 16. Despite this the best age should be when
you feel comfotable and when you are prepared to take or fix the
consequences.**

Do your parents have an influence on whether or not you have sex?
Not much

Does your religion have an influence on whether or not you have sex?
Not at all

How important is it for you to have an emotional connection with your sexual partner? **Very important**

Is there anything else at all that you would like to say about sex or your own sexual experiences?

I am glad that my partner and myself have sex because it brings us closer and makes us more open to each other. Also its good to 'get it out'.

Girl, 17, Queensland, straight

How old were you when you first heard about sex? **11**

What was the first thing you heard about sex?

That it can get you pregnant if you dont use contraception of some sort. You can get sexually transmitted diseases from having unsafe sex, but on the good side i learned that sex is supposed to be an intimate and special activity.

How old were you when you started masturbating? **14**

On average, how many times a week do you masturbate?

Four times a week

How do you masturbate?

Usually on my bed, sometimes in the shower/bath. Usually im absentmindedly playing with my pussy just stroking it, but when im horny i get myself wet by stroking my pussy and clit, and fingering myself. I then use my virbrator finger and clit stimulator or a hard long object such as a hairbrush to make myself orgasm. I also find that rubbing ice down my pussy or putting water pressure on my clit while in the shower is really kinky.

How does masturbating make you feel? **Very good**

Describe your sexual fantasies, even if they seem weird or boring or whatever.

I want to have sex on a secluded beach in all positions possible, just on sunset with my partner at the time. Also i wouldnt mind being touched and played with by several guys-threesome or foursome.

How old were you when you had your first sexual experience with someone else? **14**

What happened in this first sexual experience with another person?

Dont really remember, just kissed my crush/then boyfriend on the lips at a school dance- i got pushed into it by my friends, wasnt really good.

How old were you when you first had oral sex? **15**

Describe what happened during this oral sex, and how you felt about it.

Um a guy fingered me, went down on me and licked me out. Then i gave him a handjob then a blowjob to make him cum.

On average, how many times a week do you have oral sex? **Twice a week**

How old were you when you first had sexual intercourse? **16**

Describe what happened during intercourse, and how you felt about it emotionally.

It was perfect, we just went slow in missionary position, feeling each other out, kissing, rocking.

How old were you when you first had anal sex? **Never**

On average, how many times a week do you have intercourse?

Less than once a week

Would you like to have more sex? **Yes**

How do you think sex could be better for you?

gaining more experience, and being more confident of my body.

When you have intercourse, do you use protection? **Yes**

What kind of protection do you use? **partner-condom**

How often are your sexual experiences with someone of the same sex or gender as you? **Never**

You think of yourself as … **Straight**

How old were you when you first saw pornography or erotica? **14**

What kind of pornography have you seen?

short clips on the internet, photos on web, magazine

Does porn excite you sexually? **A bit**

Does porn give you ideas about how to have sex? **Sometimes**

Do you think sexy films, music videos or advertising encourage you to have sex? **Sometimes**

Examples of media encouraging sex:

music/films clips involving sex scenes (making it look oh so good and perfect) never see them using protection.

Have you ever had phone sex, that is, sexually exciting yourself and someone else over the phone? **Yes**

Have you ever sent or received sexual text messages? **Yes**

Have you had a sexual experience in an internet chat room? **Yes**

If so, did you also meet up with that person in real life? **Yes**

Have you ever had a sexual experience with an adult? **No**

Have you ever had a sexual experience with more than one person at a time? **No**

Have you ever been pressured or forced into having sex? **No**

How often do you have sex while using drugs or alcohol? **Sometimes**

Do drugs or alcohol make sex better or worse? **Neither**

Does what you learn in sex education classes at school help you with your actual sexual experiences? **Not much**

Do you think teenagers should be taught more or less about sex at school? **More**

What do you think is the best age to start having sexual experiences? **experiencing, experimenting with kissing touching- anywhere from 13 onwards, oral sex- about 15, sex from 15, 16 onwards. I just dont think kids under 15 are responsible enough and abuse the meaning of sex.**

Do your parents have an influence on whether or not you have sex? **Not much**

Does your religion have an influence on whether or not you have sex? **Not at all**

How important is it for you to have an emotional connection with your sexual partner? **Very important**

Is there anything else at all that you would like to say about sex or your own sexual experiences? **I believe sex is a special intimate activity that should always make you happy and feel loved, but unfortunately for some people its not always good or wanted for that matter. I think if you want to have sex, you have to be absolutely ready and you always have to take responsibility. I have a loving caring relationship with my boyfriend and we are sexually active, and our experiences are always romantic with sexy foreplay to excite us. Although sex is great it doesnt need to be had all the time, sometimes its just good to cuddle and kiss.**

Boy, 17, Western Australia, straight

How old were you when you first heard about sex? **8**

What was the first thing you heard about sex?

its how you make babies

How old were you when you started masturbating? **8**

On average, how many times a week do you masturbate?

Five times a week

How do you masturbate? **in bed, rubbing my dick**

How does masturbating make you feel? **Good**

Describe your sexual fantasies, even if they seem weird or boring or whatever.

i just think of hot chicks and doing them in different positions

How old were you when you had your first sexual experience with someone else? **6**

What happened in this first sexual experience with another person?

it was fun, i was young, nothing wrong with it

How old were you when you first had oral sex? **15**

Describe what happened during this oral sex, and how you felt about it.

i licked out my girl friend and she have me a head job. i felt good about it. felt grown up

On average, how many times a week do you have oral sex?

Less than once a week

If less frequent, how many times approximately has it occurred? **Ten times**

How old were you when you first had sexual intercourse? **15**

Describe what happened during intercourse, and how you felt about it emotionally.

me n a girl had sex at a party and found out people were watching us through a hole in the wall. it was pretty embaressing but at the time it made me a hero so i didnt really care. i kind of regret it now because she ment nothing to me.

How old were you when you first had anal sex? **Never**

Describe what happens during anal sex and how you feel about having it.

i want to try it but neva had the chance.

On average, how many times a week do you have intercourse?

Three times a week

Would you like to have more sex? **Not sure**

How do you think sex could be better for you?

   i get bored of the same position, would be cool to try some new ones

When you have intercourse, do you use protection? **Sometimes**

What kind of protection do you use? **condom, girlfriend takes the pill.**

How often are your sexual experiences with someone of the same sex or
   gender as you? **Sometimes**

You think of yourself as ... **Straight**

How old were you when you first saw pornography or erotica? **12**

What kind of pornography have you seen?

   films, photos, magazines, websites, live shows

Does porn excite you sexually? **A bit**

Does porn give you ideas about how to have sex? **Sometimes**

Do you think sexy films, music videos or advertising encourage you to have
   sex? **Sometimes**

Have you ever had phone sex, that is, sexually exciting yourself and
   someone else over the phone? **No**

Have you ever sent or received sexual text messages? **Yes**

Have you had a sexual experience in an internet chat room? **No**

Have you ever had a sexual experience with an adult? **No**

Have you ever had a sexual experience with more than one person at a
   time? **No**

Have you ever been pressured or forced into having sex? **No**

How often do you have sex while using drugs or alcohol? **Sometimes**

Do drugs or alcohol make sex better or worse? **Worse**

Does what you learn in sex education classes at school help you with your
   actual sexual experiences? **Not much**

Do you think teenagers should be taught more or less about sex at school?
   More

What do you think is the best age to start having sexual experiences?

   **i think around 16 is a good time to start anything minus anal sex. save
   that till your older.**

Do your parents have an influence on whether or not you have sex?
   Not at all

Does your religion have an influence on whether or not you have sex?

Not at all

How important is it for you to have an emotional connection with your sexual partner? **Somewhat important**

Is there anything else at all that you would like to say about sex or your own sexual experiences?

i find it alot better when you really like the person your doing it with and sharing it with them. i used to just go out and pick up sluts, at the time it was fun but now i have a good girlfriend i regret that and much prefer staying with her

Girl, 17, New South Wales, straight

What was the first thing you heard about sex?

that the penis and the vagina come together to make babies

How old were you when you started masturbating? **Never**

Describe your sexual fantasies, even if they seem weird or boring or whatever.

i don't really have any specific sexual fantasies, however often i think about specific positions or places that really turn me on.

How old were you when you had your first sexual experience with someone else? **3**

What happened in this first sexual experience with another person?

when i first learnt about sex from my older sister and older cousin, told me and my younger cousin (male) so we decided that we would try it out ...

How old were you when you first had oral sex? **15**

Describe what happened during this oral sex, and how you felt about it.

i gave a long-term boyfriend a blowjob. i really didn't enjoy this ... i still don't enjoy it much more, but i am getting more and more in to it ...

On average, how many times a week do you have oral sex? **Once a week**

How old were you when you first had sexual intercourse? **15**

Describe what happened during intercourse, and how you felt about it emotionally.

when i first had sex, it was with my second long-term boyfriend ... i had previously thought that i might have had sex with my boyfriend before, but was still a little unsure ... it turned out that when i had sex for the first time, with my then and still now boyfriend i knew i was still a virgin ... it was painful, hard to get into a certain rhythm, and enjoy it because i was in quite a bit of pain, but still so eager to make it enjoyable for my boyfriend ...

How old were you when you first had anal sex? **17**

How often does this happen? **Less than once a week**

Describe what happens during anal sex and how you feel about having it.

i only recently tried to have anal sex with my boyfriend ... i really didn't enjoy it ... i feel uncomfortable, and really hate the feeling of it ... all i can think about is that my poo is getting pushed further and further back inside me ... gross!

On average, how many times a week do you have intercourse? **Twice a week**

Would you like to have more sex? **Not sure**

How do you think sex could be better for you?

sex for me at this stage is like something that can only be done on the weekend, cause im still at school as well as my boyfriend, and both in year 12, so we both try to only see each other on the weekend ... this makes it feel like a must to have sex on the weekend ... sometimes i don't feel like it, but i feel guilty for my boyfriend ... but it works both ways, because there are then times when i really really feel like, and maybe he doesn't but he will ... we have been together for almost two years now, so we have worked out what we both like the best ...

When you have intercourse, do you use protection? **Yes**

What kind of protection do you use?

i take the pill, but every now and again, i will forget to take a pill or two ... in that case, my boyfriend will just withdraw his penis before climaxing. i realise this is stupid ...

How often are your sexual experiences with someone of the same sex or gender as you? **Sometimes**

You think of yourself as … **Straight**

What kind of pornography have you seen?

websites, movies … magazines …

Does porn excite you sexually? **A bit**

Does porn give you ideas about how to have sex? **Sometimes**

Do you think sexy films, music videos or advertising encourage you to have sex? **Sometimes**

Examples of media encouraging sex:

christina agulira - Dirty … sooooooooo erotic

Have you ever had phone sex, that is, sexually exciting yourself and someone else over the phone? **No**

Have you ever sent or received sexual text messages? **Yes**

Have you had a sexual experience in an internet chat room? **No**

Have you ever had a sexual experience with an adult? **No**

Have you ever had a sexual experience with more than one person at a time? **Yes**

If so, describe what happened and how you felt about it.

i had a sexual experience, with two girls … very close friends … it was just a bit of fun, and we all knew that …

Have you ever been pressured or forced into having sex? **No**

How often do you have sex while using drugs or alcohol? **Sometimes**

Do drugs or alcohol make sex better or worse? **Neither**

Does what you learn in sex education classes at school help you with your actual sexual experiences? **Not much**

Do you think teenagers should be taught more or less about sex at school? **More**

What do you think is the best age to start having sexual experiences?

i think both people have to have the maturity to know what they're doing, as well as the consequences of having un-protected sex etc.
i think sex is a very intimate thing, that should be done with very strong feelings … i dont think there should be specific age, but i do think people should take sex as a serious thing, that should not be handed out as free to all …

Do your parents have an influence on whether or not you have sex?

Not at all

Does your religion have an influence on whether or not you have sex?
Not at all
How important is it for you to have an emotional connection with your sexual
partner? **Very important**

Boy, 17, Queensland, straight

How old were you when you first heard about sex? **9**
What was the first thing you heard about sex?
that is where babies come from
How old were you when you started masturbating? **13**
On average, how many times a week do you masturbate?
Four times a week
How do you masturbate?
no lubricants. on the toilet, in the shower or in bed.
How does masturbating make you feel? **Good**
Describe your sexual fantasies, even if they seem weird or boring or whatever.
in a sauna, two georgeous girls, a blonde and a brunette ...
How old were you when you had your first sexual experience with someone
else? **10**
What happened in this first sexual experience with another person? **kissing.**
How old were you when you first had oral sex? **Never had oral sex**
How old were you when you first had sexual intercourse? **16**
Describe what happened during intercourse, and how you felt about it
emotionally.
**it was very slow as it was also her first time. it went from kissing fully
clothed to taking clothes off and doing the deed. It was an amazing
emotional moment as we had been together for about 4 months and
were pretty serious.**
How old were you when you first had anal sex? **Never**
On average, how many times a week do you have intercourse?
Less than once a week
Would you like to have more sex? **Yes**

How do you think sex could be better for you?

its great. i suppose if i were a bit fitter it could be better.

When you have intercourse, do you use protection? **Yes**

What kind of protection do you use? **condom and the pill, hopefully.**

How often are your sexual experiences with someone of the same sex or gender as you? **Never**

You think of yourself as … **Straight**

How old were you when you first saw pornography or erotica? **12**

What kind of pornography have you seen?

All of the above [list of examples was provided].

Does porn excite you sexually? **A lot**

Does porn give you ideas about how to have sex? **Sometimes**

Do you think sexy films, music videos or advertising encourage you to have sex? **Sometimes**

Examples of media encouraging sex: **Cant think of any at the moment.**

Have you ever had phone sex, that is, sexually exciting yourself and someone else over the phone? **Yes**

Have you ever sent or received sexual text messages? **Yes**

Have you had a sexual experience in an internet chat room? **No**

Have you ever had a sexual experience with an adult? **No**

Have you ever had a sexual experience with more than one person at a time? **No**

Have you ever been pressured or forced into having sex? **No**

How often do you have sex while using drugs or alcohol? **Sometimes**

Do drugs or alcohol make sex better or worse? **Neither**

Does what you learn in sex education classes at school help you with your actual sexual experiences? **A bit**

Do you think teenagers should be taught more or less about sex at school? **Same as now**

What do you think is the best age to start having sexual experiences? **kissing- 13, using your hands- 14 to 15, sex/oral- 16ish**

Do your parents have an influence on whether or not you have sex? **Not at all**

Does your religion have an influence on whether or not you have sex? **Not at all**

How important is it for you to have an emotional connection with your sexual partner? **Somewhat important**

Is there anything else at all that you would like to say about sex or your own sexual experiences?

i have been lucky in tha fact that i have an older sister, as being around her friends, who are pretty good looking group of girls, from a young age got me used to talking to girls and not going through that faze of being scared. i have always been confident around certain types of girls. It is a bit sadening to see how girls nowadays act, they are too slutty! There are not enough girls that are good looking and a bit more quiet. Im a believer in the 'fun is in the chase' style. where a girl lets you know that she is interested but doesnt want to lick your face, and when grog gets a hold of a girl that has tendancies to be a bit wild, it is a touch scary.

Girl, 17, South Australia, bisexual

How old were you when you first heard about sex? **6**

What was the first thing you heard about sex? **it makes babies**

How old were you when you started masturbating? **7**

On average, how many times a week do you masturbate? **Once a week**

How does masturbating make you feel? **Very good**

Describe your sexual fantasies, even if they seem weird or boring or whatever.

1.to have a man dominate me and over power me. 2.to tie up a guy and tease him with another girl and then have a 3some with both of them. 3. to have sex with jared leto.

How old were you when you had your first sexual experience with someone else? **12**

What happened in this first sexual experience with another person?

it was my first kiss! it felt kind of strange at first but i liked the guy :)

How old were you when you first had oral sex? **14**

Describe what happened during this oral sex, and how you felt about it.

i sucked a guys cock for the first time when i was 14. i didnt have any emotional attatchments to the guy. i didnt let him go down on me.

On average, how many times a week do you have oral sex?

Less than once a week

How old were you when you first had sexual intercourse? **14**

Describe what happened during intercourse, and how you felt about it emotionally.

i was 14 turning 15 and i really thought i loved the guy at the time. i went to his house when his parents werent home and we had sex. it was ok i guess but it was painful and it didnt go on for very long.

How old were you when you first had anal sex? **Never**

On average, how many times a week do you have intercourse?

Less than once a week

Would you like to have more sex? **Yes**

How do you think sex could be better for you?

if i do it with a person i really like or love or if theres a lot of sexual attraction. im really picky about who i have sex with cause i cant just do it with anyone.

When you have intercourse, do you use protection? **Yes**

What kind of protection do you use? **condoms**

How often are your sexual experiences with someone of the same sex or gender as you? **Sometimes**

You think of yourself as ... **Bisexual**

How old were you when you first saw pornography or erotica? **13**

What kind of pornography have you seen?

films, photos, internet, magazines, stories, drawings.

Does porn excite you sexually? **A bit**

Does porn give you ideas about how to have sex? **Sometimes**

Do you think sexy films, music videos or advertising encourage you to have sex? **Sometimes**

Have you ever had phone sex, that is, sexually exciting yourself and someone else over the phone? **Yes**

Have you ever sent or received sexual text messages? **Yes**

Have you had a sexual experience in an internet chat room? **Yes**

If so, did you also meet up with that person in real life? **No**

Have you ever had a sexual experience with an adult? **Yes**

If so, describe what happened and how you felt about it emotionally.

well it was my ex boyfriend i was 16 and he was 20 at the time so it is legal. we had sex and it was great i really loved him. ive never had a sexual experience with an adult over 21.

Have you ever had a sexual experience with more than one person at a time? **Yes**

If so, describe what happened and how you felt about it.

ive had a few 3somes with my best friend and other guy but not full on ones where we have sex, pretty much just touching n making out. it was fun ive also had a few 3somes with 3 girls where we fingered and licked each other out. i enjoyed it, we were all just friends having fun.

Have you ever been pressured or forced into having sex? **No**

If so, describe what happened and how you felt about it emotionally.

ive had guys pressure me for sex but if i dont want it i say no.

How often do you have sex while using drugs or alcohol? **Sometimes**

Do drugs or alcohol make sex better or worse? **Neither**

Does what you learn in sex education classes at school help you with your actual sexual experiences? **A bit**

Do you think teenagers should be taught more or less about sex at school? **More**

What do you think is the best age to start having sexual experiences?

its impossible to give a specific age because it depends on the person and when they mature and what feels right for them. when a person has sexual experiences they should be mature enough to make that decision for themselves and know that its what they want. if they are unsure then they shouldnt do it.

Do your parents have an influence on whether or not you have sex? **Not at all**

Does your religion have an influence on whether or not you have sex? **Not at all**

How important is it for you to have an emotional connection with your sexual partner? **Somewhat important**

Boy, 17, Victoria, straight

How old were you when you first heard about sex? **6**

What was the first thing you heard about sex? **cant remember**

How old were you when you started masturbating? **12**

On average, how many times a week do you masturbate?

Four times a week

How do you masturbate? **With my hand most of the time in bed**

How does masturbating make you feel? **Very good**

Describe your sexual fantasies, even if they seem weird or boring or whatever.

lesbians

How old were you when you had your first sexual experience with someone

else? **11**

What happened in this first sexual experience with another person?

i felt good and happy. made me feel confident

How old were you when you first had oral sex? **13**

Describe what happened during this oral sex, and how you felt about it.

very horney. i like it very much

On average, how many times a week do you have oral sex?

Less than once a week

If less frequent, how many times approximately has it occurred?

More than twenty

How old were you when you first had sexual intercourse? **14**

Describe what happened during intercourse, and how you felt about it

emotionally.

i was very drunk and was told the next day. i cant remember it very

clearly

How old were you when you first had anal sex? **Never**

On average, how many times a week do you have intercourse?

Less than once a week

Would you like to have more sex? **Yes**

How do you think sex could be better for you? **attractive girl, nice and likes**

me

When you have intercourse, do you use protection? **Sometimes**

What kind of protection do you use? **condom**

How often are your sexual experiences with someone of the same sex or gender as you? **Never**

You think of yourself as … **Straight**

How old were you when you first saw pornography or erotica? **7**

What kind of pornography have you seen? **photos, magazines**

Does porn excite you sexually? **A lot**

Does porn give you ideas about how to have sex? **Sometimes**

Do you think sexy films, music videos or advertising encourage you to have sex? **Sometimes**

Examples of media encouraging sex:

the ones with hot girls dancing usally or when they are wearin not much clothing

Have you ever had phone sex, that is, sexually exciting yourself and someone else over the phone? **Yes**

Have you ever sent or received sexual text messages? **Yes**

Have you had a sexual experience in an internet chat room? **Yes**

If so, did you also meet up with that person in real life? **No**

Have you ever had a sexual experience with an adult? **No**

Have you ever had a sexual experience with more than one person at a time? **No**

Have you ever been pressured or forced into having sex? **Yes**

If so, describe what happened and how you felt about it emotionally.

fine. i was with the girl at the time so it wasnt bad

How often do you have sex while using drugs or alcohol? **Sometimes**

Do drugs or alcohol make sex better or worse? **Better**

Does what you learn in sex education classes at school help you with your actual sexual experiences? **Not at all**

Do you think teenagers should be taught more or less about sex at school? **More**

What do you think is the best age to start having sexual experiences?

15. it is a good age. just sex with a partner would prob be best.

Do your parents have an influence on whether or not you have sex?

Not at all

Does your religion have an influence on whether or not you have sex?

Not at all

How important is it for you to have an emotional connection with your sexual partner? **Not important at all**

Is there anything else at all that you would like to say about sex or your own sexual experiences? **i like sex, i dont want to give it up**

Boy, 17, South Australia, straight

How old were you when you first heard about sex? **14**

What was the first thing you heard about sex? **u can make babies**

How old were you when you started masturbating? **13**

On average, how many times a week do you masturbate?
Five times a week

How do you masturbate? **just over porn**

How does masturbating make you feel? **Good**

Describe your sexual fantasies, even if they seem weird or boring or whatever.
having sex with chicks with big tits

How old were you when you had your first sexual experience with someone else? **12**

What happened in this first sexual experience with another person?
kissed my girlfriend in primary school. i got rep from my mates

How old were you when you first had oral sex? **16**

Describe what happened during this oral sex, and how you felt about it.
she sucked my dick

On average, how many times a week do you have oral sex?
Less than once a week

If less frequent, how many times approximately has it occurred? **Three times**

How old were you when you first had sexual intercourse? **17**

Describe what happened during intercourse, and how you felt about it emotionally.
had sex with my girlfriend she was in too much pain to do alot. she wasnt a virgin but apparently i was too big. 6 months later she still is hurting

How old were you when you first had anal sex? **Never**

On average, how many times a week do you have intercourse?
Less than once a week

Would you like to have more sex? **Yes**

When you have intercourse, do you use protection? **Yes**

What kind of protection do you use? **shes on the pill**

How often are your sexual experiences with someone of the same sex or gender as you? **Never**

You think of yourself as … **Straight**

How old were you when you first saw pornography or erotica? **12**

What kind of pornography have you seen? **everything**

Does porn excite you sexually? **A bit**

Does porn give you ideas about how to have sex? **Sometimes**

Do you think sexy films, music videos or advertising encourage you to have sex? **Sometimes**

Have you ever had phone sex, that is, sexually exciting yourself and someone else over the phone? **No**

Have you ever sent or received sexual text messages? **Yes**

Have you had a sexual experience in an internet chat room? **No**

Have you ever had a sexual experience with an adult? **No**

Have you ever had a sexual experience with more than one person at a time? **No**

Have you ever been pressured or forced into having sex? **No**

How often do you have sex while using drugs or alcohol? **Sometimes**

Do drugs or alcohol make sex better or worse? **Better**

Does what you learn in sex education classes at school help you with your actual sexual experiences? **Not much**

Do you think teenagers should be taught more or less about sex at school?
More

Do your parents have an influence on whether or not you have sex?
Not at all

Does your religion have an influence on whether or not you have sex?
Not at all

How important is it for you to have an emotional connection with your sexual partner? **Not very important**

Girl, 17, South Australia, straight

How old were you when you first heard about sex? **12**

What was the first thing you heard about sex?

When you have sex for the first time u break your hymen and bleed.

How old were you when you started masturbating? **Never**

Describe your sexual fantasies, even if they seem weird or boring or whatever.

having sex with with a man with an irish, english, foreign accent talking to me during sex. having sex in an isolated place and making all the noise we want

How old were you when you had your first sexual experience with someone else? **15**

What happened in this first sexual experience with another person?

i went to a party with a close mate (male) and we ended up getting drunk and havin oral sex in some guys bedroom. i felt pretty weird about it all coz a couple of people walked in on us. i had never gotten close to a penis so giving this boy head was a pretty big sexual step for me.

How old were you when you first had oral sex? **15**

Describe what happened during this oral sex, and how you felt about it.

i gave a boy head and he fingered me i thought it was easier than expected and it just came naturally. i was nervous about my body because i didnt have the biggest boobs or the most tended to bush.

On average, how many times a week do you have oral sex? **Twice a week**

How old were you when you first had sexual intercourse? **16**

Describe what happened during intercourse, and how you felt about it emotionally.

his penis wouldnt fit in the beginning and it was a bit frustrating to begin with.

How old were you when you first had anal sex? **Never**

On average, how many times a week do you have intercourse? **Once a week**

Would you like to have more sex? **Not sure**

How do you think sex could be better for you?

if my boyfriend had a bigger penis. if my boyfriend and i lived out of home and had our own privacy

When you have intercourse, do you use protection? **Sometimes**

What kind of protection do you use? **condoms the contraceptive pill**

How often are your sexual experiences with someone of the same sex or gender as you? **Never**

You think of yourself as … **Straight**

How old were you when you first saw pornography or erotica? **14**

What kind of pornography have you seen? **films, websites, magazines**

Does porn excite you sexually? **Not at all**

Does porn give you ideas about how to have sex? **Never**

Do you think sexy films, music videos or advertising encourage you to have sex? **Always**

Examples of media encouraging sex:

ads about alcohol film clips with chicks dirty dancing and wearing hardly anything

Have you ever had phone sex, that is, sexually exciting yourself and someone else over the phone? **No**

Have you ever sent or received sexual text messages? **Yes**

Have you had a sexual experience in an internet chat room? **No**

Have you ever had a sexual experience with an adult? **Yes**

If so, describe what happened and how you felt about it emotionally.

they were only 19 and 20 so not much different to someone my own age really. i have never had sex with anyone under 18.

Have you ever had a sexual experience with more than one person at a time? **No**

Have you ever been pressured or forced into having sex? **Yes**

If so, describe what happened and how you felt about it emotionally.

i would give it to him (ex boyfriend) because he would just be in a bad mood and it was worth giving him wat he wanted so he would leave me alone. that's why we arent together anymore

How often do you have sex while using drugs or alcohol? **Most of the time**

Do drugs or alcohol make sex better or worse? **Better**

Does what you learn in sex education classes at school help you with your actual sexual experiences? **Not much**

Do you think teenagers should be taught more or less about sex at school? **More**

What do you think is the best age to start having sexual experiences?

i dont believe there is a right or wrong age to start having sex. i just believe it should be with someone u care about and you know that's not the only thing they want from you.

Do your parents have an influence on whether or not you have sex?

Not at all

Does your religion have an influence on whether or not you have sex?

Not at all

How important is it for you to have an emotional connection with your sexual partner? **Very important**

Is there anything else at all that you would like to say about sex or your own sexual experiences?

young girls should never be forced into having sex. getting to know the person before having sexual contact with them is very important if u dont know ur partners history u should always use a condom

Boy, 17, South Australia, straight

How old were you when you first heard about sex? **9**

What was the first thing you heard about sex?

You put the penis in the vagina

How old were you when you started masturbating? **14**

On average, how many times a week do you masturbate?

More than five times a week

How do you masturbate?

In bed, either in the morning or when everyone else has gone to bed. Usually to my own thoughts about a girl.

How does masturbating make you feel? **Good**

Describe your sexual fantasies, even if they seem weird or boring or whatever.

Just sex.

How old were you when you had your first sexual experience with someone else? **14**

What happened in this first sexual experience with another person?

Unfortunately I cant remember it because I consumed large quantities of alcohol that night. I felt juvilant.

How old were you when you first had oral sex? **14**

Describe what happened during this oral sex, and how you felt about it.

As above, I had drunk so heavily that half an hour after it happened i couldnt even remember it.

On average, how many times a week do you have oral sex?

Less than once a week

If less frequent, how many times approximately has it occurred? **Once**

How old were you when you first had sexual intercourse? **Never**

How old were you when you first had anal sex? **Never**

Would you like to have more sex? **Yes**

How do you think sex could be better for you? **... If i had it.**

How often are your sexual experiences with someone of the same sex or gender as you? **Never**

You think of yourself as ... **Straight**

How old were you when you first saw pornography or erotica? **13**

What kind of pornography have you seen?

Films, Photos, Magazines, internet Websites.

Does porn excite you sexually? **A bit**

Does porn give you ideas about how to have sex? **Always**

Do you think sexy films, music videos or advertising encourage you to have sex? **Sometimes**

Examples of media encouraging sex:

Gimme that Nut - Eazy E

Have you ever had phone sex, that is, sexually exciting yourself and someone else over the phone? **No**

Have you ever sent or received sexual text messages? **No**

Have you had a sexual experience in an internet chat room? **No**

Have you ever had a sexual experience with an adult? **No**

Have you ever had a sexual experience with more than one person at a time? **No**

Have you ever been pressured or forced into having sex? **No**

Does what you learn in sex education classes at school help you with your
actual sexual experiences? **A bit**

Do you think teenagers should be taught more or less about sex at school?
More

What do you think is the best age to start having sexual experiences?
**The time for sex is determined by a persons maturity, however most
people who think they are mature are really just kidding themselves.**

Do your parents have an influence on whether or not you have sex?
Not at all

Does your religion have an influence on whether or not you have sex?
Not at all

How important is it for you to have an emotional connection with your sexual
partner? **Not very imporant**

Boy, 17, (no postcode given), straight

How old were you when you first heard about sex? **1**

What was the first thing you heard about sex?
It began with a man and woman who loved each other very much ...

How old were you when you started masturbating? **13**

How does masturbating make you feel? **Not very good**

Describe your sexual fantasies, even if they seem weird or boring or whatever.
Aliens, Secretaries, you name it, I've dreamed it.

How old were you when you had your first sexual experience with someone
else? **14**

What happened in this first sexual experience with another person?
oral sex, how did it feel? Have a guess.

How old were you when you first had oral sex? **14**

Describe what happened during this oral sex, and how you felt about it.
**I didnt have to do anything, it was great and she wasnt drunk either so
there were no regrets.**

On average, how many times a week do you have oral sex?
Less than once a week

If less frequent, how many times approximately has it occurred? **Four times**

How old were you when you first had sexual intercourse? **16**

Describe what happened during intercourse, and how you felt about it
emotionally.

**I was drunker then she was and her parents were out so I went back to
hers after a party. She took over from there.**

How old were you when you first had anal sex? **Never**

On average, how many times a week do you have intercourse?

Less than once a week

Would you like to have more sex? **Yes**

How do you think sex could be better for you?

**If I could last longer. Or if I could find more people interested in one
night stands.**

When you have intercourse, do you use protection? **Yes**

What kind of protection do you use?

Condom, they're usually on the pill or whatnot

How often are your sexual experiences with someone of the same sex or
gender as you? **Never**

You think of yourself as … **Straight**

How old were you when you first saw pornography or erotica? **5**

What kind of pornography have you seen?

Flipping through pictures in magazines at the newsagent.

Does porn excite you sexually? **A bit**

Does porn give you ideas about how to have sex? **Never**

Do you think sexy films, music videos or advertising encourage you to have
sex? **Sometimes**

Examples of media encouraging sex:

Four seasons condoms, doesnt get much more obvious then that.

Have you ever had phone sex, that is, sexually exciting yourself and
someone else over the phone? **No**

Have you ever sent or received sexual text messages? **No**

Have you had a sexual experience in an internet chat room? **No**

Have you ever had a sexual experience with an adult? **No**

If so, describe what happened and how you felt about it emotionally.

Sadly not, but tommorows a new day

Have you ever had a sexual experience with more than one person at a time? **No**

Have you ever been pressured or forced into having sex? **No**

If so, describe what happened and how you felt about it emotionally.
If only.

How often do you have sex while using drugs or alcohol? **Most of the time**

Do drugs or alcohol make sex better or worse? **Neither**

Does what you learn in sex education classes at school help you with your actual sexual experiences? **Not at all**

Do you think teenagers should be taught more or less about sex at school?
Same as now

What do you think is the best age to start having sexual experiences?
I dont think there's any minimum as long its not forced upon them and preferably with people the same age. Then again, when I was 15 I dreamed of making it with my best mates mum ...

Do your parents have an influence on whether or not you have sex?
Not at all

Does your religion have an influence on whether or not you have sex?
Not at all

How important is it for you to have an emotional connection with your sexual partner? **Not very important**

Is there anything else at all that you would like to say about sex or your own sexual experiences?
I think theirs too much hype, nothing needs to change and people will always have their opinions.

Girl, 17, South Australia, straight

How old were you when you first heard about sex? **12**

What was the first thing you heard about sex?
i really cant remember what the first ever thing i learnt was. Just that i knew that babies came from people having sex. I never understood or realised that it was something that people did because they enjoyed it.

I imagined it more as a chore. u had sex if u wanted to have a child. Oh how wrong i was!

How old were you when you started masturbating? **17**

On average, how many times a week do you masturbate? **Once a week**

How do you masturbate?

Masturbating is not something i do regularly but have had an increasing desire to do because it has been ages since ive had sex. I enjoy it while im doing it but often feel dirty later. I usually masturbate late at night when everyone is asleep. it always happens in bed and with no objects or lubricant.

How does masturbating make you feel? **Very good**

Describe your sexual fantasies, even if they seem weird or boring or whatever.

I dont have sexual fantasies. like no desires for threesomes or anything. usually thinking about having sex with a guy im keen on gets me going but apart from that, no real fantasies.

How old were you when you had your first sexual experience with someone else? **12**

What happened in this first sexual experience with another person?

12 years old was my first full on hook up, kiss. it was with a guy from school who i know i liked heaps but all my mates were standing around egging us on so it wasnt very romantic!! coz i liked him i guess i was stoked but probably would have prefered it to be under better, more private circumstances

How old were you when you first had oral sex? **15**

Describe what happened during this oral sex, and how you felt about it.

it was with my first real boyfriend. Id always been nervous about oral sex and im not sure why. it was along time ago now but coz my boyfriend had been with others before me i kept wanting to make sure i was doing everything right and not embarrassing myself. everything went ok but he didnt finish, the thought of him cumming in my mouth made me want to vomit. i still have never allowed it to happen. the first time he gave me oral sex i was just as awkward but i thoroughly enjoyed it. it feels just as good as sex. if not better

On average, how many times a week do you have oral sex?

Less than once a week

If less frequent, how many times approximately has it occurred?

More than twenty

How old were you when you first had sexual intercourse? **15**

Describe what happened during intercourse, and how you felt about it emotionally.

**i was nervous. but i had been with the guy for over a year and i trusted
and loved him alot so i felt comfortable. we had talked about it alot and
i knew that the time was right. i didnt want to regret having sex. I cant
remember it clearly but i know it was slow and awkward because i had
never done it before and my boyfriend was continuously checking that
i was ok and nothing was hurting or anything. it didnt go for long and
i dont think either of us came, I didnt get a huge amout of enjoyment
out of the first couple of times, but sex definatly got better as i began to
feel comfortable and gained experience. The entire time that i was
having sex i felt guilty because i was lieing to my mum who i told i
wasnt having sex. I know now that it restricted the amount of enjoyment
i was having during intercourse. I didnt want to feel guilty but i did even
though, emotionally everything else was right. I think it is so important
that a person feels comfortable and safe the first time they have sex.
I would hate to look back now and regret who and when i had sex. Im
glad i did it when and who i did it with.**

On average, how many times a week do you have intercourse?

Less than once a week

Would you like to have more sex? **Yes**

How do you think sex could be better for you?

**Ive only had two sexual partners and sex was better with the second
partner because i didnt have the feeling of guilt for sneaking behind my
mums back. I was able to totally relax and enjoy the moment. Im also
more confident now and willing to experiment, i think sex is better in
different positions. Sex could be better if it were more spontaneous and
in different locations. the beach etc.**

When you have intercourse, do you use protection? **Yes**

What kind of protection do you use?

**condoms. and im looking into going on the pill. because even though im
using a condom there hav been many occassions where ive convinced**

myself that im pregnant and have driven mysef insane thinking about it until i get my period and am so so relieved.

How often are your sexual experiences with someone of the same sex or gender as you? **Never**

You think of yourself as … **Straight**

How old were you when you first saw pornography or erotica? **16**

What kind of pornography have you seen?

photos (mostly on internet) a few films, magazines

Does porn excite you sexually? **A lot**

Does porn give you ideas about how to have sex? **Sometimes**

Do you think sexy films, music videos or advertising encourage you to have sex? **Never**

Have you ever had phone sex, that is, sexually exciting yourself and someone else over the phone? **Yes**

Have you ever sent or received sexual text messages? **Yes**

Have you had a sexual experience in an internet chat room? **No**

Have you ever had a sexual experience with an adult? **Yes**

If so, describe what happened and how you felt about it emotionally.

he was 22. which is 5 years older then i am. it was exciting and he was so goodlooking. but we got on really well and i just thoroughly enjoyed spending time with him. i met him on an interstate trip over a weekend and we ended up having sex. because we had so much in common and we got on so well age didnt really matter, infact we got on like we would if he was my age so i didnt see it as being any different because he was older

Have you ever had a sexual experience with more than one person at a time? **No**

Have you ever been pressured or forced into having sex? **No**

How often do you have sex while using drugs or alcohol? **Sometimes**

Do drugs or alcohol make sex better or worse? **Neither**

Does what you learn in sex education classes at school help you with your actual sexual experiences? **Not at all**

Do you think teenagers should be taught more or less about sex at school? **More**

What do you think is the best age to start having sexual experiences?

it depends on the circumstance because everyone is different. some would say that 15 is too young but thats when i had sex and sure if i had had sex with some random on a drunken night out id think 15 was far too young aswell but because i was with a steady boyfriend who i trusted i think 15 is ok. having said that id be thinking twice if a 13 yr old told me she was having sex regardless or not if she had a boyfriend. also, people have different standards. all of my friends have only had sex when theyve had a boyfriend while i know other girls just have sex with randoms when they feel like it. id say a good time to have sex is when your about 16 or 17. most people are mentally mature enough to deal with everything that comes with it. someone once told me that if you can say vagina and then penis without giggling then your mature enough to have sex. but i know 20 year olds who still laugh ... so i dont know. i think if your comfortable and feel ready then do it. i just wish everyone had the luxury of actually wanting to have sex the first time.

Do your parents have an influence on whether or not you have sex? **A bit**

Does your religion have an influence on whether or not you have sex?
Not at all

How important is it for you to have an emotional connection with your sexual partner? **Somewhat important**

Is there anything else at all that you would like to say about sex or your own sexual experiences?

schools need to teach better sex education. they need young people in year 9 class rooms teaching kids about sex because there are plenty of 12 and 13 year olds having sexual intercourse and encounters at that age. and i think i would have benefitted from sexual education that is relevent from a younger age. People who are in their early 20s would be listened to more then older teachers would as kids can relate to and would feel more comfortable talking to a person closer to their age.

Boy, 17, South Australia, straight

How old were you when you first heard about sex? **9**

What was the first thing you heard about sex? **that u make babies**

How old were you when you started masturbating? **14**

On average, how many times a week do you masturbate? **Twice a week**

How do you masturbate? **pull my penis**

How does masturbating make you feel? **Okay**

Describe your sexual fantasies, even if they seem weird or boring or whatever.
　meh

How old were you when you had your first sexual experience with someone
　else? **12**

What happened in this first sexual experience with another person?
　felt schweet!

How old were you when you first had oral sex? **15**

Describe what happened during this oral sex, and how you felt about it.
　it was awesome i spoofed

On average, how many times a week do you have oral sex?
　Less than once a week

If less frequent, how many times approximately has it occurred? **Ten times**

How old were you when you first had sexual intercourse? **Never**

How old were you when you first had anal sex? **Never**

Would you like to have more sex? **Yes**

How do you think sex could be better for you? **relaxes you**

When you have intercourse, do you use protection? **Yes**

What kind of protection do you use? **condom**

How often are your sexual experiences with someone of the same sex or
　gender as you? **Never**

You think of yourself as … **Straight**

How old were you when you first saw pornography or erotica? **13**

What kind of pornography have you seen? **films, mags, books, websites**

Does porn excite you sexually? **A bit**

Does porn give you ideas about how to have sex? **Sometimes**

Do you think sexy films, music videos or advertising encourage you to have
　sex? **Sometimes**

Examples of media encouraging sex: **girls in skimpy clothes**

Have you ever had phone sex, that is, sexually exciting yourself and
　someone else over the phone? **Yes**

Have you ever sent or received sexual text messages? **Yes**

Have you had a sexual experience in an internet chat room? **No**

Have you ever had a sexual experience with an adult? **No**

Have you ever had a sexual experience with more than one person at a time? **No**

Have you ever been pressured or forced into having sex? **No**

How often do you have sex while using drugs or alcohol? **Never**

Do drugs or alcohol make sex better or worse? **Neither**

Does what you learn in sex education classes at school help you with your actual sexual experiences? **A bit**

Do you think teenagers should be taught more or less about sex at school? **More**

What do you think is the best age to start having sexual experiences? **about 17-20 for intercourse so you know what you are doing Oral sex probably about 15**

Do your parents have an influence on whether or not you have sex? **Not at all**

Does your religion have an influence on whether or not you have sex? **A bit**

How important is it for you to have an emotional connection with your sexual partner? **Somewhat important**

Girl, 17, New South Wales, straight

How old were you when you first heard about sex? **7**

What was the first thing you heard about sex? **its how men and women make their babies**

How old were you when you started masturbating? **Never**

How old were you when you had your first sexual experience with someone else? **12**

What happened in this first sexual experience with another person? **kissing properly for the first time, it was exciting**

How old were you when you first had oral sex? **14**

Describe what happened during this oral sex, and how you felt about it.

the first time i had oral sex it was performed on me and i didn't enjoy it that much because i hadn't really wanted it to happen.

On average, how many times a week do you have oral sex?

Less than once a week

If less frequent, how many times approximately has it occurred?

More than twenty

How old were you when you first had sexual intercourse? **16**

Describe what happened during intercourse, and how you felt about it emotionally.

it happened in a car and i didnt really want it to happen so i regretted it. since then ive been very comfortable with my sexual experiences and haven't regretted anything that has happened since then.

How old were you when you first had anal sex? **Never**

On average, how many times a week do you have intercourse?

Twice a week

Would you like to have more sex? **Yes**

How do you think sex could be better for you?

i would like to try different positions just to experiment.

When you have intercourse, do you use protection? **Yes**

What kind of protection do you use?

birth control pills or condoms. usually both.

How often are your sexual experiences with someone of the same sex or gender as you? **Never**

You think of yourself as … **Straight**

How old were you when you first saw pornography or erotica? **14**

What kind of pornography have you seen?

ive never owned porn but i have seen it on other peoples computers, magazines, movies etc

Does porn excite you sexually? **A bit**

Does porn give you ideas about how to have sex? **Sometimes**

Do you think sexy films, music videos or advertising encourage you to have sex? **Sometimes**

Examples of media encouraging sex:

calvin klein fragance adds, some dior adds, a lot of music video clips

Have you ever had phone sex, that is, sexually exciting yourself and someone else over the phone? **No**

Have you ever sent or received sexual text messages? **Yes**

Have you had a sexual experience in an internet chat room? **No**

Have you ever had a sexual experience with an adult? **Yes**

If so, describe what happened and how you felt about it emotionally.

it was a kiss with someone in their early twenties that i was attracted to, it didnt go any further than that and it made me feel good.

Have you ever had a sexual experience with more than one person at a time? **Yes**

If so, describe what happened and how you felt about it.

didn't really enjoy it, i felt uncomfortable.

Have you ever been pressured or forced into having sex? **Yes**

If so, describe what happened and how you felt about it emotionally.

it was my first time and i didnt really want it to happen at that point but i felt pressured but ive never had an experience like that since then.

How often do you have sex while using drugs or alcohol? **Sometimes**

Do drugs or alcohol make sex better or worse? **Worse**

Does what you learn in sex education classes at school help you with your actual sexual experiences? **Not much**

Do you think teenagers should be taught more or less about sex at school?
Same as now

What do you think is the best age to start having sexual experiences?

whenever you feel ready the age doesn't matter so much as the individuals maturity in that area. people generally start experimenting sexually in their early teens which is when you are most curious about that kind of stuff and i think for the most part thats fine. intercourse should wait until the person has found someone they care about n want to share such a thing with but id say 16-17 is a reasonable age when people are able to make sensible decisions in regard to having intercourse.

Do your parents have an influence on whether or not you have sex?
Not much

Does your religion have an influence on whether or not you have sex?
Not at all

How important is it for you to have an emotional connection with your sexual partner? **Very important**

Boy, 17, South Australia, bisexual

How old were you when you first heard about sex? **11**

How old were you when you started masturbating? **12**

On average, how many times a week do you masturbate?
Three times a week

How do you masturbate?
usually lay in bed and fantasize, use two hands, sometimes ill talk to people online sometimes when i have my shower in the morning

How does masturbating make you feel? **Very good**

Describe your sexual fantasies, even if they seem weird or boring or whatever.
im bisexual, and most of my fantasies involve my best friend who i have a major crush on. they usually just involve us foolin around or experimenting.

How old were you when you had your first sexual experience with someone else? **16**

What happened in this first sexual experience with another person?
i went to a new school and had a girl allocated to show me around. we spent like 2 weeks together and really really liked eachother. we used to skip school and go to her house while her parents were at work, she had just broken up with a bf, thought it was cute i was a virgin, and "showed me the ropes" so to speak. my virginity didn't mean much to me, but it did mean something. i probably wouldn't have done it had i not been in a particularly depressed and lonely state of mind.

How old were you when you first had oral sex? **16**

Describe what happened during this oral sex, and how you felt about it.
when first giving oral sex i thought it was a lot of fun, especially because my partner got into it alot, i felt empowered, i felt i was doing it well.

On average, how many times a week do you have oral sex?
Less than once a week

If less frequent, how many times approximately has it occurred? **Ten times**

How old were you when you first had sexual intercourse? **16**

Describe what happened during intercourse, and how you felt about it emotionally.

didn't heaps know what i was doin. it felt a lot better for me and my partner doing all other sexual things more than actual intercourse. there was little intimacy when i first had intercourse.

How old were you when you first had anal sex? **16**

How often does this happen? **Less than once a week**

Describe what happens during anal sex and how you feel about having it.

ive had a partner finger me, but no more. i assumed that sorta still counted as anal sex. i enjoyed it, and i think my partner enjoyed the empowerment of being able to 'fuck' me when it was usually the other way round.

On average, how many times a week do you have intercourse?

Less than once a week

Would you like to have more sex? **Yes**

How do you think sex could be better for you?

i dont have a partner at the moment, so first i would need one. i havn't been very close to my partners in the past, and i think i rushed into things too quickly. id like to know my partners better, that i might feel more comfortable with them in a sexual situation

When you have intercourse, do you use protection? **Yes**

What kind of protection do you use?

condoms, thats usually all i believe is necessary

How often are your sexual experiences with someone of the same sex or gender as you? **Sometimes**

You think of yourself as ... **Bisexual**

If you're gay or lesbian, are you 'out'? **Yes**

If you're gay or lesbian and you came out, was it hard? **Not very hard**

Describe what happened when you came out and how you felt about it.

i told my best friend, he did not take it well at first, but was fine only days later. i think he feared that knowing it would ruin our friendship, which it didn't at all. our friendship was pretty much unaffected. he also didn't understand why i felt i had to tell him. it was a part of myself that

i wanted to explore and so i guess i just needed to talk to somebody about it. i was not ashamed of it, and i felt i should be able to talk about it freely.

How old were you when you first saw pornography or erotica? **12**

What kind of pornography have you seen?

i think it was photos, i dont really remember.

Does porn excite you sexually? **Not much**

Does porn give you ideas about how to have sex? **Sometimes**

Do you think sexy films, music videos or advertising encourage you to have sex? **Sometimes**

Examples of media encouraging sex: **plenty of films and tv shows glorify sex.**

Have you ever had phone sex, that is, sexually exciting yourself and someone else over the phone? **No**

Have you ever sent or received sexual text messages? **No**

Have you had a sexual experience in an internet chat room? **Yes**

If so, did you also meet up with that person in real life? **No**

Have you ever had a sexual experience with an adult? **No**

Have you ever had a sexual experience with more than one person at a time? **No**

Have you ever been pressured or forced into having sex? **No**

How often do you have sex while using drugs or alcohol? **Sometimes**

Do drugs or alcohol make sex better or worse? **Neither**

Does what you learn in sex education classes at school help you with your actual sexual experiences? **A bit**

Do you think teenagers should be taught more or less about sex at school? **Same as now**

What do you think is the best age to start having sexual experiences?

young girls going out with old guys is creepy and wrong. thats the only sexual age issue i have a problem with.

Do your parents have an influence on whether or not you have sex?

Not at all

Does your religion have an influence on whether or not you have sex?

Not at all

How important is it for you to have an emotional connection with your sexual partner? **Very important**

Girl, 17, New South Wales, bisexual

How old were you when you first heard about sex? **5**

What was the first thing you heard about sex?

> **my grandma told me that as i got older, sometimes i would want to sleep with people to make them like me, but i shouldn't.**

How old were you when you started masturbating? **13**

On average, how many times a week do you masturbate?

> **Three times a week**

How do you masturbate?

> **in my bedroom, on my bed, in my chair ... wherever. Usually when reading.. i find mild sex scenes in books that are absolutely not pornographic turn me on (time traveller's wife has a good one). I have a pink vibrator that an ex boyfriend gave me as a joke, which comes in handy.**

How does masturbating make you feel? **Good**

How old were you when you had your first sexual experience with someone else? **12**

What happened in this first sexual experience with another person?

> **i kissed the boy i liked at a friend's bar mitzvah party, which was held in the basement of his house. The romantic interest in question had a girlfriend, so we ended up kissing in the bathroom while enrique iglesias's 'hero' was playing in the next room. My most vivid memory of the kiss was that i had my eyes open and was looking at a drum kit which had been stored in the bathtub. Emotionally it messed me up, because even though he broke up with his girlfriend and i ended up dating the guy for 2 years, i will never be happy that my first kiss hurt another girl.**

How old were you when you first had oral sex? **14**

Describe what happened during this oral sex, and how you felt about it.

> **I was drunk and at the ski club in thredbo. I was kissing a boy who we all thought was very cool, and he sort of moved things into the dorm he was staying in. he took my top off (although there was absolutely nothing to see), but then one of the mothers staying at the ski club walked in and threw us out. We went outside and started making out in**

the snow, behind a bench next to a massive snow covered bush. He started undoing my jeans and i was so drunk and cold that i didn't even think. He started going down on me, and had absolutely no idea what he was doing! i was cold and uncomfortable. I ended up making my phone ring, pretending it was my dad, and just before i left he said the cheeseyest thing i have ever heard … "don't go … one more lick babygirl". I felt so sick!! I cried and felt like a slut, and to this day i regret telling my friends about that seedy line, because the "babygirl" nickname sort of stuck.

On average, how many times a week do you have oral sex?

Five times a week

How old were you when you first had sexual intercourse? **15**

Describe what happened during intercourse, and how you felt about it emotionally.

a close friend of mine was at my country house helping out with my brothers party. that night we got pissed and ended up having sex. it was not good, and i didn't have any emotions about it. Only two years later have i started to wish i had waited for someone i loved not just someone i trusted.

How old were you when you first had anal sex? **16**

How often does this happen? **Less than once a week**

Describe what happens during anal sex and how you feel about having it.

lots of kissing to make sure i'm very turned on. my ex boyfriend would go down on me first, and while doing that put lube on his fingers and put them inside. he'd come up and turn me over, but keep kissing my neck and stroking my hair. He would slowly ease inside me, but i would hold his hand and squeeze if it hurt. I have only done it twice … the first two times i enjoyed it and thought nothing of it, but the last time i started crying. It didn't hurt, and i still don't know why i cried, but i got sort of overwhelmed.

On average, how many times a week do you have intercourse?

Less than once a week

Would you like to have more sex? **Yes**

How do you think sex could be better for you?

Well getting a new boyfriend would be a start, as i don't want to go sleep with some random.

When you have intercourse, do you use protection? **Yes**

What kind of protection do you use? **contraceptive pill**

How often are your sexual experiences with someone of the same sex or gender as you? **Sometimes**

You think of yourself as … **Bisexual**

How old were you when you first saw pornography or erotica? **14**

What kind of pornography have you seen?

various boys have insisted ive watched porn, looked at hustler etc.

I have 2 erotic novels of my own, but they sort of just make me laugh.

Does porn excite you sexually? **A bit**

Does porn give you ideas about how to have sex? **Sometimes**

Do you think sexy films, music videos or advertising encourage you to have sex? **Always**

Examples of media encouraging sex:

dirrty by christina aguillera. Films such as basic instinct..because so many boys love the movies and love the main women, girls feel that if they act like that (don't wear pants etc) boys will by default like them too.

Have you ever had phone sex, that is, sexually exciting yourself and someone else over the phone? **Yes**

Have you ever sent or received sexual text messages? **Yes**

Have you had a sexual experience in an internet chat room? **No**

Have you ever had a sexual experience with an adult? **Yes**

If so, describe what happened and how you felt about it emotionally.

A few weeks ago i kissed a guy who was 27. He was very nice and fun and clever, but lived in london and was going back in a week. He was very gentlemanly, didn't expect anything more of me and took me out for two nice dinners with his sister and his friends.

Have you ever had a sexual experience with more than one person at a time? **No**

Have you ever been pressured or forced into having sex? **No**

How often do you have sex while using drugs or alcohol? **Sometimes**

Do drugs or alcohol make sex better or worse? **Worse**

Does what you learn in sex education classes at school help you with your actual sexual experiences? **Not at all**

Do you think teenagers should be taught more or less about sex at school? **More**

What do you think is the best age to start having sexual experiences? **it sounds corny, but whenever is right. I started at 15 and think that was too young for me, but i have friends who are still too young now, and other friends who were fine with sex at 14 or younger.**

Do your parents have an influence on whether or not you have sex? **A bit**

Does your religion have an influence on whether or not you have sex? **Not at all**

How important is it for you to have an emotional connection with your sexual partner? **Very important**

Is there anything else at all that you would like to say about sex or your own sexual experiences? **I find i am increasingly confused about sex, and instead of it getting clearer as i grow up it is all becoming more hazy. I have a real madonna/whore complex. I want sex but i somehow feel guilty or violated by it, which is totally nonsensical as i wanted it in the first place. another major issues is sexism in regard to sex. It is an obvious and well known fact that a guy can sleep with as many people as he wants and be admired, while a girl is a slut. It has taken me too long to realise that the guys couldnt care less about what a girl does, and it is girls ourselves who ruin the lives of other girls. this needs to stop, and the only way it can happen is for girls to stop being dickheads and respect each other. a way this could happen is for more respected figures such as teachers, celebrities (though ones like catherine zeta jones, not trashy ones like britney) etc to talk about their experiences and make young people realise that people can do whatever the hell they want and you can never judge people by what makes them happy in the bedroom. the happiest times in my life were having sex with my ex boyfriend. I loved him, and being so close to him and knowing he loved me too was amazing. Sex is so important because it can bring you so close to someone you love.**

Girl, 17, South Australia, straight

How old were you when you first heard about sex? **11**

What was the first thing you heard about sex? **can't remember**

How old were you when you started masturbating? **16**

On average, how many times a week do you masturbate?
Three times a week

How do you masturbate?
but i don't anymore it doesn't feel right when you have a boyfriend so i havn't for 1 month and a bit now

How does masturbating make you feel? **Very good**

Describe your sexual fantasies, even if they seem weird or boring or whatever.
i only tell certain people that

How old were you when you had your first sexual experience with someone else? **5**

What happened in this first sexual experience with another person?
Kissing. Now that i look back at it and that i still know the person weird but it is a learning thing. so yer

How old were you when you first had oral sex? **Never had oral sex**

How old were you when you first had sexual intercourse? **13**

Describe what happened during intercourse, and how you felt about it emotionally. **don't talk about it**

How old were you when you first had anal sex? **Never**

Would you like to have more sex? **Not sure**

How do you think sex could be better for you?
haven't had sex yet. i wouldn't say better for it shouldn't be done to fix things it should happen with two people who love each other and is showing and making love with each other. So it wouldn't make me better just experience and show someone how much i love them and experience the greatest thing two people could ever do and be as close to someone as i can

How often are your sexual experiences with someone of the same sex or gender as you? **Never**

You think of yourself as … **Straight**

How old were you when you first saw pornography or erotica? **13**

What kind of pornography have you seen? **posters**

Does porn excite you sexually? **A bit**

Does porn give you ideas about how to have sex? **Sometimes**

Do you think sexy films, music videos or advertising encourage you to have sex? **Sometimes**

Examples of media encouraging sex:

40 days and 40 nights did abit but if someone sees people having sex on t.v who wouldn't think about doing it????!!!!

Have you ever had phone sex, that is, sexually exciting yourself and someone else over the phone? **Yes**

Have you ever sent or received sexual text messages? **Yes**

Have you had a sexual experience in an internet chat room? **No**

Have you ever had a sexual experience with an adult? **No**

Have you ever had a sexual experience with more than one person at a time? **No**

Have you ever been pressured or forced into having sex? **Yes**

If so, describe what happened and how you felt about it emotionally.

i hated it and found out that the guy only wanted one thing so i dumped him. No names

How often do you have sex while using drugs or alcohol? **Never**

Does what you learn in sex education classes at school help you with your actual sexual experiences? **Not at all**

Do you think teenagers should be taught more or less about sex at school? **More**

What do you think is the best age to start having sexual experiences? **it changes when you feel ready and no pressure from peers, friends or family it's all about you**

Do your parents have an influence on whether or not you have sex? **Not much**

Does your religion have an influence on whether or not you have sex? **Not at all**

How important is it for you to have an emotional connection with your sexual partner? **Very important**

Is there anything else at all that you would like to say about sex or your own sexual experiences?

Be careful with what you do and make sure thet you know what your doing before you do it. Have fun.

By the age of 18, respondents to the survey generally agreed that sexual experiences improve with practice as well as emotional intimacy. As one 18-year-old said, 'the more you do it, the better it gets.' Boys at this age have become much more descriptive of their emotions, and the bravado that often characterised the younger ones is less evident. Admissions of feelings of inadequacy and even impotence are made amid frequent complaints about expectations that are just too high.

Although both boys and girls are still often insecure about their bodies, there is a greater desire to be adventurous and get more out of sex. And even though 18-year-olds can still feel taken advantage of, there is more independent thinking and self-awareness than ever before. Happily, most at this age have learned from their mistakes.

Boy, 18, South Australia, straight

How old were you when you first heard about sex? **7**

What was the first thing you heard about sex? **what it was, pretty factual**

How old were you when you started masturbating? **16**

On average, how many times a week do you masturbate?
More than five times a week

How do you masturbate? **just normal handjob, sitting in bed before i sleep**

How does masturbating make you feel? **Very good**

Describe your sexual fantasies, even if they seem weird or boring or whatever.
normal ... lesbians

How old were you when you had your first sexual experience with someone else? **15**

What happened in this first sexual experience with another person?
kissed my girlfriend. i got very excited about it

How old were you when you first had oral sex? **17**

Describe what happened during this oral sex, and how you felt about it.

i was drunk and she couldnt get me to ejaculate. i had to finish myself off. it wasnt a big deal, i had a laugh

On average, how many times a week do you have oral sex?

Less than once a week

If less frequent, how many times approximately has it occurred? **Twice**

How old were you when you first had sexual intercourse? **17**

Describe what happened during intercourse, and how you felt about it emotionally.

again i was drunk and my erection kept going down while i was getting the condom on. it worked after a few goes though. after that i didnt last as long as i would have liked but i wasnt that bad. i loved it physically and it made her and i closer emotionally. it was at my house in my bed after a party, my mum was cool with it

How old were you when you first had anal sex? **Never**

On average, how many times a week do you have intercourse?

Less than once a week

Would you like to have more sex? **Yes**

How do you think sex could be better for you?

fitness, less tension, just generally happier, higher confidence

When you have intercourse, do you use protection? **Yes**

What kind of protection do you use?

condom first 2 times, and the second time the girl was on the pill

How often are your sexual experiences with someone of the same sex or gender as you? **Never**

You think of yourself as … **Straight**

How old were you when you first saw pornography or erotica? **10**

What kind of pornography have you seen? **files from the internet**

Does porn excite you sexually? **A lot**

Does porn give you ideas about how to have sex? **Always**

Do you think sexy films, music videos or advertising encourage you to have sex? **Always**

Examples of media encouraging sex:

music videos in particular, and any sort of sexual reference from tv, movies, advertising … books too

Have you ever had phone sex, that is, sexually exciting yourself and someone else over the phone? **No**

Have you ever sent or received sexual text messages? **Yes**

Have you had a sexual experience in an internet chat room? **No**

Have you ever had a sexual experience with an adult? **No**

Have you ever had a sexual experience with more than one person at a time? **No**

Have you ever been pressured or forced into having sex? **No**

How often do you have sex while using drugs or alcohol? **Sometimes**

Do drugs or alcohol make sex better or worse? **Neither**

Does what you learn in sex education classes at school help you with your actual sexual experiences? **A bit**

Do you think teenagers should be taught more or less about sex at school? **Same as now**

What do you think is the best age to start having sexual experiences?
16 or 17 is best in my opinion. before then may lead to stupid decisions that compromise your future, and you may hurt people easily without realising it, and especially in girls cases they may not be able to "handle the pressures" and get labled a slut etc

Do your parents have an influence on whether or not you have sex?
Not at all

Does your religion have an influence on whether or not you have sex?
Not at all

How important is it for you to have an emotional connection with your sexual partner? **Somewhat important**

Is there anything else at all that you would like to say about sex or your own sexual experiences?
although school sex education hasnt really helped me when having sex (apart from protection) i am glad that i was told everything that i was in school. this sex education was done when i was in year six (12 yrs old) and it was very graphic and to the point. it showed me that sex was a very adult thing, and although i wanted sex before the age of 16, i was aware that it would come in time and gave me the patience and maturity to make the right decisions when it came to sex.

Girl, 18, Queensland, bisexual

How old were you when you first heard about sex? **10**

What was the first thing you heard about sex?

that its how babies were made.

How old were you when you started masturbating? **18**

On average, how many times a week do you masturbate? **Once a week**

How do you masturbate? **bed. vibrator.**

How does masturbating make you feel? **Good**

Describe your sexual fantasies, even if they seem weird or boring or whatever.

i want to have sex in public. a nightclub, public pool, park.

How old were you when you had your first sexual experience with someone
else? **15**

What happened in this first sexual experience with another person?

**i was really in love with the boy it was awesome. as if we were
becoming one.**

How old were you when you first had oral sex? **16**

Describe what happened during this oral sex, and how you felt about it.

its great. possibly my fav thing. i cum so quickly n so much.

On average, how many times a week do you have oral sex?

Four times a week

How old were you when you first had sexual intercourse? **15**

Describe what happened during intercourse, and how you felt about it
emotionally.

it hurt. but was beautiful. we were in love.

How old were you when you first had anal sex? **Never**

On average, how many times a week do you have intercourse?

Four times a week

Would you like to have more sex? **Yes**

How do you think sex could be better for you?

be more emotional and intimate.

When you have intercourse, do you use protection? **Yes**

What kind of protection do you use? **implanon**

How often are your sexual experiences with someone of the same sex or
gender as you? **Sometimes**

You think of yourself as ... **Bisexual**

If you're gay or lesbian, are you 'out'? **Yes**

If you're gay or lesbian and you came out, was it hard? **Not very hard**

Describe what happened when you came out and how you felt about it.

i was like ... i like boys and girls ... everyone was like thats nice.

How old were you when you first saw pornography or erotica? **12**

What kind of pornography have you seen?

films. photos. mags. internet. stories.

Does porn excite you sexually? **A lot**

Does porn give you ideas about how to have sex? **Sometimes**

Do you think sexy films, music videos or advertising encourage you to have sex? **Sometimes**

Examples of media encouraging sex: **Cruel Intentions**

Have you ever had phone sex, that is, sexually exciting yourself and someone else over the phone? **No**

Have you ever sent or received sexual text messages? **Yes**

Have you had a sexual experience in an internet chat room? **No**

Have you ever had a sexual experience with an adult? **Yes**

If so, describe what happened and how you felt about it emotionally.

it was fucked.

Have you ever had a sexual experience with more than one person at a time? **No**

Have you ever been pressured or forced into having sex? **Yes**

If so, describe what happened and how you felt about it emotionally.

it was fucked.

How often do you have sex while using drugs or alcohol? **Sometimes**

Do drugs or alcohol make sex better or worse? **Worse**

Does what you learn in sex education classes at school help you with your actual sexual experiences? **Not much**

Do you think teenagers should be taught more or less about sex at school? **More**

What do you think is the best age to start having sexual experiences?

15 is a good age. you are able to make the right choices. and young enough to grow stronger from it all.

Do your parents have an influence on whether or not you have sex?

Not much

Does your religion have an influence on whether or not you have sex?

Not at all

How important is it for you to have an emotional connection with your sexual partner? **Very important**

Is there anything else at all that you would like to say about sex or your own sexual experiences?

i love oral sex. guys out there … if you dont give head alotta girls wont want you. and public sex should be considered natural not illegal.

Girl, 18, South Australia, straight

How old were you when you first heard about sex? **7**

What was the first thing you heard about sex?

That it was how babies were made … I went and told this to my best friend with a conversation that went like so: ME: "Guess what!?" Best Friend (BF): "What!?!?" ME: "Your parents had SEX to have you!!" BF: "Really!?" ME: "Yep!!" *BF goes home and asks parents then comes back to my house* BF: "You're wrong!!" ME: "No I'm not … " BF: "Well my mum says I was born in the cabbage patch!!" We were both thoroughly confused and concluded that maybe we came from different places …

How old were you when you started masturbating? **10**

On average, how many times a week do you masturbate? **Once a week**

How does masturbating make you feel? **Good**

How old were you when you had your first sexual experience with someone else? **8**

What happened in this first sexual experience with another person?

My friends brother and I went behind the shed and rubbed tummies … Our simulation of sex … I felt happy … Haha …

How old were you when you first had oral sex? **15**

Describe what happened during this oral sex, and how you felt about it.

It's pretty self explanitory ... I felt excited because I was taking the next step with my boyfriend.

On average, how many times a week do you have oral sex? **Twice a week**

How old were you when you first had sexual intercourse? **17**

Describe what happened during intercourse, and how you felt about it emotionally.

It was really clumsy but we both wanted to do it, and when we did we were really excited about it!

On average, how many times a week do you have intercourse?

Twice a week

Would you like to have more sex? **Not sure**

When you have intercourse, do you use protection? **Yes**

What kind of protection do you use? **Condoms and/or The Pill**

How often are your sexual experiences with someone of the same sex or gender as you? **Never**

You think of yourself as ... **Straight**

How old were you when you first saw pornography or erotica? **11**

What kind of pornography have you seen?

Magazines, films, stories, websites

Does porn excite you sexually? **Not much**

Does porn give you ideas about how to have sex? **Sometimes**

Do you think sexy films, music videos or advertising encourage you to have sex? **Sometimes**

Examples of media encouraging sex:

Ones targeted at younger teens can make them feel pressured.

Have you ever had phone sex, that is, sexually exciting yourself and someone else over the phone? **No**

Have you ever sent or received sexual text messages? **Yes**

Have you had a sexual experience in an internet chat room? **Yes**

If so, did you also meet up with that person in real life? **No**

Have you ever had a sexual experience with an adult? **No**

Have you ever had a sexual experience with more than one person at a time? **No**

Have you ever been pressured or forced into having sex? **No**

How often do you have sex while using drugs or alcohol? **Sometimes**

Do drugs or alcohol make sex better or worse? **Worse**

Does what you learn in sex education classes at school help you with your actual sexual experiences? **A bit**

Do you think teenagers should be taught more or less about sex at school? **More**

What do you think is the best age to start having sexual experiences?

Well I don't think there is any "best" age ... It all depends on whether the person is ready and how they feel about it. As far as anything beyond kissing goes- I think a person should be completely comfortable with themselves and the person they're doing it with, and they shouldn't feel pressured.

Do your parents have an influence on whether or not you have sex?

Not at all

Does your religion have an influence on whether or not you have sex?

Not at all

How important is it for you to have an emotional connection with your sexual partner? **Somewhat important**

Is there anything else at all that you would like to say about sex or your own sexual experiences?

I always wanted my first of everything (e.g. oral sex, mutual masturbation, intercourse etc.) to be with my first serious boyfriend, and it was. That's how I planned it, and that's how it happened. I followed my own brain and stuck to my beliefs, no matter what others around me thought. That's the best advice teens can get, stick to your own feelings and follow them.

Girl, 18, New South Wales, straight

How old were you when you first heard about sex? **10**

What was the first thing you heard about sex?

my friend told me that when you kiss like mumies and daddies that you got a baby.

How old were you when you started masturbating? **Never**

Describe your sexual fantasies, even if they seem weird or boring or whatever.

having passionate sex in a pool at night with the hot, sexy life guard

How old were you when you had your first sexual experience with someone else? **9**

What happened in this first sexual experience with another person?

a boy and i pashed at school. (same age) it was amazing, i felt a bit naughty and exciting. the boy and and i became best friends, we became more connected.

How old were you when you first had oral sex? **16**

Describe what happened during this oral sex, and how you felt about it.

I liked it but it made me feel wierd, it was with a boy i met a few times before who was really cute and really nice. I was curious i guess. i went down on him, didnt mind, then he did it to me, i just felt, oh my god, is he really enjoying this? cause i think vaginas are just wierd and maybe he found mine gross and wasnt saying anything but would go and tell his mates about this foul vagina

On average, how many times a week do you have oral sex?

Less than once a week

If less frequent, how many times approximately has it occurred? **Twice**

How old were you when you first had sexual intercourse? **15**

Describe what happened during intercourse, and how you felt about it emotionally.

i was raped. my boyfriend took me to a public toilet in the middle of nowhere and forced me onto him. I felt so helpless, weakened and sick/damaged. i was emtionally crippled, never trusting anyone, crying myself to sleep. i have grown since then and it has made me a stronger, firmer person.

How old were you when you first had anal sex? **Never**

On average, how many times a week do you have intercourse?

Less than once a week

Would you like to have more sex? **Yes**

How do you think sex could be better for you?

i want to experience a real connection between the man and i. no meaningless sex

When you have intercourse, do you use protection? **Yes**

What kind of protection do you use? **pill and condom**

How often are your sexual experiences with someone of the same sex or gender as you? **Never**

You think of yourself as … **Straight**

How old were you when you first saw pornography or erotica? **16**

What kind of pornography have you seen?

film, net photos, stories in sealed section in Cosmo

Does porn excite you sexually? **A lot**

Does porn give you ideas about how to have sex? **Sometimes**

Do you think sexy films, music videos or advertising encourage you to have sex? **Sometimes**

Examples of media encouraging sex:

film clips especially with naked sexy females and half-naked men.

Have you ever had phone sex, that is, sexually exciting yourself and someone else over the phone? **No**

Have you ever sent or received sexual text messages? **Yes**

Have you had a sexual experience in an internet chat room? **Yes**

If so, did you also meet up with that person in real life? **No**

Have you ever had a sexual experience with an adult? **Yes**

If so, describe what happened and how you felt about it emotionally.

he was 24 and i was 17. we really liked each other and we had to keep it secret but wed meet up and talk and go to the beach and then one night we had sex … it was really amazing, i felt connected and wanted. he helped me to trust other guys and not fear sex or guys.

Have you ever had a sexual experience with more than one person at a time? **No**

Have you ever been pressured or forced into having sex? **Yes**

If so, describe what happened and how you felt about it emotionally.

i was taken into a public toilet by my boyfriend, thinking i was going to give him head, then he held my mouth and forced himself in me, i was pressed against the wall and after i felt like i was dirty, contaminated and i thought he could do it cause he was my boyfriend. I then broke up with him and he got angry and started name calling and then said he in fact broke up with me. my heart was broken, how could someone i know, do that? i was really confused if he had raped me or if it was me.

i did keep telling him to stop but i dont no if he heard cause his hand was over my mouth. i couldnt trust boys and i sort of feared them.

How often do you have sex while using drugs or alcohol? **Never**

Does what you learn in sex education classes at school help you with your actual sexual experiences? **Not much**

Do you think teenagers should be taught more or less about sex at school? **More**

What do you think is the best age to start having sexual experiences?
i think its ok to have sex, so long as its with someone you really know and trust. having a pash is fine when you're 13-15, any other sexual experience i think should not be started untill say 15 because you have your whole life to have sex and these experiences and to hold onto your childhood as long as possible cause once its gone, you cant get it back

Do your parents have an influence on whether or not you have sex?
Not much

Does your religion have an influence on whether or not you have sex?
Not at all

How important is it for you to have an emotional connection with your sexual partner? **Very important**

Boy, 18, (no postcode given), straight

What was the first thing you heard about sex?
all girls are sluts and easy, cept a few, their easy to root

How old were you when you started masturbating? **14**

On average, how many times a week do you masturbate? **Five times a week**

How do you masturbate? **just hands**

How does masturbating make you feel? **Very good**

Describe your sexual fantasies, even if they seem weird or boring or whatever.
fuckin chicks anywhere and everywhere

How old were you when you had your first sexual experience with someone else? **16**

What happened in this first sexual experience with another person?
it was awsum fingered her and kisst her

How old were you when you first had oral sex? **16**

Describe what happened during this oral sex, and how you felt about it.

she was my gf sucked my cock good

On average, how many times a week do you have oral sex? **Twice a week**

How old were you when you first had sexual intercourse? **16**

Describe what happened during intercourse, and how you felt about it emotionally.

it was awsum i was with the girl for ages she was a virgin 2 so it was pretty close

How old were you when you first had anal sex? **Never had anal sex**

On average, how many times a week do you have intercourse?

Four times a week

Would you like to have more sex? **Yes**

How do you think sex could be better for you?

hot chick more attached and she aint a slut

When you have intercourse, do you use protection? **Sometimes**

What kind of protection do you use?

sumtimes nothin, just spit on the cock and put it in but usually use dingaz

How often are your sexual experiences with someone of the same sex or gender as you? **Never**

You think of yourself as … **Straight**

How old were you when you first saw pornography or erotica? **12**

What kind of pornography have you seen? **everythin**

Does porn excite you sexually? **A lot**

Does porn give you ideas about how to have sex? **Always**

Do you think sexy films, music videos or advertising encourage you to have sex? **Always**

Examples of media encouraging sex: **most tv and society**

Have you ever had phone sex, that is, sexually exciting yourself and someone else over the phone? **Yes**

Have you ever sent or received sexual text messages? **Yes**

Have you had a sexual experience in an internet chat room? **Yes**

If so, did you also meet up with that person in real life? **Yes**

Have you ever had a sexual experience with an adult? **Yes**

If so, describe what happened and how you felt about it emotionally.

good experience cause ima guy i can only gain not lose

Have you ever had a sexual experience with more than one person at a time? **Yes**

If so, describe what happened and how you felt about it.

5 chicks and i was the only guy it was awsum no wonder im the pimp king at school

Have you ever been pressured or forced into having sex? **No**

How often do you have sex while using drugs or alcohol? **Never**

Does what you learn in sex education classes at school help you with your actual sexual experiences? **A bit**

Do you think teenagers should be taught more or less about sex at school? **Less**

What do you think is the best age to start having sexual experiences?

after marriage cause today sex means nothin thats y every1 is divorced cause ur bond is not strong i could go on but cbf

Do your parents have an influence on whether or not you have sex? **A bit**

Does your religion have an influence on whether or not you have sex? **A bit**

How important is it for you to have an emotional connection with your sexual partner? **Not very important**

Is there anything else at all that you would like to say about sex or your own sexual experiences?

ive fukt so many girls its mad i hate most chicks cause theyre dumb and easy ima pretty smart guy know the world is full of easy ppl and weak minded creature take advantage of it

Girl, 18, New South Wales, straight

How old were you when you first heard about sex? **7**

What was the first thing you heard about sex?

From a book called "Where did I come from" with cartoon illustrations. The book said sex was fun, good exercise, and was had between a man and a woman who loved each other very much. It also explained very basically how reproduction worked.

How old were you when you started masturbating? **14**

How do you masturbate?

> **I've only masturbated once since I became sexually active. Before that, I used to masturbate up to five times a week but sometimes not for a couple of weeks at a time. I usually masturbated in my bedroom through clitoral stimulation with a small rounded object.**

How does masturbating make you feel? **Very good**

Describe your sexual fantasies, even if they seem weird or boring or whatever.

> **I used to fantasise about guys I liked - usually older men because I didn't know many guys my own age. This included teachers and my brother's friends.**

How old were you when you had your first sexual experience with someone else? **15**

What happened in this first sexual experience with another person?

> **I kissed a guy at my year 10 formal after party. I didn't particularly like him but we were dancing and we talked for a while and then he kissed me. It went on for ages and I wasn't enjoying it at all - probably because neither of us knew what we were doing - but I didn't want to be rude and tell him to stop. I didn't see him after that night for a while, but that didn't bother me. He text messaged me the next day and made excuses about not asking me out, but I didn't really care. I didn't kiss anyone else (for lack of opportunity) until I was 18 at university - so at least it was good that I hadn't "never been kissed" before.**

How old were you when you first had oral sex? **18**

Describe what happened during this oral sex, and how you felt about it.

> **I had oral sex with my first boyfriend (the first guy I had sex with) some time after we first started having intercourse. I can't exactly remember it that well (I wasn't drunk or anything, I just don't remember), but I wanted to do it and he was more sexually experienced than me so I got him to show me how to do it better. I enjoyed it.**

On average, how many times a week do you have oral sex? **Twice a week**

How old were you when you first had sexual intercourse? **18**

Describe what happened during intercourse, and how you felt about it
emotionally.

**I first had intercourse with my first boyfriend. It was my first time but it
wasn't his. It hurt a bit - I bled a bit. It wasn't great but I could tell that it
would get better. We both really liked each other and I felt very loved
and cared for. He knew what he was doing and he didn't rush me.**

On average, how many times a week do you have intercourse?

More than five times a week

Would you like to have more sex? **No**

How do you think sex could be better for you?

**I don't know - sex is usually pretty good for me! When I say "more than
five times a week" I mean when I have a boyfriend and I'm not on my
period.**

When you have intercourse, do you use protection? **Yes**

What kind of protection do you use?

**I'm on the pill so that takes care of birth control (hopefully). I haven't
been using condoms which I know is stupid, but I really don't like
them (what a silly excuse). I went to FPA and had a screen for STDs
and a pap smear, and found out I had human papilloma virus. So I
guess any sex I have with new sexual partners should be more
protected as I'd feel irresponsible about passing something on now
that I know I've got it.**

How often are your sexual experiences with someone of the same sex or
gender as you? **Never**

You think of yourself as … **Straight**

How old were you when you first saw pornography or erotica? **11**

What kind of pornography have you seen?

**Books of my parents' that I found (with drawings and photographs),
internet websites.**

Does porn excite you sexually? **A bit**

Does porn give you ideas about how to have sex? **Sometimes**

Do you think sexy films, music videos or advertising encourage you to have
sex? **Never**

Have you ever had phone sex, that is, sexually exciting yourself and
someone else over the phone? **No**

Have you ever sent or received sexual text messages? **No**

Have you had a sexual experience in an internet chat room? **Yes**

If so, did you also meet up with that person in real life? **No**

Have you ever had a sexual experience with an adult? **No**

If so, describe what happened and how you felt about it emotionally.

> **I'm 18 and the only real sexual experiences I've had have been with adults.**

Have you ever had a sexual experience with more than one person at a time? **Yes**

If so, describe what happened and how you felt about it.

> **While I was going out with this guy we decided it would be fun to have a threesome but we couldn't really decide who we'd want to have it with - I wanted another guy (not a girl) and he seemed happy enough with that. Then we broke up, but we were still having sex occasionally. One night he and I and another mutual guy friend of ours were in my room and my ex-boyfriend started making suggestions. Our friend said he was up for it so we started mucking around, kissing each other (no homosexual activity took place) and removing clothes. Before it got very far, I decided I didn't want to because of other factors (involving emotional relationships with someone else who I was interested in) - I certainly had nothing against the idea and it was fun, exciting, and a bit different. We tentatively planned to do it again in a few months when my other factors were sorted out.**

Have you ever been pressured or forced into having sex? **Yes**

If so, describe what happened and how you felt about it emotionally.

> **When my ex-boyfriend and I broke up he was really upset and I was the cause of his distress (i.e. I cheated on him amongst other things). We were both pissed off with the way the other had reacted to the situation, but we still liked each other a lot. We still spent time together, and when you're watching a movie in someone's room at 3am, lying on their bed with them, things are bound to happen. Because I like someone else and had come to a tentative agreement when I broke up with my boyfriend, I felt a bit guilty like I was cheating even though I wasn't going out with the other guy yet. Sometimes I didn't want to, but my ex-boyfriend really wanted me sometimes and when he turned me on**

I sometimes found it hard to say no. After the first time, he tried again even when he knew I didn't want to. He never forced me and I was always consensual, but sometimes I'd regret it a bit afterwards. The sex itself was still very good though.

How often do you have sex while using drugs or alcohol? **Never**

Do drugs or alcohol make sex better or worse? **Neither**

Does what you learn in sex education classes at school help you with your actual sexual experiences? **Not much**

Do you think teenagers should be taught more or less about sex at school? **Same as now**

What do you think is the best age to start having sexual experiences?

I don't know - it's completely up to the individual. As long as you feel ready yourself. I know I started probably too late at 18 when I moved away from home for uni and finally met some guys my own age. Being at a single sex school meant I didn't meet any guys while I was at school, even though I was probably ready to be sexually active.

Do your parents have an influence on whether or not you have sex?

Not much

Does your religion have an influence on whether or not you have sex?

Not at all

How important is it for you to have an emotional connection with your sexual partner? **Somewhat important**

Is there anything else at all that you would like to say about sex or your own sexual experiences?

I like sex a lot. It's fun, and the more you do it, the better it gets. I've had intercourse with three different guys, only two of whom I was emotionally involved with. I wouldn't say that having sex with someone you're not emotionally involved with is any better or worse than with someone you are. Sex can be emotional, or it can be just sex - both types are good. I find it frustrating that there are stigmas attached to girls who have a lot of sexual partners. There's a huge double standard. If you're a guy it's a good thing, if you're a girl you can be labelled a slut. I've been warned by my ex-boyfriend that I have to be careful about getting labelled and "ruining my reputation". He acknowledges there's a double standard but still. I'd like to have as much sex as I want without being judged.

Boy, 18, Victoria, straight

How old were you when you first heard about sex? **10**

What was the first thing you heard about sex? **Can't remember**

How old were you when you started masturbating? **13**

On average, how many times a week do you masturbate?

Four times a week

How do you masturbate?

With porn magazines. Lie down on my bed and wank with my right hand while flicking the pages with my left.

How does masturbating make you feel? **Good**

Describe your sexual fantasies, even if they seem weird or boring or whatever.

The girl or girls have to have big tits. We fuck on a secluded tropical beach and go to wash the sand off in the water naked and we fuck out there in the water some more. We fuck for hours and its complete ecstasy for hours. Starts slow and as we build up we peak and max amount of pleasure for hours. I have a super strong stamina!

How old were you when you had your first sexual experience with someone else? **15**

What happened in this first sexual experience with another person?

It was my first kiss. It was great. All my friends had kissed people all the time and i felt like shit coz i hadn't yet and then when it happened i was over the moon and felt like i had finally got rid of the burden i had of not kissing someone.

How old were you when you first had oral sex? **18**

Describe what happened during this oral sex, and how you felt about it.

The girl giving the oral sex to me was doing a good job. It got me relaxed as she was doing it. I felt great coz i didn't have to do anything. I just lay back and let her do it all. I was feeling really great and she was going for a while and then she pulled out before i cummed. I hadn't quite peaked yet which was a bit annoying but it felt great all the same

On average, how many times a week do you have oral sex?

Less than once a week

If less frequent, how many times approximately has it occurred? **Once**

How old were you when you first had sexual intercourse? **16**

Describe what happened during intercourse, and how you felt about it emotionally.

It wasn't the best time i've ever had. I felt pretty flat. We were both silent the whole time with no music or nothing. It was pitch black and my expectations were pretty high about sex and then i didn't enjoy it as much as what i thought it would be like. And wen we finished up my ex-girlfriend said "Don't freak out if theres blood everywhere" when it was pitch black and couldn't see nothing so i was frozen still for a while. It wasn't the best thing to say after sex

How old were you when you first had anal sex? **Never**

On average, how many times a week do you have intercourse?

Less than once a week

Would you like to have more sex? **Yes**

How do you think sex could be better for you?

I'd like to be able to go for longer and not get so tired so quickly. I wish i could give a girl real pleasure. I haven't given a girl an orgasm yet.

When you have intercourse, do you use protection? **Yes**

What kind of protection do you use?

Condoms pretty much all the time but the girl was on the pill once and i didn't have any condoms on me

How often are your sexual experiences with someone of the same sex or gender as you? **Never**

You think of yourself as … **Straight**

How old were you when you first saw pornography or erotica? **12**

What kind of pornography have you seen?

Pics on the internet and magazines

Does porn excite you sexually? **A bit**

Does porn give you ideas about how to have sex? **Sometimes**

Do you think sexy films, music videos or advertising encourage you to have sex? **Sometimes**

Examples of media encouraging sex:

Britney video clips is about all i can think of atm.

Have you ever had phone sex, that is, sexually exciting yourself and someone else over the phone? **No**

Have you ever sent or received sexual text messages? **No**

Have you had a sexual experience in an internet chat room? **Yes**

If so, did you also meet up with that person in real life? **Yes**

Have you ever had a sexual experience with an adult? **No**

Have you ever had a sexual experience with more than one person at a time? **No**

Have you ever been pressured or forced into having sex? **No**

How often do you have sex while using drugs or alcohol? **Never**

Do drugs or alcohol make sex better or worse? **Neither**

Does what you learn in sex education classes at school help you with your actual sexual experiences? **A bit**

Do you think teenagers should be taught more or less about sex at school? **More**

What do you think is the best age to start having sexual experiences? **about 15 or 16. Any earlier and its too young and too immature to know wats realy going on and wat they are doing. This is talking about intercourse.**

Do your parents have an influence on whether or not you have sex? **Not at all**

Does your religion have an influence on whether or not you have sex? **Not at all**

How important is it for you to have an emotional connection with your sexual partner? **Not very imporant**

Is there anything else at all that you would like to say about sex or your own sexual experiences? **I need more practice to get better and i'm looking for more girls to practice with! Wish me luck!**

Boy, 18, Queensland, bisexual

How old were you when you first heard about sex? **10**

What was the first thing you heard about sex? **how the penis enters the pussy**

How old were you when you started masturbating? **13**

On average, how many times a week do you masturbate?

Three times a week

How do you masturbate?

looking at porn on the internet or with my girlfriend when we are home alone

How does masturbating make you feel? **Very good**

Describe your sexual fantasies, even if they seem weird or boring or whatever.

being dominated by a woman. having a huge orgy in a pool

How old were you when you had your first sexual experience with someone else? **16**

What happened in this first sexual experience with another person?

it was on a pool table it was kinda weird cause we didnt know what to do

How old were you when you first had oral sex? **16**

Describe what happened during this oral sex, and how you felt about it.

it was on the pool table i got a blow job and it felt great

On average, how many times a week do you have oral sex?

Less than once a week

If less frequent, how many times approximately has it occurred? **Three times**

How old were you when you first had sexual intercourse? **16**

Describe what happened during intercourse, and how you felt about it emotionally.

it was weird cause we were inexperienced but we started pashing then ripping off each others clothes before long i was fucking her and was loving it

How old were you when you first had anal sex? **17**

How often does this happen? **Less than once a week**

Describe what happens during anal sex and how you feel about having it.

it hurt a lot but felt really good after

On average, how many times a week do you have intercourse?

Less than once a week

Would you like to have more sex? **Yes**

How do you think sex could be better for you?

if we knew all the best positions

When you have intercourse, do you use protection? **Sometimes**

What kind of protection do you use? **condoms**

How often are your sexual experiences with someone of the same sex or gender as you? **Sometimes**

You think of yourself as … **Bisexual**

If you're gay or lesbian, are you 'out'? **No**

Describe what happened when you came out and how you felt about it.

i have never came "out" but i suppose it would be hard

How old were you when you first saw pornography or erotica? **13**

What kind of pornography have you seen?

movies mags internet websites photos

Does porn excite you sexually? **A lot**

Does porn give you ideas about how to have sex? **Sometimes**

Do you think sexy films, music videos or advertising encourage you to have sex? **Sometimes**

Examples of media encouraging sex:

some of the rap stars music videos

Have you ever had phone sex, that is, sexually exciting yourself and someone else over the phone? **Yes**

Have you ever sent or received sexual text messages? **Yes**

Have you had a sexual experience in an internet chat room? **No**

Have you ever had a sexual experience with an adult? **Yes**

If so, describe what happened and how you felt about it emotionally.

it was my 1st and only gay sex i was 17 and i felt sick after but during it i was so horny i didnt care

Have you ever had a sexual experience with more than one person at a time? **Yes**

If so, describe what happened and how you felt about it.

my girlfriend and her friend came over and we had sex. i felt great fucking someone i didnt know very well and seeing my gf being leso

Have you ever been pressured or forced into having sex? **No**

How often do you have sex while using drugs or alcohol? **Sometimes**

Do drugs or alcohol make sex better or worse? **Neither**

Does what you learn in sex education classes at school help you with your actual sexual experiences? **Not much**

Do you think teenagers should be taught more or less about sex at school?
More

What do you think is the best age to start having sexual experiences?
16 cause having normal sex with a chick

Do your parents have an influence on whether or not you have sex?
Not at all

Does your religion have an influence on whether or not you have sex?
Not at all

How important is it for you to have an emotional connection with your sexual partner? **Somewhat important**

Is there anything else at all that you would like to say about sex or your own sexual experiences? **i love my gf and her big tits they are great to fuck**

Boy, 18, South Australia, straight

How old were you when you first heard about sex? **5**

What was the first thing you heard about sex? **u make babies**

How old were you when you started masturbating? **12**

On average, how many times a week do you masturbate? **Once a week**

How do you masturbate? **in the toilet**

How does masturbating make you feel? **Very good**

Describe your sexual fantasies, even if they seem weird or boring or whatever.
having sex with a chick

How old were you when you had your first sexual experience with someone else? **17**

What happened in this first sexual experience with another person?
i got 3 bjs in one night! It felt great! i was on a high from it.

How old were you when you first had oral sex? **17**

Describe what happened during this oral sex, and how you felt about it.
i ate out a chick ... felt real good

On average, how many times a week do you have oral sex? **Twice a week**

How old were you when you first had sexual intercourse? **17**

Describe what happened during intercourse, and how you felt about it emotionally. **the best thing i ever did**

How old were you when you first had anal sex? **Never**

Would you like to have more sex? **Yes**

How do you think sex could be better for you?
should feel good and both people should be really into it emotionally

When you have intercourse, do you use protection? **Yes**

What kind of protection do you use? **condoms**

How often are your sexual experiences with someone of the same sex or gender as you? **Never**

You think of yourself as … **Straight**

Does porn excite you sexually? **A bit**

Does porn give you ideas about how to have sex? **Sometimes**

Do you think sexy films, music videos or advertising encourage you to have sex? **Sometimes**

Have you ever had phone sex, that is, sexually exciting yourself and someone else over the phone? **Yes**

Have you ever sent or received sexual text messages? **Yes**

Have you had a sexual experience in an internet chat room? **Yes**

If so, did you also meet up with that person in real life? **Yes**

Have you ever had a sexual experience with an adult? **No**

Have you ever had a sexual experience with more than one person at a time? **No**

Have you ever been pressured or forced into having sex? **No**

How often do you have sex while using drugs or alcohol? **Sometimes**

Do drugs or alcohol make sex better or worse? **Worse**

Does what you learn in sex education classes at school help you with your actual sexual experiences? **Not at all**

Do you think teenagers should be taught more or less about sex at school? **More**

What do you think is the best age to start having sexual experiences?
around 18 is the best age because you have the freedom to do more things and it's more understandable by peers at that age.

Do your parents have an influence on whether or not you have sex?
Not at all

Does your religion have an influence on whether or not you have sex?
Not at all

How important is it for you to have an emotional connection with your sexual
partner? **Very important**

Is there anything else at all that you would like to say about sex or your own
sexual experiences?

**i enjoy having sex alot. i cant get enough of it. even though i had it
2 times in four days the other week. I STILL WANT MORE!**

Girl, 18, New South Wales, straight

How old were you when you first heard about sex? **13**

What was the first thing you heard about sex? **to always use protection**

How old were you when you started masturbating? **16**

On average, how many times a week do you masturbate? **Twice a week**

How do you masturbate?

**i often am watching kissing/sex scenes in movies or tv shows and that
usually leads to me touching myself**

How does masturbating make you feel? **Good**

Describe your sexual fantasies, even if they seem weird or boring or whatever.

**to have someone blindfold, massage me, kiss me from head to toe and
just pleasure me til i cum and reach my peak.**

How old were you when you had your first sexual experience with someone
else? **Never**

What happened in this first sexual experience with another person?

**never had any sexual experience. never been kissed. only thought
about it.**

How old were you when you first had oral sex? **Never had oral sex**

How old were you when you first had sexual intercourse? **Never**

How old were you when you first had anal sex? **Never**

Would you like to have more sex? **Not sure**

How do you think sex could be better for you?

**physically I'd feel if someone wanted to have sex with me, then that
would mean they find me attractive physically so therefore i would be**

less insecure about the way i look and i might be more confident about myself.

What kind of protection do you use?

if i were to have sex, i would always use condoms.

How often are your sexual experiences with someone of the same sex or gender as you? **Never**

You think of yourself as … **Straight**

How old were you when you first saw pornography or erotica? **18**

What kind of pornography have you seen?

stories, magazines, internet websites

Does porn excite you sexually? **A lot**

Does porn give you ideas about how to have sex? **Sometimes**

Do you think sexy films, music videos or advertising encourage you to have sex? **Sometimes**

Examples of media encouraging sex:

mostly rnb videos - their lyrics and video content are (usually) mainly about sex and what the artist would like to be done to them, etc - for example "candy shop" by 50 cent.

Have you ever had phone sex, that is, sexually exciting yourself and someone else over the phone? **No**

Have you ever sent or received sexual text messages? **No**

Have you had a sexual experience in an internet chat room? **Yes**

If so, did you also meet up with that person in real life? **No**

Have you ever had a sexual experience with an adult? **No**

Have you ever had a sexual experience with more than one person at a time? **No**

Have you ever been pressured or forced into having sex? **No**

How often do you have sex while using drugs or alcohol? **Never**

Do drugs or alcohol make sex better or worse? **Neither**

Does what you learn in sex education classes at school help you with your actual sexual experiences? **Not much**

Do you think teenagers should be taught more or less about sex at school? **More**

What do you think is the best age to start having sexual experiences?

18 - when they are legal. that way, they may have learnt more about the issue by this age and know whether or not they still want to go through it.

Do your parents have an influence on whether or not you have sex?

Not much

Does your religion have an influence on whether or not you have sex?

Not at all

How important is it for you to have an emotional connection with your sexual partner? **Very important**

Is there anything else at all that you would like to say about sex or your own sexual experiences?

I think sex is something that should be taken seriously. People should not advertise their bodies if they want to sexual intercourse with somebody. When people have sex, the two people involved should have a connection with each other - most times it should be about doing it with someone you love. Sex is not an issue to be taken lightly. Everyone should make their first time special and let it be something that they'll always remember. Something they'll look back on and be happy about not something that they'll look back on and regret later in their life. Sex is a topic talked about almost everyday by teenagers, young adults, etc. As long as they know what they are getting themselves into and the consequences that may follow, they should do what their heart tells them, not what their head or hormones are persuading them to go ahead with. Always use protection - it could save your life in the end.

Boy, 18, (no postcode given), straight

How old were you when you first heard about sex? **5**

What was the first thing you heard about sex?

That it was mostly about love, and something done by couples for procreation.

How old were you when you started masturbating? **14**

On average, how many times a week do you masturbate? **Twice a week**

How do you masturbate? **In the shower, sometimes in my bedroom to porn.**

How does masturbating make you feel? **Good**

Describe your sexual fantasies, even if they seem weird or boring or whatever.
Usually just celebrities from TV (Paris Hilton, etc) and sometimes female teachers at my school.

How old were you when you had your first sexual experience with someone else? **Never**

How old were you when you first had oral sex? **Never had oral sex**

How old were you when you first had sexual intercourse? **Never**

How old were you when you first had anal sex? **Never**

Would you like to have more sex? **Yes**

How often are your sexual experiences with someone of the same sex or gender as you? **Never**

You think of yourself as … **Straight**

How old were you when you first saw pornography or erotica? **15**

What kind of pornography have you seen?
internet websites, some magazines.

Does porn excite you sexually? **A lot**

Does porn give you ideas about how to have sex? **Sometimes**

Do you think sexy films, music videos or advertising encourage you to have sex? **Sometimes**

Examples of media encouraging sex:
I don't think they really encourage you to have sex - I think they're exploiting our urges for sex by attaching their products to sex. Just ads for anything from fast food outlets (young couple on a beach holding each other) to furniture (women lying suggestively on a couch, stroking chairs and tables, etc). Obviously theres the more blatantly sexual products like condoms, and phone sex lines ads which come on later at night, but that's to be expected from advertising those specifically sexual things. Music videos don't encourage you to have sex, but they've really become hot. Things like the film clip for Eric Prydz's "Call on me", it's got chicks in 80's leotards. It's not encouraging sex, there's no flashing lights saying "HAVE SEX NOW OR DIE". Everyone I know can't keep their eyes away from that music clip, myself included. And there's lots of clips like it - watch most rap videos and there are women

shaking like nothing else. I think it's just supposed to keep your attention to the song (and I think it works).

Have you ever had phone sex, that is, sexually exciting yourself and someone else over the phone? **No**

Have you ever sent or received sexual text messages? **No**

Have you had a sexual experience in an internet chat room? **No**

Have you ever had a sexual experience with an adult? **No**

Have you ever had a sexual experience with more than one person at a time? **No**

Have you ever been pressured or forced into having sex? **No**

Do you think teenagers should be taught more or less about sex at school?
More

Do your parents have an influence on whether or not you have sex?
A lot

Does your religion have an influence on whether or not you have sex?
Not much

How important is it for you to have an emotional connection with your sexual partner? **Very important**

Is there anything else at all that you would like to say about sex or your own sexual experiences?

I feel that every time i enter a relationship with any girl, it's expected of me that i have to have sex. It's not a negotiable thing, I feel like once im in the relationship, she will expect it of me, and my mates will assume I am sexually active with the girl. As a virgin, this is sort of a worrying thing for me, because it always makes me hesitant - if its expected of me, will i be okay in bed? I don't really know much about the actual practical act of sex because i have never done it, so how am i going to tell her i'm a virgin? Will she reject me outright because of this? It's not like i don't want to have sex, i do, a lot – it's just that the thought of screwing it up or being turned down frightens me. The fact that those expectations can taint the basis of a relationship from the very start kind of angers me. I think there's more to a relationship than sex, and i wish people would stop plugging it as what i HAVE to do. I do want to have sex (I'm not frigid) - I just don't want it to be this obligatory thing, and i want to be able to discuss exactly what i feel about sex with my

girlfriend, like the things i list above. I get the feeling that I am a rare case, and also that it's going to be hard to find a girl who feels the same way.

Girl, 18, New South Wales, straight

What was the first thing you heard about sex?

that everyone seemed to be doing it, cant exactly remember the details of learning about it but our school was pretty big on sex education and gave us almost evry detail ... enough to scare us any way!

How old were you when you started masturbating? **Never**

Describe your sexual fantasies, even if they seem weird or boring or whatever.

these sorts of things are thought up randomly but nothing specific.

How old were you when you had your first sexual experience with someone else? **14**

What happened in this first sexual experience with another person?

before this there were things like playing kiss and catch and stuff when we were little but other than that it was just small things with the boyfriend i had at that particullar time, i wasnt afraid of this but i chose not to lose my virginity for a while

How old were you when you first had oral sex? **15**

Describe what happened during this oral sex, and how you felt about it.

i still cant remember this sort of thing, being blonde i have a goldfish memory

On average, how many times a week do you have oral sex? **Once a week**

How old were you when you first had sexual intercourse? **15**

Describe what happened during intercourse, and how you felt about it emotionally.

i was almost 16 but i was with a boyfriend that i felt comfortable with and there were no regrets as we were together for 2 years after that.

How old were you when you first had anal sex? **Never**

On average, how many times a week do you have intercourse?

Four times a week

Would you like to have more sex? **Not sure**

How do you think sex could be better for you?

> confidence, mainly with a new partner u cant do it to ur full 'potential'
> i guess u feel judged especially when u were with the same person for
> such a long time before this one.

When you have intercourse, do you use protection? **Never**

What kind of protection do you use? **Pill**

How often are your sexual experiences with someone of the same sex or
gender as you? **Never**

You think of yourself as ... **Straight**

How old were you when you first saw pornography or erotica? **13**

What kind of pornography have you seen?

> the first one i saw was a movie that my friends dad accidently left in the
> vcr. But i have seen magazines and photos, movies just about anything
> except live.

Does porn excite you sexually? **A bit**

Does porn give you ideas about how to have sex? **Never**

Do you think sexy films, music videos or advertising encourage you to have
sex? **Sometimes**

Examples of media encouraging sex: **movies with major sex scenes**

Have you ever had phone sex, that is, sexually exciting yourself and
someone else over the phone? **No**

Have you ever sent or received sexual text messages? **Yes**

Have you had a sexual experience in an internet chat room? **Yes**

If so, did you also meet up with that person in real life? **No**

Have you ever had a sexual experience with an adult? **No**

Have you ever had a sexual experience with more than one person at a
time? **No**

Have you ever been pressured or forced into having sex? **No**

How often do you have sex while using drugs or alcohol? **Sometimes**

Do drugs or alcohol make sex better or worse? **Neither**

Does what you learn in sex education classes at school help you with your
actual sexual experiences? **Not much**

Do you think teenagers should be taught more or less about sex at school?
Same as now

What do you think is the best age to start having sexual experiences?

16 ... for all of it, coz ur old enough to know what ur doing

Do your parents have an influence on whether or not you have sex?

Not at all

Does your religion have an influence on whether or not you have sex?

Not at all

How important is it for you to have an emotional connection with your sexual partner? **Very important**

Boy, 18, South Australia, straight

How old were you when you first heard about sex? **4**

What was the first thing you heard about sex?

That sperm goes into the egg and makes babys.

How old were you when you started masturbating? **8**

On average, how many times a week do you masturbate?

More than five times a week

How do you masturbate?

I lie on my back and use my hands. I feel bad about doing it the same way everytime because I heard it decreases your ability to become aroused in a variety of ways in later life - so I try to do it differently some times e.g standing up.

How does masturbating make you feel? **Good**

Describe your sexual fantasies, even if they seem weird or boring or whatever.

I sometimes think about going to a strip club and the stripper finding me so attractive that we go into a back room and have sex.

How old were you when you had your first sexual experience with someone else? **14**

What happened in this first sexual experience with another person?

I kissed a girl who i met at a party, we were both fairly drunk, then we went for a walk to keep kissing. While kissing I semi pulled down my pants and she rubbed my penis, but it wasn't fully erect. Later I briefly licked her vagina and then she sucked my penis, but it was still not fully erect and I was not even close to coming. I felt strange after we went

back to the party. I felt like I hadn't lived up to what ever sex was meant to be like and i guess I felt inadequate.

How old were you when you first had oral sex? **14**

Describe what happened during this oral sex, and how you felt about it.

When i recieved the oral sex it did not feel that good - as in it wasn't that sexually exciting for me. It also hurt a little bit when teeth were involved. Overall it was a bit of a let down.

On average, how many times a week do you have oral sex?

Less than once a week

If less frequent, how many times approximately has it occurred? **Twice**

How old were you when you first had sexual intercourse? **17**

Describe what happened during intercourse, and how you felt about it emotionally.

I put my penis inside and just started thrusting wildly, I fell out a couple of times to begin with. The girl was older so she just sort of laughed and gave me directions, like to go slower. There were unexpected things - like when entering the vagina its a different process, and the feeling of cumming inside. To be honest the main feeling after finishing was relief and happiness, it had been a source of anxiety and stress so to finally do it was very relaxing. Emotionally I felt positive towards the girl, even though we never sustained a relationship following it. I felt happy that we had spent that act together.

How old were you when you first had anal sex? **Never**

On average, how many times a week do you have intercourse?

Less than once a week

Would you like to have more sex? **Yes**

How do you think sex could be better for you?

If I was in a relationship with someone who i actually liked that would improve it. Particulary if sex was not preceeded by the act of trying to procure it! I would love to just have sex on its own terms, just because I want to with some one who likes me and i like.

When you have intercourse, do you use protection? **Never**

How often are your sexual experiences with someone of the same sex or gender as you? **Never**

You think of yourself as … **Straight**

How old were you when you first saw pornography or erotica? **8**

What kind of pornography have you seen?

> **internet sites, magazines, hard and soft core videos. And I have been to strippers.**

Does porn excite you sexually? **A lot**

Does porn give you ideas about how to have sex? **Sometimes**

Do you think sexy films, music videos or advertising encourage you to have sex? **Always**

Examples of media encouraging sex:

> **Teen movies like 'American Pie' where all the guys are on a quest to 'get laid' makes me think I should be having more sex.**

Have you ever had phone sex, that is, sexually exciting yourself and someone else over the phone? **No**

Have you ever sent or received sexual text messages? **Yes**

Have you had a sexual experience in an internet chat room? **No**

Have you ever had a sexual experience with an adult? **Yes**

If so, describe what happened and how you felt about it emotionally.

> **I took adult to mean someone over 18. The girl I was with was 20 and I did not feel different to if it had been someone who was my own age.**

Have you ever had a sexual experience with more than one person at a time? **No**

Have you ever been pressured or forced into having sex? **No**

How often do you have sex while using drugs or alcohol? **Most of the time**

Do drugs or alcohol make sex better or worse? **Worse**

Does what you learn in sex education classes at school help you with your actual sexual experiences? **Not at all**

Do you think teenagers should be taught more or less about sex at school? **More**

What do you think is the best age to start having sexual experiences?

> **I think it really is an individual decision - even though that sounds like a cop out, its actually based on my own experience. I felt like I had to have sex early, yet when i did finally do it I felt much better that I did it when i was more comfortable with it as a concept. So I think young people can have sex at any time in their teen years, i also think oral sex**

or other experiences are not very different to intercourse and the same applies to them.

Do your parents have an influence on whether or not you have sex?

Not at all

Does your religion have an influence on whether or not you have sex?

Not at all

How important is it for you to have an emotional connection with your sexual partner? **Somewhat important**

Is there anything else at all that you would like to say about sex or your own sexual experiences?

The first time I had sex i was in a 'semi-relationship' as in we knew each other fairly well, and had what could be described as a fling - a short but passionate period of sexual activity. It felt great! It really did, I enjoyed sex. So when I got home from interstate where I had the fling, in the first week back I was at a drunken gathering and ended up having sex with a girl I know fairly well but am not close with. We were both pretty drunk and the sex, in my eyes, just had none of the special quality of the other one. It was just sweaty and hot. The next day we didn't even kiss goodbye. I just felt so bad! Even though i wasn't in love with the first girl, we did have an emotional connection of some sort - I was just utterly struck by how bad I felt after the second girl. They should warn you in school how bad you feel after a one night stand! On a seperate note, I struggled with impotence from about 14 to 17. I even visited a psychologist and a GP who specialised in erectile dysfunction. It was basically based on intial encounters I had had where I failed to perform, and was then anxious about it in subsequent situations. It prevented me becoming sexually active earlier and was a huge burden as I had only heard about old men having trouble 'getting it up'. Eventually I got over it after persistant attempts with a girl until basically I was comfortable with my body and being sexual with someone.

Girl, 18, New South Wales, lesbian

How old were you when you first heard about sex? **12**

How old were you when you started masturbating? **Never**

Describe your sexual fantasies, even if they seem weird or boring or whatever.
truthfully don't have any!

How old were you when you had your first sexual experience with someone else? **13**

What happened in this first sexual experience with another person?
a kiss … we were going out and just hooked up one afternoon, only thing i can remember was me having to bend down cause i was taller than him!!

How old were you when you first had oral sex? **17**

Describe what happened during this oral sex, and how you felt about it.
was her birthday and she just went down on me … was different i guess … first time i gave it was quite intimidating cause i had no clue what i was doing!

On average, how many times a week do you have oral sex? **Once a week**

How old were you when you first had sexual intercourse? **Never**

Describe what happened during intercourse, and how you felt about it emotionally. **i haven't slept with a guy**

How old were you when you first had anal sex? **Never**

On average, how many times a week do you have intercourse?
Twice a week

Would you like to have more sex? **Not sure**

How do you think sex could be better for you?
kinda go through the same routine now … would be good to mix it up, even if it was having sex not in the bed!

When you have intercourse, do you use protection? **Never**

How often are your sexual experiences with someone of the same sex or gender as you? **Always**

You think of yourself as … **Lesbian**

If you're gay or lesbian, are you 'out'? **Yes**

If you're gay or lesbian and you came out, was it hard? **A bit hard**

Describe what happened when you came out and how you felt about it.
i came out to my close friends and it was all good, then i was seeing someone and they got really drunk and told everyone about it so thats how everyone else found out, which really pissed me off and made it

more difficult. i found people that knew me were fine with it because i'm still the same person and all that but i find it difficult telling new people in certain situations (ie at uni because its a very conservative campus) i still haven't come out to my parents but they've got to have an idea now ... i plan on telling them soon though

How old were you when you first saw pornography or erotica? **15**

What kind of pornography have you seen?

found my brothers magazine and some websites he'd visited ... went to sexpo this year

Does porn excite you sexually? **Not at all**

Does porn give you ideas about how to have sex? **Never**

Do you think sexy films, music videos or advertising encourage you to have sex? **Sometimes**

Examples of media encouraging sex:

a lot of music videos exploit females by portraying them as sexual objects just to appeal to their audience, which obviously will make people think of sex.

Have you ever had phone sex, that is, sexually exciting yourself and someone else over the phone? **No**

Have you ever sent or received sexual text messages? **No**

Have you had a sexual experience in an internet chat room? **No**

Have you ever had a sexual experience with an adult? **No**

Have you ever had a sexual experience with more than one person at a time? **No**

Have you ever been pressured or forced into having sex? **No**

How often do you have sex while using drugs or alcohol? **Sometimes**

Do drugs or alcohol make sex better or worse? **Neither**

Does what you learn in sex education classes at school help you with your actual sexual experiences? **Not much**

Do you think teenagers should be taught more or less about sex at school? **Same as now**

What do you think is the best age to start having sexual experiences?

it depends on the maturity of the person. it disturbs me to hear that kids in year 7 are happily going around and giving oral just because thats such an intimate sexual experience and it just seems like its a social

thing now and they really don't know much ... they're a bit too innocent for my liking! i think if people feel comfortable about what they're doing, and they are aware of it then age shouldn't dictate completely ...

Do your parents have an influence on whether or not you have sex?

Not much

Does your religion have an influence on whether or not you have sex?

Not at all

How important is it for you to have an emotional connection with your sexual partner? **Somewhat important**

Boy, 18, Victoria, other (curious)

How old were you when you first heard about sex? **8**

What was the first thing you heard about sex? **Im not sure.**

How old were you when you started masturbating? **14**

On average, how many times a week do you masturbate?

Four times a week

How do you masturbate?

Normal masturbation in my room while watching various porn movies. Sometimes changing hand positions and speed etc

How does masturbating make you feel? **Good**

Describe your sexual fantasies, even if they seem weird or boring or whatever.

I have fantasies about 2 different teachers at school. Both are young and attractive but the power thing is so hot. I want to have sex with a mother daughter combo and twins.

How old were you when you had your first sexual experience with someone else? **14**

What happened in this first sexual experience with another person?

I kissed my gf from school before rubbing her up on the outside.

How old were you when you first had oral sex? **15**

Describe what happened during this oral sex, and how you felt about it.

We were kissing and she slowly undid my pants and i was kindve hoping she would give me oral. She did and it was awesome. I ended up ejaculating into her mouth and she swollowed which was great.

On average, how many times a week do you have oral sex?

Less than once a week

If less frequent, how many times approximately has it occurred? **Ten times**

How old were you when you first had sexual intercourse? **15**

Describe what happened during intercourse, and how you felt about it emotionally.

It was kindve rushed and on the spot thing. It was my first time but she was a lot more experienced and i regret it now.

How old were you when you first had anal sex? **17**

How often does this happen? **Less than once a week**

Describe what happens during anal sex and how you feel about having it.

It was the best sex i had ever experienced. The feeling is so much better then normal intercourse.

On average, how many times a week do you have intercourse?

Less than once a week

Would you like to have more sex? **Yes**

How do you think sex could be better for you?

I would like to last longer in bed. Apart from that im fine.

When you have intercourse, do you use protection? **Sometimes**

What kind of protection do you use? **Condoms and the pill if the girl is on it**

How often are your sexual experiences with someone of the same sex or gender as you? **Never**

You think of yourself as … **Other: Curious**

If you're gay or lesbian, are you 'out'? **No**

How old were you when you first saw pornography or erotica? **14**

What kind of pornography have you seen?

Films, Photos, Magazines, Stories, Books, Strippers, internet photos and movies.

Does porn excite you sexually? **A lot**

Does porn give you ideas about how to have sex? **Sometimes**

Do you think sexy films, music videos or advertising encourage you to have sex? **Sometimes**

Examples of media encouraging sex:

Movies like American Pie push me to have as much sex as i can

Have you ever had phone sex, that is, sexually exciting yourself and someone else over the phone? **Yes**

Have you ever sent or received sexual text messages? **Yes**

Have you had a sexual experience in an internet chat room? **Yes**

If so, did you also meet up with that person in real life? **Yes**

Have you ever had a sexual experience with an adult? **No**

Have you ever had a sexual experience with more than one person at a time? **No**

Have you ever been pressured or forced into having sex? **No**

How often do you have sex while using drugs or alcohol? **Sometimes**

Do drugs or alcohol make sex better or worse? **Worse**

Does what you learn in sex education classes at school help you with your actual sexual experiences? **Not at all**

Do you think teenagers should be taught more or less about sex at school? **More**

What do you think is the best age to start having sexual experiences?
I think kids should be able to make decisions about when they should be having sex. Obviously it is a big decision to make so before it happens they should be sorting help from parents/school to make sure everything is fine

Do your parents have an influence on whether or not you have sex? **Not much**

Does your religion have an influence on whether or not you have sex? **Not at all**

How important is it for you to have an emotional connection with your sexual partner? **Not very imporant**

Is there anything else at all that you would like to say about sex or your own sexual experiences? **I wish i had more sex is pretty much all.**

Girl, 18, Queensland, lesbian

How old were you when you first heard about sex? **5**

What was the first thing you heard about sex?

That to produce a child, a man and a woman must have sex - it was a book called "where do i come from"

How old were you when you started masturbating? **12**

On average, how many times a week do you masturbate? **Five times a week**

How do you masturbate?

Until the age of 18, masturbation was just general rubbing of the pelvic area against a hand or the bed (clothed), more recently, it has involved clitoral stimulation, penetration of both holes, use of lubricant, watching of porn and the use of some dildos etc with the view to a broadening range of "toys"

How does masturbating make you feel? **Okay**

Describe your sexual fantasies, even if they seem weird or boring or whatever.

My fantasies are wide and varied, sometimes i will assume the role of a gay male, straight male, straight woman, but rarely a gay woman. they include bondage, latex, leather, whipping, gang-bangs, torture, fisting, role-play, use of food items, but as a rule are a variation of a situation seen on a tv show or in porn. generally the fantasies involve multiple participants with at least one under duress

How old were you when you had your first sexual experience with someone else? **16**

What happened in this first sexual experience with another person?

it was on a science camp and was a naive attempt by me to make a boy more comfortable around girls (knowing myself to be gay i thought this was a sacrifice i was willing to take). It was awkward, and involved him exploring my body (hands only), and him fingering me. only one kiss resulted at the end. it left me feeling used and dirty the next day, although he claims that he'll never forget the experience i gave him.

i saw him kissing a girl the next day and experienced envy

How old were you when you first had oral sex? **Never had oral sex**

How old were you when you first had sexual intercourse? **Never**

How old were you when you first had anal sex? **Never**

Would you like to have more sex? **Yes**

When you have intercourse, do you use protection? **Never**

How often are your sexual experiences with someone of the same sex or
     gender as you? **Always**

You think of yourself as … **Gay**

If you're gay or lesbian, are you 'out'? **Yes**

If you're gay or lesbian and you came out, was it hard? **Very hard**

How old were you when you first saw pornography or erotica? **18**

Does porn excite you sexually? **A lot**

Does porn give you ideas about how to have sex? **Sometimes**

Do you think sexy films, music videos or advertising encourage you to have
     sex? **Sometimes**

Have you ever had phone sex, that is, sexually exciting yourself and
     someone else over the phone? **No**

Have you ever sent or received sexual text messages? **No**

Have you had a sexual experience in an internet chat room? **No**

If so, did you also meet up with that person in real life? **No**

Have you ever had a sexual experience with an adult? **No**

Girl, 18, New South Wales, other

How old were you when you first heard about sex? **13**

What was the first thing you heard about sex?

> **what the term virginity meant … it ended up not being true!!!**

How old were you when you started masturbating? **6**

How do you masturbate?

> **When i was 6 i started using my Barbie's foot to masturbate … though
> I didn't know what the sensation was that I got from it. Then i moved
> onto using my pillow to get me off … I would kind of hump it like it was
> a person. Now I rarely masturbate coz I have a boyfriend who pleases
> me … though sometimes I do it to get him hot but it doesn't give me
> any pleasure.**

How does masturbating make you feel? **Not very good**

Describe your sexual fantasies, even if they seem weird or boring or whatever.

> **I don't really have any fantasies as such coz I play them all out. I love
> holding my bfs hands down when we are having sex so that he can't**

touch me. Sometimes I dream about having sex with another girl, though I don't know if I would ever actually do it coz I don't know if it would be weird.

How old were you when you had your first sexual experience with someone else? **8**

What happened in this first sexual experience with another person?

Me and my best friend (a girl) used to close the door when we were at each other's house and kind of dry hump each other n kiss n stuff. I guess at the time I felt kinda naughty coz we knew that what we were doing was bad but I guess I loved it at the same time. Now I just feel disgusted by it, I guess coz I still think it's really wrong and also coz I'm not friends with her anymore. I always wonder if she remembers what we did and I get embarrassed bout it. I have never told anyone about it either.

How old were you when you first had oral sex? **14**

Describe what happened during this oral sex, and how you felt about it.

I can't remember exactly the first time that it happened but I know that I used to love it when my bf did it to me.

On average, how many times a week do you have oral sex? **Once a week**

How old were you when you first had sexual intercourse? **14**

Describe what happened during intercourse, and how you felt about it emotionally.

I had been with my bf for about 6 months. This was the longest relationship I had ever had and I really felt like I loved him. It was his first time too and we both felt like we were with the right people. I had had a bit to drink, I think he had too but I'm not sure. We had been to a party and I was staying the night at his house. We didn't use a condom coz it was one of those embarrassing things but I don't think he blew. I remember I was really sore the next day and I started to bleed a bit so I was feeling sorry for myself the next day but I didn't regret it and never have to this day.

How old were you when you first had anal sex? **Never**

On average, how many times a week do you have intercourse?

Twice a week

Would you like to have more sex? **Yes**

How do you think sex could be better for you?

Me and my bf have the best sex ever ... the act itself couldn't get any better coz we talk about everything and experiment with new stuff only when the other person agrees. The only thing that could get better is that over the past few months I haven't wanted to have sex with him as much as I used to. We used to have it every second day pretty much but now we only have it once or twice a week (if he's lucky!!) I think it's coz I'm trying to deal with some issues in our relationship and I think I may have developed some hard feelings towards him because of these issues. So I'm rarely in the mood to have sex now and he's always complaining to me that I never let him touch me now. But once we get started I don't hold back ... I love it and it makes me feel closer to him afterwards.

When you have intercourse, do you use protection? **Yes**

What kind of protection do you use? **Condoms**

How often are your sexual experiences with someone of the same sex or gender as you? **Never**

You think of yourself as ...

Other: straight but I may have bisexual tendencies

If you're gay or lesbian, are you 'out'? **No**

How old were you when you first saw pornography or erotica? **16**

What kind of pornography have you seen?

I've seen parts of films on Foxtel and have seen some stuff in magazines and on those pop-ups that are on the internet. Overall I haven't really seen much but me and my bf are looking at hiring a few pornos.

Does porn excite you sexually? **A bit**

Does porn give you ideas about how to have sex? **Sometimes**

Do you think sexy films, music videos or advertising encourage you to have sex? **Sometimes**

Examples of media encouraging sex:

I can't really be specific but just ones that are really sexy ... if there are people doing stuff in a film or video sometimes it turns me on or if there are really sexy looking people with not many clothes in it gets me a bit excited.

Have you ever had phone sex, that is, sexually exciting yourself and
    someone else over the phone? **Yes**

Have you ever sent or received sexual text messages? **Yes**

Have you had a sexual experience in an internet chat room? **Yes**

If so, did you also meet up with that person in real life? **Yes**

Have you ever had a sexual experience with an adult? **Yes**

If so, describe what happened and how you felt about it emotionally.

> **Well not so much with an adult but I have had sex with a couple of guys**
> **who were 19 when I was 16 so if that counts then I have. I was going**
> **out with both of them so I was cool with it, though one of the guys was**
> **a bit of an asshole and I felt a bit used by him. There was also one night**
> **when he took me to his friends house and they got me drunk and his**
> **friend took me into the spare room and started fingering me and then he**
> **tried to have sex with me but I didn't want him to so he didn't. That time**
> **I really felt dirty and like I had been used.**

Have you ever had a sexual experience with more than one person at a
    time? **Yes**

If so, describe what happened and how you felt about it.

> **I was at a party and I got really drunk and with that got really horny.**
> **I pretty much had sex with the first guy that I saw that would have sex**
> **with me. He was younger than me and practically carried me into the**
> **garage where there was a mattress and we had sex while one of his**
> **friends watched and I gave him a hand job. While we were having sex**
> **some of my guy friends walked in and saw and before I knew it**
> **everyone at the party knew about it. One of my friends started calling**
> **me a slut so I started punching into him but coz he was so drunk as**
> **well he didn't feel it. Then I tried to run into the kitchen and grab a knife**
> **coz I told him I was going to kill him coz he had called me that and also**
> **coz I think I was so embarrassed by what had happened, but two guys**
> **stopped me. I then left the party and walked down the road with the**
> **guy I had given the hand job to and I told him I wanted to go and lie on**
> **the train tracks and die. I also tried to call my ex who I still loved and**
> **who I am back with today coz I wanted him to come and get me coz I**
> **felt so lousy. I am still embarrassed by what happened to this day and**
> **I regret it.**

Have you ever been pressured or forced into having sex? **Yes**

If so, describe what happened and how you felt about it emotionally.

I have already explained the bf that I was with who was an asshole and was just using me for sex and the time his friend tried to have sex with me but there have been other times too. There was this guy that I met over the internet and we talked for months on end and really liked each other though he lived in Qld and I live in Nsw. Eventually he bought a ticket and came down to see me and we went to one of my friends parties. I have to admit as soon as I saw him in person I was kinda freaked out so I tried to avoid him for the rest of the night. Eventually my friends mum kicked us out of the party coz she didn't like this guy and didn't trust him. So we were stuck outside in the freezing cold and I was half an hour's train trip from home plus there were no trains running at that time so I was stranded. We ended up walking down the road a bit and we had sex on the side of the road. The only reason I did it was coz he was pressuring me and I wanted to keep him happy. There was also another time where I wasn't actually verbally pressured into having sex but I felt like I was obliged to do it. There was this guy at work that I had thought was hot for ages but never paid much attention to coz he hadn't given me any signs. Then at the Xmas party he started flirting with me and I started flirting back. We texted each other for a while and we ended up meeting up one night and having sex in my car. He was a shit root but all he wanted to do was please me and he gave good oral so it was alright. We kept on texting each other but then I felt bad coz I already had a bf and had cheated on him and I think it was also a case of where I chased the guy and as soon as I got him I didn't want him anymore. So anyway I didn't really want to have sex with him again but he wanted to so I met up with him again just coz I felt like I couldn't say no to him and I also wanted to have a friendship with him coz we had never really had that before.

How often do you have sex while using drugs or alcohol? **Sometimes**

Do drugs or alcohol make sex better or worse? **Better**

Does what you learn in sex education classes at school help you with your actual sexual experiences? **Not much**

Do you think teenagers should be taught more or less about sex at school?
More

What do you think is the best age to start having sexual experiences?
Well I can't really say coz I was 14 when I first had sex and although when I look back on it now I think I was too young, I still don't regret it at all coz it was with a guy that I have been with for nearly 3 years in total now and I love him with all my heart. I was just lucky but that I didn't regret it later and that I never fell pregnant. Ideally it would be good to say that maybe 16 is when you should first have sex, but the world's not perfect is it!!!

Do your parents have an influence on whether or not you have sex?
Not at all

Does your religion have an influence on whether or not you have sex?
Not at all

How important is it for you to have an emotional connection with your sexual partner? **Very important**

Boy, 18, Western Australia, straight

How old were you when you first heard about sex? **10**
What was the first thing you heard about sex? **It's where we came from.**
How old were you when you started masturbating? **16**
On average, how many times a week do you masturbate?
Three times a week

How do you masturbate?
I grip my penis with my right hand and move it tightly up and down the shaft while I view pornography or fantasise. I do this until I ejaculate, then I clean up with tissues. 90 percent of the time this happens in my room, but 10 percent is in the family study.

How does masturbating make you feel? **Very good**

Describe your sexual fantasies, even if they seem weird or boring or whatever.
Involving my unreachable female friends or anybody I know really.

How old were you when you had your first sexual experience with someone else? **16**

What happened in this first sexual experience with another person?

I licked BBQ sauce off a girls breast, but it was a girl I wasnt interested in at the time so it was exciting to the level that I was doing something to a girl.

How old were you when you first had oral sex? **17**

Describe what happened during this oral sex, and how you felt about it.

my girlfriend was over, and we were naked in bed together and then she proceeded to kiss me down and down until eventually she was sucking and licking and kissing my penis. She did that for a while ... but I found it too hard to ejacualte this way so we stopped. Then I did it to her ... basically I stayed on her clitorous, drawing the alphabet and running my tongue up and down ... I did this for a while then I gave up as well. It was a good experience overall.

On average, how many times a week do you have oral sex? **Once a week**

How old were you when you first had sexual intercourse? **17**

Describe what happened during intercourse, and how you felt about it emotionally.

It took heaps of attempts for me to actually get it in the right area, we laughed about it as I made more and more mistakes, but we were both quite mature so I didnt let it hurt my pride or anything like that. After a while I got it in, she gave a big gasp and winced ... I got a rythum going, it lasted about 3 minutes then I quickly pulled out and about 2 seconds later I ejaculated. Later that day I felt really happy and couldnt get the smile off my face. I felt really proud.

How old were you when you first had anal sex? **17**

How often does this happen? **Less than once a week**

Describe what happens during anal sex and how you feel about having it.

I go in really gently, I let her guide me most of the way in, and then I start going in and out gently, eventually building up rythum and speed. We do it lying sideways, with her back facing me. I feel awkward having it with her, but sometime it's more fun for me, and she doesn't seem to mind, from what I can tell.

On average, how many times a week do you have intercourse?

Three times a week

Would you like to have more sex? **Not sure**

How do you think sex could be better for you?

I consider it a good way to *release* stress and relax with someone you love. It burns heaps of calories and it helps me feel like a better person after I make someone else feel good.

When you have intercourse, do you use protection? **Sometimes**

What kind of protection do you use?

Recently my partner went on the pill and I stopped using condoms (simply because we couldnt be bothered) but before that, we always used condoms and were very careful.

How often are your sexual experiences with someone of the same sex or gender as you? **Never**

You think of yourself as … **Straight**

How old were you when you first saw pornography or erotica? **15**

Does porn excite you sexually? **A bit**

Does porn give you ideas about how to have sex? **Never**

Do you think sexy films, music videos or advertising encourage you to have sex? **Sometimes**

Examples of media encouraging sex:

Pussycat Dolls - Don't Cha or whatever it is … Lots of sexually-oriented scenes. Austin Powers While showing sex in a humourous light, lots of small kids watch these films and it lets them think it is cool and something you should do to become better.

Have you ever had phone sex, that is, sexually exciting yourself and someone else over the phone? **No**

Have you ever sent or received sexual text messages? **No**

Have you had a sexual experience in an internet chat room? **Yes**

If so, did you also meet up with that person in real life? **No**

Have you ever had a sexual experience with an adult? **No**

Have you ever had a sexual experience with more than one person at a time? **No**

Have you ever been pressured or forced into having sex? **No**

How often do you have sex while using drugs or alcohol? **Never**

Do drugs or alcohol make sex better or worse? **Neither**

Does what you learn in sex education classes at school help you with your actual sexual experiences? **A bit**

Do you think teenagers should be taught more or less about sex at school?
Same as now

What do you think is the best age to start having sexual experiences?
I believe everyone is different and should start when they believe they are ready, not when everyone else their age is doing it. However, the best age to START THINKING about having sex would probably be around 16, cause by then you should be aware of the main principals and things you should know about sex and know the consequences of your actions.

Do your parents have an influence on whether or not you have sex? **A lot**

Does your religion have an influence on whether or not you have sex?
Not at all

How important is it for you to have an emotional connection with your sexual partner? **Somewhat important**

Is there anything else at all that you would like to say about sex or your own sexual experiences?
Sex is a part of growing up that most will have to face at some point in their young lives. It doesnt matter if your 16 or 25, its still the same thing happening with regards to semen, orgasms and everything in both cases and as long as teenagers can understand the realities and consequences of their actions, and know what they have to do to be safe and respectful, they can have sex at a young age and turn out just FINE. I'm living proof of that.

Girl, 18, New South Wales, lesbian

How old were you when you first heard about sex? **7**

What was the first thing you heard about sex?
That it was the ultimate way of showing love to someone ...

How old were you when you started masturbating? **10**

On average, how many times a week do you masturbate?
Four times a week

How does masturbating make you feel? **Very good**

Describe your sexual fantasies, even if they seem weird or boring or whatever.

Varies from use of toys to risky situations to BD/SM, depending on my moods.

How old were you when you had your first sexual experience with someone else? **7**

What happened in this first sexual experience with another person?

Unwilling intercourse. I was terrified and distraught.

How old were you when you first had oral sex? **12**

Describe what happened during this oral sex, and how you felt about it.

I performed fellatio on a then-boyfriend, didn't like it but was willing to for the sake of experience.

On average, how many times a week do you have oral sex? **Twice a week**

How old were you when you first had sexual intercourse? **7**

How old were you when you first had anal sex? **14**

How often does this happen? **Less than once a week**

Describe what happens during anal sex and how you feel about having it.

It was willingly experimenting with a then-girlfriend, but it's not my thing.

On average, how many times a week do you have intercourse?

Less than once a week

Would you like to have more sex? **Yes**

How do you think sex could be better for you?

Being able to trust my lover implicitly, as well as being in a loving relationship.

When you have intercourse, do you use protection? **Never**

How often are your sexual experiences with someone of the same sex or gender as you? **Always**

You think of yourself as … **Gay**

If you're gay or lesbian, are you 'out'? **Yes**

If you're gay or lesbian and you came out, was it hard? **A bit hard**

Describe what happened when you came out and how you felt about it.

I felt relieved to have the people that I cared about accept me, developed deeper bonds with some friends and learned others were not really true friends.

How old were you when you first saw pornography or erotica? **9**

What kind of pornography have you seen?
Magazines, pictures, videos & literature from different sources.
Does porn excite you sexually? **A bit**
Does porn give you ideas about how to have sex? **Sometimes**
Do you think sexy films, music videos or advertising encourage you to have sex? **Always**
Have you ever had phone sex, that is, sexually exciting yourself and someone else over the phone? **Yes**
Have you ever sent or received sexual text messages? **Yes**
Have you had a sexual experience in an internet chat room? **Yes**
If so, did you also meet up with that person in real life? **Yes**
Have you ever had a sexual experience with an adult? **Yes**
If so, describe what happened and how you felt about it emotionally.
They were supposedly a trusted relation and I wasn't willing to participate but was convinced to ...
Have you ever had a sexual experience with more than one person at a time? **Yes**
If so, describe what happened and how you felt about it.
It's happened a few times, all willingly, with people I've been close to. Enjoyed it thoroughly.
Have you ever been pressured or forced into having sex? **Yes**
If so, describe what happened and how you felt about it emotionally.
A few times completely unwillingly physically forced.
How often do you have sex while using drugs or alcohol? **Sometimes**
Do drugs or alcohol make sex better or worse? **Better**
Does what you learn in sex education classes at school help you with your actual sexual experiences? **Not at all**
Do you think teenagers should be taught more or less about sex at school?
More
What do you think is the best age to start having sexual experiences?
I don't think there is a set age or kind of sex. It should happen when all persons involved are emotionally ready and willing.
Do your parents have an influence on whether or not you have sex?
Not at all

Does your religion have an influence on whether or not you have sex?

Not at all

How important is it for you to have an emotional connection with your sexual partner? **Somewhat important**

Boy, 18, Western Australia, straight

How old were you when you first heard about sex? **9**

How old were you when you started masturbating? **11**

On average, how many times a week do you masturbate? **Five times a week**

How do you masturbate?

with hand, no lube, in shower, to porn on computer

How does masturbating make you feel? **Very good**

Describe your sexual fantasies, even if they seem weird or boring or whatever.

anal, facial cumshot, having sex in public places

How old were you when you had your first sexual experience with someone else? **9**

What happened in this first sexual experience with another person?

kissed girl, did something similar to dry-sex in underwear. was fun

How old were you when you first had oral sex? **13**

On average, how many times a week do you have oral sex?

Less than once a week

If less frequent, how many times approximately has it occurred?

More than twenty

How old were you when you first had sexual intercourse? **15**

Describe what happened during intercourse, and how you felt about it emotionally.

didn't last quite 5 minutes, was embarrased, but didn't show that embarrasment to girl

How old were you when you first had anal sex? **17**

How often does this happen? **Less than once a week**

Describe what happens during anal sex and how you feel about having it.

feel in control of girl

On average, how many times a week do you have intercourse?
   More than five times a week

Would you like to have more sex? **Not sure**

When you have intercourse, do you use protection? **Never**

What kind of protection do you use? **girlfriend uses birthcontrol pill**

How often are your sexual experiences with someone of the same sex or
   gender as you? **Never**

You think of yourself as … **Straight**

How old were you when you first saw pornography or erotica? **10**

What kind of pornography have you seen?
   magazines, internet websites, films, stories, photos

Does porn excite you sexually? **A lot**

Does porn give you ideas about how to have sex? **Sometimes**

Do you think sexy films, music videos or advertising encourage you to have
   sex? **Sometimes**

Have you ever had phone sex, that is, sexually exciting yourself and
   someone else over the phone? **No**

Have you ever sent or received sexual text messages? **Yes**

Have you had a sexual experience in an internet chat room? **No**

Have you ever had a sexual experience with an adult? **No**

Have you ever had a sexual experience with more than one person at a
   time? **No**

Have you ever been pressured or forced into having sex? **No**

How often do you have sex while using drugs or alcohol? **Sometimes**

Do drugs or alcohol make sex better or worse? **Worse**

Does what you learn in sex education classes at school help you with your
   actual sexual experiences? **Not much**

Do you think teenagers should be taught more or less about sex at school?
   More

What do you think is the best age to start having sexual experiences?
   15-17 for sexual intercourse & anal, 14 for oral

Do your parents have an influence on whether or not you have sex?
   Not at all

Does your religion have an influence on whether or not you have sex?
   Not at all

How important is it for you to have an emotional connection with your sexual partner? **Somewhat important**

Boy, 18, New South Wales, straight

How old were you when you first heard about sex? **5**

What was the first thing you heard about sex?

that sex was totally normal and a good thing

How old were you when you started masturbating? **12**

On average, how many times a week do you masturbate?

Three times a week

How do you masturbate?

mostly in the shower. sometimes in bed. i have only used lubricants a few times

How does masturbating make you feel? **Very good**

Describe your sexual fantasies, even if they seem weird or boring or whatever.

... me having sex with hot girls ... or two hot girls having sex with each other

How old were you when you had your first sexual experience with someone else? **16**

What happened in this first sexual experience with another person?

it was just a kiss ... i felt pretty good

How old were you when you first had oral sex? **16**

Describe what happened during this oral sex, and how you felt about it.

a girl invited me to her house and we had a couple of drinks then we went to her room and we started kissing ... i fingered her then she gave me a blow job.

On average, how many times a week do you have oral sex?

Less than once a week

If less frequent, how many times approximately has it occurred? **Five times**

How old were you when you first had sexual intercourse? **Never**

How old were you when you first had anal sex? **Never**

Would you like to have more sex? **Yes**

How do you think sex could be better for you?

i dont know ... i've never had sex

You think of yourself as ... **Straight**

How old were you when you first saw pornography or erotica? **12**

What kind of pornography have you seen?

films, photos, magazines, stories, internet, tv shows

Does porn excite you sexually? **A lot**

Does porn give you ideas about how to have sex? **Sometimes**

Do you think sexy films, music videos or advertising encourage you to have sex? **Sometimes**

Examples of media encouraging sex:

like film clips with sexy girls wearing not much clothing. they just get boys turned on.

Have you ever had phone sex, that is, sexually exciting yourself and someone else over the phone? **Yes**

Have you ever sent or received sexual text messages? **Yes**

Have you had a sexual experience in an internet chat room? **No**

Have you ever had a sexual experience with an adult? **No**

Have you ever had a sexual experience with more than one person at a time? **Yes**

If so, describe what happened and how you felt about it.

i was at the school dance and i was kissing 2 girls at the same time ... they were both hot so i was pretty happy with it. it made me feel good about myself.

Have you ever been pressured or forced into having sex? **No**

How often do you have sex while using drugs or alcohol? **Never**

Do you think teenagers should be taught more or less about sex at school? **More**

What do you think is the best age to start having sexual experiences?

i think kissing is fine when people get into high school, so 12 or 13 ... they should wait till they are 15 till they get fingered or get a wristy ... wen they are 16 it is ok to give and recieve oral sex, and have sex.

Do your parents have an influence on whether or not you have sex?

Not at all

Does your religion have an influence on whether or not you have sex?

Not at all

How important is it for you to have an emotional connection with your sexual

partner? **Somewhat important**

Girl, 18, Queensland, lesbian

How old were you when you first heard about sex? **11**

What was the first thing you heard about sex?

that a guy inserts his part into the female part and good things happen

How old were you when you started masturbating? **15**

On average, how many times a week do you masturbate?

More than five times a week

How do you masturbate?

In my bed, sometimes with toys with my hand and fingers going up into myself and fiddling with my diddle until I orgasm.

How does masturbating make you feel? **Very good**

Describe your sexual fantasies, even if they seem weird or boring or whatever.

Doing it in public with a hot teacher or some mature woman. At a bar or club or on the beach.

How old were you when you had your first sexual experience with someone

else? **15**

What happened in this first sexual experience with another person?

I got with this lady who was very much older than I was and she told me to go down on her and I didnt have a clue what she was talking about but she taught me the correct method and the night became a lot more interesting. Then she went down on me. I felt weird I hadnt come to accept my sexuality I felt dirty and I didnt want to do it again. But ... I did and I do.

How old were you when you first had oral sex? **15**

Describe what happened during this oral sex, and how you felt about it.

After I went down on her she went down on me. Feeling was kind of same as above

On average, how many times a week do you have oral sex?

More than five times a week

How old were you when you first had sexual intercourse? **Never**

How old were you when you first had anal sex? **Never**

Would you like to have more sex? **Yes**

How do you think sex could be better for you?

I think it could be better if the ladies I choose understood me more. If they knew that although I am young I'm not stupid and I know my way around their bodies. If they knew that i wasnt just there for the bang then it could be a more relaxed situation. I mean they get nervous around an 18 year old.

When you have intercourse, do you use protection? **Never**

What kind of protection do you use? **I dont have sex with guys**

How often are your sexual experiences with someone of the same sex or gender as you? **Always**

You think of yourself as … **Lesbian**

If you're gay or lesbian, are you 'out'? **Yes**

If you're gay or lesbian and you came out, was it hard? **Very hard**

Describe what happened when you came out and how you felt about it.

I felt like the lowest piece of dirt on the planet. It was just swept under the carpet and then excuses like your too young to know were pulled out. I finally accepted me and my family couldnt. I felt like jumping back into the closet and bolt it shut.

How old were you when you first saw pornography or erotica? **12**

What kind of pornography have you seen? **everything possible**

Does porn excite you sexually? **A bit**

Does porn give you ideas about how to have sex? **Sometimes**

Do you think sexy films, music videos or advertising encourage you to have sex? **Sometimes**

Examples of media encouraging sex:

films hell yeah which film doesnt encourage sex, Rap videos, perfume ads all, some clothing ads designer wear, and even food ads yuk. Cant really be more specific.

Have you ever had phone sex, that is, sexually exciting yourself and someone else over the phone? **Yes**

Have you ever sent or received sexual text messages? **Yes**

Have you had a sexual experience in an internet chat room? **Yes**

If so, did you also meet up with that person in real life? **Yes**

Have you ever had a sexual experience with an adult? **Yes**

If so, describe what happened and how you felt about it emotionally.

> **Um i felt small and insignificant. She was so sophisticated and she knew what she was doing. I didn't want to do it but she kind of persuaded me to like it and now I do, it grew on me.**

Have you ever had a sexual experience with more than one person at a time? **Yes**

If so, describe what happened and how you felt about it.

> **ah I didnt like it too much, too much competition. I walked out.**

Have you ever been pressured or forced into having sex? **Yes**

If so, describe what happened and how you felt about it emotionally.

> **My first time I got with a lady so much older than me, I didnt want to do it but I felt obligated. I did it, felt sick, angry, helpless but I got over it.**

How often do you have sex while using drugs or alcohol? **Most of the time**

Do drugs or alcohol make sex better or worse? **Neither**

Does what you learn in sex education classes at school help you with your actual sexual experiences? **A bit**

Do you think teenagers should be taught more or less about sex at school? **More**

What do you think is the best age to start having sexual experiences?

> **er 17-18 for girls why? because girls are so much more mature at 17-18 at 16 its all about sex come on what do they know. Any type of sex is good at 17-18 you know a lot more about yourself and other people. I mean whats the hurry you have years to do it.**

Do your parents have an influence on whether or not you have sex? **Not at all**

Does your religion have an influence on whether or not you have sex? **Not at all**

How important is it for you to have an emotional connection with your sexual partner? **Very important**

Is there anything else at all that you would like to say about sex or your own sexual experiences?

Sex is fun sometimes its made out to be the enemy not at all its the people doing it. Sex is not evil, people are. some people chose to abuse what they have. sex cant be made out to be some satanic ritual it just misleads people who are easily mislead. You have sex if you both consent if you dont thats rape not sex. Sex isnt evil people are. its not if you have sex you will get raped thats bullshit it can happen to anyone. You can have sex and not get pregnant everyone knows this yet when it comes time to do it that fact slips away with some teens. And whats with the all the limits on Homosexual relations come on 18 for a girl to have sex with a girl and same with the guys???? why is everyone against people who like the same sex ... If anything homsexuals are more educated on the matter than a sex worker. We arent the enemy here we are everyday people we could be the office clown or the coffee machine whiz. what happens in the bedroom doesnt represent us as a person we arent sick or perverted. You get a hand full that are but thats from both gay and lesbian and the straight community. We dont all have sex with children and we wont turn you teenage daughter if she doesnt want it goddamit, we are not vampires.

Girl, 18, Western Australia, straight

How old were you when you first heard about sex? **8**
What was the first thing you heard about sex?

that it can lead to making babies. I cant say i really remember it
How old were you when you started masturbating? **Never**
Describe your sexual fantasies, even if they seem weird or boring or whatever.

just having a night where everything that happened was amazing and that i can look back and go oh yeah that was the best time i had sex
How old were you when you had your first sexual experience with someone else? **16**

What happened in this first sexual experience with another person?

i was really drunk and i kissed this old friend who used to be my boyfriend in yr 7 and we catched up after not [seeing] each other for about 3 years and we kissed and that [led] on to other things. I wasnt too happy about what happened that night cos it was my first real kiss and i was drunk. So all in all it wasnt a good experience.

How old were you when you first had oral sex? **16**

Describe what happened during this oral sex, and how you felt about it.

this happened when i had my first kiss the night that i was very drunk. I just ended up giving him oral but i cant remember why because i had no idea how to do it. I wasnt pressured to do it, i just did it which was really weird and which im not really happy about.

On average, how many times a week do you have oral sex? **Once a week**

How old were you when you first had sexual intercourse? **16**

Describe what happened during intercourse, and how you felt about it emotionally.

i was with my boyfriend for about a month when we decided to do it. we really were into each other which was good. but it was too much like okay lets do it now sort of situation. it really hurt but he looked after me. We both now wish it happened differently but we are still together so im alright with how it happened.

How old were you when you first had anal sex? **18**

How often does this happen? **Less than once a week**

Describe what happens during anal sex and how you feel about having it.

it really hurt the first time but he really looks after me when we do it. After a while i get used to it and start to enjoy it. But i do like doing it because it makes him happy and yeah i like doing it because its different but i wouldn't do it all the time

On average, how many times a week do you have intercourse?

Twice a week

Would you like to have more sex? **No**

How do you think sex could be better for you?

if he could go for longer. We decided a couple of weeks ago that if you take longer with the foreplay this being kissing as well, sex becomes so much better so yeah now its good. and it always so much better if you

have your cuddling time after wards cos theres nothing worse then just having to leave after sex

When you have intercourse, do you use protection? **Sometimes**

What kind of protection do you use?

condom and pulling out before he comes

How often are your sexual experiences with someone of the same sex or gender as you? **Never**

You think of yourself as … **Straight**

How old were you when you first saw pornography or erotica? **15**

What kind of pornography have you seen?

Films, magazines, internet, photos, and live shows

Does porn excite you sexually? **A bit**

Does porn give you ideas about how to have sex? **Sometimes**

Do you think sexy films, music videos or advertising encourage you to have sex? **Sometimes**

Have you ever had phone sex, that is, sexually exciting yourself and someone else over the phone? **No**

Have you ever sent or received sexual text messages? **Yes**

Have you had a sexual experience in an internet chat room? **Yes**

If so, did you also meet up with that person in real life? **No**

Have you ever had a sexual experience with an adult? **No**

Have you ever had a sexual experience with more than one person at a time? **No**

Have you ever been pressured or forced into having sex? **No**

How often do you have sex while using drugs or alcohol? **Sometimes**

Do drugs or alcohol make sex better or worse? **Better**

Does what you learn in sex education classes at school help you with your actual sexual experiences? **Not at all**

Do you think teenagers should be taught more or less about sex at school? **Same as now**

What do you think is the best age to start having sexual experiences?

first kiss should be from 10 onwards. Oral should come at the same time as intercourse which should be at about the age of 16. just because you are a little bit more mature at that age and you know what you are getting yourself into.

Do your parents have an influence on whether or not you have sex? **A bit**

Does your religion have an influence on whether or not you have sex?
Not much

How important is it for you to have an emotional connection with your sexual
partner? **Very important**

Boy, 18, South Australia, straight

How old were you when you first heard about sex? **9**

What was the first thing you heard about sex?
the penis has to insert the vigana

How old were you when you started masturbating? **13**

On average, how many times a week do you masturbate? **Once a week**

How do you masturbate?
in the shower, standin up, and i use conditioner

How does masturbating make you feel? **Okay**

Describe your sexual fantasies, even if they seem weird or boring or whatever.
**Tits i can't get enough of them they need to be shaking in my face ...
hahaha and they have to at least be a C cup, i don't mind smaller but
the bigger the better**

How old were you when you had your first sexual experience with someone
else? **5**

What happened in this first sexual experience with another person?
a kiss ... i dunno i think i got a boner afterwards

How old were you when you first had oral sex? **16**

Describe what happened during this oral sex, and how you felt about it.
i went down on a chick and it was alright

On average, how many times a week do you have oral sex?
Less than once a week

If less frequent, how many times approximately has it occurred?
More than twenty

How old were you when you first had sexual intercourse? **15**

Describe what happened during intercourse, and how you felt about it emotionally.

not much really happened she just sat on my cock and did her thing it was pretty damn good

How old were you when you first had anal sex? **Never**

Describe what happens during anal sex and how you feel about having it.

not really interested, might give it a go on a long term relationship

On average, how many times a week do you have intercourse?

Less than once a week

Would you like to have more sex? **Not sure**

How do you think sex could be better for you?

maybe if i was smaller in height, cos it isn't easy to give doggy-style, i kinda need to sqwat which isn't comfortable

When you have intercourse, do you use protection? **Yes**

What kind of protection do you use?

rubber band and glad wrap ... hahaha nah just kidding Large & ribbed

How often are your sexual experiences with someone of the same sex or gender as you? **Never**

You think of yourself as ... **Straight**

How old were you when you first saw pornography or erotica? **13**

What kind of pornography have you seen? **movies, mags and the net**

Does porn excite you sexually? **A lot**

Does porn give you ideas about how to have sex? **Always**

Do you think sexy films, music videos or advertising encourage you to have sex? **Sometimes**

Have you ever had phone sex, that is, sexually exciting yourself and someone else over the phone? **Yes**

Have you ever sent or received sexual text messages? **Yes**

Have you had a sexual experience in an internet chat room? **No**

Have you ever had a sexual experience with an adult? **Yes**

If so, describe what happened and how you felt about it emotionally.

one thing leads to another, it was pretty scary to start off with cos she was older then i just relaxed and did my thing

Have you ever had a sexual experience with more than one person at a time? **Yes**

If so, describe what happened and how you felt about it.

i was with three girls which was kinda lucky and i hooked up with all of them and fingered all of them

Have you ever been pressured or forced into having sex? **Yes**

If so, describe what happened and how you felt about it emotionally.

my ex-girlfriend it was a first cos usually i'm the horny one but this time she was and she wasn't takin no for an answer which was all good and i got the job done

How often do you have sex while using drugs or alcohol? **Sometimes**

Do drugs or alcohol make sex better or worse? **Neither**

Does what you learn in sex education classes at school help you with your actual sexual experiences? **A bit**

Do you think teenagers should be taught more or less about sex at school? **Same as now**

What do you think is the best age to start having sexual experiences? **if you have morals follow them and tryin to make it someone that is worthwhile**

Do your parents have an influence on whether or not you have sex? **Not at all**

Does your religion have an influence on whether or not you have sex? **Not at all**

How important is it for you to have an emotional connection with your sexual partner? **Somewhat important**

Is there anything else at all that you would like to say about sex or your own sexual experiences?

I'd shag all day if a had the chance but it's always better to get it every now and then, you appreciate it more

Girl, 18, New South Wales, lesbian

How old were you when you first heard about sex? **10**

What was the first thing you heard about sex? **that it produces babies**

How old were you when you started masturbating? **14**

On average, how many times a week do you masturbate?

Three times a week

How do you masturbate?

Using hands only. Purely clitoris no penetration. At home when noone is around. Usually in the shower.

How does masturbating make you feel? **Okay**

Describe your sexual fantasies, even if they seem weird or boring or whatever.

Not so much sex as just being affectionate with someone. I imagine what they'd say to me and how they would seduce me. It can be all different places, clubs, houses, on a train, in my car.

How old were you when you had your first sexual experience with someone else? **13**

What happened in this first sexual experience with another person?

I was pashed by a guy. I felt awkward because I'm gay, and I already knew that but hadn't admitted it to myself. We were set up by some mates so I felt like I had to prove something because I'd been copping a lot [of] flack for looking 'butch', I wanted to show them I wasn't.

How old were you when you first had oral sex? **16**

Describe what happened during this oral sex, and how you felt about it.

It was with a girl. I went down on her and she was very uncomfortable because it was her first time too. It felt foreign but not unpleasant. I was completely lost and worried I wasn't doing the right thing but kept going anyway.

On average, how many times a week do you have oral sex?

Less than once a week

If less frequent, how many times approximately has it occurred?

More than twenty

How old were you when you first had sexual intercourse? **17**

Describe what happened during intercourse, and how you felt about it emotionally.

It wasn't a penis, it was a strap on so I don't know if that counts. Emotionally it was right because it was a long term relationship. I just felt weird because it was a piece of rubber, it takes away a certain level of intimacy.

How old were you when you first had anal sex? **Never**

On average, how many times a week do you have intercourse?

Less than once a week

Would you like to have more sex? **Not sure**

How do you think sex could be better for you?

Sex could have more emotional attachment. I've had one night stands, they satisfy you physically but I feel used and dirty for a few days afterwards.

When you have intercourse, do you use protection? **Sometimes**

What kind of protection do you use? **dams, condoms on toys**

How often are your sexual experiences with someone of the same sex or gender as you? **Always**

You think of yourself as … **Lesbian**

If you're gay or lesbian, are you 'out'? **Yes**

If you're gay or lesbian and you came out, was it hard? **A bit hard**

Describe what happened when you came out and how you felt about it.

I came out over a long time. At school everyone already called me gay so I just agreed with them and it was fine. My parents were harder. They are still a bit worried but they trust I can handle myself. I felt happier when my friends knew but my parents I felt worse because now they wonder about every girl I know and constantly ask if they are gay or not. I'm still being lectured about how 'unsavoury' the gay world can be, it makes me feel guilty that I may have made the wrong choice but its not a choice.

How old were you when you first saw pornography or erotica? **12**

What kind of pornography have you seen?

magazines (although I work in a newsagency so I probably never would have), photos, films, stories

Does porn excite you sexually? **A bit**

Does porn give you ideas about how to have sex? **Sometimes**

Do you think sexy films, music videos or advertising encourage you to have sex? **Always**

Examples of media encouraging sex:

American Pie, any sexually targetted advertising particularly deodorant or cosmetics

Have you ever had phone sex, that is, sexually exciting yourself and someone else over the phone? **No**

Have you ever sent or received sexual text messages? **No**

Have you had a sexual experience in an internet chat room? **No**

Have you ever had a sexual experience with an adult? **No**

Have you ever had a sexual experience with more than one person at a time? **No**

Have you ever been pressured or forced into having sex? **Yes**

If so, describe what happened and how you felt about it emotionally.

I was raped. I fell pregnant and had an abortion. I will never be the same. Psychologists try to justify my lesbianism due to this experience but I was gay before it happened. I dont trust drinking alcohol around anyone I don't know. I'm wary of being by myself. I felt horrible, but the abortion was far worse.

How often do you have sex while using drugs or alcohol? **Sometimes**

Do drugs or alcohol make sex better or worse? **Neither**

Does what you learn in sex education classes at school help you with your actual sexual experiences? **Not at all**

Do you think teenagers should be taught more or less about sex at school? **More**

What do you think is the best age to start having sexual experiences?

I think the maturity of people can not be judged by their age. If people are mature enough they can. I've met 16 year olds who are very self aware and I'd say go for it but I also know 19 year olds who are still getting drunk at parties and doing it because they are dared to. All in all I think I was a bit young, I was lost and confused by the situation.

Do your parents have an influence on whether or not you have sex? **Not at all**

Does your religion have an influence on whether or not you have sex? **Not at all**

How important is it for you to have an emotional connection with your sexual partner? **Somewhat important**

Is there anything else at all that you would like to say about sex or your own
sexual experiences?

**I think sex education at school should talk about homosexuality more.
I was clueless and I don't think the word was even mentioned. I went to
a normal public school, not a catholic school or anything. There are 180
people in my grade (I've just finished year 12). We advertised and held a
coming out of sexual preferences group purely so we could all have
support and there were 19 gay/lesbian/bisexual kids there. Thats 12%,
at 12% of the grade population we have some right to education too.**

Boy, 18, South Australia, straight

How old were you when you first heard about sex? **7**
What was the first thing you heard about sex? **How sex is done.**
How old were you when you started masturbating? **11**
On average, how many times a week do you masturbate?
   More than five times a week
How do you masturbate?
   Usually My bedroom. Used to use a lubricant. Usually to porn.
How does masturbating make you feel? **Good**
Describe your sexual fantasies, even if they seem weird or boring or whatever.
   **Being able to have sex with almost any girl i chose, whenever, wherever!
   I think about lots of different positions and places basically.**
How old were you when you had your first sexual experience with someone
   else? **16**
What happened in this first sexual experience with another person?
   **I had oral sex with a girl on the beach and then tried to have sex but we
   didnt have any lube!**
How old were you when you first had oral sex? **16**
Describe what happened during this oral sex, and how you felt about it.
   **I had stage fright, i didnt end up having an orgasm- but it felt really
   good anyway.**
On average, how many times a week do you have oral sex?
   Less than once a week

If less frequent, how many times approximately has it occurred? **Five times**

How old were you when you first had sexual intercourse? **16**

Describe what happened during intercourse, and how you felt about it emotionally.

It felt really good. It felt just like i expected it and better. It didnt really hit me until after i did it that i lost my virginity, and i sorta felt proud but didnt really care that much.

How old were you when you first had anal sex? **Never**

On average, how many times a week do you have intercourse?

Less than once a week

Would you like to have more sex? **Yes**

How do you think sex could be better for you?

Sex would be awesome if i had a bigger penis, even though im satisfied with mine at the moment. You watch the pornos and they do it with so much ease because they have a huge one!! I think if i found the right girl it would be a better feeling as well, instead of just doing it for the hell of it.

When you have intercourse, do you use protection? **Yes**

How often are your sexual experiences with someone of the same sex or gender as you? **Never**

You think of yourself as … **Straight**

How old were you when you first saw pornography or erotica? **11**

What kind of pornography have you seen?

films, photos, magazines, internet sites

Does porn excite you sexually? **A lot**

Does porn give you ideas about how to have sex? **Sometimes**

Do you think sexy films, music videos or advertising encourage you to have sex? **Sometimes**

Have you ever had phone sex, that is, sexually exciting yourself and someone else over the phone? **Yes**

Have you ever sent or received sexual text messages? **No**

Have you had a sexual experience in an internet chat room? **Yes**

If so, did you also meet up with that person in real life? **No**

Have you ever had a sexual experience with an adult? **No**

Have you ever had a sexual experience with more than one person at a
    time? **No**

Have you ever been pressured or forced into having sex? **No**

How often do you have sex while using drugs or alcohol? **Most of the time**

Do drugs or alcohol make sex better or worse? **Worse**

Does what you learn in sex education classes at school help you with your
    actual sexual experiences? **Not at all**

Do you think teenagers should be taught more or less about sex at school?
    Same as now

What do you think is the best age to start having sexual experiences?
    **I think mine was about the right age. Of course i would have liked to do
    it earlier but it just didnt really happen.**

Do your parents have an influence on whether or not you have sex?
    Not at all

Does your religion have an influence on whether or not you have sex?
    Not at all

How important is it for you to have an emotional connection with your sexual
    partner? **Not very imporant**

Is there anything else at all that you would like to say about sex or your own
    sexual experiences?
    **I think sex is a perfectly chilled thing to do. I think that you need to be
    careful about how you do it as far as protection etc and I know alot of
    friends that go too far, male and female, and take too many risks. I think
    I am fairly safe when it comes to sex. At the moment I will only have sex
    with either someone I really like and think i can persue a relationship
    with or a complete random, because i Dont want to give the girl the
    wrong impression. Ive learnt that sex can mean more for other people
    than it does for me and I have to be very careful with whom i play
    around with. In one instance, I had sex with a virgin and now she throws
    sex around like its nothing, just because i hurt her for not wanting to do
    it again. I don't know what she was thinking at the time but i have learnt
    that sex can be a very powerful tool of destruction!****

Boy, 18, South Australia, straight

How old were you when you first heard about sex? **9**

What was the first thing you heard about sex? **Can't remember.**

How old were you when you started masturbating? **13**

On average, how many times a week do you masturbate?

Four times a week

How do you masturbate? **Prefer not to disclose.**

How does masturbating make you feel? **Very good**

Describe your sexual fantasies, even if they seem weird or boring or whatever.

Females in general as I am a heterosexual. But I especially love the lower part of their bodies namely the legs and feet. My main fantasy is having a woman rub me off with her feet so I can climax all over them. No one really knows about footsex here in this country, a huge shame. The above activity I described is called a footjob. Basically I like pretty females, and it's a huge plus if they have pretty feet. I like soft wrinkled soles and bright nailpolish is a huge turn on.

How old were you when you had your first sexual experience with someone else? **Never**

How old were you when you first had oral sex? **Never had oral sex**

How old were you when you first had sexual intercourse? **Never**

How old were you when you first had anal sex? **Never**

Would you like to have more sex? **Yes**

How do you think sex could be better for you?

I think it could be better if I actually did have it!

How often are your sexual experiences with someone of the same sex or gender as you? **Never**

You think of yourself as … **Straight**

How old were you when you first saw pornography or erotica? **15**

What kind of pornography have you seen? **Websites.**

Does porn excite you sexually? **A bit**

Does porn give you ideas about how to have sex? **Sometimes**

Do you think sexy films, music videos or advertising encourage you to have sex? **Sometimes**

Examples of media encouraging sex:

Certain music videos of attractive female singers.

Have you ever had phone sex, that is, sexually exciting yourself and
someone else over the phone? **No**

Have you ever sent or received sexual text messages? **No**

Have you had a sexual experience in an internet chat room? **No**

Have you ever had a sexual experience with an adult? **No**

Have you ever had a sexual experience with more than one person at a
time? **No**

If so, describe what happened and how you felt about it.

I haven't had this great experience unfortunately.

Have you ever been pressured or forced into having sex? **No**

How often do you have sex while using drugs or alcohol? **Never**

Do drugs or alcohol make sex better or worse? **Worse**

Does what you learn in sex education classes at school help you with your
actual sexual experiences? **Not at all**

Do you think teenagers should be taught more or less about sex at school?
More

What do you think is the best age to start having sexual experiences?

**Even as young as 14 and 15 is fine I think because there are so many
sexual activities other than intercourse that can be done so the risks of
pregnancy can be totally eliminated. But STI's are still dangerous and
that's where more education at school's comes in. Anything other than
intercourse/anal (and perhaps oral due to STI risks) should be fairly safe
at any age.**

Do your parents have an influence on whether or not you have sex?
Not at all

Does your religion have an influence on whether or not you have sex?
Not at all

How important is it for you to have an emotional connection with your sexual
partner? **Somewhat important**

Is there anything else at all that you would like to say about sex or your own
sexual experiences?

**Its a shame that no one here in this country is really interested in sexual
activities, at least it seems that way to me. School's should deliver a**

better education program regarding this topic area. I am unhappy and unsatisfied with my experiences. Maybe if I moved to the USA I would become more experienced; Australian women seem uninterested.

Boy, 18, South Australia, bisexual

How old were you when you first heard about sex? **12**

What was the first thing you heard about sex?

that sex is for making babies and that it should only be performed within a marrige

How old were you when you started masturbating? **13**

On average, how many times a week do you masturbate?

More than five times a week

How do you masturbate?

i grasp myself reasonably tightly and move my hand up and down the shaft of my penis. sometimes i focus purely on the head and use a lubricant of some sort.

How does masturbating make you feel? **Very good**

Describe your sexual fantasies, even if they seem weird or boring or whatever.

making sweet love to the girl of my dreams, who has a name but i will not mention it. i have been quietly in love with her since i met her.

How old were you when you had your first sexual experience with someone else? **14**

What happened in this first sexual experience with another person?

i was making out and petting with my girlfriend on the basketball courts at school. it was dark and really exciting.

How old were you when you first had oral sex? **14**

Describe what happened during this oral sex, and how you felt about it.

being the first time physically it didnt feel like much but seeing as how it was both my girlfriend's and mine first time at oral sex we enjoyed purely sharing a new experience and being that extra bit closer to each others bodies

On average, how many times a week do you have oral sex? **Twice a week**

How old were you when you first had sexual intercourse? **14**

Describe what happened during intercourse, and how you felt about it emotionally.

being my first time once again physically it was terrible and we were both scared of getting caught as we were at a friends house. afterwards i felt terrible because i wanted nothin more than to show the girl i loved just how much i loved her.

How old were you when you first had anal sex? **17**

How often does this happen? **Less than once a week**

Describe what happens during anal sex and how you feel about having it.

we hav only tried once and it kind of hurt us both. we havnt tried it since

On average, how many times a week do you have intercourse?

Twice a week

Would you like to have more sex? **Yes**

How do you think sex could be better for you?

if there was less concern about getting caught. also if my girlfriend had a better connection to me spiritually, because sometimes i feel as though she doesnt know what is going on inside me even though i know what is happening inside her

When you have intercourse, do you use protection? **Yes**

What kind of protection do you use? **condoms**

How often are your sexual experiences with someone of the same sex or gender as you? **Sometimes**

You think of yourself as … **Bisexual**

How old were you when you first saw pornography or erotica? **13**

What kind of pornography have you seen?

apart from live shows i have seen almost everything. through seeing all forms of erotica i have come to appreciate the female form and its beauty. i have found that typical pornography that degrades women makes me sick. degrading porn is a big turn off

Does porn excite you sexually? **A bit**

Does porn give you ideas about how to have sex? **Sometimes**

Do you think sexy films, music videos or advertising encourage you to have sex? **Sometimes**

Examples of media encouraging sex:

i think all forms of media often attempt to encourage people into having sex. however i try to not let the views of corporate executives push me into doing things i dont want to

Have you ever had phone sex, that is, sexually exciting yourself and someone else over the phone? **Yes**

Have you ever sent or received sexual text messages? **Yes**

Have you had a sexual experience in an internet chat room? **Yes**

If so, did you also meet up with that person in real life? **Yes**

Have you ever had a sexual experience with an adult? **No**

Have you ever had a sexual experience with more than one person at a time? **No**

Have you ever been pressured or forced into having sex? **No**

How often do you have sex while using drugs or alcohol? **Sometimes**

Do drugs or alcohol make sex better or worse? **Neither**

Does what you learn in sex education classes at school help you with your actual sexual experiences? **Not much**

Do you think teenagers should be taught more or less about sex at school? **More**

What do you think is the best age to start having sexual experiences?

with the right educational knowledge to ensure that people stay safe and pregnancy free. i think that there is no specific age that you should start off … the important thing is having the necessary respect for the other person and their feelings so that everyone can be safe and happy

Do your parents have an influence on whether or not you have sex? **A bit**

Does your religion have an influence on whether or not you have sex? **Not at all**

How important is it for you to have an emotional connection with your sexual partner? **Very important**

Girl, 18, New South Wales, bisexual

How old were you when you first heard about sex? **8**

What was the first thing you heard about sex? **that it makes babies**

How old were you when you started masturbating? **11**

On average, how many times a week do you masturbate? **Twice a week**

How do you masturbate? **in bed, with my hands or dildo**

How does masturbating make you feel? **Very good**

How old were you when you had your first sexual experience with someone else? **5**

What happened in this first sexual experience with another person?

we were in the bath and i was pulling his penis and he was touching me and we kissed.

How old were you when you first had oral sex? **12**

Describe what happened during this oral sex, and how you felt about it.

i gave the boy a blow job but not for long because i didnt like it

On average, how many times a week do you have oral sex?

Four times a week

How old were you when you first had sexual intercourse? **13**

Describe what happened during intercourse, and how you felt about it emotionally.

it was the first time i got drunk and we had sex and i didnt like it because it hurt

How old were you when you first had anal sex? **17**

How often does this happen? **Less than once a week**

Describe what happens during anal sex and how you feel about having it.

he puts it in my ass i like it

On average, how many times a week do you have intercourse?

More than five times a week

Would you like to have more sex? **Yes**

How do you think sex could be better for you? **if it lasted longer**

When you have intercourse, do you use protection? **Sometimes**

What kind of protection do you use? **pill**

How often are your sexual experiences with someone of the same sex or gender as you? **Sometimes**

You think of yourself as … **Bisexual**

If you're gay or lesbian, are you 'out'? **No**

How old were you when you first saw pornography or erotica? **13**

What kind of pornography have you seen?

films, photos, magazine, books, internet, live

Does porn excite you sexually? **A bit**

Does porn give you ideas about how to have sex? **Never**

Do you think sexy films, music videos or advertising encourage you to have sex? **Sometimes**

Have you ever had phone sex, that is, sexually exciting yourself and someone else over the phone? **Yes**

Have you ever sent or received sexual text messages? **Yes**

Have you had a sexual experience in an internet chat room? **No**

Have you ever had a sexual experience with an adult? **Yes**

If so, describe what happened and how you felt about it emotionally.

i had sex with my boss and then i quit because he knew my family really well

Have you ever had a sexual experience with more than one person at a time? **Yes**

If so, describe what happened and how you felt about it.

with my best friend we ate each other out while our boyfriends were watching and then they joined in. and then another time we both gave this guy head and then i had sex with him.

Have you ever been pressured or forced into having sex? **No**

How often do you have sex while using drugs or alcohol? **Sometimes**

Do drugs or alcohol make sex better or worse? **Better**

Does what you learn in sex education classes at school help you with your actual sexual experiences? **Not much**

Do you think teenagers should be taught more or less about sex at school? **More**

What do you think is the best age to start having sexual experiences? **15**

Do your parents have an influence on whether or not you have sex? **Not much**

Does your religion have an influence on whether or not you have sex? **Not at all**

How important is it for you to have an emotional connection with your sexual partner? **Not very imporant**

Is there anything else at all that you would like to say about sex or your own sexual experiences? **i love sex**

Boy, 18, South Australia, straight

How old were you when you first heard about sex? **12**

What was the first thing you heard about sex? **puberty**

How old were you when you started masturbating? **14**

On average, how many times a week do you masturbate?
Three times a week

How do you masturbate? **Bedroom, just my hand. into a box of tissues**

How does masturbating make you feel? **Okay**

Describe your sexual fantasies, even if they seem weird or boring or whatever.
two blonde twins

How old were you when you had your first sexual experience with someone
else? **12**

What happened in this first sexual experience with another person?
just kissed. I thought it was lame

How old were you when you first had oral sex? **17**

Describe what happened during this oral sex, and how you felt about it.
**We played with each others private parts. I was boozed so didnt feel
much**

On average, how many times a week do you have oral sex?
Less than once a week

If less frequent, how many times approximately has it occurred? **Twice**

How old were you when you first had sexual intercourse? **Never**

How old were you when you first had anal sex? **Never**

You think of yourself as … **Straight**

How old were you when you first saw pornography or erotica? **12**

What kind of pornography have you seen? **video, man on women**

Does porn excite you sexually? **A bit**

Does porn give you ideas about how to have sex? **Always**

Do you think sexy films, music videos or advertising encourage you to have
sex? **Always**

Examples of media encouraging sex: **music clips**

Have you ever had phone sex, that is, sexually exciting yourself and
someone else over the phone? **No**

Have you ever sent or received sexual text messages? **No**

Have you had a sexual experience in an internet chat room? **Yes**

If so, did you also meet up with that person in real life? **No**

Have you ever had a sexual experience with an adult? **No**

Have you ever had a sexual experience with more than one person at a time? **No**

Have you ever been pressured or forced into having sex? **No**

How often do you have sex while using drugs or alcohol? **Never**

Do drugs or alcohol make sex better or worse? **Neither**

Does what you learn in sex education classes at school help you with your actual sexual experiences? **A lot**

Do you think teenagers should be taught more or less about sex at school? **Same as now**

What do you think is the best age to start having sexual experiences? **when you are ready. And your dick is big enough**

Do your parents have an influence on whether or not you have sex? **A bit**

Does your religion have an influence on whether or not you have sex? **Not at all**

How important is it for you to have an emotional connection with your sexual partner? **Not very imporant**

Boy, 18, New South Wales, straight

How old were you when you first heard about sex? **10**

What was the first thing you heard about sex? **women turned me on**

How old were you when you started masturbating? **13**

On average, how many times a week do you masturbate? **Twice a week**

How do you masturbate?
in the shower fantasise, mainly about past experiences

How does masturbating make you feel? **Okay**

How old were you when you had your first sexual experience with someone else? **6**

What happened in this first sexual experience with another person?
kissed, i cant really remember

How old were you when you first had oral sex? **15**

Describe what happened during this oral sex, and how you felt about it.

in the movies, absolutely awesome

On average, how many times a week do you have oral sex?

Three times a week

How old were you when you first had sexual intercourse? **16**

Describe what happened during intercourse, and how you felt about it emotionally.

first time i was drunk dont remember much, second time was with an experienced girlfriend and i wasnt very attracted to her so it wasnt very good.

How old were you when you first had anal sex? **17**

How often does this happen? **Less than once a week**

Describe what happens during anal sex and how you feel about having it.

did it out of curiosity, never again

On average, how many times a week do you have intercourse?

More than five times a week

Would you like to have more sex? **No**

How do you think sex could be better for you? **threesome**

When you have intercourse, do you use protection? **Yes**

What kind of protection do you use? **me girls on the pill**

How often are your sexual experiences with someone of the same sex or gender as you? **Never**

You think of yourself as … **Straight**

How old were you when you first saw pornography or erotica? **7**

What kind of pornography have you seen? **pictures in magazines**

Does porn excite you sexually? **Not much**

Does porn give you ideas about how to have sex? **Always**

Do you think sexy films, music videos or advertising encourage you to have sex? **Always**

Examples of media encouraging sex:

music videos, ads use a lot of sex and it makes it really hard to watch tv without thinkin bout it

Have you ever had phone sex, that is, sexually exciting yourself and someone else over the phone? **Yes**

Have you ever sent or received sexual text messages? **Yes**

Have you had a sexual experience in an internet chat room? **Yes**

If so, did you also meet up with that person in real life? **No**

Have you ever had a sexual experience with an adult? **No**

Have you ever had a sexual experience with more than one person at a time? **No**

Have you ever been pressured or forced into having sex? **Yes**

If so, describe what happened and how you felt about it emotionally.

my woman was in the mood

How often do you have sex while using drugs or alcohol? **Sometimes**

Do drugs or alcohol make sex better or worse? **Worse**

Does what you learn in sex education classes at school help you with your actual sexual experiences? **A bit**

Do you think teenagers should be taught more or less about sex at school? **More**

What do you think is the best age to start having sexual experiences?

kissing 12/13, mutual mastubation 14/15, oral and intercourse around 16/17

Do your parents have an influence on whether or not you have sex? **Not much**

Does your religion have an influence on whether or not you have sex? **Not at all**

How important is it for you to have an emotional connection with your sexual partner? **Somewhat important**

Is there anything else at all that you would like to say about sex or your own sexual experiences?

i feel i want sex all the time except when i am actually doing it. and ive asked around and a lot of guys feel the same. Girls enjoy sex a lot more than guys and actually enjoy doing it.

Boy, 18, South Australia, straight

How old were you when you first heard about sex? **10**

What was the first thing you heard about sex? **Put the penis in the chick**

How old were you when you started masturbating? **11**

On average, how many times a week do you masturbate?
Five times a week
How do you masturbate? **slap the old sausage in front of the computer**
How does masturbating make you feel? **Very good**
Describe your sexual fantasies, even if they seem weird or boring or whatever.
Lots of babes like threesomes and slutty outfits aka nurse and teacher
How old were you when you had your first sexual experience with someone
else? **12**
What happened in this first sexual experience with another person?
Just kissing. Didn't really feel emotions just kissing
How old were you when you first had oral sex? **18**
Describe what happened during this oral sex, and how you felt about it.
Just got the dong rubbed which felt good i must admit
How old were you when you first had sexual intercourse? **Never**
How old were you when you first had anal sex? **Never**
Would you like to have more sex? **Yes**
How do you think sex could be better for you? **Just having it for starters**
How often are your sexual experiences with someone of the same sex or
gender as you? **Never**
You think of yourself as … **Straight**
How old were you when you first saw pornography or erotica? **8**
What kind of pornography have you seen?
All kinds from movies to magazines
Does porn excite you sexually? **A bit**
Does porn give you ideas about how to have sex? **Always**
Do you think sexy films, music videos or advertising encourage you to have
sex? **Sometimes**
Have you ever had phone sex, that is, sexually exciting yourself and
someone else over the phone? **No**
Have you ever sent or received sexual text messages? **No**
Have you had a sexual experience in an internet chat room? **Yes**
If so, did you also meet up with that person in real life? **No**
Have you ever had a sexual experience with an adult? **No**
Have you ever had a sexual experience with more than one person at a
time? **No**

Have you ever been pressured or forced into having sex? **No**

Does what you learn in sex education classes at school help you with your actual sexual experiences? **A lot**

Do you think teenagers should be taught more or less about sex at school? **More**

What do you think is the best age to start having sexual experiences? **When ever u can get it**

Do your parents have an influence on whether or not you have sex? **Not at all**

Does your religion have an influence on whether or not you have sex? **Not at all**

Is there anything else at all that you would like to say about sex or your own sexual experiences? **Get me more**

Girl, 18, (no postcode given), lesbian

How old were you when you first heard about sex? **13**

What was the first thing you heard about sex? **It's fun**

How old were you when you started masturbating? **14**

On average, how many times a week do you masturbate? **More than five times a week**

How do you masturbate? **Rub clitoris gently, then rub progressively harder ... depends on mood.**

How does masturbating make you feel? **Very good**

Describe your sexual fantasies, even if they seem weird or boring or whatever. **My girlfriend**

How old were you when you had your first sexual experience with someone else? **14**

What happened in this first sexual experience with another person? **Had intercourse with a boy. Felt good.**

How old were you when you first had oral sex? **15**

Describe what happened during this oral sex, and how you felt about it. **Got licked by a girl. Felt incredible.**

On average, how many times a week do you have oral sex?

More than five times a week

How old were you when you first had sexual intercourse? **14**

Describe what happened during intercourse, and how you felt about it emotionally. **Was with a boy. Felt good.**

How old were you when you first had anal sex? **Never**

On average, how many times a week do you have intercourse?

More than five times a week

Would you like to have more sex? **Not sure**

How do you think sex could be better for you? **No my girlfriend is perfect.**

When you have intercourse, do you use protection? **Never**

How often are your sexual experiences with someone of the same sex or gender as you? **Always**

You think of yourself as … **Lesbian**

If you're gay or lesbian, are you 'out'? **Yes**

If you're gay or lesbian and you came out, was it hard? **Not very hard**

Describe what happened when you came out and how you felt about it.

My parents must have guessed because they just came out with it and asked. Said yes.

How old were you when you first saw pornography or erotica? **15**

What kind of pornography have you seen? **Magazines, films, photos**

Does porn excite you sexually? **A bit**

Does porn give you ideas about how to have sex? **Never**

Do you think sexy films, music videos or advertising encourage you to have sex? **Sometimes**

Examples of media encouraging sex: **Herbal Essences commercial**

Have you ever had phone sex, that is, sexually exciting yourself and someone else over the phone? **No**

Have you ever sent or received sexual text messages? **Yes**

Have you had a sexual experience in an internet chat room? **No**

Have you ever had a sexual experience with an adult? **Yes**

If so, describe what happened and how you felt about it emotionally.

It was sex. It was good.

Have you ever had a sexual experience with more than one person at a time? **No**

Have you ever been pressured or forced into having sex? **No**

How often do you have sex while using drugs or alcohol? **Never**

Do drugs or alcohol make sex better or worse? **Neither**

Does what you learn in sex education classes at school help you with your actual sexual experiences? **Not much**

Do you think teenagers should be taught more or less about sex at school? **Same as now**

What do you think is the best age to start having sexual experiences? **It's entirely up to the individual. Whenever you are ready and have found the right person.**

Do your parents have an influence on whether or not you have sex? **Not at all**

Does your religion have an influence on whether or not you have sex? **Not at all**

How important is it for you to have an emotional connection with your sexual partner? **Very important**

Is there anything else at all that you would like to say about sex or your own sexual experiences? **I love it.**

Boy, 18, New South Wales, straight

How old were you when you first heard about sex? **6**

What was the first thing you heard about sex?
A mans penis had to go into the womens vagina.

How old were you when you started masturbating? **12**

On average, how many times a week do you masturbate? **Twice a week**

How do you masturbate? **I rub my penis, in the shower, no lubricant.**

How does masturbating make you feel? **Good**

Describe your sexual fantasies, even if they seem weird or boring or whatever.
Having sex with multiple women.

How old were you when you had your first sexual experience with someone else? **12**

What happened in this first sexual experience with another person?
We pashed at a party. it was cool.

How old were you when you first had oral sex? **14**

Describe what happened during this oral sex, and how you felt about it.

She sucked on my penis. :) My friend was sleeping next to us! Thats where it ended.

On average, how many times a week do you have oral sex?

Three times a week

How old were you when you first had sexual intercourse? **14**

Describe what happened during intercourse, and how you felt about it emotionally.

My penis went in her vagina and then out again and then in again for quite some time. It then ended and i was on an emotional high.

How old were you when you first had anal sex? **Never**

On average, how many times a week do you have intercourse?

Three times a week

Would you like to have more sex? **Not sure**

How do you think sex could be better for you?

Wish the girl would come more often. She doesn't fake it or anything, it just doesn't happen.

When you have intercourse, do you use protection? **Yes**

What kind of protection do you use? **pill**

How often are your sexual experiences with someone of the same sex or gender as you? **Never**

You think of yourself as … **Straight**

How old were you when you first saw pornography or erotica? **11**

What kind of pornography have you seen? **most kinds.**

Does porn excite you sexually? **A bit**

Does porn give you ideas about how to have sex? **Sometimes**

Do you think sexy films, music videos or advertising encourage you to have sex? **Sometimes**

Examples of media encouraging sex:

The kind with girls and guys dancing half naked.

Have you ever had phone sex, that is, sexually exciting yourself and someone else over the phone? **Yes**

Have you ever sent or received sexual text messages? **Yes**

Have you had a sexual experience in an internet chat room? **No**

Have you ever had a sexual experience with an adult? **No**

Have you ever had a sexual experience with more than one person at a time? **No**

Have you ever been pressured or forced into having sex? **No**

How often do you have sex while using drugs or alcohol? **Sometimes**

Do drugs or alcohol make sex better or worse? **Neither**

Does what you learn in sex education classes at school help you with your actual sexual experiences? **A bit**

Do you think teenagers should be taught more or less about sex at school? **More**

What do you think is the best age to start having sexual experiences? **It's quite different for every person.**

Do your parents have an influence on whether or not you have sex? **Not at all**

Does your religion have an influence on whether or not you have sex? **A bit**

How important is it for you to have an emotional connection with your sexual partner? **Somewhat important**

Is there anything else at all that you would like to say about sex or your own sexual experiences? **If you can't be good be careful but if you can't be carefull, name the first one after me.**

Boy, 18, New South Wales, straight

How old were you when you first heard about sex? **7**

What was the first thing you heard about sex? **make babies**

How old were you when you started masturbating? **10**

On average, how many times a week do you masturbate? **More than five times a week**

How do you masturbate? **no lubricants. anywhere and anytime. Need a wank to get to sleep. otherwise i spend hours trying to get to sleep.**

How does masturbating make you feel? **Very good**

Describe your sexual fantasies, even if they seem weird or boring or whatever.

being with a hot teacher at school. being with a tutor in my school boarding house. Being with my friends mums

How old were you when you had your first sexual experience with someone else? **12**

What happened in this first sexual experience with another person?

i kissed a girl. It felt good because it made me feel like a man

How old were you when you first had oral sex? **15**

Describe what happened during this oral sex, and how you felt about it.

i got a blowjob on a couch at a party. Of course it felt good, its a blowjob!!

On average, how many times a week do you have oral sex? **Once a week**

How old were you when you first had sexual intercourse? **16**

Describe what happened during intercourse, and how you felt about it emotionally.

i was blind drunk. i remember very little. I remember sitting on my bed naked, and i remember watching the roof spin.

How old were you when you first had anal sex? **Never**

Describe what happens during anal sex and how you feel about having it.

Dick in arse. I would have it if the girl had a good arse and id definitly wear a condom and apparently lubricant is needed

On average, how many times a week do you have intercourse?

More than five times a week

Would you like to have more sex? **No**

How do you think sex could be better for you? **nothing at the moment**

When you have intercourse, do you use protection? **Sometimes**

What kind of protection do you use? **condom**

How often are your sexual experiences with someone of the same sex or gender as you? **Never**

You think of yourself as … **Straight**

How old were you when you first saw pornography or erotica? **9**

What kind of pornography have you seen? **everything**

Does porn excite you sexually? **A bit**

Does porn give you ideas about how to have sex? **Always**

Do you think sexy films, music videos or advertising encourage you to have sex? **Always**

Examples of media encouraging sex:

music videos are very sexually orientated and films constantly use sex (eg. original sin)- this puts ideas in my head and even just makes me feel like having sex at the time

Have you ever had phone sex, that is, sexually exciting yourself and someone else over the phone? **No**

Have you ever sent or received sexual text messages? **Yes**

Have you had a sexual experience in an internet chat room? **No**

Have you ever had a sexual experience with an adult? **No**

Have you ever had a sexual experience with more than one person at a time? **No**

Have you ever been pressured or forced into having sex? **No**

How often do you have sex while using drugs or alcohol? **Sometimes**

Do drugs or alcohol make sex better or worse? **Neither**

Does what you learn in sex education classes at school help you with your actual sexual experiences? **Not at all**

Do you think teenagers should be taught more or less about sex at school? **More**

What do you think is the best age to start having sexual experiences?

I think everyone should experience sexual acts before 18. I think society should lift the stigma that sex before then is bad etc.

Do your parents have an influence on whether or not you have sex? **Not much**

Does your religion have an influence on whether or not you have sex? **Not at all**

How important is it for you to have an emotional connection with your sexual partner? **Not very important**

Unsurprisingly, boys and girls at the age of 19 show the greatest degree of confidence about their sexuality, no matter what variety. A higher percentage declare themselves gay or lesbian, and some even describe their zoosexuality, or sexual encounters with animals. One 19-year-old announces her unhappiness at still being a virgin, as she feels that she has missed out on some important aspects of adolescence.

A satisfying sex life is obviously important to 19-year-olds, and there is a sense that most got through those often tricky sexual experiences in their teen years in reasonable shape, in spite of the lack of enough useful information and guidance from parents, teachers, or anyone who doesn't sponsor websites with names like monsterdicks.com.

Boy, 19, Western Australia, straight

What was the first thing you heard about sex?
its good and girls get pregnant from it
How old were you when you started masturbating? **Never**
Describe your sexual fantasies, even if they seem weird or boring or whatever.
mine usually involve a girl i like, they're not weird, theyre usually romantic. sometimes i involve the story lines of final fantasy [a video game] but incorporate my life into it
How old were you when you had your first sexual experience with someone else? **13**
What happened in this first sexual experience with another person?
i kissed a girl, she grabbed my dick. emotionally it was good, coz she was my girlfriend
How old were you when you first had oral sex? **14**
Describe what happened during this oral sex, and how you felt about it.
i sprogged in her face after about 10 minutes
On average, how many times a week do you have oral sex? **Once a week**
How old were you when you first had sexual intercourse? **14**

Describe what happened during intercourse, and how you felt about it
emotionally. **we had sex 3 times, i loved her.**

How old were you when you first had anal sex? **Never**

On average, how many times a week do you have intercourse?
Three times a week

Would you like to have more sex? **No**

How do you think sex could be better for you?
it relieves frustration, making me more well rounded.

When you have intercourse, do you use protection? **Yes**

What kind of protection do you use? **condom**

How often are your sexual experiences with someone of the same sex or
gender as you? **Never**

You think of yourself as … **Straight**

What kind of pornography have you seen? **movie**

Does porn excite you sexually? **Not much**

Does porn give you ideas about how to have sex? **Sometimes**

Do you think sexy films, music videos or advertising encourage you to have
sex? **Sometimes**

Have you ever had phone sex, that is, sexually exciting yourself and
someone else over the phone? **No**

Have you ever sent or received sexual text messages? **Yes**

Have you had a sexual experience in an internet chat room? **Yes**

If so, did you also meet up with that person in real life? **Yes**

Have you ever had a sexual experience with an adult? **Yes**

If so, describe what happened and how you felt about it emotionally.
nothing really emotional, just had sex with my girlfriends mum

Have you ever had a sexual experience with more than one person at a
time? **Yes**

If so, describe what happened and how you felt about it.
it was with my girlfriend and her sister.

Have you ever been pressured or forced into having sex? **No**

How often do you have sex while using drugs or alcohol? **Sometimes**

Do drugs or alcohol make sex better or worse? **Neither**

Does what you learn in sex education classes at school help you with your
actual sexual experiences? **Not much**

Do you think teenagers should be taught more or less about sex at school?
Same as now

What do you think is the best age to start having sexual experiences?
whenever

Do your parents have an influence on whether or not you have sex?
Not at all

Does your religion have an influence on whether or not you have sex?
Not at all

How important is it for you to have an emotional connection with your sexual
partner? **Somewhat important**

Is there anything else at all that you would like to say about sex or your own
sexual experiences? **nope**

Girl, 19, Western Australia, 'bi-curious'

How old were you when you first heard about sex? **11**

What was the first thing you heard about sex? **was kissing naked**

How old were you when you started masturbating? **17**

On average, how many times a week do you masturbate? **Five times a week**

How do you masturbate?
**in bed, in the shower, with fingers lying on my stomach. i sometimes use
vaseline.**

How does masturbating make you feel? **Good**

Describe your sexual fantasies, even if they seem weird or boring or whatever.
guys going down on girls, footy players

How old were you when you had your first sexual experience with someone
else? **17**

What happened in this first sexual experience with another person?
**we were dancing closely at a club and he full on kissed me it was foul
and i dont mean the animal!**

How old were you when you first had oral sex? **18**

Describe what happened during this oral sex, and how you felt about it.
**it was a 69er and i didnt know how to do it, i told the guy i did it before
but i lied, and apparently i was too rough. it was shit**

On average, how many times a week do you have oral sex?

Less than once a week

If less frequent, how many times approximately has it occurred?

More than twenty

How old were you when you first had sexual intercourse? **19**

Describe what happened during intercourse, and how you felt about it emotionally.

i was going out with a boy and he asked me if i wanted to have sex and i said i hadn't had it and he was surprised. We were seeing each other for about 3 weeks then broke up and then met up one nite for drinks and started foreplay. he asked if i wanted to have sex with him and i said no, then we got a bit frisky and then i said i would have sex. he put his dick in and then felt guilty and then apoligised and we just cuddled. i felt ok, my best mate was a little displeased at me, but supportive. The next time was with someone i really loved and it was proper, so i will take it from that time on.

How old were you when you first had anal sex? **19**

How often does this happen? **Less than once a week**

Describe what happens during anal sex and how you feel about having it.

only once and lasted 1 sec it was painful and sucked badly! i thought we were doggy styling and then he put it in my bum. i didnt like it one bit!

On average, how many times a week do you have intercourse?

Less than once a week

Would you like to have more sex? **Yes**

How do you think sex could be better for you?

if i can find someone a fuck buddy or something but in secret, or if i find a really really nice boyfriend to treat me good.

When you have intercourse, do you use protection? **Sometimes**

What kind of protection do you use? **condoms or pill**

How often are your sexual experiences with someone of the same sex or gender as you? **Sometimes**

You think of yourself as … **Other: bi curious**

If you're gay or lesbian, are you 'out'? **No**

How old were you when you first saw pornography or erotica? **16**

What kind of pornography have you seen?

old ones that are funny, i masturbate to them sometimes. lots of pussy licking and girls rubbing themselves i like watching that

Does porn excite you sexually? **A lot**

Does porn give you ideas about how to have sex? **Sometimes**

Do you think sexy films, music videos or advertising encourage you to have sex? **Sometimes**

Examples of media encouraging sex:

movies with sex in them i guess it makes me wanna bone

Have you ever had phone sex, that is, sexually exciting yourself and someone else over the phone? **Yes**

Have you ever sent or received sexual text messages? **Yes**

Have you had a sexual experience in an internet chat room? **Yes**

If so, did you also meet up with that person in real life? **No**

Have you ever had a sexual experience with an adult? **No**

Have you ever had a sexual experience with more than one person at a time? **Yes**

If so, describe what happened and how you felt about it.

i have had 3 threesomes once with a girl best friend and boy i really had a crush on. I felt jealous and stole away the attention from the girl. The other time i was asked by a couple i was mates with. She was going ok then felt a bit weird so we stopped i didnt have sex. The 3rd was with the boy at the 1st time and his best mate a boy. Again we kinda left his best mate out and he walked away feeling shit. I think its hard and is overated. I don't think u should b emotionally involved with anyone u do it with. if its just for fun then go for it! i was drunk all three times

Have you ever been pressured or forced into having sex? **Yes**

If so, describe what happened and how you felt about it emotionally.

he was fingering me and i was giving him a handjob then he slipped his dick in without me saying any thing. I told him i didnt want to and he said ok and then i left.

How often do you have sex while using drugs or alcohol? **Most of the time**

Do drugs or alcohol make sex better or worse? **Worse**

Does what you learn in sex education classes at school help you with your actual sexual experiences? **Not much**

Do you think teenagers should be taught more or less about sex at school?

Same as now

What do you think is the best age to start having sexual experiences?

i think when u feel like having it and are mature enough to know what is going on. I think the 1st time should be around 17-19 depending on attitude

Do your parents have an influence on whether or not you have sex?

Not at all

Does your religion have an influence on whether or not you have sex?

Not at all

How important is it for you to have an emotional connection with your sexual partner? **Very important**

Is there anything else at all that you would like to say about sex or your own sexual experiences?

i love sex!! and am promiscuous, its fun! but its better with someone u really like.

Boy, 19, New South Wales, gay

How old were you when you first heard about sex? **6**

What was the first thing you heard about sex?

Mum and dads have sex to make babies

How old were you when you started masturbating? **12**

On average, how many times a week do you masturbate?

Four times a week

How do you masturbate?

just with my hand in the bed. dont use lubricants, Have tissues on my stomach

How does masturbating make you feel? **Good**

Describe your sexual fantasies, even if they seem weird or boring or whatever.

Just people i have met or know having sex with them.

How old were you when you had your first sexual experience with someone else? **11**

What happened in this first sexual experience with another person?

I played around with a friend. felt good at the time but because it was a boy i felt that i was doing somethin wrong

How old were you when you first had oral sex? **13**

Describe what happened during this oral sex, and how you felt about it.

Was with another boy. yeah felt great but also the feeling after the sexual experience that there was something wrong that i was doing seeing it was a boy

On average, how many times a week do you have oral sex?

Less than once a week

If less frequent, how many times approximately has it occurred? **More than twenty**

How old were you when you first had sexual intercourse? **18**

Describe what happened during intercourse, and how you felt about it emotionally.

It felt good. was not with anyone i loved but because i at least knew the person. felt better then early sexual experiences because was fine with my sexuality and was comfortable

How old were you when you first had anal sex? **18**

How often does this happen? **Less than once a week**

Describe what happens during anal sex and how you feel about having it.

It still hurts me because i have not had it enough but its starting to feel alot better. I love to give it though

On average, how many times a week do you have intercourse?

Less than once a week

Would you like to have more sex? **Yes**

How do you think sex could be better for you?

If it was with someone that i was fully in love with and felt comfortable with.

When you have intercourse, do you use protection? **Sometimes**

What kind of protection do you use? **condoms**

How often are your sexual experiences with someone of the same sex or gender as you? **Always**

You think of yourself as … **Gay**

If you're gay or lesbian, are you 'out'? **Yes**

If you're gay or lesbian and you came out, was it hard? **Not very hard**

Describe what happened when you came out and how you felt about it.

I came out after school which was a good idea. Everyone was really supportive. i did not come out at school because didnt want to be known as the gay guy. when i first admitted to myself i was gay in high school i had suicidal thoughts.

How old were you when you first saw pornography or erotica? **10**

What kind of pornography have you seen?

magazines, videos, internet websites

Does porn excite you sexually? **A bit**

Does porn give you ideas about how to have sex? **Sometimes**

Do you think sexy films, music videos or advertising encourage you to have sex? **Sometimes**

Examples of media encouraging sex:

film clips of music that are really sexual

Have you ever had phone sex, that is, sexually exciting yourself and someone else over the phone? **Yes**

Have you ever sent or received sexual text messages? **No**

Have you had a sexual experience in an internet chat room? **Yes**

If so, did you also meet up with that person in real life? **No**

Have you ever had a sexual experience with an adult? **No**

Have you ever had a sexual experience with more than one person at a time? **No**

Have you ever been pressured or forced into having sex? **Yes**

If so, describe what happened and how you felt about it emotionally.

Just when i was drunk and my casual sex partner wanted sex. i had made the decision that i didnt really want sex with them again. i like i was more above him afterwards because i didnt really want it and gave him sex through pity

How often do you have sex while using drugs or alcohol? **Sometimes**

Do drugs or alcohol make sex better or worse? **Neither**

Does what you learn in sex education classes at school help you with your actual sexual experiences? **Not at all**

Do you think teenagers should be taught more or less about sex at school? **More**

What do you think is the best age to start having sexual experiences?

From about 15 upwards. Any type of sex as long as it is with someone you really like. because any age below that you are too young to understand all that comes with sex

Do your parents have an influence on whether or not you have sex?

Not at all

Does your religion have an influence on whether or not you have sex? **A lot**

How important is it for you to have an emotional connection with your sexual partner? **Somewhat important**

Girl, 19, South Australia, straight

How old were you when you first heard about sex? **7**

What was the first thing you heard about sex?

That you could catch AIDS and that you should always wear a condom.

How old were you when you started masturbating? **11**

On average, how many times a week do you masturbate? **Twice a week**

How do you masturbate? **at home in my bed**

How does masturbating make you feel? **Very good**

Describe your sexual fantasies, even if they seem weird or boring or whatever.

Mostly with guys I know or famous people, but sometimes with strangers. Mainly the same thing- having hot, sweaty passionate sex.

How old were you when you had your first sexual experience with someone else? **17**

What happened in this first sexual experience with another person?

I hooked up with this guy at a party and spent the night making out on a couch, but it didn't go any further. It made me feel special and attractive, something that I hadn't felt before.

How old were you when you first had oral sex? **Never had oral sex**

How old were you when you first had sexual intercourse? **Never**

How old were you when you first had anal sex? **Never**

Would you like to have more sex? **Yes**

How do you think sex could be better for you?

If I was actually getting sex from another person!

How often are your sexual experiences with someone of the same sex or gender as you? **Never**

You think of yourself as … **Straight**

How old were you when you first saw pornography or erotica? **15**

What kind of pornography have you seen? **movies, magazines**

Does porn excite you sexually? **Not much**

Does porn give you ideas about how to have sex? **Never**

Do you think sexy films, music videos or advertising encourage you to have sex? **Never**

Have you ever had phone sex, that is, sexually exciting yourself and someone else over the phone? **No**

Have you ever sent or received sexual text messages? **Yes**

Have you had a sexual experience in an internet chat room? **No**

Have you ever had a sexual experience with an adult? **No**

Have you ever had a sexual experience with more than one person at a time? **No**

Have you ever been pressured or forced into having sex? **No**

How often do you have sex while using drugs or alcohol? **Never**

Does what you learn in sex education classes at school help you with your actual sexual experiences? **Not at all**

Do you think teenagers should be taught more or less about sex at school? **More**

What do you think is the best age to start having sexual experiences? **I don't think there is an age, it depends on the level of maturity.**

Do your parents have an influence on whether or not you have sex? **Not at all**

Does your religion have an influence on whether or not you have sex? **Not at all**

How important is it for you to have an emotional connection with your sexual partner? **Somewhat important**

Is there anything else at all that you would like to say about sex or your own sexual experiences? **It sucks being a nineteen year-old virgin. I want to have sex but I don't want to throw away my virginity on some guy who isn't worth it. I also** feel like I have missed out on some very important parts of adolescence by not having very many sexual experiences.

Boy, 19, Queensland, straight

How old were you when you first heard about sex? **13**

What was the first thing you heard about sex? **babies**

How old were you when you started masturbating? **12**

On average, how many times a week do you masturbate?

Four times a week

How do you masturbate?

Watch porn and masturbate at home.

How does masturbating make you feel? **Okay**

Describe your sexual fantasies, even if they seem weird or boring or whatever.

my fantasy is being the best male lover of all time, i have three girls surrounding me and all of them leave in a wheel chair.

How old were you when you had your first sexual experience with someone else? **15**

What happened in this first sexual experience with another person?

It went not so smoothly i felt like i was doing something wrong eg. hurting her.

How old were you when you first had oral sex? **15**

Describe what happened during this oral sex, and how you felt about it.

It was the best thing ever, it came as a complete surprise, she just went down on me and i remember thinking "holy shit is she realy gonna do what i think she is gonna do".

On average, how many times a week do you have oral sex?

Four times a week

How old were you when you first had sexual intercourse? **15**

Describe what happened during intercourse, and how you felt about it emotionally.

the girl of my dreams came over one day and we did it. during it was quiet and awkward being naked in front of the opposite sex.

How old were you when you first had anal sex? **18**

On average, how many times a week do you have intercourse?
Three times a week

Would you like to have more sex? **Yes**

How do you think sex could be better for you?
if i had some kind of device that told me everytime she was "really" enjoying it.

When you have intercourse, do you use protection? **Never**

What kind of protection do you use? **pill, not me personally.**

How often are your sexual experiences with someone of the same sex or gender as you? **Never**

You think of yourself as … **Straight**

How old were you when you first saw pornography or erotica? **9**

What kind of pornography have you seen? **dvd's,websites and magz.**

Does porn excite you sexually? **A bit**

Does porn give you ideas about how to have sex? **Always**

Do you think sexy films, music videos or advertising encourage you to have sex? **Sometimes**

Examples of media encouraging sex:
most film clips do but they're only showing us what is already out there and how it is sometimes.

Have you ever had phone sex, that is, sexually exciting yourself and someone else over the phone? **No**

Have you ever sent or received sexual text messages? **No**

Have you had a sexual experience in an internet chat room? **No**

Have you ever had a sexual experience with an adult? **No**

Have you ever had a sexual experience with more than one person at a time? **Yes**

If so, describe what happened and how you felt about it.
we got drunk at my gf's house and then she asked her friend if she wanted to join us. Her friend is Bi/Lez and thought my gf was hot so she said yes.

Have you ever been pressured or forced into having sex? **No**

How often do you have sex while using drugs or alcohol? **Most of the time**

Do drugs or alcohol make sex better or worse? **Neither**

Does what you learn in sex education classes at school help you with your actual sexual experiences? **Not much**

Do you think teenagers should be taught more or less about sex at school? **More**

What do you think is the best age to start having sexual experiences? **prolly around grade 11-12, maybe grade 10 like myself both oral and intercourse.**

Do your parents have an influence on whether or not you have sex? **Not at all**

Does your religion have an influence on whether or not you have sex? **A bit**

How important is it for you to have an emotional connection with your sexual partner? **Very important**

Is there anything else at all that you would like to say about sex or your own sexual experiences? **There isn't much to say, but if this is a survay on teaching minors about sex make sure u mention that having a conection makes it easier on both partners and it's the only way to realy get the most of what sex is realy about.**

Girl, 19, Queensland, other

How old were you when you first heard about sex? **15**

What was the first thing you heard about sex? **I guess i kinda taught myself. But, i clearly remember reading a book which my mum had given me about sex which stated a lot of myths and true facts. That book helped me more than my parents could have I believe.**

How old were you when you started masturbating? **15**

How do you masturbate? **I don't masterbate, I have a partner.**

Describe your sexual fantasies, even if they seem weird or boring or whatever. **One of my fantasies would be role playing with a man kidnapping me and having intercourse with me, calling me dirty names & squeezing my nipples and choking me a little. Thats soo hot!**

How old were you when you had your first sexual experience with someone else? **15**

What happened in this first sexual experience with another person?

I fell in love! And we're still together to this present day having sex. Since 2001.

How old were you when you first had oral sex? **15**

Describe what happened during this oral sex, and how you felt about it.

It felt awkward, and i had no clue. But neither did he. It was good to teach each other where the right places are and what not.

On average, how many times a week do you have oral sex?

Five times a week

How old were you when you first had sexual intercourse? **15**

Describe what happened during intercourse, and how you felt about it emotionally.

It hurt, it was passionate. I thought i was the most beautiful and luckiest girl ever. Not only because of the sex, but because I wanted the guy so much. I was head over heals for him.

How old were you when you first had anal sex? **19**

How often does this happen? **Less than once a week**

Describe what happens during anal sex and how you feel about having it.

I dont like having it that much ... But when im feeling REALLY kinky and raunchy then i usually want it, or tell my bf to bring out the anal toys.

On average, how many times a week do you have intercourse?

Four times a week

Would you like to have more sex? **No**

How do you think sex could be better for you?

Im happy with what I have. Haven't had better. Honestly.

When you have intercourse, do you use protection? **Never**

What kind of protection do you use? **I take the pill.**

How often are your sexual experiences with someone of the same sex or gender as you? **Sometimes**

You think of yourself as ... **Other: I'd do a girl, but i wouldn't date her.**

What kind of pornography have you seen?

Films, pics, mags, stories, internet ...

Does porn excite you sexually? **A bit**

Does porn give you ideas about how to have sex? **Sometimes**

Do you think sexy films, music videos or advertising encourage you to have sex? **Always**

Examples of media encouraging sex:

Golddigger by kanye west. Thats number one atm ... Also, snoop dogg "drop it like it's hot". Most R&B songs are nothing but big ass big tittie girls wearing nothing and shaking it everywhere ... I hate my bf watching it, I get annoyed. I think girls should have more respect about their bodies.

Have you ever had phone sex, that is, sexually exciting yourself and someone else over the phone? **No**

Have you ever sent or received sexual text messages? **Yes**

Have you had a sexual experience in an internet chat room? **Yes**

If so, did you also meet up with that person in real life? **No**

Have you ever had a sexual experience with an adult? **Yes**

If so, describe what happened and how you felt about it emotionally.

Not good, he used me. I thought older men were supose to be more mature and respect people.

Have you ever had a sexual experience with more than one person at a time? **Yes**

If so, describe what happened and how you felt about it.

At my home, my boyfriend, myself and a girl. Drinking alcohol and then "truth or dare" came along ... Then we had a 3some ... It was ok, but i felt jealous seeing my man do another girl ... wasn't so great. Havent done it again.

Have you ever been pressured or forced into having sex? **Yes**

If so, describe what happened and how you felt about it emotionally.

I felt violated, used and worthless. I slept at my soon to be bf's house (in the process of dating). And he forced me face down into the pillow and clasped my hands behind my back and had sex with me ...

How often do you have sex while using drugs or alcohol? **Most of the time**

Do drugs or alcohol make sex better or worse? **Better**

Does what you learn in sex education classes at school help you with your actual sexual experiences? **A bit**

Do you think teenagers should be taught more or less about sex at school?

Same as now

What do you think is the best age to start having sexual experiences?

Whenever you feel ready to have sex.

Do your parents have an influence on whether or not you have sex?

Not at all

Does your religion have an influence on whether or not you have sex?

Not at all

How important is it for you to have an emotional connection with your sexual partner? **Very important**

Boy, 19, Victoria, gay

How old were you when you first heard about sex? **7**

What was the first thing you heard about sex? **It was where I came from**

How old were you when you started masturbating? **7**

On average, how many times a week do you masturbate?

More than five times a week

How do you masturbate?

Usually on a chair facing the computer screen. Usually with porn movies playing. Through my track pants with my right hand

How does masturbating make you feel? **Very good**

Describe your sexual fantasies, even if they seem weird or boring or whatever.

My boss against the glasses shelves as they smash on the floor. I'm hanging on him with my legs on his hips and my arms holding the shelf and shoulders.

How old were you when you had your first sexual experience with someone else? **7**

What happened in this first sexual experience with another person?

Me and another boy rubbed penises together in a cubicle while laughing.

How old were you when you first had oral sex? **16**

Describe what happened during this oral sex, and how you felt about it.

I was in a car outside my house and I felt adult. I felt very sexual but still scared I was fucking up.

On average, how many times a week do you have oral sex?
Less than once a week
How old were you when you first had sexual intercourse? **19**
Describe what happened during intercourse, and how you felt about it emotionally.
I was at his place and I penetrated him and it was very different than how I thought it would feel. I thought it would feel better. More acute. It just felt warm and a little desensitised. I think I used too much lube. Emotionally I felt a bit alienated.
How old were you when you first had anal sex? **19**
How often does this happen? **Less than once a week**
Describe what happens during anal sex and how you feel about having it.
I'm inside them and it feels great. When they're inside me I'm scared, I think I should stop in case I shit myself but want more.
On average, how many times a week do you have intercourse?
Less than once a week
Would you like to have more sex? **Yes**
How do you think sex could be better for you?
Safety with the person. I should know them more. I should learn more things to do technique-wise.
When you have intercourse, do you use protection? **Yes**
What kind of protection do you use? **Condoms**
How often are your sexual experiences with someone of the same sex or gender as you? **Always**
You think of yourself as … **Gay**
If you're gay or lesbian, are you 'out'? **Yes**
If you're gay or lesbian and you came out, was it hard? **Not very hard**
Describe what happened when you came out and how you felt about it.
I told everyone and they were fine. They were like "Finally!" Except my dad. When told him he said, after a long silence, "What makes you think that?" As if he didn't think I could make that decision. As if it's a decision. I didn't speak to him for three weeks.
How old were you when you first saw pornography or erotica? **10**
What kind of pornography have you seen? **Films, Photos, Mags, Webcams**
Does porn excite you sexually? **A lot**

Does porn give you ideas about how to have sex? **Always**

Do you think sexy films, music videos or advertising encourage you to have sex? **Always**

Examples of media encouraging sex:

A lot of hip-hop culture male-dominated hip-hop culture is about women being prizes and/or badges of pride.

Have you ever had phone sex, that is, sexually exciting yourself and someone else over the phone? **Yes**

Have you ever sent or received sexual text messages? **Yes**

Have you had a sexual experience in an internet chat room? **Yes**

If so, did you also meet up with that person in real life? **No**

Have you ever had a sexual experience with an adult? **Yes**

If so, describe what happened and how you felt about it emotionally.

I had sex in an alley way with a 34 yo guy I picked up in a bar I was working at. I felt great about it but I would've liked a better location.

Have you ever had a sexual experience with more than one person at a time? **Yes**

If so, describe what happened and how you felt about it.

It was with my brother's ex-boyfriend and another guy he had picked up and it was in a drained-out pond in a park near the club we were at. I felt guilty for having sex with my Bro's Ex. Other than that I felt hurt that the other guy never called me after that coz he was really sweet and nice.

Have you ever been pressured or forced into having sex? **No**

How often do you have sex while using drugs or alcohol? **Sometimes**

Do drugs or alcohol make sex better or worse? **Neither**

Does what you learn in sex education classes at school help you with your actual sexual experiences? **Not at all**

Do you think teenagers should be taught more or less about sex at school? **Same as now**

What do you think is the best age to start having sexual experiences?

I think it's subjective. Personally I started having "experience" when I was 15. It was right for me. Some need time. Some need less.

Do your parents have an influence on whether or not you have sex? **Not at all**

Does your religion have an influence on whether or not you have sex?
Not at all

How important is it for you to have an emotional connection with your sexual partner? **Somewhat important**

Is there anything else at all that you would like to say about sex or your own sexual experiences?

I think that schools give the spin that sex is necessary yet slightly wrong. I believe that the only thing that makes you feel good about sex is a safe environment and experience. If you don't know what you're doing down there then it feels akward and you're uncomfortable. When school teaches us about sex they give biological facts and slightly "old school" opinions. As opposed to the truth which is it's fun. It can be casual and that's nothing bad or immoral as long as you are responsible. If you enjoy it and it doesn't hurt you or anyone else it is ok. I feel patronised when I get taught about sex as well as the feeling that I'm not getting the whole story. I feel comfortable having sex now. and school did next to nothing for that to happen. I found out through my own blunders. School never taught me anything I didn't know except disease info. And we need more learning about diseases HPV is still unknown in most schools as well as forms of contraction. Some people believe (adults i have met as well as school kids) that HIV/AIDS cannot be contracted by swallowing semen because your stomach acids destroy the virus. There has been a huge increase in HIV/AIDS infection in younger people. You do the maths. There are many dangers to having sex so the most sensible thing to do is not to "shield" the kids from them but give them the tools to shield themselves.

[Oral sex and swallowing semen are fairly low-risk activities. You can become infected with HIV if you've got cuts in your mouth but it's much more unlikely than unprotected anal or vaginal intercourse.]

Girl, 19, Queensland, straight

How old were you when you first heard about sex? **7**

What was the first thing you heard about sex?

that its only meant to be with someone special or that u love

How old were you when you started masturbating? **4**

On average, how many times a week do you masturbate? **Twice a week**

How does masturbating make you feel? **Good**

Describe your sexual fantasies, even if they seem weird or boring or whatever.

sex with 2 guys sex in a cupboard

How old were you when you had your first sexual experience with someone else? **14**

What happened in this first sexual experience with another person?

full on pashing, alcohol involved. how did i feel? excitement but also knew how far i wanted to go with it

How old were you when you first had oral sex? **Never had oral sex**

How old were you when you first had sexual intercourse? **19**

Describe what happened during intercourse, and how you felt about it emotionally.

i got a pounding. it was with some random i met at a club. i felt that i may as well get it over with so that i can move on with my life. i didnt care about them. wasnt even attracted to them. i was completely sore for the week following and had bleeding that i was afraid wouldnt stop. i did it because i was ashamed to be a virgin and sick of waiting for the right person to come along. the month following i was depressed, wanted to kill myself. but now i dont have that cloud of shame over my head

How old were you when you first had anal sex? **Never**

On average, how many times a week do you have intercourse?

Less than once a week

Would you like to have more sex? **Yes**

How do you think sex could be better for you?

perhaps if i loved them. i dont have sex with people that im attracted to as i dont want to form an attachment

When you have intercourse, do you use protection? **Yes**

What kind of protection do you use? **condoms, pill**

How often are your sexual experiences with someone of the same sex or gender as you? **Never**

You think of yourself as … **Straight**

How old were you when you first saw pornography or erotica? **9**

What kind of pornography have you seen?

    films, magazines, internet, live shows

Does porn excite you sexually? **Not at all**

Does porn give you ideas about how to have sex? **Sometimes**

Do you think sexy films, music videos or advertising encourage you to have sex? **Sometimes**

Have you ever had phone sex, that is, sexually exciting yourself and someone else over the phone? **No**

Have you ever sent or received sexual text messages? **Yes**

Have you had a sexual experience in an internet chat room? **No**

Have you ever had a sexual experience with an adult? **Yes**

Have you ever had a sexual experience with more than one person at a time? **No**

Have you ever been pressured or forced into having sex? **No**

How often do you have sex while using drugs or alcohol? **Most of the time**

Do drugs or alcohol make sex better or worse? **Neither**

Does what you learn in sex education classes at school help you with your actual sexual experiences? **Not much**

Do you think teenagers should be taught more or less about sex at school? **More**

What do you think is the best age to start having sexual experiences?

    16 or older for sex, when the person has a mature mind to deal with it

Do your parents have an influence on whether or not you have sex? **Not much**

Does your religion have an influence on whether or not you have sex? **Not at all**

How important is it for you to have an emotional connection with your sexual partner? **Very important**

Is there anything else at all that you would like to say about sex or your own sexual experiences?

    it seems to be the 'in' thing to have sex at a young age and it just alienates those who put it off because theyre waiting for someone who deserves this moment in a girls life. i see kissing as just practice so

therefore i dont form attachments to that person. ive always kept myself at an emotional distance. i dont give head- only once but stopped as i was bored. oral is more personal than sex. and for that reason havnt allowed anyone to perform oral on me. i have too much respect for myself to sink that low for a near stranger give them head. most guys arnt worth it and my challange isnt to impress or please them, thats their challange. if i was with someone who id love then i probably would. id want to try everything with them. im at a stage where im after a companion not just a one nite stand- i value myself too much

Girl, 19, Queensland, lesbian

How old were you when you first heard about sex? **4**

What was the first thing you heard about sex?

that men and women did it only to have babies.

How old were you when you started masturbating? **10**

On average, how many times a week do you masturbate?

More than five times a week

How do you masturbate?

i started out masturbating (even though i didn't know what i was doing) by grinding against bed sheets and pillows while in bed, often fully clothed. i would lie on my back or stomach and hump something. usually it only took a few minutes to climax, but i didn't realise/believe it was actually an orgasm until i was about 17. last year i started using the detachable shower head. i twist the nozzle to almost full-force spray and stimulate my clitoris while sitting down in the shower. so now i usually do it everytime i have a shower, unless i'm in a real hurry.

How does masturbating make you feel? **Good**

How old were you when you had your first sexual experience with someone else? **4**

What happened in this first sexual experience with another person?

my family was very close to another family, and they had a little boy who was about six months younger than me. we were good friends. one night while the adults were having fun, my mother put their son and

myself into my bed to go to sleep (which i think was normal practice). we were talking and playing 'truth or dare' and i think it was my idea to dare him to show me his penis. he did and i touched it and we laughed about how funny it looked and felt. and then he said "show me your secret part" so i did, casually, and he touched it and we ended up going back and forth for about five minutes doing this. then just as we stopped my older sister and his older sister came into the room and started teasing us about liking each other and i felt really guilty and embarrassed and for years i was scared that they had seen us!

How old were you when you first had oral sex? **Never had oral sex**

How old were you when you first had sexual intercourse? **Never**

How old were you when you first had anal sex? **Never**

Would you like to have more sex? **Yes**

How do you think sex could be better for you?

umm, perhaps actually having sexual intercourse! hah

How often are your sexual experiences with someone of the same sex or gender as you? **Always**

You think of yourself as … **Lesbian**

If you're gay or lesbian, are you 'out'? **No**

If you're gay or lesbian and you came out, was it hard? **A bit hard**

Describe what happened when you came out and how you felt about it.

i'm only out to my very close friends and their partners if they have one (about 13 people probably know). in highschool my friends were very liberal and accepting and most of us admitted to being bi/gay. in college, i've only made a handfull of close friends and i've only told two so far. none of my family know, as it would be too awkward. we don't talk about anything deep or sexual at all and my dad and brother are homophobic so i won't tell them until i've moved out of home and have a serious partner. sometimes i hide it from new people i meet at college because i sense that they will feel awkward (other girls) and think that i like them or not like me as much. so i pretend to like guys. it kind of sucks, and i know some girls think i'm weird because i don't rave on about guys like they do. i can sense when someone won't be very accepting of my sexuality, and i guess it stops me from making a lot of friends.

How old were you when you first saw pornography or erotica? **7**

What kind of pornography have you seen?

a book, stories (fanfic mostly), internet websites.

Does porn excite you sexually? **A lot**

Does porn give you ideas about how to have sex? **Always**

Do you think sexy films, music videos or advertising encourage you to have
sex? **Sometimes**

Examples of media encouraging sex:

**i think the majority of movies encourage sex because producers know
that 'sex sells' and they often use sex in their movies to incite people to
see it. sex is almost always idealised in movies and portrayed as being
'cool'. a lot of music videos do the same thing.**

Have you ever had phone sex, that is, sexually exciting yourself and
someone else over the phone? **No**

Have you ever sent or received sexual text messages? **Yes**

Have you had a sexual experience in an internet chat room? **Yes**

If so, did you also meet up with that person in real life? **No**

Have you ever had a sexual experience with an adult? **No**

Have you ever had a sexual experience with more than one person at a
time? **No**

Have you ever been pressured or forced into having sex? **No**

How often do you have sex while using drugs or alcohol? **Never**

Do drugs or alcohol make sex better or worse? **Neither**

Does what you learn in sex education classes at school help you with your
actual sexual experiences? **Not at all**

Do you think teenagers should be taught more or less about sex at school?
More

What do you think is the best age to start having sexual experiences?

**i think 12-15 year olds should be allowed to explore their sexuality by
kissing/making out. i don't think it's healthy to repress sexuality. 16+
teens should be allowed to have oral sex and intercourse. i don't think
that there is a definite answer though, because everyone has different
maturity levels. some sixteen year olds may be emotionally mature
enough to handle sex, others are probably not.**

Do your parents have an influence on whether or not you have sex?

Not at all

Does your religion have an influence on whether or not you have sex?

Not at all

How important is it for you to have an emotional connection with your sexual partner? **Somewhat important**

Boy, 19, ACT, zoosexual

How old were you when you first heard about sex? **9**

What was the first thing you heard about sex?

My penis would continue to grow as I masturbated

How old were you when you started masturbating? **11**

On average, how many times a week do you masturbate?

Three times a week

How do you masturbate?

Mostly just in bed early mornings without anything except my hand (I close my foreskin at ejaculation to catch it, then contain it till I get to the toilet)

How does masturbating make you feel? **Good**

Describe your sexual fantasies, even if they seem weird or boring or whatever.

Long lazy session of sex with a female Llama out in a field on a pleasantly sunny day.

How old were you when you had your first sexual experience with someone else? **Never**

What happened in this first sexual experience with another person?

Not applicable, since this asks about another *person*

How old were you when you first had oral sex? **15**

Describe what happened during this oral sex, and how you felt about it.

While masturbating a Golden Retriever I decided to see what it tasted like. He enjoyed it a lot more which turned me on greatly.

On average, how many times a week do you have oral sex?

Five times a week

How old were you when you first had sexual intercourse? **16**

Describe what happened during intercourse, and how you felt about it
emotionally.

**A neighbour's Red Setter that had been sneaking in to find me for oral
sex was learning to mount, but was turning off me too early, so I
positioned myself under him with my feet on the wall behind him to
achieve intromission. I knew about the knot and didn't intend to take it,
so it was progressive and he was happy to how it went and we rested
afterwards sprawled over each other. Utter bliss.**

How old were you when you first had anal sex? **16**

How often does this happen? **Less than once a week**

Describe what happens during anal sex and how you feel about having it.

**I only take the knot with smaller dogs as it's just not comfortable
with larger breeds. The sheer glee dogs have when they realise I
accept their advances never gets old. But a dog that is experienced
is much better because I know he won't try to pull the knot out too
early, so I can lie back and let the feeling of completeness wash
over me.**

On average, how many times a week do you have intercourse?

Less than once a week

Would you like to have more sex? **Yes**

How do you think sex could be better for you?

**If I owned my own place, I could keep my own animals. Not for any
control/power issue, just because of the privacy and having as much
time as I wanted with them whenver they want sex, instead of just well
timed opportunistic sex.**

When you have intercourse, do you use protection? **Never**

What kind of protection do you use?

**No need, since no zoonosis diseases can be transmitted exclusively via
intercourse that can't be transmitted by normal contact. So normal
hygiene is all that is needed.**

How often are your sexual experiences with someone of the same sex or
gender as you? **Never**

You think of yourself as … **Other: Zoosexual**

How old were you when you first saw pornography or erotica? **15**

What kind of pornography have you seen?

films, photos, magazines, stories, books, internet websites. Human porn does nothing for me, so I have to fake interest when my mates are watching it. I don't think I'll ever let them see any animal porn.

Does porn excite you sexually? **Not at all**

Does porn give you ideas about how to have sex? **Sometimes**

Do you think sexy films, music videos or advertising encourage you to have sex? **Never**

Have you ever had phone sex, that is, sexually exciting yourself and someone else over the phone? **No**

Have you ever sent or received sexual text messages? **No**

Have you had a sexual experience in an internet chat room? **No**

Have you ever had a sexual experience with an adult? **Yes**

If so, describe what happened and how you felt about it emotionally.

All the animals I have sex with are adults. I feel this question is a bit irrelavant to me.

Have you ever had a sexual experience with more than one person at a time? **No**

Have you ever been pressured or forced into having sex? **No**

How often do you have sex while using drugs or alcohol? **Never**

Does what you learn in sex education classes at school help you with your actual sexual experiences? **A lot**

Do you think teenagers should be taught more or less about sex at school? **More**

What do you think is the best age to start having sexual experiences?

I'm only just finding out the deeper emotional attachments with animals, and I don't think many people will be able to acknowledge their emotions at any younger than 18-19 if they're having any kind of sex with animals. Emotional maturity is scientifically shown not to happen until after the teenage years, and I am seeing the evidence of that.

Do your parents have an influence on whether or not you have sex?

Not at all

Does your religion have an influence on whether or not you have sex?

Not at all

How important is it for you to have an emotional connection with your sexual
partner? **Very important**

Is there anything else at all that you would like to say about sex or your own
sexual experiences?

**I've found that I have significantly increased my ability to understand
communication with animals through having sex with them. The very
nature of intimacy it requires means they taught me a lot about body
language, subtle signals and acknowledging feedback. In return I have
researched how to best care for them, and also taken an interest in
other activities like pet massage. I've realised that society's
neotenisation of our pets as childlike means that in general they will
never accept zoosexuality despite evidence of neurochemical
similarities in all mammals that affect bonding, oxytocin being just one
of those.**

Girl, 19, New South Wales, lesbian

How old were you when you first heard about sex? **13**

What was the first thing you heard about sex? **how to have safe sex**

How old were you when you started masturbating? **18**

On average, how many times a week do you masturbate? **Once a week**

How do you masturbate? **in bed, lubricants some time, with hands.**

How does masturbating make you feel? **Okay**

Describe your sexual fantasies, even if they seem weird or boring or whatever.
having sex with other women

How old were you when you had your first sexual experience with someone
else? **Never**

How old were you when you first had oral sex? **Never had oral sex**

How old were you when you first had sexual intercourse? **Never**

How old were you when you first had anal sex? **Never**

On average, how many times a week do you have intercourse?
Less than once a week

Would you like to have more sex? **Yes**

How do you think sex could be better for you? **if i had a girlfriend**

When you have intercourse, do you use protection? **Never**

How often are your sexual experiences with someone of the same sex or gender as you? **Always**

You think of yourself as … **Lesbian**

If you're gay or lesbian, are you 'out'? **Yes**

If you're gay or lesbian and you came out, was it hard? **Very hard**

Describe what happened when you came out and how you felt about it.
my father tried killing me and i havent seen him since i came out about 2 years ago and my mother hates me and can barely speak to me. my sisters hate me. my mother physicaly abuses me and verbally abuses me.

How old were you when you first saw pornography or erotica? **18**

What kind of pornography have you seen? **magazine, internet.**

Does porn excite you sexually? **A bit**

Does porn give you ideas about how to have sex? **Always**

Do you think sexy films, music videos or advertising encourage you to have sex? **Sometimes**

Examples of media encouraging sex: **cant remember**

Have you ever had phone sex, that is, sexually exciting yourself and someone else over the phone? **No**

Have you ever sent or received sexual text messages? **Yes**

Have you had a sexual experience in an internet chat room? **No**

Have you ever had a sexual experience with an adult? **No**

Have you ever had a sexual experience with more than one person at a time? **No**

Have you ever been pressured or forced into having sex? **No**

How often do you have sex while using drugs or alcohol? **Never**

Do drugs or alcohol make sex better or worse? **Neither**

Does what you learn in sex education classes at school help you with your actual sexual experiences? **Not much**

Do you think teenagers should be taught more or less about sex at school? **More**

What do you think is the best age to start having sexual experiences? **16**

Do your parents have an influence on whether or not you have sex? **A lot**

Does your religion have an influence on whether or not you have sex?
Not much

How important is it for you to have an emotional connection with your sexual partner? **Very important**

Is there anything else at all that you would like to say about sex or your own sexual experiences?

i at the moment am not ready to have sex but wen i find the right person i will and being a lesbian is harder. i do want to have sex even if its just a one night stand but wen i'm ready.

Boy, 19, New South Wales, straight

How old were you when you first heard about sex? **13**

What was the first thing you heard about sex? **Sex ed in year 7**

How old were you when you started masturbating? **14**

On average, how many times a week do you masturbate?

More than five times a week

How do you masturbate?

sometimes as many as 6 times a day. Normally just with my hand(s). Nothing fancy.

How does masturbating make you feel? **Very good**

Describe your sexual fantasies, even if they seem weird or boring or whatever.

Normally sex with young women i have met/know, current or past lovers

How old were you when you had your first sexual experience with someone else? **14**

What happened in this first sexual experience with another person?

I sat on the bus with my girlfriend and from underneath a newspaper masterbated her ... regularly.

How old were you when you first had oral sex? **15**

Describe what happened during this oral sex, and how you felt about it.

She went down on me as she did not want to do intercourse. felt fantastic.

On average, how many times a week do you have oral sex? **Once a week**

How old were you when you first had sexual intercourse? **15**

Describe what happened during intercourse, and how you felt about it emotionally.

I hardly knew her but she was seriously horny and mildly attractive. After work we went somewhere quiet and tried to have sex. i was nervous and had difficulty getting it up. Neither of us had condoms. She told me she was infertile. Eventually i got it hard enough to penetrate, i wasn't sure if it was actually in but it felt good. i ejacualted and pulled out. After sex, she put her legs on her chest like she was trying to conceive! I was horrified and fled. I think she lied to me. I am not proud of this experience and would rather have lost virginity another way.

How old were you when you first had anal sex? **17**

How often does this happen? **Less than once a week**

Describe what happens during anal sex and how you feel about having it.

I have never had it up the arse but have had anal sex with two differnet girlfriends, one once and the other twice. I enjoyed it - felt good, but the pain it caused my partner made me feel bad about it. All precautions were made, lube, arousal, she orgasming, then we tried it. Again it was pleasurable, but probably not worth the effort. It was a thrill and glad to have tried it.

On average, how many times a week do you have intercourse?

Four times a week

Would you like to have more sex? **Yes**

How do you think sex could be better for you?

Emotional connection. A responsive and intuitive lover. good communication. sharing experiences - give and take. More oral sex, more often and more fun ... never theless its still great to be doing it. And on the whole fantastic.

When you have intercourse, do you use protection? **Yes**

What kind of protection do you use? **Condoms until she gets onto the pill**

You think of yourself as ... **Straight**

How old were you when you first saw pornography or erotica? **13**

What kind of pornography have you seen?

Magazines, internet pictures, films

Does porn excite you sexually? **A bit**

Does porn give you ideas about how to have sex? **Sometimes**

Do you think sexy films, music videos or advertising encourage you to have sex? **Always**

Examples of media encouraging sex:

Id see a music video and the females in it are behaving in ways that excite me, then i imagine shagging them quite easily. Its exciting to see a girl on a video wear little and wiggle or stretch herself and pose in sexually suggestive ways. Britney spears "hit me baby one more time" was sexy, as is many other singers.

Have you ever had phone sex, that is, sexually exciting yourself and someone else over the phone? **Yes**

Have you ever sent or received sexual text messages? **No**

Have you had a sexual experience in an internet chat room? **No**

Have you ever had a sexual experience with an adult? **Yes**

If so, describe what happened and how you felt about it emotionally.

I have no problems with dating older women.

Have you ever had a sexual experience with more than one person at a time? **No**

Have you ever been pressured or forced into having sex? **Yes**

If so, describe what happened and how you felt about it emotionally.

The lover at the time seriously wanted to have sex. i did not. i shagged her to shut her up. Didn't particularly enjoy it but it was not so bad.

How often do you have sex while using drugs or alcohol? **Never**

Does what you learn in sex education classes at school help you with your actual sexual experiences? **A lot**

Do you think teenagers should be taught more or less about sex at school? **More**

What do you think is the best age to start having sexual experiences?

age of consent is 16, i still think intercourse for only over 16's and if 15 yo's want to fool about then i guess thats ok. I have a problem with people 14 yo or even under doing anything beyond kissing/hugging. I have serious concerns when people significantly older go for 16 yo's or younger. I suppose that 17 up is the better age for sexual encounters. Despite what people say, i don't think people are ready until after they are over 17.

Do your parents have an influence on whether or not you have sex? **A lot**

Does your religion have an influence on whether or not you have sex?
Not at all

How important is it for you to have an emotional connection with your sexual partner? **Somewhat important**

Is there anything else at all that you would like to say about sex or your own sexual experiences?
Its much better when there is a "love-like" connection. However generally lust is ok and has its place.

No age given

How old were you when you first heard about sex? **8**

What was the first thing you heard about sex?

That the penis had to go into the vagina to make babies.

How old were you when you started masturbating? **13**

On average, how many times a week do you masturbate?

More than five times a week

How do you masturbate?

Usually once a day, generally anywhere that I have enough privacy and time to quickly squeeze one out— whether it be in my bedroom, public toilet, shower ...

How does masturbating make you feel? **Good**

Describe your sexual fantasies, even if they seem weird or boring or whatever.

I really like the idea of women that ejaculate when they come for some reason. I've always thought that I'd like a woman to do that on my face while I was licking her out. Also, for ME to come all over a woman's face while she's kneeling and giving me head is high on the list. And I also find this weird enjoyment for watching girls pee.

How old were you when you had your first sexual experience with someone else? **6**

What happened in this first sexual experience with another person?

Myself and a girl classmate used to sit outside our year one classroom and talk about and practice, kissing. We'd discuss what we'd try next, whether it felt good or not, whether we should put the tongue in "like they do in the movies", all that sorta stuff ... It was really fun, because it was exciting, and while I didn't really "get off" on it, I knew it was somehow related to "naughtiness". Also, in my younger years before that, I was a very big fan of the game—"you show me yours and I'll show you mine", even though I had way too many a girl break that promise after I had gone through with my end of the deal.

How old were you when you first had oral sex? **15**

Describe what happened during this oral sex, and how you felt about it.

> **It was exciting because I was getting it, rather than how it felt. There's this stigma attatched to all the different steps (ie. Hand-Job, Blow-Job, Sex) that you think you'll go through, but I missed the first one and all of a sudden she was putting her mouth around it. It felt good but it was her first time doing it as well (at least that's what she told ME!), so we were both fairly fumbly. I'd never fingered a girl either (which is what i was doing) so I was feeling all these things at once that I'd never felt before and it's hard to concentrate on any single one.**

On average, how many times a week do you have oral sex? **Twice a week**

How old were you when you first had sexual intercourse? **15**

Describe what happened during intercourse, and how you felt about it emotionally.

> **It was alright. Emotionally, I wasn't exactly "in love", but I did like the girl and I was attracted to her, and I certainly don't have any regrets, it's just my mind was focused more on the fact that I was actually losing my virginity than the passion that we were sharing. It felt fucking good and she had a fairly small vagina so it was nice, warm and tight, however, my cock kept popping out with every few strokes because I couldn't tell how far I should pull back each thrust.**

How old were you when you first had anal sex? **Never**

On average, how many times a week do you have intercourse? **Once a week**

Would you like to have more sex? **No**

How do you think sex could be better for you?

> **There's something about sex that I don't really care for. I've been in a relationship with my girlfriend for 11 months now, and sometimes we'll have sex three times a day, and sometimes we won't have sex for a fortnight, and either scenario really doesn't bother me. I always feel like, if I need to get a load off, then I can always just masturbate to keep my nerves at ease. I think I enjoy the IDEA, and dirty images and thoughts, and taboo, and messiness that sex provides, rather than the actually participation of it.**

When you have intercourse, do you use protection? **Yes**

What kind of protection do you use?

> Condoms. I don't like my GF using the pill because I've heard from other female friends about the adverse effects it had on their emotional and physical health. Sometimes Condoms ARE a hassle, but the tension has never been so intense that we haven't been able to hold off, or compensate with oral sex. It's not worth the risk ...

How often are your sexual experiences with someone of the same sex or gender as you? **Never**

You think of yourself as ... **Straight**

How old were you when you first saw pornography or erotica? **9**

What kind of pornography have you seen?

> All of the ones listed above. I used to go into the newsagency across the road from where I lived, and stand a little bit down from where the porno mags were. I'd read the video game mags and wait for someone to go to the porno section and browse. Then I'd pretend to continue reading my magazine while I was actually looking over the other guys shoulder. I'd end up getting this raging hard-on, and had no idea what to do with it. It was exciting as hell, but frustrating as fuck at the same time.

Does porn excite you sexually? **A bit**

Does porn give you ideas about how to have sex? **Sometimes**

Do you think sexy films, music videos or advertising encourage you to have sex? **Sometimes**

Examples of media encouraging sex:

> Music film clips always have sex in them. It's certainly a selling point in most places, but it's also the cheap way out.

Have you ever had phone sex, that is, sexually exciting yourself and someone else over the phone? **Yes**

Have you ever sent or received sexual text messages? **No**

Have you had a sexual experience in an internet chat room? **No**

Have you ever had a sexual experience with an adult? **Yes**

If so, describe what happened and how you felt about it emotionally.

> I freaked the fuck out! I was 19, she was 34. I was wasted, she was drunk. I like older women, she likes younger men. I kept trying to rush things, she kept slowing them down. I woke up naked and jumped out

of bed. I tried to leave the room, but she woke up and was like "where are you going" and I said "I've just gotta go" and she said "why don't you just stay for a bit?" and I said "really, I'd love to, but I can't, my dad wants me home" and just fucking bolted out! I should have just stuck around though— shown some respect. I know the lady and do like her, it was just my first one-night-stand as well as my first significantly older sexmate and all of a sudden, after waking up and trying to figure out where I was, everything was a bit too overwhelming for me.

Have you ever had a sexual experience with more than one person at a time? **Yes**

If so, describe what happened and how you felt about it.

One of the best experiences of my life. Driving two girls home, I was able to convince them into taking their tops off. Then they started kissing each other, and I started fingering them, and then they started sucking my cock, and swapping turns while one fingered themself and kissed me and the other went down on me. We were all fairly good friends so it wasn't weird or anything like that. We've talked about it since and we all seem to agree how much fun it was and how exciting and "on the edge" it seemed to be at the time.

Have you ever been pressured or forced into having sex? **No**

How often do you have sex while using drugs or alcohol? **Sometimes**

Do drugs or alcohol make sex better or worse? **Neither**

Does what you learn in sex education classes at school help you with your actual sexual experiences? **Not much**

Do you think teenagers should be taught more or less about sex at school? **More**

What do you think is the best age to start having sexual experiences?

I think masturbation should begin around end of primary school, start of high school, because that's when you actually become REALLY interested in girls, but really don't know how to do anything with them. Hand jobs and fingering are a definite year 9 and 10 thing. It's a way of being sexually experimental without the risks of sex. People can tell each other their stories, and you can find out how different everyone's genetalia is. Depending on what kind of person you are, I see year 11 and 12 as the "sucking and fucking" years (I just made that term up—

feel free to use that shit in your book!). This is because you're wanting to try these things before you go out into the big bad world of college interaction with the opposite sex, and also, by this stage, your mind is so goddamn curious as to what is SO GOOD about this frigging SEX thing!

Do your parents have an influence on whether or not you have sex?

Not at all

Does your religion have an influence on whether or not you have sex?

Not at all

How important is it for you to have an emotional connection with your sexual partner? **Somewhat important**

Is there anything else at all that you would like to say about sex or your own sexual experiences?

We really need to start learning about what genetalia looks like, and how people's can differ! I had no idea about labia majora's and minora's and all that bullshit with flaps, and clits, and openings and ALL THAT KINDA STUFF! Same goes with penises. Everyone needs to know that their sexual organs are normal no matter what they look like.

Girl, Tasmania, bisexual (no age given)

How old were you when you first heard about sex? **8**

What was the first thing you heard about sex? **how babys are made**

How old were you when you started masturbating? **11**

On average, how many times a week do you masturbate?

Three times a week

How do you masturbate?

usaly just in my bedroom. just sort of touch it gently

How does masturbating make you feel? **Good**

Describe your sexual fantasies, even if they seem weird or boring or whatever.

this sounds sort of weird but id have to go with u know, lether and whip and boot type thing? yea

How old were you when you had your first sexual experience with someone else? **12**

What happened in this first sexual experience with another person?

it was only a kiss, but it was amazing. like there was this whole adreniline rush though my body

How old were you when you first had oral sex? **14**

Describe what happened during this oral sex, and how you felt about it.

i guess i sort of regrett it cuz i think i was too young, never the less, it was the best feeling ...

On average, how many times a week do you have oral sex? **Twice a week**

How old were you when you first had sexual intercourse? **12**

Describe what happened during intercourse, and how you felt about it emotionally. **i was raped 1st time round.**

How old were you when you first had anal sex? **Never**

On average, how many times a week do you have intercourse?

Less than once a week

Would you like to have more sex? **Not sure**

How do you think sex could be better for you? **i think im way too young**

When you have intercourse, do you use protection? **Yes**

What kind of protection do you use? **condom**

How often are your sexual experiences with someone of the same sex or gender as you? **Sometimes**

You think of yourself as ... **Bisexual**

If you're gay or lesbian and you came out, was it hard? **Not hard at all**

Describe what happened when you came out and how you felt about it.

well im not a lesbian, im bisexual, but coming out with my sexualty wasnt very hard

How old were you when you first saw pornography or erotica? **12**

What kind of pornography have you seen? **well, most really**

Does porn excite you sexually? **A lot**

Does porn give you ideas about how to have sex? **Sometimes**

Do you think sexy films, music videos or advertising encourage you to have sex? **Sometimes**

Have you ever had phone sex, that is, sexually exciting yourself and someone else over the phone? **Yes**

Have you ever sent or received sexual text messages? **Yes**

Have you had a sexual experience in an internet chat room? **Yes**

If so, did you also meet up with that person in real life? **No**

Have you ever had a sexual experience with an adult? **Yes**

If so, describe what happened and how you felt about it emotionally.

im fully awere it was the wrong thing but i dun really care. he was 24.

Have you ever had a sexual experience with more than one person at a time? **Yes**

Have you ever been pressured or forced into having sex? **Yes**

If so, describe what happened and how you felt about it emotionally.

i felt dirty.

How often do you have sex while using drugs or alcohol? **Sometimes**

Do drugs or alcohol make sex better or worse? **Better**

Does what you learn in sex education classes at school help you with your actual sexual experiences? **Not at all**

Do you think teenagers should be taught more or less about sex at school? **Same as now**

What do you think is the best age to start having sexual experiences?

i think older than i am.

Do your parents have an influence on whether or not you have sex? **A bit**

Does your religion have an influence on whether or not you have sex?

Not at all

How important is it for you to have an emotional connection with your sexual partner? **Not important at all**

Girl, Victoria, straight (no age given)

How old were you when you first heard about sex? **6**

What was the first thing you heard about sex?

i learnt it from my friends: babies were born by pressing your tummy button then i learned that a man put his manly part in a womans girly bit

How old were you when you started masturbating? **Never**

Describe your sexual fantasies, even if they seem weird or boring or whatever.

i once dreamt of hooking up with a boy i liked

How old were you when you had your first sexual experience with someone else? **6**

What happened in this first sexual experience with another person?

me and my friend were playing "snakes" in the bath

How old were you when you first had oral sex? **Never had oral sex**

How old were you when you first had sexual intercourse? **Never**

How old were you when you first had anal sex? **Never**

Would you like to have more sex? **No**

How do you think sex could be better for you?

i think i need to mature mentally before i have sex

You think of yourself as … **Straight**

How old were you when you first saw pornography or erotica? **12**

What kind of pornography have you seen?

i accedentally saw it i thought the girl was desgusting and rude it made me sick and i think she musnt have much pride in herself

Does porn excite you sexually? **Not at all**

Does porn give you ideas about how to have sex? **Never**

Do you think sexy films, music videos or advertising encourage you to have sex? **Sometimes**

Have you ever had phone sex, that is, sexually exciting yourself and someone else over the phone? **No**

Have you ever sent or received sexual text messages? **No**

Have you had a sexual experience in an internet chat room? **Yes**

If so, did you also meet up with that person in real life? **No**

Have you ever had a sexual experience with an adult? **No**

Have you ever had a sexual experience with more than one person at a time? **No**

Have you ever been pressured or forced into having sex? **No**

How often do you have sex while using drugs or alcohol? **Never**

Do you think teenagers should be taught more or less about sex at school?

Same as now

What do you think is the best age to start having sexual experiences?

probably about 16 for sex and 9 upwords if you want to masterbate

Do your parents have an influence on whether or not you have sex? **A lot**

Does your religion have an influence on whether or not you have sex?

Not at all

How important is it for you to have an emotional connection with your sexual partner? **Very important**

Is there anything else at all that you would like to say about sex or your own sexual experiences? **sex scares me!!!!!!!**

Girl, Western Australia, straight (age not given)

How old were you when you first heard about sex? **5**

What was the first thing you heard about sex?

the first thing i learned about sex was that a man had to lie ontop of the woman for it happen. and it seemed that only the man would enjoy it.

How old were you when you started masturbating? **8**

On average, how many times a week do you masturbate? **Once a week**

How do you masturbate?

I sometimes masturbate with a pillow between my legs, other times i just use my hands. Usually on my bed at nights but sometimes in the shower (with my hands). Most of the time its just to relieve stress, but other times i do it because i really feel sexed up and those times i caress my whole body really lightly with my finger tips and climaxing with hand movements on the clitoris and fingers inside the vagina.

How does masturbating make you feel? **Good**

Describe your sexual fantasies, even if they seem weird or boring or whatever.

Having the person i really admire at that time - usually a famous person near me and then touching me all over. I suppose i like this because it makes me feel loved. It has to make me feel like i am loved by the other person.

How old were you when you had your first sexual experience with someone else? **17**

What happened in this first sexual experience with another person?

I was at a friend's halloween party and there was a guy there that was friends with my friend's boyfriend. I knew he liked me cos he was flirting heaps with me, and as i started to drink more, i started flirting back with him. Finally, something happened with my friend - she got pretty drunk

and smashed her bottle on the floor, so i took her inside. She was really embarrassed, and after a while her boyfriend and his friend followed us inside. The friend stayed and he made us laugh, and then eventually he got to kiss me. It was nice.

How old were you when you first had oral sex? **18**

Describe what happened during this oral sex, and how you felt about it.

We were in the guys bedroom and he had taken me back here after a party. We were kissing pretty agressively on his bed. and then he started to take my clothes off, he pulled my knickers off and immediately started to lick down there and make wierd reptile movements with his tongue. It didnt turn me on at all, because it felt so rushed even though i tried to.

On average, how many times a week do you have oral sex?

Less than once a week

If less frequent, how many times approximately has it occurred? **Three times**

How old were you when you first had sexual intercourse? **Never**

How old were you when you first had anal sex? **Never**

Would you like to have more sex? **Not sure**

How do you think sex could be better for you?

When ever anyone came close to having sex with me it just felt like they were there for one thing. They were all guys that i hardly knew, and i didnt want to be used in that way. i DO want to have sex but not until i am certain the man i am with loves me.

How often are your sexual experiences with someone of the same sex or gender as you? **Never**

You think of yourself as ... **Straight**

How old were you when you first saw pornography or erotica? **16**

What kind of pornography have you seen?

photos on playing cards, magazines, stories, books, videos and websites.

Does porn excite you sexually? **A bit**

Does porn give you ideas about how to have sex? **Sometimes**

Do you think sexy films, music videos or advertising encourage you to have sex? **Sometimes**

Examples of media encouraging sex:

For example the teen movies where you know all the kids in them are having sex, and its not even questioned whether they should or shouldnt - it just is. they treat it as a step higher towards adult life. American pie, scream, etc

Have you ever had phone sex, that is, sexually exciting yourself and someone else over the phone? **No**

Have you ever sent or received sexual text messages? **Yes**

Have you had a sexual experience in an internet chat room? **Yes**

If so, did you also meet up with that person in real life? **No**

Have you ever had a sexual experience with an adult? **Yes**

If so, describe what happened and how you felt about it emotionally.

I was already over 18 at the time so it didnt affect me mentally or anything. He was a boyfriend a year older than me.

Have you ever had a sexual experience with more than one person at a time? **No**

Have you ever been pressured or forced into having sex? **No**

How often do you have sex while using drugs or alcohol? **Never**

Do drugs or alcohol make sex better or worse? **Neither**

Does what you learn in sex education classes at school help you with your actual sexual experiences? **A bit**

Do you think teenagers should be taught more or less about sex at school? **More**

What do you think is the best age to start having sexual experiences?

It really depends on the emotional maturity of the person, and for that reason i dont think people should have sexual intercourse before the age of 18. With the experiences ive had and of others, i know that teens have sex at a young age for the sake of it because they have that urge to and also because the whole highschool thing pressures them into it because its cool and makes you more powerful in the school society. Kissing and stuff is a good thing, because as a teen you really do need some kind of love factor, but friendship with the other person is the most important because without it, your whole relationship is all about sex.

Do your parents have an influence on whether or not you have sex? **A bit**

Does your religion have an influence on whether or not you have sex? **A lot**

How important is it for you to have an emotional connection with your sexual partner? **Very important**

Boy, Victoria, gay/straight (no age given)

How old were you when you first heard about sex? **9**

What was the first thing you heard about sex?

> **Sex makes babies.. basic reproductive information**

How old were you when you started masturbating? **11**

On average, how many times a week do you masturbate? **Five times a week**

How do you masturbate?

> **Usually just with a hand ... stroking off. Have recently been introduced to toys by a friend ... not much usage yet.**

How does masturbating make you feel? **Good**

Describe your sexual fantasies, even if they seem weird or boring or whatever.

> **Most tend to involve zoophilia or furry concepts, usually heterosexual acts, occasionally with genders swapped. Fantasised frequently about dolphins, lionesses and tigresses ... occasionally dogs.**

How old were you when you had your first sexual experience with someone else? **10**

What happened in this first sexual experience with another person?

> **It could be described basically as sexual exploration ... staying over at a friend's place, staying up till late then talking about sex; stripping off; and looking at each other. There was a bit of playful humping, but nothing more.**

How old were you when you first had oral sex? **15**

Describe what happened during this oral sex, and how you felt about it.

> **I was rather sensitive at the time ... almost to the point of squirming. Started off with a bit of fondling, and ended up with my boyfriend at the time licking, then sucking. As to question 12 (frequency of oral sex), the times per week are low due to a long distance relationship.**

On average, how many times a week do you have oral sex?

> **Less than once a week**

If less frequent, how many times approximately has it occurred?

More than twenty

How old were you when you first had sexual intercourse? **15**

Describe what happened during intercourse, and how you felt about it emotionally.

My first experience was with a mare. I was staying with a friend (who later became my boyfriend) in a semi-rural area, and he'd previously explained to me (about a year or so beforehand) about what he'd done; his attraction to non-humans, and it pretty much clicked with how I feel, something of an explanation. Late at night, we wandered out, probably walking at least 10km to a quiet area with a few paddocks. The intercourse itself was almost laughable, looking back on it now ... many false starts, falling out ... but lasted a good half hour, including the cuddling afterwards.

How old were you when you first had anal sex? **19**

How often does this happen? **Less than once a week**

Describe what happens during anal sex and how you feel about having it.

Somewhat painful initially after being mounted ... but pleasurable after a little while. I tend to be the one on top as the couple of friends I've slept with have tended to have more experience, and gotten past the initial stretching issues. It tends to alternate between the extremes of lust and affection, usually within the space of 30 seconds or so ... but the time spent, and not just with sex, with the friends tends to make me feel loved and content. I'm in something of a precarious position ... my boyfriend's overseas, so I'm occasionally staying around with a close circle of friends who are either single or with someone.

On average, how many times a week do you have intercourse?

Less than once a week

Would you like to have more sex? **Yes**

How do you think sex could be better for you?

Physically, it takes me far too long to climax, something I have in common with a few friends, so we usually either end up giving up, or masturbating then going back to intercourse for the final bit. Emotionally, it's fine ... there's nothing better than curling up with someone before and afterwards, and being affectionate.

When you have intercourse, do you use protection? **Sometimes**

What kind of protection do you use? **Condoms, typically.**

How often are your sexual experiences with someone of the same sex or
gender as you? **Always**

You think of yourself as …

Other: Pretty much gay with humans, straight otherwise

If you're gay or lesbian, are you 'out'? **No**

If you're gay or lesbian and you came out, was it hard? **A bit hard**

Describe what happened when you came out and how you felt about it.

**I've came out to my close friends; but that was helped because 30-40%
of them are gay as well. It wasn't so much a coming out as everyone
realising that the others weren't straight either. Also, when I came out to
my mum, shocked would be the best word to describe it. She was in
denial for a good few months, and only in the last 6 or so months has
she accepted it. I do worry about coming out to my other friends
though … lack of knowledge about how they'd react, and also the
difficulty of how to place it - you don't hear others saying "hey … I'm
straight!"; so how do you tell them you're not so straight?**

How old were you when you first saw pornography or erotica? **13**

What kind of pornography have you seen?

**Mainly photos and videos downloaded from the internet, as well as a
magazine or two at friends' places. I was dragged along to a strip club
for a friend's bucks' night … but it was terrifying, to be honest. It was
just so tacky … and I was disturbed by it to the extent of physically
shaking.**

Does porn excite you sexually? **Not much**

Does porn give you ideas about how to have sex? **Never**

Do you think sexy films, music videos or advertising encourage you to have
sex? **Sometimes**

Examples of media encouraging sex:

**Music videos targeted at the teen market, especially with female
vocalists, tend to be sexually suggestive, something that tends to get
bloody annoying.**

Have you ever had phone sex, that is, sexually exciting yourself and
someone else over the phone? **No**

Have you ever sent or received sexual text messages? **Yes**

Have you had a sexual experience in an internet chat room? **Yes**

If so, did you also meet up with that person in real life? **Yes**

Have you ever had a sexual experience with an adult? **No**

Have you ever had a sexual experience with more than one person at a
time? **Yes**

If so, describe what happened and how you felt about it.

It was fairly recent … a few weeks ago. A friend had his boyfriend down
for the weekend (another long-distance relationship), and we were
sharing the same bed for a weekend (I came up for the weekend,
travelling interstate, to catch up). There were heavily suggestive
comments from all in the week leading up to it, and we ended up going
out to a club the first night, and coming back in a great mood. After
having a shower and such, we all slipped into bed, and started cuddling
and talking. We ended up having anal sex with the three of us … but, as
per the earlier answer, it was probably 70% cuddling, 30% sex or such.
We'd been close friends for a fair while, and ecstatic would best sum up
how I felt.

Have you ever been pressured or forced into having sex? **No**

How often do you have sex while using drugs or alcohol? **Never**

Do drugs or alcohol make sex better or worse? **Neither**

Does what you learn in sex education classes at school help you with your
actual sexual experiences? **Not much**

Do you think teenagers should be taught more or less about sex at school?
Same as now

What do you think is the best age to start having sexual experiences?

I'd say around 14 or 15, probably oral sex, fondling, or non-reproductive
intercourse. At that age, while fairly mentally developed, there's still a
level of immaturity, and I'd say that straight vaginal sex would be a bad
idea unless the concept of contraception is well known with both
parties. Teenage pregnancy can be a real issue in some socioeconomic
groups, and education could help to address this. Sex isn't going to be
stopped between individuals, regardless of age, so education is the
better attitude to take. Additionally, sex ed needs to emphasise the
emotional side of relationships and sexual experiences, which I feel are

more important than the physical act itself. Additionally, there were a non-insignificant group of my peers back at school who were either homosexual or zoosexual; whilst these may be unappealing to the population at large, some education on both needs to occur. Going back to the initial topic, I think that around 13-15, individuals start to get hormonal in terms of sexual development, so it's best that individuals can experience it, but in a safe manner, rather than suppressing what comes naturally.

Do your parents have an influence on whether or not you have sex?

Not much

Does your religion have an influence on whether or not you have sex?

Not at all

How important is it for you to have an emotional connection with your sexual partner? **Very important**

Is there anything else at all that you would like to say about sex or your own sexual experiences?

My experience has not been typical, from what I can tell, with being introduced to homosexuality, zoophilia, furry and bondage between 15 and 17. I'd think that my opinions are somewhat liberal, so probably needs to be taken with a grain of salt. More than anything though, the emotional side of relationships and sex are important to me, and the physical side's pretty much just a way to relax.

Postscript

I'm happy to say that I got answers to all the questions that got me going on this project in the first place. I now feel pretty well equipped to advise writers of fiction about contemporary teenage sexual habits. But it's a small thing compared to the warmth and gratitude I feel towards all the girls and boys who took part and shared their intimate thoughts and histories. I have enormous affection for them, with all their desires and confusion and insecurities, and I am deeply heartened that there was only one example of blatant homophobia, one misogynist, and one possible paedophile-in-the-making.

Most of the teenagers who answered the questionnaire displayed a sense of morality, a yearning for emotional closeness, an ability to understand their mistakes and the desire to change when they know they've done wrong. Far from being the aimless, amoral hedonists depicted in some alarmist and overly simplistic films such as *Thirteen*, most kids seem to be on the right track.

Another conclusion that no-one could help but reach when looking at the survey responses is the triumph of diversity. Whether exemplified by their behaviours, their fantasies or the way they define their sexual preferences, Australian teenagers defy stereotypes. Even within minority groups whether they be bisexuals, zoosexuals or foot fetishists, these kids will not be pigeonholed. As you read the individual histories, just when you think you have someone pegged, they surprise you. Exceptions are the rule. There is variety within diversity, and the concept of what is 'normal' or 'average' becomes meaningless the more you listen to teens speak.

Now that teenagers have spoken, they need to *keep* speaking. They need to be as open with each other as they've been in the survey. Girls should talk to each other about the whole issue of sexual double standards, whereby they label each other 'sluts' while boys are just 'experienced'. Boys should talk to each other about their insecurities when it comes to girls, and the sad effects of too much beer on their ability to perform. Girls and boys need to talk to each other. There is a gaping gender divide that's often defined by girls and their emotional needs on one side, and boys and their physical needs on the other. A little exchange of information will go a long way.

Teens also need to speak to their parents if their parents haven't had the nerve to speak to them about sex. And if those teens have younger siblings, they should encourage their parents to be open with them about sexuality before it's too late. Teens should speak to their school counsellors and whoever is running sex education classes and tell them what they want to know. Older teens should be able to talk to younger teens about their experiences in these classes, sometimes without any adults in the room. A climate of safety, privacy and inclusion should prevail.

Most teenagers are having some kind of sexual experiences, and most of those who aren't, want to. This is healthy and natural. Trying to prevent them will only fail and result in the reverse of what is intended: they will not be protected but left vulnerable. To paraphrase Kinsey, after rape and paedophilia, the only sexual perversion is abstinence. Why preach against it? As young people enter adolescence, they should be armed with information and a healthy attitude to sexuality that's grounded in meaningful communication between them and their parents from the moment they're born. That's how they'll learn to protect themselves. And also enjoy the greatest pleasure two people can share. Especially, as one girl said, with some hot music playing in the background.

Part III

Resources

Resources for teens

The phone numbers, addresses and websites listed in the following resource section were current when this book went to press, but please be aware that they may change.

Also remember that different advice-givers may have their own agenda, and always find out as much as you can about an organisation before going to them for help.

National

Kids Help Line
www.kidshelp.com.au
Freecall: 1800 55 1800
For young people from anywhere in Australia, 24 hours, toll-free.

Lifeline
www.lifeline.org.au
Phone: 13 11 14
Anyone can ring Lifeline about any issue. Lifeline provides free, confidential support and advice.

Australian Bisexual Network (ABN)
http://members.optusnet.com.au/
~ausbinet/
Phone: 07 3857 2500
Freecall: 1800 653 223
Mobile: 0416 068 532
ABN is based in Brisbane, but provides information about associated groups around Australia.

Australian Drug Information Network (ADIN)
www.adin.com.au
ADIN's website gives a state-by-state list of services and resources related to alcohol and other drugs.

ALSORTS
www.also.org.au/alsorts
ALSORTS is a booklet available in hardcopy or pdf. It contains a wealth of information for gay, lesbian, bisexual, transgender and intersex young people, covering such topics as sexuality and gender, common myths, homophobia, family, disability, religion, health (physical and mental) and the law.

Health Matters
www.abc.net.au/health/library/
sexualhealth.htm
Australian Broadcasting Corporation's 'Health Matters' website – lots of good information about sex and sexual health.

Pregnancy Help Line
www.pregnancysupport.com.au
Phone: 1300 13 93 13
Pregnancy Help Line doesn't offer direct counselling, but can help callers find a helpline or other service within their own state.

Violence against women: Australia says no – Confidential Helpline
www.australiasaysno.gov.au
Phone: 1800 200 526

ACT and region

ACT Youth Services
The following youth centres are all listed at this website:
www.makingcontact.net.au

Axis Youth Centre
Queanbeyan Park
(off Campbell Street)
Queanbeyan NSW 2620
Phone: 02 6297 2921
Mobile: 0408 404 181

U-Turn Youth Services Belconnen
Cnr Chandler Street and
Swanson Court
Belconnen ACT 2617
www.belcomserv.com.au/youth
Phone: 02 6264 0260
Email: uturn@belcomserv.com.au

Gugan Gulwan Youth Aboriginal Corporation
Grattan Court
Wanniassa ACT 2903
Phone: 02 6231 9555

Gungahlin Youth Centre
Ernest Cavanagh Street
Gungahlin ACT 2912
www.gungahlin.org
Phone: 02 6123 4411
Email: grcsyth@gungahlin.org

Northside Community Service
Majura Community Centre
2 Rosevear Place
Dickson ACT 2602
www.nside.org.au
Phone: 02 6257 2255
Email: headoffice@northside.asn.au

YWCA Mura Lanyon Youth and Community Centre
Cnr Norman Lindsay and Sidney
Nolan Streets
Conder ACT 2906
Phone: 02 6294 4633
lyacc@ywca-canberra.org.au

Tuggeranong Youth Centre
Cnr Pitman and Howell Streets
Tuggeranong ACT 2901
www.commsatwork.org
Phone: 02 6293 2146
Email: youthservices@commsatwork.org

Weston Creek Youth Centre
Parkinson Street
Weston ACT 2611
www.commsatwork.org
Phone: 02 6288 0709
Email: youthservices@commsatwork.org

Woden Youth Centre
www.beanbag.net.au/woden
Callam Street
Woden ACT 2606
Phone: 02 6282 3037
Email: wodenyouth@wcs.org.au

Youth in the City
Cnr Ballumbir and Petrie Streets
Civic ACT 2612
Phone: 02 6232 2444

AIDS Action Council ACT
Westlund House
16 Gordon Street
Acton ACT 2601
www.aidsaction.org.au
Phone: 02 6257 2855

Sexual Health and Family Planning ACT
Level 1, 28 University Avenue
Civic ACT 2601
www.shfpact.org.au
Phone: 02 6247 3077
SMS: 0400 770 999

NSW

Family Planning NSW

www.fpahealth.org.au

Ashfield Centre
328–336 Liverpool Road
Ashfield NSW 2131
Phone: 02 9716 6099

Dubbo Centre
221 Darling Street
Dubbo NSW 2830
Phone: 02 6885 1544

Fairfield Health Multicultural Services
Suite 5, Level 2
Neeta City Shopping Centre
Smart Street
Fairfield NSW 2165
Phone: 02 9754 1322

Newcastle Centre
15–19 Queen Street
Cooks Hill NSW 2300
Phone: 02 4929 4485

The Warehouse Youth Health Centre
13 Reserve Street
Penrith NSW 2750
Phone: 02 4721 8330

Illawarra Centre
2/26 Park Road
Woonona NSW 2517
Phone: 02 4283 2877

AIDS Council of NSW (ACON)

9 Commonwealth Street
Surry Hills NSW 2010
www.acon.org.au
Phone: 02 9206 2000
Freecall: 1800 063 060
Email: acon@acon.org.au

Gay and Lesbian Counselling Service of NSW

www.glcsnsw.org.au
Phone: 02 8594 9596
Freecall: 1800 18 4527

Twenty10

45 Bedford Street
Newtown NSW 2042
www.twenty10.org.au
Phone: 02 8594 9555
Freecall: 1800 65 2010
Email info@twenty10.org.au
Twenty10 is an organisation that helps young gay, lesbian, bisexual, transgender and same-sex attracted and gender-questioning people who are having problems at home or have recently become homeless.

Youth Block Health and Resource Service

142 Carillon Avenue (cnr Church Street)
Camperdown NSW 2050
Phone: 02 9516 2233
Email: youthblock@email.cs.nsw.gov.au
Youth Block Health and Resource Service provides counselling; medical and dental therapy services; and health, visual arts and music programs.

Northern Territory

Northern Territory AIDS and Hepatitis Council

www.ntahc.org.au
Email: info@ntahc.org.au

Darwin Head Office
46 Woods Street
Darwin NT 0800
Phone: 08 8941 1711

Centralian Office
14 Railway Terrace
Alice Springs NT 0870
Phone: 08 8953 3172

Family Planning Welfare Association of the NT Inc
Darwin Head Office
Unit 2, The Clock Tower
Dick Ward Drive
Coconut Grove NT 0810
Phone: 08 8948 0144
Email: admin@fpwnt.com.au

Outreach Centre – Alice Springs
Eurilpa House
25 Todd Street Mall
Alice Springs NT 0870
Phone: 08 8953 0288
Please note: the Alice Springs office is closed as this book goes to print, but there are plans to reopen it in 2007. Call the Darwin office on 08 8948 0144 for further information.

Outreach Centre – Katherine
Katherine Community Care Centre
Government Centre
First Street
Katherine NT 0850
Phone: 08 8971 3153 (answering machine)

Outreach Centre – Palmerston
Palmerston Community Care Centre
Palmerston Health Precinct
Cnr Temple Terrace and
Roystonea Avenue
Palmerston NT 0830
Phone: 08 8948 0144

Queensland

Family Planning Queensland (FPQ)
www.fpq.com.au

Brisbane
100 Alfred Street
Fortitude Valley QLD 4006
Phone: 07 3250 0200
Email: enquiries@fpq.com.au

Bundaberg
Thabeban State School
270 Goodwood Road
Bundaberg QLD 4670
(Visitors must report to the School Administration Office before entering school.)
Phone: 07 4151 1556
Email: bundabergedu@fpq.com.au

Cairns
37 McLeod Street
Cairns QLD 4870
Phone: 07 4051 3788
Email: cnsclinic@fpq.com.au

Gold Coast
Suite 1/47 Nerang Street
(cnr Davenport Street)
Southport QLD 4215
Phone: 07 5531 2636
Email: gcoastedu@fpq.com.au

Ipswich
Ipswich Health Plaza
Bell Street
Ipswich QLD 4305
Phone: 07 3281 4088
Email: ipsclinic@fpq.com.au

Rockhampton
83 Bolsover Street
Rockhampton QLD 4700
Phone: 07 4927 3999
Email: rckclinic@fpq.com.au

Sunshine Coast
6/96 Aerodrome Rd
Maroochydore QLD 4558
Phone: 07 5479 0755
Email: scoastedu@fpq.com.au

Tablelands
DPI Building
21 James Street
Malanda QLD 4885
Phone: 07 4096 6376
Email: malandaedu@fpq.com.au

Toowoomba
First Floor
4 Duggan Street
Toowoomba QLD 4350
Phone: 07 4632 8166
Email: twbclinic@fpq.com.au

Townsville
45 Eyre Street
North Ward QLD 4810
Phone: 07 4771 2005
Email: tvlclinic@fpq.com.au

Queensland Association for Healthy Communities (formerly the Queensland AIDS Council)
30 Helen Street
Newstead QLD 4006
www.qahc.org.au
Phone: 07 3017 1777
Freecall: 1800 177 434
Email: info@qahc.org.au

South Australia

SHINE – Sexual Health Information, Networking and Education (formerly known as Family Planning South Australia)
www.shinesa.org.au

Sexual healthline
Phone: 08 8364 0444
Freecall: 1800 188 171
Email:
SexualHealthHotline@health.sa.gov.au

AIDS Council of South Australia
www.acsa.org.au
Darling House
64 Fullarton Road
Norwood SA 5067
Phone: 08 8334 1611
Freecall: 1800 888 559
Email: information@acsa.org.au

Rape and Sexual Assault Service
Norwich Centre
Level 2, 55 King William Road
North Adelaide 5006
www.yarrowplace.sa.gov.au/rape.htm
Phone: 08 8226 8777
Freecall: 1800 817 421
After Hours Emergency Line:
08 8226 8787

Sobering Up Unit
Hindmarsh Centre
35 Richard Street
Hindmarsh SA 5007
Phone: 08 8346 4015
Mission Australia provides an overnight, non-medical sobering-up unit for young people at risk.

Gay and Lesbian Community Services of SA Inc
www.glcssa.org.au
Phone: 08 8422 8400
Freecall: 1800 182 233
Email: glcs@glcssa.org.au

Tasmania

Family Planning Tasmania
www.fpt.asn.au
www.fpt.asn.au/youth

Hobart
2 Midwood Street
New Town TAS 7008
Phone: 03 6228 5244
Email: info@fpt.asn.au

Launceston
269 Wellington St
Launceston TAS 7250
Phone: 03 6343 4566
Email: lton@fpt.asn.au

North West
1 Pine Ave
Upper Burnie TAS 7320
Phone: 03 6431 7692
Email: burnie@fpt.asn.au

Tasmanian Council on AIDS, Hepatitis and Related Diseases (TasCAHRD)
319 Liverpool Street
Hobart TAS 7000
www.tascahrd.org.au
Phone: 03 6234 1242
Email: mail@tascahrd.org.au

Victoria

Victorian AIDS Council/Gay Men's Health Centre (VAC/GMHC)
www.vicaids.asn.au
Email: enquiries@vicaids.asn.au

St Kilda Clinic
77 Fitzroy Street (rear)
St Kilda VIC 3182
Phone: 03 9525 5866

Northcote Clinic
42 Separation Street
Northcote VIC 3070
Phone: 03 9481 7155

Peter Knight Centre
6 Claremont Street
South Yarra VIC 3141
Phone: 03 9865 6700
Freecall: 1800 134 840

Bi-Victoria
www.bi-victoria.org
Email: info@bi-victoria.org
A support and social group for bisexuals and their friends.

Gay and Lesbian Switchboard Victoria
http://home.vicnet.net.au/~glswitch/
Phone: 03 9827 8544
Freecall: 1800 184 527
Email: admin@switchboard.org.au

Family Planning Victoria (FPV)
www.fpv.org.au
Email: fpv@fpv.org.au

Action Centre for Young People
Level 1, 92–94 Elizabeth Street
Melbourne VIC 3000
Phone: 03 9654 4766
Freecall: 1800 013 952
Email: action@fpv.org.au
Action Centre for Young People is
FPV's clinic for people under 25. The
centre can provide callers from outside
Melbourne with referrals to services in
their area.

Box Hill Head Office
901 Whitehorse Road
Box Hill VIC 3128
Phone: 03 9257 0100
Email: fpv@fpv.org.au

Hoppers Crossing
82 Derrimut Road
Hoppers Crossing VIC 3029
Phone: 03 9742 8155

Cranbourne
140–154 Sladen Street
Cranbourne VIC 3977
Phone: 03 5990 6789

Goulburn Valley Health
Shepparton
Graham Street
Shepparton VIC 3630
Phone: 03 5832 2460

Western Australia

WA AIDS Council
664 Murray Street
West Perth WA 6005
www.waaids.com
Phone: 08 9482 0000
Email: waac@waaids.com

FPWA Sexual Health Services
70 Roe Street (cnr Lake Street)
Northbridge WA 6003
www.fpwa.org.au
Phone: 08 9227 6177

Sexual Health Helpline
Phone: 08 9227 6178
Freecall: 1800 198 205

Quarry Health Centre for under 25s
7 Quarry Street (rear)
Fremantle WA 6160
www.fpwa.org.au/services/quarry
Phone: 08 9430 4544

Pride Western Australia Inc.
36 Brisbane Street
Perth WA 6000
www.pridewa.asn.au
Phone: 08 9427 0828
Email: pride@pridewa.asn.au

Bibliography

Australian Clearing House for Youth Studies, 'Sexual health', available at: www.youthfacts.com.au

Australian Clearing House for Youth Studies, 'Sexuality', available at: www.youthfacts.com.au

BBC News World Edition, 'Beauty is in the eye of the beerholder', 18 August 2002, available at: http://news.bbc.co.uk

Brody, J, 'Children, media and sex: a big book of blank pages', *The New York Times*, 31 January 2006, available at: www.nytimes.com

Carey, B, 'Crazy for you – here's the scan to prove it', *The Sydney Morning Herald*, 1 June 2005, available at: www.smh.com.au

Connell, R and Dowsett, G, *Rethinking Sex: social theory and sexuality research*, Melbourne University Press, Carlton, Vic., Australia, 1992

Costello, S, 'Sexual consent laws in Australia', *Novo*, issue 9, November 2000, available at: http://users.tpg.com.au/users/taboo/Novo/Issue9

Couch, M, Dowsett, G, et al., *Looking for More: a review of social and contextual factors affecting young people's sexual health*, Australian Research Centre in Sex, Health and Society, La Trobe University, Melbourne, 2006, pp 32–33, available at: www.latrobe.edu.au/arcshs/assets/downloads/reports/looking_for_more.pdf

Cox Newspapers, 'Sex better than cash in the happiness stakes', *The Sydney Morning Herald*, 14 March 2005, available at: www.smh.com.au

Darvill, W and Powell, K, *What Shall We Tell The Children?*, Hodder Headline Australia Pty Ltd, Rydalmere, NSW, Australia, 1995

Fawcett, A, 'The search for satisfaction', *The Sydney Morning Herald*, 31 March 2005, available at: www.smh.com.au

Forrest, S, 'The pleasure principle', *The Sydney Morning Herald*, 7–8 May 2005, available at: www.smh.com.au

Friday, N, *Women on Top*, Arrow Books, London, 1992

Hite, S, *The Hite Report on Female Sexuality*, Pandora, London, 1989

Hite, S, *The Hite Report on Male Sexuality*, Ballantine Books, New York, 1982

Horin, A, 'Coming out getting easier for gay teenagers', *The Sydney Morning Herald*, 25 May 2005, available at: www.smh.com.au

Houston, M, 'They Grow Up Fast', Sunday Life, *The Sun Herald*, 17 April 2005

Jones, JH, *Alfred C. Kinsey*, W. W. Norton & Co. Inc., New York, 1997

Kinsey, AC, et al., *Sexual Behavior in the Human Female*, Indiana University Press, Bloomington, Indiana, 1998

Kinsey, AC, Pomeroy, WB, Martin, CE, *Sexual Behavior in the Human Male*, Indiana University Press, Bloomington, Indiana, 1998

Kovner, G, 'Shared secrets expose teens to risk of sexual predators', *The Sydney Morning Herald*, 24 December 2005, available at: www.smh.com.au

Mascarenhas, A, 'Tantra mantra', *The Sydney Morning Herald*, 22–23 October 2005

Masters, WH, Johnson, VE, Kolodny, RC, *Masters and Johnson on Sex and Human Loving*, Little, Brown & Co., Boston, Mass., USA, 1982

Mayle, P, *Where Did I Come From?*, Pan Macmillan, Chippendale, NSW, Australia, 1991

News-Medical.Net, 'Oral sex not sex say teens', 4 April 2005, available at: www.news-medical.net

News-Medical.Net, 'Sex education delivered by teenagers for teenagers', 23 July 2004, available at: www.news-medical.net

Phelps, K, *Sex: confronting sexuality*, HarperCollins Publishers, Pymble, NSW, Australia, 1993

Pikul, C, 'The girls are all right', *Salon*, 20 April 2005, available at: http://dir.salon.com/story/mwt/feature/2005/04/20/stabiner/index.html

Plibersek, T, 'Pressure point for teens who test limits', *The Sydney Morning Herald*, 22 March 2006, available at: www.smh.com.au

Pollard, R, 'Soaring infections hidden by lack of screening', *The Sydney Morning Herald*, 6 June 2006

Richters, J and Rissel, C, *Doing It Down Under: the sex lives of Australians*, Allen & Unwin, Crows Nest, NSW, Australia, 2005

Selinger-Morris, S, 'I'll have what she's having', *The Sydney Morning Herald*, 22 June 2006, available at: www.smh.com.au

Singer, P, 'Heavy Petting', *Nerve*, 2001, available at: www.utilitarian.net/singer/by/2001----.htm

Smith, A, Agius, P, Dyson, S, et al., *Secondary Students & Sexual Health*, The Australian Research Centre in Sex, Health & Society, La Trobe University Melbourne, 2003

Smith, D, 'Big bang theory', *The Sydney Morning Herald*, 11 June 2005, available at: www.smh.com.au

Stevenson, DB, 'Freud's Psychosexual Stages of Development', available at: www.victorianweb.org/science/freud/develop.html

Storm, A, 'Lauren Winner: reformed sinner or canny opportunist?', *Soma Review*, 24 May 2005, available at: www.somareview.com/laurenwinner.cfm

TeenPregnancy.org, 'Teens say parents most influence their sexual decisions' (press release), 3 June 2005, available at: http://parentingteens.about.com/od/teensexuality/a/teen_sex7.htm

Totaro, P, 'Silk and lace turn little girls into eye candy', *The Sydney Morning Herald*,18–19 February 2006, available at: www.smh.com.au

Weis, D, et al., 'Interpersonal heterosexual behaviors', available at: www2.hu-berlin.de/sexology/GESUND/ARCHIV/IES/USA08.HTM

Wikipedia, 'Zoophilia', available at: http://en.wikipedia.org/wiki/Zoophilia

Womack, S, 'Image-conscious boys join girls in unhappy reflection', *The Sydney Morning Herald*, 25 May 2005, available at: www.smh.com.au

Zuckerman, D, 'Boys to men', National Research Center for Women & Families, October 2001, available at: www.center4research.org/children12.html

Notes

1   J Richters and C Rissel, *Doing It Down Under: the sexual lives of Australians*, Allen & Unwin, Sydney, 2005, p 144

2   J Richters and C Rissel, *Doing It Down Under: the sexual lives of Australians*, Allen & Unwin, Sydney, 2005, p 34

3   D Blanchflower and A Oswald, 'Money, sex and happiness: an empirical study', *Scandinavian Journal of Economics*, vol. 106, issue 3, September 2004, pp 393–415, quoted in 'Sex better than cash in the happiness stakes', *The Sydney Morning Herald*, 14 March 2005, available at: www.smh.com.au/news/World/Sex-better-than-cash-in-the-happiness-stakes/2005/03/13/1110649061304.html

4   M Couch, G Dowsett et al., *Looking for More: a review of social and contextual factors affecting young people's sexual health*, Australian Research Centre in Sex, Health and Society, La Trobe University, Melbourne, 2006, pp 32–33, available at: www.latrobe.edu.au/arcshs/assets/downloads/reports/looking_for_more.pdf

5   Wikipedia, 'Zoophilia', available at: http://en.wikipedia.org/wiki/Zoophilia

6   Wikipedia, 'Zoophilia', available at: http://en.wikipedia.org/wiki/Zoophilia

7   S Womack, 'Image-conscious boys join girls in unhappy reflection', *The Sydney Morning Herald*, 25 May 2005, available at: www.smh.com.au/news/World/Imageconscious-boys-join-girls-in-unhappy-reflection/2005/05/24/1116700712126.html

8   G Kovner, 'Shared secrets expose teens to risk of sexual predators', *The Sydney Morning Herald*, 24 December 2005, available at: www.smh.com.au/news/technology/shared-secrets-expose-teens-to-sexual-predators/2005/12/23/1135032186808.html

9   BBC News World Edition, 'Beauty is in the eye of the beerholder', 18 August 2002, available at: http://news.bbc.co.uk/2/hi/uk_news/scotland/2201198.stm

10 News-Medical.Net, 'Sex education delivered by teenagers for teenagers', 23 July 2004, available at: www.news-medical.net/?id=3512

Acknowledgements

A thousands thanks to …

Julie Catt, psychologist and my brilliant and huge-hearted consultant on the book, who was always ready with expert information, advice, opinions and a smile.

Deb Callaghan, my wonderful agent, who has always gone above and beyond the call of duty to support me and my ideas.

Jane Palfreyman and Meredith Curnow, publishers with tons of intelligence, enthusiasm and heart.

Editorial coordinator Elizabeth Cowell and dream editor Siobhán Cantrill, who both took great care to make me look good.

Designer Nanette Backhouse for her gorgeous design.

Powerhouse Random House publicists Karen Reid and Peta Levett.

All the young people who handed out leaflets – a scarier job than you might think! Without them, no one would know about the survey and there would be no book. A round of applause, please, for Cadence Barkelew-Catt, Matt Okine, Penny Kershaw, Hugh Varga, Katie McLernon, Burak Oguz, Anna Richardson, Reuben Krum, Anna and Alex Garling and Ruby Heery.

My lawyer and comic relief, Shaun Miller, of Marshalls & Dent, and my barrister, Dr Ian Freckelton, who informed me of the legal issues involved with the survey and its publication.

The ever helpful and quick-to-respond Matt Fenton and Roy Cablewski of Monkii Media in Melbourne, who designed and built the website and collected the data. Without them, teenspeak would not have flown.

Others helped, advised, supported … Sally and Ernie Dingo, Dr Gemma O'Brien, Sadie Chrestman, Jeremy Saunders, Phil McAloon, Katrina Gunn, Mariel Beros, Dasha Ross, Ruth Cullen, Karin Altman, Serhat Caradee, Paul Busch and Amanda Higgs.

About the author

Joan Sauers is the author of eight published books in the areas of health, parenting and relationships including *Gut Reactions*; *The Little Back Book*; *Brothers and Sisters*; *Teething, Tantrums and Tattoos*; *Ageing Disgracefully*; and the best-selling *A Grown-up Girl's Guide to Life*. She is a screenwriter as well as a script editor on films such as *Caterpillar Wish*, *The Heartbreak Kid*, *Feeling Sexy* and *Hey, Hey, It's Esther Blueburger*, and television series including *Heartbreak High*, *The Ferals* and *The Little Things* with Antonia Kidman. She has also had articles published in *The Sydney Morning Herald*, *The Age*, *The Australian*, *Vogue* and *Marie Claire*, and was associate producer for a documentary based on her book, *Brothers and Sisters*, made for the ABC and broadcast to wide critical acclaim.

For the last six years Joan has been a mentor and lecturer for *Pygmalion*, a European workshop that develops television series and films for children and adolescents. She is also an adviser for the Australian script workshops SPARK and IndiVision. In her recent work as script editor on several films that deal with teenage sexuality, she realised that adults make a lot of assumptions about what teenagers do and how they feel, without really having any idea. Wanting to know the truth was her inspiration for *Sex Lives of Australian Teenagers*.

About the consultant

Julie Catt is a psychologist and writer specialising in sexual and psychological health. Working for many years for Planned Parenthood in the USA, Julie created workshops for young people including Girl and Boy Scouts, students and adolescents in the juvenile justice system, aimed at increasing sexual health awareness, social skills and self-esteem, as well as demystifying sexually transmitted diseases, safer sex and contraception.

Since moving to Australia in 1994, Julie has worked as a journalist, as a psychologist in private practice, and as director of counselling in a women's sexual health clinic. She has also run writing workshops for people living with mental illness. She and her husband are incredibly busy managing their blended family, which includes six children, a dog and two cats, and she spends her spare time writing her own book about the whole escapade.

Index